We Are Each Other's Liberation

BLACK AND ASIAN FEMINIST SOLIDARITIES

Edited by
Rachel Kuo, Jaimee A. Swift, and TD Tso

Haymarket Books
Chicago, IL

Published in 2025 by
Haymarket Books
P.O. Box 180165
Chicago, IL 60618
www.haymarketbooks.org

ISBN: 979-8-88890-372-8

Distributed to the trade in the US through Consortium Book Sales and Distribution (www.cbsd.com) and internationally through Ingram Publisher Services International (www.ingramcontent.com).

This book was published with the generous support of Lannan Foundation, Wallace Action Fund, and Marguerite Casey Foundation.

Special discounts are available for bulk purchases by organizations and institutions. Please email info@haymarketbooks.org for more information.

Cover design by Rachel Cohen.

Printed in Canada by union labor.

Library of Congress Cataloging-in-Publication data is available.

10 9 8 7 6 5 4 3 2 1

FSC www.fsc.org MIX Paper | Supporting responsible forestry FSC® C103567

Praise for **We Are Each Other's Liberation**

"*We Are Each Other's Liberation* is a beacon of kinship, movement wisdom, and insurgent possibility for all of us struggling with despair in fascist times. Rooted in Black and Third World feminism as queer, disability justice, abolitionist, and transnational interconnection, this vital collection defies stereotypical notions of identity and reductive concepts of solidarity. By delving into our radical inheritances of political struggle—the beauty and the messiness, the expansiveness and the intimacies—the book conjures up a prophetic yet practical path toward collective liberatory futures."

—**HARSHA WALIA**, author of *Border and Rule: Global Migration, Capitalism, and the Rise of Racist Nationalism*

"A powerful collection that puts past, present, and theory in conversation, *We Are Each Other's Liberation* urges us to reexamine Black and Asian community dynamics through the lens of woman of color feminisms. The gift that this book gives us is a guide for how to think about power—how we wield it, how it is used against us, how we can use it to oppose those who are out to destroy us. *We Are Each Other's Liberation* is a gathering of essential answers to the question of where we go from here."

—**CHANDA PRESCOD-WEINSTEIN**, author of *The Disordered Cosmos: A Journey into Dark Matter, Spacetime, and Dreams Deferred*

"Two principles of disability justice are cross-movement organizing and collective liberation. *We Are Each Other's Liberation* is a comprehensive anthology featuring a wide range of essays from a feminist racial justice lens. A must-read for organizers in need of hope in these difficult times."

—**ALICE WONG**, author of *Year of the Tiger: An Activist's Life*

"*We Are Each Other's Liberation* offers crucial stories and frameworks for overcoming cross-racial divisions, building on past legacies, and expanding the possibilities of solidarity and liberation. Essential and groundbreaking, it will equip organizers to harness the power of relationships for revolutionary change."

—**NADINE NABER**, author of *Arab America: Gender, Cultural Politics, and Activism*

CONTENTS

PREFACE

Toward Black and Asian Feminist Solidarities

Rachel Kuo, Jaimee A. Swift, and TD Tso

> *I believe that we need each other and need to learn from one another now more than ever.*
>
> —Jaimee A. Swift, Letter from Black Women Radicals to the Asian American Feminist Collective, April 2020

In early 2020, the global COVID-19 pandemic marked the beginning of a mass disabling event that saw the collapse of social support systems and an intensification of racist violence. We witnessed both disproportionate death and illness in Black communities due to state neglect and incidents of violence against Asians due to racist scapegoating and xenophobia. In April 2020, Jaimee A. Swift of Black Women Radicals reached out to the Asian American Feminist Collective to hold a public conversation on the necessity of cross-racial feminist solidarity. This simple act of reaching out with an invitation to come together and engage in dialogue allowed us to build political alignment and a longer-term relationship and commitment to one another.

A month later, the murder of George Floyd sparked uprisings against police violence in the United States and globally. We saw widespread demands for the dismantling of carceral systems and calls for solidarity with Black liberation movements. One year later, in March 2021, a mass shooter targeted Asian women working in spas and massage parlors in Atlanta, which escalated law enforcement responses to "stop Asian hate," despite the long history of police violence against communities of color and momentum for police and prison abolition.

We continue to be caught in a series of crises that produce solidarities as well as divisions. Since we have started this anthology, we have seen the stripping of reproductive rights and the criminalization of bodily autonomy with the overturning of *Roe v. Wade* and banning of gender-affirming care in states. We have also seen the repeal of affirmative action, in part due to some Asian American internalizations of the model minority myth and desires for proximities to whiteness, as well as ongoing attacks on curriculum about race, gender, and sexuality in education. We continue to see the ways that the unending war on terror justifies mass death, violence, and militarism. We are in the midst of ongoing genocides and state-sanctioned violence in Palestine, Sudan, Democratic Republic of Congo, Haiti, Tigray, Kashmir, and West Papua. We are experiencing the suppression and punishment of activist voices in calls for justice, ceasefire, and decolonization, including the use of police force against student protestors and the uses of detention and deportation systems to target dissent. We have reckoned with grief, loss, and death at multiple scales. At the same time, we witness the creative imagination of communities coming together to take care of each other, to organize and experiment, and to dismantle broken systems and build worlds anew.

Our long-standing struggles toward liberation are connected as we create radical change together. We are united in the fight to dismantle the oppressive and connected systems of imperialism, patriarchy, white supremacy, and capitalism. This anthology offers reflections and meditations on the difficult and necessary work of feminist solidarity. We bring together writing by an intergenerational and transnational group of contributors located across various sites of political struggle, including perspectives from activists, community organizers, journalists, creative writers, artists, poets, scholars, and educators. We hope to stir, shake, disrupt, and dismantle historical and stereotypical notions of Black and Asian interactions and relationships that often only depict negative interactions and tokenizing representations. We hope that in learning about our collective struggles, past and present, we can plant a seed for the radical futurity of Black and Asian feminist movement building and inspire others to do the same.

This collection brings together various texts, ideas, histories, and movement stories that have informed our work together and helped grow our own political analysis and practice. The politics emergent from the longer histories of Black radical feminism and Third World feminist politics have always approached women of color as an insurgent political formation with alignment against empire and state violence, rather than as a description of identity or place. As Barbara Smith, through her work at the Kitchen Table Press and the Combahee River Collective, has shown us, the most radical of political agendas and visions can surface our lived experiences to bring us together in collective struggle. Yet, over time, the revolutionary possibilities of identity politics have been co-opted into reactionary individual demands for recognition and surface-level representations based on institutionalized categories of difference and tokens of diversity and inclusion. Our framework for solidarity seeks to understand the ways we relate and connect to one another politically, including the ways those relations can be fractious.

Our anthology is organized into six parts to speak to the interconnected themes that have emerged in our ongoing explorations and conversations about feminist solidarity.

Part 1, "Our Tensions," looks at political conflict and frictions between Black and Asian communities, on both global and granular levels. What are the sources of the ruptures, silences, and violences between us, and how do we name, challenge, and abolish them? Spanning politics, culture, the public, and the quotidian, Black and Asian communities encounter each other across geographies of empire and everyday sites, such as the nail salon and laundromat. We honor Latasha Harlins, a 15-year-old Black girl who was fatally shot by Soon Ja Du, a 49-year-old Korean convenience store owner, in South Central Los Angeles in 1991. Moreover, we explore the enduring legacies of anti-Blackness in transnational and intimate domains, such as in Chandanie Somwaru's piece. To understand the root causes and structures of racial conflict, Talila A. Lewis highlights dis/ableism as a structuring force of white supremacy and urges us to develop disability justice and anti-ableist politics as central to fostering cross-community solidarity. "Our Tensions" causes us to think about how what bell hooks calls "imperialist white supremacist capitalist patriarchy" has been used to thwart and divide us.[1] In catalyzing true solidarities, we must reckon with historical messiness, challenges, and pain to move forward.

Part 2, "Our Lineages," focuses on radical histories of cross-racial organizing as a response to these tensions. Black and Asian interactions and solidarities are deeply shaped by histories of slavery, labor exploitation, and colonialism. We look to a long tradition of internationalist and revolutionary movement building, including reflections on the legacies of feminists before us, such as Claudia Jones, Barbara Smith, the Third World Women's

Alliance, and the Organisation of Women of African and Asian Descent. We explore archives of queer community building between Asian and African diasporas. Through remembering histories of feminist friendships, alliances, and coalitions, we learn how our pasts and futures are tied together.

Part 3, "Our Liberation," shows us how these legacies of Black and Asian feminist solidarity are alive and well today in abolitionist movements, including calls for decolonization and demilitarization, the decriminalization of sex work, and transformative justice. These struggles for freedom and bodily autonomy shape our politics and provide us with the tools that allow us to imagine a better world. We look to examples from contemporary case studies, such as how South Asian American communities engage with abolitionist organizing across issues such as caste, immigration, and domestic violence, as covered in Mon M.'s and Salonee Bhaman's pieces. The voices in this part include those of sex workers, poets, scholars, and those who provide support for incarcerated people—all of whom urge us to look "beyond gilded cages" and toward the myriad ways our fights for radical world transformation come together.

Part 4, "Our Interconnections," traces the various relations and entanglements that bring us together, from deep interpersonal bonds, such as the nurturing of a long-distance friendship across two coasts, and familial and community kinships, such as Akemi Kochiyama-Ladson's memories of her grandmother Yuri Kochiyama, to transnational ties, such as the urgency of "taking up each other's cause" between Tigray, Kashmir, and Palestine. The section opens with TD Tso's reflections on the Atlanta spa massacres through recounting the creation of transnational networks of care in global sex worker organizing as a counter to narratives of victimization and takes us to Jamy Drapeza and Shaé Smith's meditations on queer intimacies and principled practices in relationship building. How are we brought together (and pulled apart) by diaspora? By the places we inhabit? How do we find each other and hold each other close when the world tries so hard to keep us apart? Building and sustaining solidarities is difficult, uncomfortable, and messy but crucial work, and the bonds that are created are often both precarious and precious. This part highlights the interconnectedness of different movements across struggles and geographies as well as in day-to-day intimacies and encounters.

Part 5, "Our Joy," recenters the pleasure, love, and joy in our movements. As feminists of color, we often find ourselves connecting through our shared oppression and traumas; in this section, we spotlight the "rebellious joy" found within our connections with one another and practices of radical love that sustain us. We look to conduits of joy such as cooking ancestral food with friends, as Rosa Bordallo writes about in her essay. TD Tso writes on how Dr. Margo Okazawa-Rey, aka DJ MOR Love and Joy, models building transnational feminist solidarity through virtual dance parties. Yin Q and J Wortham come together to discuss their reconnections with nature and explorations of kink, among other modalities of healing. Self-love is defined through language shifts about autism in Jane Shi's "mother tongue," Chinese, and through Sonya Renee Taylor's "unapologetic agreements." In a world that devalues, erases, and enacts violence against us, we must be committed to our own survival, which necessitates intentional practices of pleasure, love, and joy.

Part 6, "Our Futures," looks to radical possibilities of catalyzing and imagining cross-racial feminist solidarities. How do we dream, experiment, and build new worlds and realities for ourselves? What revolutions must we make within ourselves and with each other to create the world we want to see? How do we sustain our revolutions into the future? This section highlights radical feminist practices and frameworks for movement building so that we can truly get free. Priscillia Kounkou-Hoveyda of the Collective for Black Iranians reminds us to reflect on the voices we have left behind in our previous movements and ways to build critical consciousness and understanding of histories and stories that have been erased. We also draw on feminist voices who have come before us, such as those of Loretta Ross and Grace Lee Boggs, as ways to practice for our revolutionary feminist future.

As we stand firm on the feminisms that keep us grounded in our praxis, what wisdom from these frameworks should we take with us—and what must be added, subtracted, and multiplied from them? How will we be committed to our radical postures and positionalities yet remain humble and vulnerable to the fact that we do not have all the answers? And that we might fail in the process?

As Mariame Kaba says, hope is a discipline—solidarity is, too. Solidarity requires study. It requires constructive critique. It requires political communion. It requires a radical imagination, even when this world tries to crush our dreams. It requires us to not allow our dreams of a new world to be deferred or to fester. Instead, solidarity pushes us to keep watering those dreams so they can develop, ripen, and grow into ultimate realities. We hope this anthology may galvanize us all toward solidarity and, as a result, liberation.

PART 1

Our Tensions

Unpacking Conflict Through a Feminist Lens

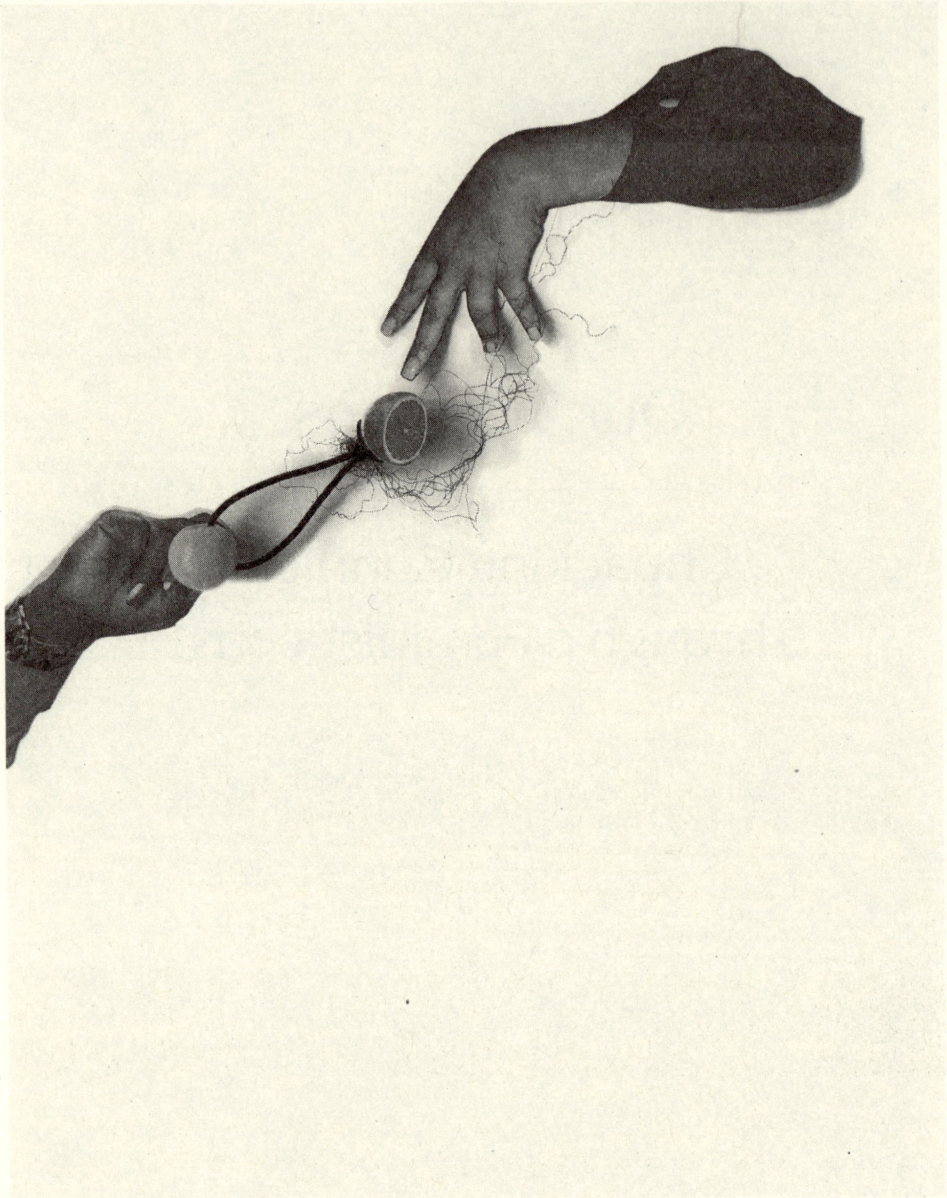

Five Memorials for Latasha. Image by Courtney Faye Taylor.

Mural of Latasha Harlins at the Algin Sutton Recreation Center (Los Angeles, California), painted by artist Victoria Cassinova in 2021. Image by Courtney Faye Taylor.

1.

Five Memorials for Latasha

Courtney Faye Taylor

The following excerpt comes from poet Courtney Faye Taylor's hybrid essay in *Concentrate* (Graywolf Press, 2022), in which she visits five locations in Los Angeles that are vital to the memory of Latasha Harlins, a 15-year-old Black girl killed by Korean American grocer Soon Ja Du after being falsely accused of shoplifting a bottle of orange juice.

The epicenter of my curiosity is 91st and Figueroa, the lot on which Empire Liquor Market stood. Empire: a collection of states under one dominion; omnipotent premises; a territory implying power and power implying those who die in the course of courting it.

On 91st and Figueroa stood a structure, a system akin to a kingdom.

Business never resumed after Latasha Harlins was killed inside. Vacancy made it a feasible target. On the first night of revolution, there were several attempts to incinerate it. But Black residents living next door at the Webb Motel stayed up into the wee hours, filling garbage cans with water. Living so close by, barely two feet from the store, they knew the fate of Empire would have also been the fate of their home. To save their own lives, they had to save this monument of brutality. Our survival, inextricable from the structures that threaten it.

In the late 1990s, Empire's signage was peeled from the building and replaced with that of Numero Uno Market. This is the face that greets me now.

Unlike the stone-white dress of its predecessor, Numero is a pink and green shock to the street. I see a parking lot and a threshold in the back where trucks relieve themselves of cereal, seafood, juice. Inside, three officers linger by the liter sodas. I watch a butcher conceive slivers of meat. A child walks aisles freely, motherless, unhesitant. I make efforts to push my shoulders back but hesitate. I grab a grocery bag, eager for artifact. I hover at the refrigerators, eyeing a camera above the door. I walk around, consumed by questions of configuration. Is everything in the same place? Is this where Soon Ja tended the counter, a gun her clandestine companion? Evidence takes imagination now.

But those who love Latasha do imagine. In 2016, on the twenty-fifth anniversary of her loss, photos slouched against this edifice. Balloons ascended by the fence, dressing the hood in cool helium. On the sidewalk, a pastor prayed for protection, for wherewithal, for a heaven-eyed CCTV.

2.

Field Trip to the Museum of Human History

Franny Choi

With thanks to Ursula K. Le Guin

Everyone had been talking about the new exhibit,
recently unearthed artifacts from a time

no living hands remember. What twelve-year-old
doesn't love a good scary story? Doesn't thrill

at rumors of her own darkness whispering
from the canyon? We shuffled in the dim light

and gaped at the secrets buried
in clay, reborn as warning signs:

a "nightstick," so called for its use
in extinguishing the lights in one's eyes.

A machine used for scanning fingerprints
like cattle ears, grain shipments. We shuddered,

shoved our fingers in our pockets, acted tough.
Pretended not to listen as the guide said,

Ancient American society was built on competition
and maintained through domination and control.

In place of our modern-day accountability practices,
the institution known as "police" kept order

using intimidation, punishment, and force.
We pressed our noses to the glass,

strained to imagine strangers running into our homes,
pointing guns in our faces because we'd hoarded

too much of the wrong kind of "property."
Jadera asked something about redistribution,

and the guide spoke of safes, evidence rooms,
more profit. Marian asked about raiding the rich,

and the guide said, *In America, there were no greater*
protections from police than wealth and whiteness.

Finally, Zaki asked what we were all wondering:
But what if you didn't want to?

and the walls snickered and said, *Steel,*
padlock, stripsearch, hardstop.

Dry-mouthed, we came upon a contraption
of chain and bolt, an ancient torture instrument

the guide called "handcuffs." We stared
at the diagrams and almost felt

the cold metal licking our wrists, almost tasted dirt,
almost heard the siren and slammed door,

the cold-blooded click of the cocked-back pistol,
and our palms were slick with some old recognition,

as if in some forgotten dream we had lived this way,
in submission, in fear, assuming positions

of power were earned, or at least carved in steel,
that they couldn't be torn down like musty curtains,

an old house cleared of its dust and obsolete artifacts.
We threw open the doors to the museum,

shedding its nightmares on the marble steps,
and bounded into the sun, toward the school buses

or toward home, or the forests, or the fields,
or wherever our good legs could roam.

3.

Understanding Disability, Ableism, and Incarceration More Expansively

Talila A. Lewis

This essay is adapted from a two-part interview series between Talila A. Lewis and George Yancy in 2023 about the ways ableism structures systems of oppression. Lewis helps us understand how developing a nuanced and expansive analysis of disability and ableism can bring oppressed communities together in solidarity and avoid the (re)production of tensions and conflict that pit these communities against each other. The piece makes a call to action to develop our understanding of disability justice and ensure that anti-ableist politics remain at the heart of our struggles for abolition and liberation.

Disability and ableism have been misunderstood, downplayed, erased, ignored, or manipulated in discussions of social inequity and oppression. Specifically, disability is often misunderstood as an objectively defined, static identity, and ableism misunderstood as an oppression that can only be experienced by disabled people. But these conveniently and strategically limited conceptions of disability and ableism create, enable, and exacerbate all forms of inequity and hamper liberation efforts.

In truth, disability is one of the *most fluid* and complex marginalized identities, and ableism one of the oldest, most radical, and least understood systemic oppressions. Since we live under racial capitalism, settler colonialism, and white supremacy, ableism in the united states has never solely been about disability.[1] Ableism here has *always* been about *at least* race, gender, labor/productivity/capital, and dis/ability. Ableism has been used for generations to degrade, oppress, control, and disappear disabled and nondisabled people alike—especially those who are Black/Indigenous (e.g., scientific racism). Relatedly, all oppression is rooted in and dependent on ableism—especially anti-Black/Indigenous racism. Ableism plays a leading role in how we frame, understand, construct and respond to race, class, gender, sexual orientation, ethnicity, nationality, criminal status, disability, and countless other identities.

In its simplest terms, ableism is the categorization and valuation of a bodymind, behavior, characteristic, or community as inferior or superior, unworthy or worthy, useless or useful, normative or deviant.[2] In the united states context, these valuations are in/formed through the application of white supremacist, settler-colonial, cis-heteropatriarchal, capitalist ideas about race, ethnicity, dis/ability, gender, re/productivity, criminality, civility, intelligence, fitness, beauty, birth/living place, etc.[3] In other words, our identities and our purported values are both a function and byproduct of ableism.

Ableism is mutually dependent on and inclusive of *all* other oppressions—in constant conversation with one another, continuously forming, informing, and influencing the power of the other, while re/defining the identities of those affected by said oppression. State, religious, and corporate violence and oppression perpetrated against negatively racialized and educationally and economically disenfranchised communities is *deeply* rooted in ableism. As such, ending this violence requires not only an understanding of disability and disability-based oppressions but also a keen understanding of how disability exists and arises in, and interacts with, marginalized people and communities. More to the point, ending this violence demands that we understand how race-, class-, and disability-based oppressions interact with one another and precisely how seamlessly each is interwoven into social, political, economic, and legal mores and codes—written and unwritten.

I have been experimenting with using "disableism" to refer to oppression experienced by disabled people and those perceived or labeled as disabled (e.g., sanism, audism, linguicism, vidism, etc.) and using "ableism" to refer to the force from which all oppression draws power and takes refuge (i.e., the categorization/ranking/valuation of bodyminds and the consequences that flow therefrom in a given society, community, setting, etc.). Nondisabled marginalized people must understand that ableism harms them, and white and non-Black/Indigenous disabled people must also understand that racism and white supremacy harms them.

Settler-colonial, capitalist, cis-heteropatriarchal societies leverage disability in similar ways as they do ableism—to justify violence and rationalize banning anything that might make oppressed people more powerful and/or of less value to colonizers. In the united states, disability has been used to justify the imposition of enslavement and deprivation of freedom. Dis/ableism, racism, classism, and other oppressions intersect to create and shape how *all* marginalized people are made vulnerable to medical-carceral-economic surveillance, criminalization, pathologization, and incarceration.[4]

Dis/Ableist Violence and Carcerality

Disabled people have always been among the chief intended targets of all forms of incarceration and are the largest marginalized population in jails and prisons (and almost 100 percent of those confined in other locked institutions).[5] Consider: the criminal legal system targets and disadvantages disabled people at *every* phase of the criminal legal process, and carceral institutions are disabling by design (so those who enter jail, prison, and other locked institutions without disabilities almost assuredly acquire disabilities while incarcerated).

Disabled people are more likely to have catastrophic encounters with policing systems, with *at least* half of the people killed by law enforcement having disabilities and disabled people quite literally being targeted for policing, incarceration, and institutionalization.[6] An example is New York City mayor Eric Adams's 2022 "plan" to abduct and involuntarily hospitalize New Yorkers whom New York City firefighters/EMS deem disabled—most of whom would undoubtedly be Black, Latine, otherwise negatively racialized, and low-/no-income people who are unhoused.[7] Euphemistically framed as "aid," this is racist-classist-ableist through and through.

Disabled people are also disproportionately arrested, convicted, and incarcerated (often despite actual innocence) and spend disproportionately longer amounts of time incarcerated than nondisabled people.[8] They also are more likely to experience the worst these institutions have to offer due to dis/ableism.[9] It is also more difficult to free disabled people from incarceration, regardless of innocence, owing to carceral dis/ableism.[10] Reentry, "alternative," and post-carceral surveillance and control machinations and agencies (i.e., parole, probation, e-carceration) are also dis/ableist and inaccessible or known to be insurmountable for disabled people.[11] In short, disabled people are arrested and incarcerated more often, held longer, suffer more, and return more frequently and faster than nondisabled people. Disabled people with other marginalized identities fare even worse.

To be clear, carceral institutions are *designed* to cause illness, disability, dis-ease, perpetual fear, and premature death. Outside the near-constant toxic exposures and death-hastening deprivations, theft of freedom, all on its own, is disabling. Incarcerated disabled people go on living in these violent, hyperableist institutions—living as the marginalized among the hypermarginalized. While incarcerated, disabled people are targeted for punishment mercilessly for having disabilities, exposed to extreme neglect, denied access to accommodations, and forced to fight for access and basic decency (then punished for these righteous struggles). If they survive incarceration, they return to the free world with disabilities *and* immense trauma. But this comes as no surprise to those who understand jails, prisons, civil commitment, and modern psychiatric carceral institutions as progeny of plantations, asylums, poorhouses, circuses and zoos, the military, and other places to which dispossessed people have been subjected to savagery and barbarism of the "civilest" kinds.

Poverty, "criminality," and Blackness/Indigeneity—like disability—have long since been framed as heritable character flaws, moral failings, and sicknesses that need to be cured and purged.[12] Structural violence is never implicated, despite the obvious economic, social, cultural, political, medical, educational, legal, and other generational deprivation, dispossession, and depression borne by those subjected to and dying from this nation's violence. Azza Altiraifi reminds us that "work therapy" was honed during and after chattel slavery—and continues to today—employing medical authority and ableism to justify enslavement and other forms of confinement, to compel uncompensated labor, and to deny actual care while developing and assigning medical diagnoses, among other things. The links between penal, medical, and economic incarceration are striking.[13]

There are undeniable similarities, connections, and overlays between Black Codes, Indian Removal and Appropriations Acts, Jim Crow, manumission, public charge laws; unsightly beggar ordinances, antitramping, antisolicitation, and antivagrancy laws; and convict leasing, vendue, sharecropping, peonage, sheltered workshop, and modern prison labor systems.[14]

These sites, their illogics, interchangeability, and often indistinguishability, reveals the ease with which power holders leverage ableism to categorize and (re)distribute marginalized people into and across carceral institutions on the basis of purported health, criminality, and vulnerability. Some of these places include plantations, stockades, privately owned and operated "homes," and "houses of corrections" (i.e., jails/prisons); poorhouses, workhouses, poor farms, and homeless "shelters"; asylums, county infirmaries, and prison hospitals; reservations, boarding and residential "schools," orphanages, and boot and internment camps, among others. While the stated purposes of these institutions and practices always include a positive spin (e.g., aid, treatment, cure, rehabilitation, correction, discipline, vocational skills development and proving, etc.), all are carceral regardless of their euphemistic name or stated benevolent rationale or claim. *This* is the backdrop against which we must understand and challenge incarceration expansively as a form of eugenics rooted in dis/ableism.

Conditions at all of these institutions are horrifically similar, and people confined in all of these institutions were at one time or another called "inmate," even where they are now euphemistically called patient, resident, worker, or client.[15] Some of the obvious similarities include separating people from their loved ones; indoctrinating and "breaking" a person into assimilation; using violence to coerce people to push their bodymind beyond its limits; and not paying or underpaying for dangerous, disability-inducing labor being framed as character and morality building. People who refuse to quietly accept the injustices of these institutions are often deemed "maladjusted," "intransigent," or "noncompliant," then are force medicated, restrained, isolated, and punished. People who flee these places are deemed fugitives and deserters and are severely punished, even killed, to remind those who are still incarcerated in these institutions to "stay in their place," or else. The geographies, illogics, and conditions of these places, and the similarities between those confined within these purging places, make clear that the aim has always been to maintain control over populations deemed valueless, surplus, or ungovernable to expand and protect white settler-colonial power and capital. No need to repurpose a facility or institution if it is already perfectly purposefully aligned.

These are all highly effective segregating, reproduction-preventing, deprivationist, disabling, profit-extracting, killing machines. Reform-proof proven. Controlled by the state and corporations, they swallow up generationally dispossessed, patho-criminalized, multiply marginalized, and traumatized people using medical, legal, state, and corporate authority. Incarcerators swear they are doing incarcerated people and society a favor. They engage academic, medical, and scientific "professionals" to aid in "studies" that might prove their foregone conclusions. Incarcerated and formerly incarcerated people and their loved ones and communities sink further into economic depression, social degradation, and political disadvantage *for generations* as a direct result of policing, pathologization, criminalization, and incarceration.

Incarceration does not heal, make us safer, or positively transform individuals, harm, or our society. Quite the contrary. Incarceration destroys humans, families, communities, generations, and society. Incarceration makes accountability and repair for harm more difficult to achieve and perpetuates violence. We must create the conditions that bring forth a world where incarceration has no place.

Anti-Ableism, Abolition, and Cross-Community Solidarity

Disability and ableism can serve as the tie that holds oppressed communities together or the wedge that pits us against each other. Developing an anti-ableist lens and praxis lends itself to powerful cross-community solidarity and leads to incredible cross-community victories.[16] We have a lot of work to do, however. Ableism, and the disability-consciousness gap within and across social justice movements, has led and continues to lead to oppressed communities distancing themselves from disability and reinforcing the ableist notion that disability is a valid excuse for people to be exposed to injustice, inequity, and violence (e.g., suffragists of the past and even some prison reformists/abolitionists of the present).[17] The solution, of course, is not to denigrate disabled people but to debunk and dismantle popularized ableist myths of inferiority, "undeservingness," and invalidity of all oppressed peoples, disabled included.

We all must ardently contest advocacy strategies that tie people's value to their labor productivity or that establish or reinforce ranking systems of marginalized people. All social justice movements must be intentionally rooted in, *at least*, anti-ableism, antiracism, anticapitalism, and anti-imperialism. Incarceration in *all* its horrific forms must be named, shamed, and dismantled. Reparations, including guaranteed income, housing, health care, and other social benefits with the attendant and necessary support a person, family, and community needs, should be requisite for all those returning from all forms of incarceration.

Disability justice offers an entry point for many people who are just beginning this inquiry. Like many other solidarity praxes developed by Black/Indigenous, queer, feminist, and disabled people, disability justice is concerned with the kinship of our identities, communities, and struggles (with an intentional centering of those living at the margins of the margins). Disability justice is also concerned with co-creating safety and abundance and destabilizing the foundations of all structures that create and perpetuate domination, exploitation, violence, and inequity. In 2020, Angela Davis noted that "for centuries, people have been unwilling to grasp the concept that only by undoing the foundation can we build a new future." *Ableism is the foundation that must be torn asunder.*

Let us (re)commit to developing a disability politic and anti-ableist framework that invites and demands solidarity across identities, communities, and movements:

- Develop a nuanced and expansive understanding of disability and dis/ableism, studying their relationships with/in and to power, systems of oppression, domination, white supremacy, racial capitalism, settler colonialism, imperialism, law, medicine, and more. Integrate an analysis of disability and ableism into your everyday life, practice, and work.
- Assess how your communities/the communities you serve are categorized, criminalized, pathologized, or are otherwise deemed undesirable, unworthy, disposable, etc. Identify how these categorizations are connected to disability, anti-Blackness, ableism, eugenics, etc., both past and present.
- Identify how your community is seemingly pushed toward ableism in efforts to defend its humanity, and find ways to center anti-ableism and cross-community and cross-movement solidarity instead.
- Assess how disability and ableism are implicated in and/or informing your advocacy (e.g., how ableism shows up in the laws you follow and cite, the practices you engage in, the "alternatives" you propose, etc.).
- Identify common and overlapping issues and struggles within and across communities (disabled and nondisabled, for example). You might begin by asking these or similar questions:
    - Who was/is categorized together?
    - How were/are these identities created/defined/manufactured?
    - What claims were/are made about heredity?

  - What were/are acceptable actions in response to these categorizations/heredities?
  - How are different communities similarly/differently affected by this issue?
- Develop and implement access-centered practices and study and internalize disability rights, justice, and liberation to build a stronger movement and bring those who are not considered within your own community or who exist at the margins of your community to the center. Ensure your thought, work, actions, publications, movements are centering anti-ableism, disability, and disabled people. (*Always* center the "margins of the margins.")
- Do not erase disabled identities of Black/Indigenous/negatively racialized ancestors. Honor the whole humanity of those who came before us by naming their disabilities in addition to their other identities. Take note how their disabilities in/formed their lives, perspectives, freedom dreams, and work.
- For those in principled struggle: pace yourself, give yourself and others grace, take time for rest and pleasure, ever-evolve, and create your own heart- and humanity-centered metrics of "success."
- And finally, and perhaps most importantly, Black/Indigenous and other negatively racialized folks who have disabilities, there is a home for you with your Black/Indigenous disabled kin that requires nothing of you but your existence. Come home.

4.

We Want Cop-Free Communities

A Letter

Asian American Feminist Collective

In response to the spike of racialized violence against Asians during the COVID-19 pandemic, the New York Police Department announced the creation of a permanent task force to address hate crimes against Asian New Yorkers and is considering other "culture-based task forces" for the future. As members of the Asian American community in New York City, we denounce the creation of an Asian Hate Crimes Task Force by the NYPD on Tuesday, August 18, 2020. We do not believe this task force will make us safer but instead will put our communities (especially the most vulnerable) at greater risk.

We do not support any initiative that expands the power of police, nor do we believe in carceral responses to address racist violence.

The city has no right to scapegoat our communities. The NYPD and council members who voted against defunding police accuse Asians of not cooperating with the police, but the reality is, survivors of anti-Asian harassment do not cooperate with police because they are *afraid of police*. Our communities stand to face greater harm because of police.

The NYPD has a long history of perpetrating violence within Asian communities, including the murder of 16-year-old Yong Xin Huang in 1995 and attack on 84-year-old Kang Wong in 2014. In the mid-1990s, during an escalating period of anti-immigrant violence, CAAAV: Organizing Asian Communities documented seventy-one incidents of anti-Asian violence in New York City, with almost half of all cases involving law enforcement as the primary perpetrators of violence.

South Asian and Muslim communities continue to experience ongoing racial and religious profiling and surveillance by police.[1] Police have also continued to harass Asian immigrant workers, including street vendors, massage parlor workers, delivery workers, and taxi drivers, through stops, raids, and fines. They have targeted Asian sex workers and asylum seekers. The NYPD works closely with ICE to detain and deport our communities. Additionally, real estate developers have worked with NYPD to protect private property and raise property value under the guise of "safe communities," facilitating the eviction of people from their homes. We have also seen the connection between policing and gentrification through how the installation of new surveillance technologies on older buildings has created loopholes for landlords to raise rent and displace low-income tenants.

In all these ways and more, the police and prison industrial complex hurt our communities. "Culturally specific" police reforms will not help our communities.

Despite historically massive policing budgets and endless task forces, these reforms have never stopped anti-Asian racism from happening in the first place. We question the city's decision to supply more funds toward the policing of already criminalized communities rather than toward language services and free cultural competency training for business owners.

We also oppose the use of hate crime legislation to further expand systems of criminalization. Measures against hate crimes have been used to increase the power of the carceral system, responding to violence through more violence, including harsher sentencing, mandatory minimums, and the death penalty. In 2009, the Obama administration tethered the expansion of hate crime legislation (to include gender, sexuality, and disability) with the funding of US militarization by attaching the bill to the National Defense Authorization Act for 2010. This inextricably links national investments in so-called tolerance to the perpetuation of the military industrial complex, eliding the ways the military reproduces and perpetuates violence under the guise of freedom and equality.[2] Further, as the Sylvia Rivera Law Project has pointed out, "tough on crime" policies are often used against communities already marginalized. They obscure the systemic violence of policing and individualize violent actions that, in reality, are the expression of a racist structure.[3] They do not lead to justice, nor do they address the root causes of racial violence. In the long fight against racial, sexual, and gendered violence, carceral punishment is not the answer to keeping our communities safe, and we refuse to be used as another excuse to harm people of color, specifically Black folks, in our name.

We also reject both the complicity and the active participation of Asians in the expansion of policing. Since the recent resurgence of uprisings in defense of Black lives, we have seen pro-cop Asian "celebrity" activists co-opt the language of antiracist organizing to increase policing in our communities. These "activists" have continued to replicate misogynistic behavior through hypermasculinist "more arms, more police" organizing that ignores and takes for granted the consent of people they purport to rally on behalf of; to harass those who disagree with them, including youth organizers; and to disregard people's safety in public spaces.

We uplift how Asian community groups within New York City, primarily through the leadership of women and queer, trans, and gender nonconforming people, have long fought against the expansion of policing and prisons. Groups such as CAAAV, Mekong NYC, and Desis Rising Up and Moving (DRUM) have organized for economic and racial justice through antipolicing initiatives to defund the NYPD and end surveillance. Red Canary Song organizes to decriminalize sex work and address the harms of police violence and harassment against migrant sex workers. The Chinatown Art Brigade has worked in solidarity with campaigns against borough-based jail expansion, including opposing jail construction in Chinatown.

The creation of this task force is a thinly veiled operation to get more cops in Asian communities.

What do we need instead? Instead of investing more resources in the NYPD, our communities need antiviolence infrastructures that don't replicate or support systems that cage and dispose of people. For example, the Center for Anti-Violence Education has been building upstander trainings that better enable community interventions and responses for disrupting racist attacks and harassment. Rather than bilingual cops, we need more funding for language justice so our communities can have the necessary translation and interpretation for accessing care, benefits, and services. Rather than bringing more police into our homes and communities, we need safe and accessible housing. We need institutional support for street vendors, nail salon workers, and other precarious Asian American workers, including the decriminalization of sex work.

These forms of support will keep us safe.

In continuing the lineages of anti-imperialist, anticapitalist, and antiracist movements before us, we continue to demand the abolition of the police, prison, and military complex. We demand no more cops and no more cages in our communities.

Signed,
Asian American Feminist Collective
Chinatown Art Brigade
Equality Labs
Q-Wave — Building Queer & Trans API Community Since 2004
Bangladeshi Feminist Collective
Bangladeshi Americans for Political Progress (BAPP)
National Queer Asian Pacific Islander Alliance (NQAPIA)
API Rainbow Parents of PFLAG NYC
GAPIMNY — Empowering Queer & Trans Asian Pacific Islanders
The Sống Collective
Asian Womxn in the Arts (AWA)
Red Canary Song
WOW Project
Sakhi for South Asian Women
Hai Bà Trưng — NYC
Chinese Feminist Collective
Nodutdol
Slant'd
Welcome to Chinatown
Mekong NYC
Owner-members of Our House
East Coast Asian American Student Union (ECAASU)
Maynmai
CAAAV: Organizing Asian Communities
Sister Diaspora for Liberation
NAPAWF*NYC
NAWS (Neighbors Against White Supremacy) Central Queens

5.

Nail Salon Brawls and Boycotts

Unpacking the Black-Asian Conflict in America

TD Tso

As early as I can remember, my dad, an immigrant from Taiwan, would nonchalantly use the term 黑鬼 (hēi guǐ), Mandarin for "black ghost" and essentially the Chinese equivalent of the N-word, to refer to Black people. From a young age, I understood that the racial discrimination perpetuated against Black people in this country was mirrored in the sentiments of members of my community—a community that also faces intolerance in this country.

There have been ways in which this racial divide has been represented by the victimization of Asians, from biased coverage of the 1992 Los Angeles Uprising to reports of targeted attacks against Asians by Black people.[1] It could be argued that the violence is mutual, but in reality, the Asian community and Asian-owned businesses have much responsibility to bear when it comes to anti-Black violence.

On August 3, 2018, a dispute over an eyebrow wax became physical at New Red Apple Nails on Nostrand Avenue in East Flatbush, a neighborhood in Brooklyn, New York. According to a report in the *New York Post*, customer Christina Thomas was at the nail salon with her sister and grandmother when she received an unsatisfactory eyebrow waxing and refused to pay for the service. The staff ended up getting violent with the three Black women, with employees hitting them with broomsticks, dustpans, and their hands. A Facebook video of the brawl went viral, which led to protesters trying to shut down the salon, as well as other Asian-owned nail salons.[2] It also led to a movement among Black women to patronize Black-owned businesses.

The New York Healthy Nail Salons Coalition was quick to condemn the violence of New Red Apple Nails employees, stating that "at no point is any level of violence needed or justified," while Asian American community organizations banded together to call out our complicity in Black oppression.[3] "White supremacy is upheld when Asian American workers who are sometimes exploited with long days and low pay may unjustly take their frustration out with Black customers," the statement read.[4]

This incident does not stand alone. In fact, there is a long history of Black-Asian conflict in America, and tensions were especially high in the early 1990s in New York and Los Angeles. In 1990, the Flatbush boycott, also known as the Family Red Apple boycott, broke out following the assault of a Haitian woman by employees of the Korean-owned grocery in Brooklyn's predominantly Black Flatbush neighborhood. Black protesters called for the boycott of all Korean-owned stores.[5] In 1991, convenience store owner Soon Ja Du shot and killed 15-year-old Latasha Harlins after she wrongly accused Harlins of trying to shoplift a bottle of orange juice from her South Central Los Angeles store. A security camera video showed the girl had money in her hand to pay for it. Du didn't serve any jail time.[6] Alongside the police beating of Rodney King, Harlins's death is cited as a catalyst to the 1992 Los Angeles Uprising, in which Korean-owned stores were targeted, looted, and destroyed. Fast-forward to March 2017, when Black community members in Charlotte, North Carolina, protested the Missha Beauty store after owner Sung Ho Lim was filmed choking a Black female customer he suspected of stealing.[7] These infamous incidents have become emblematic of Black-Korean conflict, which has been widely documented and researched.

"Although 'Black-Korean conflict' may have largely disappeared from front page headline news, the reality of racially distinct immigrant small business entrepreneurs operating in poor, underserved minority neighborhoods persists as a formula for potential conflict," wrote scholar Miliann Kang. "The potential for misunderstandings and dissatisfaction remains high in service exchanges involving emotional and embodied dimensions across various social divisions."[8]

Each publicized incident called into question the anti-Black biases of Asian immigrants and Asian Americans. But the boycotts that followed were often xenophobia-tinged retaliations, depicting a sort of tit-for-tat cycle between communities. In the protests following the incident at New Red Apple Nails, "Where's ICE?" was heard among the chants outside of a second salon blocks away, Beautiful Red Apple Nails.[9] An employee at Beautiful Red Apple Nails told the *New York Times* that the two similarly named businesses are not owned by the same people.[10]

In 1990, the Haitian woman involved in the scuffle that began the Flatbush boycott allegedly told the cashier, "Yon Chinese, Korean motherfucker. Go back to your country," according to a report from the *New Republic*. During the ensuing protests, a Black teen bashed the skull of a Vietnamese resident with a hammer, as his accomplices yelled, "Koreans go home!"[11]

These sentiments mirror the xenophobic rhetoric often experienced by nonwhite immigrants and call to mind, for Asian Americans, the 1982 murder of Vincent Chin, a Chinese man who was murdered by two white men who mistook him for being Japanese. People of color often adopt the same anti-immigrant mentality and buy into the fear of "yellow peril" created by white supremacy and nationalism—systems that make everybody complicit to them, including the oppressed.

Sociologist Tamara K. Nopper argued against depicting these Black-Asian conflicts as "mutual misunderstanding." She writes, "The use of 'mutual' misunderstanding suggests shared status or power, with each group contributing to each other's vulnerability and suffering."[12]

Asian Americans must acknowledge and rectify the ways we uphold white supremacy, namely our anti-Blackness. Much like the United States, Asian countries suffer from colorism and caste systems within their own societies. "Anti-Blackness is foundational to the creation of America," said Diane Wong, a scholar and organizer whose research has focused on the gentrification of Chinatowns and Afro-Asian solidarities. "It's no secret then that anti-Blackness is reflected in Asian immigrant families, businesses, institutions, and interpersonal relationships on a frequent basis."[13]

In retail spaces, Black people continue to experience racism and antagonism.[14] When Asians internalize and perpetuate anti-Black racism and violence, we are reifying our complicity and driving a deeper wedge between our communities.

It's important to note that the two groups are not equally positioned in the larger structures of power, especially when one racial group is profiting off the other, which is oftentimes the case in these violent clashes between Black and Asian people. "Race is certainly a factor, but it is not the only factor," Kang said in an interview. Kang's research has focused on Asian-owned nail salons and their racially diverse customers. "Many nail salon workers are under pressure to work quickly and keep costs down, which does not create the best environment for building customer relations. The potential for tensions is heightened by the intimacy of the service, which involves direct physical contact, and the fact that many of the workers and owners are immigrants who do not speak the language or understand the culture of their customers." In these scenarios, the tension is stoked by economic stress: the salon workers often work for low wages under poor conditions, and the mostly working-class clientele cannot afford to waste money on subpar service.[15] Kang stressed the importance of putting these largely publicized conflicts in context. "I have observed hundreds of interactions in salons in this neighborhood that were very cordial and where workers and customers were very respectful and appreciative of each other," she said.

Our perspectives are largely shaped by the way Black-Asian conflict is covered in media. "There is a lot of misinformation when it comes to reporting on salient issues that affect both Black and Asian communities," Wong said.[16] However, when videos of Asian business owners and workers inflicting violence on Black customers go viral, when Asian American activists protest in support for Peter Liang, an NYPD officer who shot and killed Akai Gurley, an unarmed Black man, in a stairwell, the message received by the public is that Asians do not care about Black lives.[17]

These acts of violence are only a microcosm of the conflict between the minority groups, moments when the tension bubbles up to the surface and pops. There have been many ways statistics about Asian American achievement and the "model minority" myth have been used as a wedge between Asians and other minority groups, most notably through Ed Blum's anti–affirmative action lawsuit against Harvard University.[18] Some Asian Americans have thrown their support behind ending affirmative action and promoting standardized testing in school admission, placing their own concerns ahead of the communities marginalized by these systems, namely Black, Brown, and Indigenous peoples.

As a kid, I used to cringe when my dad, a self-proclaimed Democrat, would use slurs to refer to Black people, sometimes rolling my eyes and shouting "Daddy!" at him. Now, I realize that I must do more than just cringe. It is my generation's job to undo the legacy of anti-Black racism within our communities and to resist complicity with white supremacy—and it starts with talking about it.

6.

On Anti-Black Terror, Captivity, and Black-Korean Conflict

Tamara K. Nopper

The words "terror" and "captivity" are not commonly found in the scholarship on Asian-Black relations, particularly in the scholarship on Korean store owners and Black customers in the United States. But terror and captivity are there. Numerous studies show Black people report being watched, followed, and treated as criminals by Asian store owners. And if you go off the grid of the dominant commentary circulated and sanctioned in progressive and leftist spaces, you will hear more explicit discussions of what Black people endure as they shop in these businesses.

In response to Black people reporting in academic surveys and interviews that Asian store owners treat them as criminals, many Asian American scholars, pundits, and activists reframe these accounts as indicative of "mutual misunderstanding" or "mutual stereotyping." According to this narration, we are told, Yes, Korean immigrant store owners may have "stereotypes" about Black people as criminals, but in return, African Americans are xenophobic and treat Asians as foreigners.

Black people's desire to live with dignity and free from the constant threat of captivity gets read as Black nationalism, and Black nationalism is generally framed in Korean immigrant entrepreneurship literature as American-centric, irrational, violent, and opportunist. Boycotts, calls for community control, and organized challenges to Korean-owned liquor stores in Black neighborhoods are depicted as racist and xenophobic. On more than one occasion, Asian American scholars and writers have falsely equated Black protest targeting or affecting Korean-owned businesses with state violence and white supremacy, such as drawing parallels to the US government's internment of Japanese Americans or the 1982 beating and subsequent death of Vincent Chin.

The use of "mutual" misunderstanding suggests shared status or power, with each group contributing to each other's vulnerability and suffering. While some concede that Yes, Black people and Asian Americans don't have the same power or aren't "treated the same" (by white people or the state), they will often return to a comparative framework to suggest that we are nevertheless "similar" and that once Black people and Asian Americans realize this, Black-Asian conflict will decrease.

The employment of the mutual misunderstanding framework suggests Asian store owners desire identification with and from Black customers across class and race lines. Yet many studies of Asian immigrant store owners show they hold racist views of Black people and associate them with negative qualities purportedly absent among Asians. And when Asian Americanists emphasize that Asian store owners do identify with Black customers, the timing of such pronouncements seems preemptive. Solicited comments often appear, in print at least, when the store is considered at risk of being the target of a protest during urban uprisings, such as in Ferguson, Missouri, and Baltimore, Maryland. The fear of another 1992 Los Angeles Uprising is explicitly or implicitly expressed in such commentaries. We get quotes from Asian immigrant store owners saying some variation of, "We don't have any problems with Black people." As a preemptive gesture, we can consider how to read this as "we don't want a problem with Black people," which of course is different from "We don't want problems for Black people." This preemptive move maintains the mutual misunderstanding framework and, in the process, keeps analyses prioritizing Black suffering off the grid of progressive discourse.

What is particularly pernicious about the mutual misunderstanding approach is it recognizes Black suffering only to throw it in Black people's faces. That is, the structuring logic of the mutual misunderstanding framework requires the recognition of anti-Blackness and to a certain degree, of slavery. But the mutual misunderstanding framework simultaneously suggests Black people protesting their mistreatment are perpetrators of racism against non-Black people of color. Racial power, then, is reduced to stereotypes and not considered in terms of who is in the structural position to determine or participate in the captivity or freedom of another group. This, of course, is a variation of the "reverse racism" claim.

Related, coalitional gestures often involve Asian Americans and our allies pointing out the "immorality" of Black protest toward Asian-owned businesses, basically saying to Black people, "You should know better because you too have been oppressed." In the process, Asian Americanists suggest similarity or sameness with Black people and thus obscure Black captivity and our relationship to it. For example, among some promoting Black-Asian coalition, Black protests and political organizing directed at Asian-owned businesses are treated as examples of misdirected rage that should instead target white supremacy, corporations, or the police. According to this account, Asian Americans, non-Black people of color, and immigrant store owners have no relationship to white supremacy, corporations, or the police.

In some variations, the mutual misunderstanding framework casts Black people as akin to white people. The logic of the ethnic succession model applied to the study of Black-Korean "conflict" assumes Black political demands are driven by a territorial beef with "newcomers." According to this approach, there is likely to be tension between longtime residents, who've established themselves in an area, and new ethnic and racial groups entering the space. The ethnic succession model does not know what to do with the afterlife of slavery as it casts Black people as akin to white immigrants who have become assimilated and American, as having control of space and land they can demarcate as "Black space," and in that position, block new immigrants seeking to enter "Black space." In short, the ethnic succession model assumes Black people can defend themselves from non-Black people without political punishment. The ethnic succession model also does not know what to do with anti-Black terror, emphasizing competition and conflict between "established" groups and "newcomers."

The progressive version of the ethnic succession model suggests that Black people are settlers. While you are not likely to find the word "settler" to describe African Americans in the Black-Korean conflict literature, the accusation is embedded in the discourse regarding Black people as "misguided" in their "Black nationalism." The reading of Black nationalism as misguided is related to the assumption that Black people are not only acting like Americans but, as racially oppressed people, are confused about being American. This depiction of Black nationalism as "confused" about being American is based on a limited and strategic recognition of slavery and anti-Blackness by non-Black people, where the aforementioned sentiment of "You should know better because you too have been oppressed" is coupled with the sentiment of "Stay in your lane," which confines how Black people should trace and confront slavery and its afterlife. Black people are expected to compartmentalize their recognition of slavery as well as their political demands so as not to appropriate a suffering and political demand presumably not theirs.

The "stay in your lane" approach is the "progressive version" of the ethnic succession model because it appears to reject assimilation as a dominant framework and ideal by recognizing settler colonialism and the ongoing captivity of Native Americans. It is critical of white supremacy and Black nationalism by claiming the latter, like the former, is a colonizing politic. According to this account, Black people are not only confused about being American, they're confused about slavery and anti-Blackness. Ongoing captivity as well as the demand for space, territory, land, and sovereignty are treated as the racial formation and political domain of (non-Black) Indigenous peoples. Black people's demand for community control or other markers of Black space and sovereignty are thus taken as mimicking white people as settlers and cultural appropriators.

This critique of Black nationalism assumes Black people have no ethical standing to make political demands or claims regarding ownership to space, land, and social boundaries—or for sovereignty—because they are not Indigenous. This claim serves to reinforce the reading of Black protest toward Asian store owners as gestures of xenophobia, American-centrism, and identification with, or acting like, white people. According to this, the demand that Black lives be affirmed and bodily integrity respected, however articulated, gets read as immoral in terms of misidentifying with land, capitalism, the American project, whiteness, and settlement as well as an appropriation of an Indigenous political demand. In short, it means regardless of the ideological differences expressed by Black people, demands for dignity or political protest are usually read as suspect in some way. This then requires Black people remain vulnerable to predation and the social mobility aspirations of non-Black people of color so as not to be accused of political immorality.

The belief that Black people have no ethical standing to make political demands or claims associated with sovereignty (however constructed) or Black space or land hinges, then, on the recognition of Native Americans and Indigenous peoples in the Americas as the "original peoples," the "truly captive," and thus the "true" owners of land and claims to sovereignty. I am not suggesting that this non-Black demand, directed at Black people to "recognize" Indigenous peoples and settler colonialism, is sincerely concerned with

Native Americans or critical of ongoing genocide. Indeed, we may consider how the demand by non-Black people that Black people recognize they are not Indigenous to the United States or that they are the descendants of slaves weaponizes anti–Native American genocide to disavow anti-Blackness and capitalism—as well as fetishizes (the loss of) land and property in its "recognition" of settler colonialism, thereby ignoring internal debates among Indigenous people and between Black people and Indigenous people regarding visions of decolonization. In the process, the immigrant's status as a settler disappears from the conversation.

Think here of the way immigrant rights activists defend immigration and a desire for citizenship (and make strange communion, at least rhetorically, with Indigenous peoples) by pointing out to white xenophobes that Christopher Columbus was "the first illegal immigrant." Relevant to discussions of Black-Korean conflict, Black people—like the white xenophobes who supposedly forgot about Columbus—are depicted as seeking to exclude immigrants while purportedly forgetting that, from an "Indigenous perspective," they have no legible claim to the nation or territory—a legible claim we are told immigrants (as settlers) supposedly care about. Critics of what is constructed as Black nationalism can thus conceal their anti-Blackness by posing as pro-Indigenous, "reminding" Black people they are not the "truly captive" nor the "original owners" of land and that sovereignty is the political domain of Indigenous peoples.

This conflation of Black people who protest their treatment by Asian store owners with Americans, xenophobes, and settlers is coupled, of course, with an unwillingness to recognize the role of non-Black people of color in anti-Black terror and captivity.

I want to briefly address this here by sharing a story about my friend Jay. A few years ago, when I lived in Philadelphia, Jay and I met up to get some drinks. On the way, Jay told me about a problem he was having with a dry cleaner near where we were planning to go to happy hour. The dry cleaner had given him the wrong shirt. Not only that, the shirt they gave him had a stain on it. When Jay had told them they had given him the wrong shirt, the dry cleaning staff denied it and refused to do anything to remedy the situation.

I asked Jay if the dry cleaner was Korean owned. He said yes. I told him I should go with him to see about his shirt. For some stupid reason I thought me being Korean would matter. That I could persuade the staff to believe Jay.

We went to the dry cleaner. Jay and I stood at the counter. One of the owners, a Korean immigrant woman, approached us. She recognized Jay. He had his ticket in his hand. Again, she denied any wrongdoing. I tried to appeal to her. She and I began to argue. Then, she won.

She told us she would call the police and pointed to a camera focused on the counter. We stopped trying to make our case. Jay and I were doing nothing wrong. We were just contesting her mistake. But we knew what could happen if the police came, even though nothing would be on camera but us standing there asking questions and looking unhappy, Jay with his ticket in hand. We knew that all the cops would see is a Korean woman store owner on one side of the counter and a Black man on the other. Or perhaps the cops wouldn't bother to look at the film. They would just see Jay standing there.

We left quickly. I can't remember if we got drinks like we had planned. I just remember Jay's face. And that we felt defeated and helpless.

When I called Jay to ask him if I could write about his story for this essay, he told me that he had eventually returned to the store, and they acknowledged they had given him the wrong shirt. They offered him $25.00 as compensation. Jay accepted it even though he had purchased his shirt for almost double that. As he put it, he didn't want to be threatened with the police again. On that visit, they told him not to bring his clothes to their establishment anymore.

Jay said something to me on the phone that I want to repeat here: "I knew my shirt." A simple sentence that says so much. But that, as well as his ticket generated by the store documenting their mistake, did not matter. We also talked about other shopping experiences he has had, how often Black people are treated like shit at businesses and expected to take it for fear the police will be called. We talked about the constant navigation to not be accused or arrested or incarcerated. We talked about anti-Black terror.

Black residents in urban neighborhoods will sometimes be described as a "captive market." A concept found in discussions of "internal colonialism," notably in Kwame Ture and Charles V. Hamilton's book *Black Power,* Black residents in poor urban neighborhoods are considered a colonized group and thus captive to economic exploitation by non-Black people who find urban neighborhoods fertile ground for their social mobility. It is rare, though, that you see the idea of Black residents as a captive market taken seriously in studies on Black-Korean conflict. Such an account does not fit well with the mutual misunderstanding framework that dominates the literature.

For the most part, the captive market concept is a spatial one. It focuses on how Black people are spatially segregated and bound to urban ghettos and exploitation by non-Black people. But Jay's experience did not happen in a Black neighborhood. The dry cleaner, like many Korean-owned businesses, was located in an upscale, predominantly white neighborhood.

How, then, do we think of Black captivity? We could see Jay's experience as reinforcing the captive market model in terms of being punished for leaving a Black neighborhood; that is, we could read this as Jay being unwanted in non-Black spaces or, specifically, in upscale, predominantly white neighborhoods. That he "went out of bounds" of where he "belongs." But then, per the captive market framework, Jay would be treated badly in a Black neighborhood by Korean store owners capitalizing on the captivity of Black residents. Given this, where does Jay belong and where is he free from the threat of captivity?

Anti-Blackness followed Jay. Or it was waiting for him. Non-Black power over Black people is not spatially bound. The store owner could have pointed to a camera in the dry cleaner or in a bodega in a poor Black neighborhood. Regardless, the Korean store owner could do whatever she wanted to Jay. Wherever the camera was, wherever the store was located, the Korean immigrant store owner, as non-Black, as a person of color, as an immigrant, and as a woman, had the power to participate in Jay's criminalization and thus to play a decisive role in the future of his life and the lives of people who love him. Admitting fault and not calling the police on Jay when he returned to inquire about his shirt were not signs of her respect, they were signs of her power.

The body of scholarship on Black-Korean conflict is now a little over fifty years old, as it started to develop shortly after the 1965 Immigration Act and the noticeable establishment of Korean businesses in Black neighborhoods. Yet the way we (can) think about Black-Korean conflict is not a "done deal." Study after study tells us Black people report being treated like criminals in stores. Testimonies that appear off the grid, that is, in discourse not preoccupied with coalition or widely circulated in progressive media, tend to report this in more explicit terms than are found in survey research. How might more of us, especially those preoccupied with coalition and solidarity, seriously and ethically grapple with this reality as indicative of anti-Black terror and captivity and not "mutual misunderstanding"?

7.

I Rememory You, Zheng Xianjuan

Nana Brantuo

A Note on Rememory Work

In *Undrowned: Black Feminist Lessons from Marine Mammals*, Alexis Pauline Gumbs offers a mediation on the significance of remembrance that is at the heart of the rememory work captured in this essay. She poses: "What do we remember and what do we forget? How do we name and categorize what we can barely observe, for what purpose, with what results? . . . What do we need to remember that will push back against the forgetting encouraged by consumer culture and linear time? What can we remember that will surround us in oceans of history and potential?"[1]

Remembering and rememorying, or the simultaneous processes of "both forgetting and remembering . . . [that] transcend[s] the temporality of past, present, and future," took hold of me while exploring digitized artifacts and revisiting Sunflowers Carry Out, a Chinese American restaurant in Chillum, Maryland, where Zheng Xianjuan was shot and took her last breath.[2] Resurfacing the memories of my former classmate and revisiting the spaces where our paths crossed invoked a deep pain and grief for a life lost too soon and so violently. Remembering and rememorying her over the years, and in the years to come, will always bring me to a pause.

The haunting silence that surrounded her death has followed me for the eighteen years since that September evening in 2005. In 2018, homicide (alongside heart disease) ranked fifth as the leading cause of death for Asian American girls and women between the ages of one and nineteen.[3] Xianjuan was eighteen years old when she was murdered, the same age as a young Asian student at Indiana University who, in January 2023, was racially targeted and nearly killed on a public bus. At a rally in support of the Asian community in Indiana, Parnasi Bandyopadhyay shared with *B Square Bulletin*:

> We are perpetually foreigners. By virtue of our appearance, we do not belong. . . . We need to . . . name injustices, and make it understood that what was done was unacceptable. Without doing that, the attack on our fellow student, and the hurt that all of us have experienced in different ways, is rendered invisible.[4]

This call for safety and justice parallels those of Black women and girls who face invisibilization rooted in the history of enslavement, colonization, and anti-Black racism and misogyny and presents an opportunity for personal and communal inquiry meant to catalyze solidarity building.

To rememory Zheng Xianjuan and the intersecting histories and events that ultimately made it possible for us to share space, and to rememory the silence that surrounded her death interrogates a legacy of deprioritization of safety and justice for Black and Asian girls across the Prince George's County, Maryland, and Washington, DC, lines and our country as a whole. The personal inquiry that follows implores Black and Asian feminists to rememory intersecting histories and events and consider the following: How can rememory be in service of solidarity building for the future?

> *I was talking about time. It's so hard for me to believe in it. Some things go. Pass on. Some things just stay. I used to think it was my rememory. You know. Some things you forget. Other things you never do. But it's not. Places, places are still there. If a house burns down, it's gone, but the place—the picture of it—stays, and not just in my rememory, but out there, in the world. What I remember is a picture floating around out there outside my head.*
>
> —Toni Morrison, *Beloved*

The image of Sunflowers Carry Out as it stood nearly twenty years ago stays in my rememory, though it's no longer physically there. Revisiting my hometown and walking up Chillum Road toward the shopping center where my favorite restaurant once stood was haunting. The last time I had been there was for Zheng Xianjuan's vigil in the fall of 2005, crying quietly as her father mourned her.

Zheng Xianjuan was an upperclassman at my high school who had migrated to the United States only a few years before her life was cut short. Because of differences in age, race, and neighborhood, our paths should have never crossed. The shopping center and her father's carry out, however, served as a refuge for me—away from the chaos and violence I experienced at home.

"They think we're all thieves" is what my mother would say as I'd get ready to leave and treat myself to a lunch special. Then she'd go on to discuss Latasha Harlins and the LA Uprising, the Chinese presence in Africa, and her rememories of shop owners' prejudices. No matter what she'd say, I'd find my way there. With the little money I earned and saved from odd jobs, I'd purchase journals and stationery from neighboring dollar and convenience stores. Occasionally, I'd treat myself to a pedicure at Ti's Nails, observing and sourcing knowledge on beauty rituals in the exchanges between technicians and customers. I'd always, no matter what, save enough to purchase an orange chicken lunch special or chicken wing special with mumbo sauce on the side.

Zheng Xianjuan and I would often share awkward hellos and smiles whenever we saw and acknowledged each other's presence. More than before, I recall the times when our eyes locked, when that feeling filled the room. It was the same feeling I'd felt at Ti's Nails and the neighboring Asian immigrant-owned beauty supply store. It's the same feeling I feel now in nail salons, grocery stores, carryouts, and beauty supply stores—unspoken suspicions and tensions between Black and Asian folx, customer and owner, migrant and US citizen, and the intersections at which these identities lie. No room for conversation outside of the scope of sell and exchange. Commerce driven by white supremacy culture and capitalism set the stage for stores as the primary meeting point for our communities and constrained our ability to live with and among, and not simply coexist.

Occasionally, an adult would mediate if tensions rose too high. Other times, exchanges were brief but kind. But always brief. Sunflowers was my refuge away from the world, no matter how high tensions rose. I'd eat my meals in peace, with headphones in and a journal at hand, writing down my thoughts and planning my escape. I'd sometimes wonder if she, too, was looking for a way out of the wrong side of Prince George's County, in search of schools and neighborhoods that were clean, safe, and resourced. There's no way to know now.

While waiting for her father's shift to end that September day, Zheng Xianjuan was outside the restaurant drinking a bowl of soup when she was approached and shot multiple times by two men. Her father cradled her for the last time as her life slipped away before collapsing in tears on the ground next to her. He told the *Washington Post*, "I only have this one daughter. She was so beautiful. She was such a good student."[5]

Even now, I can remember her bloodstains were faintly visible on the sidewalk. I can still remember her face. I remember searching and listening for her name in local newspapers and news broadcasts and never seeing it. I remember her death and vigil being read out during morning announcements too quickly, the speaker mispronouncing her name along the way.

I remember how little people cared, and how she became invisible.

She was one of so many throughout my girlhood who were killed or disappeared. Years before we were enrolled at Northwestern High School, 14-year-old Nia Aisha Owens was raped and murdered in the woods behind the building. Her murderer has since been released, after serving nine years in prison.[6] During my senior year of high school, Sintia Mesa, a 25-year-old Chillum resident whose family was from the Dominican Republic and El Salvador, was strangled by her boyfriend and found naked in her car trunk miles away in Baltimore.[7]

Years later, nothing much has changed. In 2020, Fatima Kamara, a young African immigrant woman, was killed in her apartment by her boyfriend, a mile or so away from where Sunflowers used to be. Her neighbor shared with local DC news station WUSA9: "It's really scary. That's what goes through my head and my heart and my whole body, because I'm a young Black woman, I'm an immigrant as well, and you never know what could happen. We don't feel protected in our homes, and it's really sad because it happens too often."[8]

Here on the DC/Prince George's County border, less than seven miles away from the US capital, Black, Asian, Latina, immigrant, working-class women and girls' lack of access to safety has led to loss of life that is immeasurably tragic.[9] Here in the government's backyard, where genocide, slavery, and segregation were legal and where the Page Act (the first of many racialized immigration restrictions and bans) was signed into law by the Forty-Third US Congress, we embody and navigate the ironies and contradictions of citizenship.

I learned that years ago, and feel it more deeply now as I recall Zheng Xianjuan's face.

8.

Dear Indo-Caribbean People

Chandanie Somwaru

I never understood why Kali Ma was shoved in the back of my father's altar, behind the fair goddesses. Wasn't she the Hindu goddess who protected her children? Why did her tongue hanging out of her mouth and her pitch-black skin attract the words "possession," "evil," or "shame"? I had once attended mandir during Navratri to learn more about this powerful woman I prayed to. I didn't learn much, besides the fact that she realized the destruction she caused and transformed into her fairer, more "lovely" Gauri form. A form that was considered pure. Free from stigmas. Free from the hatred of Blackness.

As a half-Guyanese and half-Trinidadian New Yorker of Indo-Caribbean descent, my identity is complicated, and my community's relationship with Blackness even more so. Today, my family members are a beautiful mix of Afro-Caribbean and Indo-Caribbean descent. But underneath this mirage of multiculturalism are whispers of anti-Black racism played out through a history of political, economic, and social strife.

Back home in Guyana, my grandmother used to walk up the road to trade produce grown in her backyard. When hungry, her children would pick mangoes off trees. They would savor the last pieces of curried meat they had, not knowing when they would have the chance to eat this delicacy again. My family and their neighbors—different in religion and heritage—worked together to feed each other's children for the sake of staying alive, one cup of rice for one loaf of bread. What else was there to do when they lived in rural Guyana—surrounded by large areas of land and sugarcane—secluded from the growing tensions in the distant towns?

Maybe my father and his family were too young. Maybe they were isolated by the bushes that bordered their home. Maybe they didn't and still don't want to talk about the enmity between Indo-Guyanese and Afro-Guyanese people. Because of conflict between political parties starting in the 1940s, these communities were divided. Beatings, murders, and rapes were tallied on both sides. It seemed impossible for people to get along.

On the other side of my family, my mother, too, only remembers driving through the streets of Trinidad on a motorcycle, having beach limes, and living a calm island life before she moved to the United States. But like in Guyana, Afro-Trinidadian and Indo-Trinidadian people fought against each other to have their voices heard in the political sphere of the 1950s. Then, in 1995, when Trinidad had its first Indo-Caribbean prime minister, the appointment fueled even more hostility between Indo-Caribbean and Afro-Caribbean people.

As a child, I was once told that I looked so Black I could've been a *dougla gyal*. I didn't understand what that meant and asked family members, "What's so funny about being dougla?" What was so insulting about the term "dougla"? This derogatory term labeling a Caribbean person of mixed African and Indian descent is one of the ways people perpetuated discrimination against Blackness. The affected people were labeled too ugly, too violent. Being "too dark" pressured many women to bleach themselves to try to be whiter. Or like me, it forced us inside, where we didn't have to be seen by people or the sun.

It was under this same sun that the discrimination started. When slavery was abolished in the 1830s and Africans no longer wanted to work the land, the British had to find a new kind of labor. Indian people—who were already facing poverty, harsh working conditions, and a caste system that stereotyped and belittled people—were an easy target upon which to propagate the idea of a "better life" as an indentured servant in Guyana and Trinidad. To keep these groups apart, planters instigated jealousy and a hierarchy between them. Prejudices between the newly freed Africans and the indentured Indians blossomed in the face of both groups' lack of power and money.

The anti-Black narrative pushed by colonization and casteism in Indian culture fit right into the lifestyle practiced by the Indians who came to Guyana and Trinidad. Blackness as tainted translated into the Hindu religion and caused divine forms like Kali Ma to be associated with witchcraft and possession, when she was formerly the embodiment of power and protection. Shani Dev, a dark-skinned deity who deals with karma, came to be associated with bad luck. Gods were depicted with a blue hue instead of the "skin as dark as night" they are said to have in the texts.

Based on the caste system in India, which also draws connections between ideals of purity and skin color, Dalits (the "lowest" of the castes) were considered polluted and excluded from civil rights. In some areas of India, they are still forbidden to sit in certain places, live or walk where higher caste members are, and touch anyone or be touched. Caste and its associated overlaps with anti-Blackness extended to the Caribbean and caused us to be separated, not just ideologically but geographically as well. In Trinidad, Laventille is known to be a predominantly Afro-Caribbean area, whereas Penal, where my mother grew up, was mostly an Indo-Caribbean region. Although intermarriage is becoming more common in younger generations, it is still discouraged and looked down upon.

Even now in New York, after many Indo-Caribbean and Afro-Caribbean people migrated to the United States, the idea of separation remains in the minds of those creating a new life. One summer, I visited Island Express in Flatbush, Brooklyn, to learn how tennis rolls were made and got into an enlightening conversation about race with the bakery's owner. Her family is fused with an Afro-Guyanese and Indo-Guyanese lineage, but she still witnesses the prejudice against her loved ones who have an African ancestry. She told me, "This is what we're taught. We're taught to dislike each other."

The inheritance of this dislike is very much prevalent as aunties whisper, "Black people do crimes," and as geographic segregation continues. Richmond Hill is predominantly an area for Indo-Caribbean people, while Afro-Caribbean people are mostly located in Flatbush. However, Island Express is a safe haven and community space for workers and customers from all parts of the Caribbean.

We Caribbeans need to remember where we come from, our roots in a home infused with Indian and African traditions. Soca is the hybrid of African beats and Indian lyrics. Pepperpot is a mix of Indian and African flavors. Carnival, a time to celebrate life, is the festival where we continue to dance together, sing together, drink together, and march together, regardless of our lineages.

What creates our Caribbean heritage is not based on maliciousness but formed through shared histories of survival under unjust situations. No matter our religion, our race, our sexuality, the Caribbean is our collective home. As the Caribbean community grows in New York, I've witnessed younger generations talking back to our *macoing* aunties and organizing at the intersection of Afro- and Indo-Caribbean communities. Afro-Caribbean is still Caribbean. Indo-Caribbean is still Caribbean. We have a duty—from our culture that has always encouraged us to jump up together—to fight for and support each other.

9.

We Will Not Be Used

Mari Matsuda

In this April 1990 speech originally delivered at a fundraising banquet for the Asian Law Caucus, a public interest organization built by young radical lawyers to serve the Asian American community, critical race theorist Mari Matsuda addresses the risk of Asian Americans becoming complicit in white supremacy by playing into racial hierarchies and the model minority myth. Matsuda's words still resonate today, given the role Asian Americans played in the US Supreme Court reversal of affirmative action in 2023.[1]

I want to speak of my fear that Asian Americans are in danger of becoming the racial bourgeoisie and of my resolve to resist that path.

Marx wrote of the economic petite bourgeoisie—of the small merchants, the middle class, and the baby capitalists who were deeply confused about their self-interest. The petite bourgeoisie, he said, often emulate the manners and ideology of the big-time capitalists. They are the "wannabes" of capitalism. Struggling for riches, often failing, confused about the reasons why, the economic wannabes go to their graves thinking that the big hit is right around the corner.

Living in nineteenth-century Europe, Marx thought mostly in terms of class. Living in twentieth-century America, in the land where racism found a home, I am thinking about race. Is there a racial equivalent of the economic bourgeoisie? I fear there may be, and I fear it may be us.

If white, as it has been historically, is the top of the racial hierarchy in America, and black, historically, is the bottom, will Asians assume the place of the racial middle? The role of the racial middle is a critical one. It can reinforce white supremacy if the middle deludes itself into thinking it can be just like white if it tries hard enough. Conversely, the middle can dismantle white supremacy if it refuses to be the middle, if it refuses to buy into racial hierarchy, and if it refuses to abandon communities of black and brown people, choosing instead to forge alliances with them.

"We will not be used" is a plea to Asian Americans to think about the ways in which our communities are particularly susceptible to playing the worst version of the racial bourgeoisie role.

I remember my mother's stories of growing up on a sugar plantation on Kauai. She tells of the Portuguese *luna,* or overseer. The luna rode on a big horse and issued orders to the Japanese and Filipino workers. The luna in my mother's stories is a tragic/comic figure. He thinks he is better than the other workers, and he does not realize that the plantation owner considers the luna subhuman, just like all the other workers. The invidious stereotype of the dumb *"portagee"* persists in Hawai'i today, a holdover from the days of the luna parading around on the big horse, cloaked in self-delusion and false pride.

The double tragedy for the plantation Nisei who hated the luna is that the Sansei in Hawai'i are becoming the new luna. Nice Japanese girls from Manoa Valley are going through four years of college to get degrees in travel industry management in order to sit behind a small desk in a big hotel, to dole out marching orders to brown-skinned workers, and to take orders from a white man with a bigger desk and a bigger paycheck who never has to complicate his life by dealing with the brown people who make the beds and serve the food.[2] He need only deal with the nice-Japanese-girl-ex-cherry-blossom-queen, eager to please, who does not know she will never make it to the bigger desk.

The Portuguese luna now has the last laugh with this new, unfunny portagee joke: When the portagee was the luna, he did not have to pay college tuition to ride that horse. I would like to say to my sister behind the small desk, "Remember where you came from, and take this pledge: We will not be used."

There are a hundred ways to use the racial bourgeoisie. First is the creation of success myths and blame-the-victim ideology. When Asian Americans manage to do well, their success is used against others. Internally, it is used to erase the continuing poverty and social dislocation within Asian American communities. The media are full of stories of Asian American whiz kids.[3] Their successes are used to erase our problems and to disavow any responsibility for them. The dominant culture does not know about drug abuse in our communities, our high school dropouts, or our AIDS victims.[4] Suggestions that some segments of the Asian American community need special help are greeted with suspicion and disbelief.

Externally, our successes are used to deny racism and to put down other groups. African Americans and Latinos and poor white people are told, "Look at those Asians—anyone can make it in this country if they really try." The cruelty of telling this to workers displaced by runaway shops and to families waiting in line at homeless shelters is not something I want associated with my genealogy. Yes, my ancestors made it in this country, but they made it against the odds. In my genealogy, and probably in yours, are people who went to bed hungry, who lost land to the tax collector, who worked to exhaustion and ill health, who faced pain and relocation with the bitter stoicism that we call, in Nihongo, *gaman*.[5] Many who came down the hard road of our ancestors did not make it. Their bones are still in the mountains by the tunnels they blasted for the railroad, still in the fields where they stooped over the short-handled hoe, and still in the graveyards of Europe, where they fought for a democracy that did not include them.

Asian success was success with a dark, painful price. To use that success to discount the hardship facing poor and working people in this country today is a sacrilege to the memory of our ancestors. It is an insult to today's Asian American immigrants who work the double-triple shift, who know no leisure, who crowd two and three families to a home, and who put children and old folks alike to work at struggling family businesses or doing piecework until midnight. Yes, we take pride in our success, but we should also remember the cost. The success that is our pride is not to be given over as a weapon to use against other struggling communities. I hope we will not be used to blame the poor for their poverty.

Nor should we be used to deny employment or educational opportunity to others. A recent exchange of editorials and letters in the Asian American press reveals confusion over affirmative action.[6] Racist anti-Asian quotas at the universities can give quotas a bad name in our community. At the same time, quotas have been the only way we have been able to walk through the door of persistently discriminatory institutions like the San Francisco Fire Department.[7] We need affirmative action because there are still employers who see an Asian face and see a person who is unfit for a leadership position. In every field where we have attained a measure of success, we are underrepresented in the real power positions.[8] And yet, we are in danger of being manipulated into opposing affirmative action by those who say affirmative action hurts Asian Americans. What is really going on here? When university administrators have hidden quotas to keep down Asian admissions, this is because Asians are seen as destroying the predominantly white character of the university. Under this mentality, we cannot let in all those Asian overachievers and maintain affirmative action for other minority groups. We cannot do both because that will mean either that our universities lose their predominantly white character or that we have to fund more and better universities. To either of those prospects, I say, why not?, and I condemn the voices from my own community that are translating legitimate anger at ceilings on Asian admissions into unthinking opposition to affirmative action floors needed to fight racism.

In a period when rates of educational attainment for minorities and working-class Americans are going down, in a period when America is lagging behind other developed nations in literacy and learning, I hope we will not be used to deny educational opportunities to the disadvantaged and to preserve success for only the privileged.[9]

Another classic way to use the racial bourgeoisie is as America's punching bag. There is a lot of rage in this country, and for good reason. Our economy is in shambles. Persistent unemployment is creating new ghost towns and new soup kitchens from coast to coast. The symptoms of decay—the drugs, the homelessness, and the violence—are everywhere.

From out of this decay comes a rage looking for a scapegoat, and a traditional American scapegoat is the Oriental Menace. From the Workingmen's Party that organized white laborers around an anti-Chinese campaign in California in 1877, to the World War II incarceration fueled by resentment of the success of Issei farmers, to the murder of Vincent Chin and the terrorizing of Korean merchants, there is an unbroken line of poor and working Americans turning their anger and frustration into hatred of Asian Americans.[10] Every time this happens, the real villains—the corporations and politicians who put profits before human needs—are allowed to go about their business free from public scrutiny, and the anger that could go to organizing for positive social change goes instead to Asian bashing.

Will we be used as America's punching bag? We can prevent this by organizing to publicize and to fight racist speech and racist violence wherever we find it. More important, however, Asian Americans must take a prominent role in advocating economic justice. We must show that Asian Americans are allies of the working poor and the unemployed. If we can show our commitment to ending the economic upheaval that feeds anti-Asian sentiment, the displaced rage that terrorizes Asian Americans will turn on more deserving targets.

If we can show sensitivity to the culture and needs of other people of color when we do business in their communities, we will maintain our welcome there, as we have in the past. I hope we can do this so we can put an end to being used as America's punching bag.

The problem of displaced anger is also an internal problem for Asian Americans. You know the story: the Japanese pick on the Okinawans, the Chinese pick on the Filipinos, and the Samoans pick on the Laotians. On the plantation we scabbed on each other's strikes. In Chinatown, we have competed over space. There are Asian men who batter Asian women and Asian parents who batter their children. There is homophobia in our communities, tied to a deep fear that we are already so marginalized by white society that any additional difference is intolerable. I have heard straight Asian men say they feel so emasculated by white society that they cannot tolerate assertive women or sexually ambiguous men. This is a victim's mentality, the tragic symptom of a community so devoid of self-respect that it brings its anger home.

I love my Asian brothers, but I have lost my patience with malingering homophobia and sexism and especially with using white racism as an excuse to resist change. You know, the "I have to be Bruce Lee because the white man wants me to be Tonto" line. Yes, the J-town boys with their black leather jackets are adorable, but the pathetic need to put down straight women, gays, and lesbians is not. To anyone in our communities who wants to bring anger home, let us say, "Cut it out." We will not be used against each other.

If you know Hawaiian music, you know of the *ha'ina* line that tells of a song about to end. This speech is about to end. It will end by recalling echoes of Asian American resistance.

In antieviction struggles in Chinatown from coast to coast and in Hawai'i, we have heard the song "We Will Not Be Moved."[11] I want to remember the times when Asian Americans stood side by side with African Americans, Latinos, and progressive white people to demand social justice. I want to remember the multiracial International Longshore and Warehouse Union, which ended the plantation system in Hawai'i, and the multiracial sugar beet strikes in California that brought together Japanese, Filipino, and Chicano workers to fulfill their dream of a better life.[12] I want to remember the American Committee for Protection of the Foreign Born, which brought together progressive Okinawans, Koreans, Japanese,

Chinese, and European immigrants to fight McCarthyism and the deportation of political activists.[13] I want to remember the San Francisco State College strike and the Asian American students who stood their ground in a multiracial coalition to bring about ethnic studies and lasting changes in American academic life, changes that make it possible for me, as a scholar, to tell the truth as I see it.[14]

In remembering the San Francisco State strike, I also want to remember Dr. Hayakawa and ask what he represented.[15] For a variety of historical and cultural reasons, Asian Americans are particularly susceptible to being used by the dominant society. Nonetheless, we have resisted being used. We have joined time and again in the struggle for democracy in America. A friend sent me a news clipping from the *San Francisco Chronicle* about Asian Americans as the retailer's dream. It starts out, "They're young, they're single, they're college-educated, and on the white-collar track. And they like to shop for fun."[16] Does that describe you? Well, it may describe me, too. But I hope there is more to Asian American identity than that. I hope we will be known to history as a people who remembered the hard road of their ancestors and who shared, therefore, a special commitment to social justice.

This song is now at an end, a song of my hope that we will not be used.

10.

Recognition and Liberation for CHamoru People

A Congressional Statement

Rosa Bordallo

The following congressional statement was made on May 27, 1993, by a 9-year-old Rosa Bordallo at a hearing before the Subcommittee on National Parks, Forests and Public Lands under the Committee on Natural Resources (House of Representatives, 103rd Congress) in Washington, DC. The session was held in support of H.R. 1944, which called for additional development for the War in the Pacific National History Park in Guam, including the construction of a monument to "commemorate the loyalty of the people of Guam and the heroism of the American forces that liberated Guam," as well as the implementation of "programs to interpret experiences of the people of Guam during World War II, including oral histories of people who experienced the occupation." HR 1944 was signed into law on December 17, 1993. The oral histories of the CHamoru people of Guam are especially important to our understanding of cross-racial solidarity given the violence experienced by Pacific Islanders at the hands of multiple colonizers, including the US and Japanese—all the while being lumped into the same racial category as Asian Americans.[1] We include this testimony in the anthology not to erase or absorb CHamoru and other Pacific Islander experiences and voices but to offer an example of the kinds of struggles and forms of resistance arising out of Oceania and its diaspora and to elucidate the complex tensions and of Asian, Asian American, and Pacific Islander positions and harms caused by war-making, militarism, and imperialism.

My name is Rosalia Bordallo. I am from the Island of Guam, and I have traveled nearly nine thousand miles in twenty hours to tell the story of my father and grandfather. I am nine years old, and I am in the fourth grade at Cathedral Grade School. It is from my parents that I learned the history of my island during World War II. I hope that you decide to build this monument at the War in the Pacific Park on Guam.

On December 8, 1941, the Japanese began bombing my homeland of Guam. Two days later, they invaded and took over the entire island. It was not until July 21, 1944, that American forces returned to Guam. During these two and a half years, the people of Guam suffered greater and deeper losses than any other community in the United States during World War II. In my own family, my father, Paul Bordallo, and my grandfather, Baltazar Bordallo, were tortured and almost killed by the Kempeitai, the Japanese secret police.

On midnight of August 10, 1943, my grandfather and his family of fourteen children, most of whom were only my age or younger, were marched off their ranch at gunpoint. They were called by the Kempeitai to the central police station, where they were separated from my grandfather and thrown into an underground dungeon.

When my grandmother asked why they were imprisoned, the commander told her that the family ranch was hiding the American sailor George Tweed, who was not captured by the Japanese authorities during the occupation.

My father, who was thirteen at the time and one of the eldest children, still remembers the screams of a young CHamoru girl who was being tortured in a cell nearby. For five hours she screamed and pleaded for mercy while my grandmother and her children sat in the small cell completely terrified.

In the early morning hours, a policeman came and called for my father. Full of fear, my father answered back. He was taken out of the dark and terrible dungeon into the street in front of the police station. There he was told by the Kempeitai commander that his father had confessed that radioman George Tweed had been hidden on the family ranch.

The commander also told him that he suspected my father of delivering food and supplies to Tweed. The commander told my father that if he confessed now, he and his family would not be executed. My father did not know the whereabouts of George Tweed. The officer became angry that my father could not tell him where the American sailor was hiding.

He ordered four soldiers to hold my father while Kempeitai officers beat him on the head, back, and legs with a club. My father told me that he screamed and cried from the pain.

Soon, however, the continuous hitting stopped hurting my father. The more they kept hitting him, the less he could feel the pain. After what seemed like hours, my father lost consciousness under the torture. Later that night, the Japanese awoke him and brought him back to the dark cell where the rest of the family was kept.

He told me that he looked quietly at all his younger siblings, sat down on the dirt floor, and cried. My grandfather was treated even more harshly than my father.

After being separated from the rest of his family, my grandfather was interrogated by the Kempeitai commander about the location of George Tweed. My grandfather, who truly did not know where Mr. Tweed was hiding, was beaten by the Japanese just like my father had been.

However, the Kempeitai still did not believe that my grandfather did not know where Tweed was. They imprisoned my grandfather during the day and tortured him at night.

They would tie his hands to two poles stuck in the ground and would whip him until his back bled. When they released him ten days later, my father told me he had no skin on his back. When I asked my father why he and grandpa were beaten, he told me that the Japanese were trying to capture an American soldier.

He also told me that all people suffered during war. My father would tell me that the Japanese did those things to him because they were just as afraid of war as we CHamorus were. To him, this sailor George Tweed was hiding in the jungles of Guam because he was afraid of the Japanese. But the Japanese were just as afraid of Mr. Tweed.

Their failure to capture this lone man made the Japanese commanders lose face with their superiors.

The CHamorus hid George Tweed and gave him food. Many CHamorus were killed by the Japanese for hiding this American soldier, or for expressing hope that America would return to Guam.

Mr. Tweed later received a medal for his struggle against the Japanese. He was honored for saving himself. The Japanese commanders also sought to save themselves, if not their lives, then their honor or face.

But it was only the CHamorus who sought to give generously of themselves. It was the CHamorus who sheltered Mr. Tweed. To save their lives, as well as the lives of other CHamorus, they could easily have revealed Mr. Tweed's hiding places, but they chose not to do that.

I have heard my teacher say that George Tweed stood as a symbol of America during the war with the Japanese. The CHamorus wanted to be liberated from the bad conditions during the war. Those who hid Mr. Tweed all those years believe that the United States will come back and save Guam. My father told me that the CHamorus were liberated by the Americans because our island was important to winning the war.

The CHamorus of Guam still want recognition for the bravery of their people. My father told me that the memorial will ensure forever the memory that we are a people of worth and bravery who have been tested in battle and blood and whom history will not forget.

My father also told me that the story of the CHamoru people will live on long after its telling ceases upon the silent graves of our elders. My father told me that war is a terrible thing and what the war did to our people must not be forgotten.

PART 2

Our Lineages

Radical Histories of Cross-Racial Organizing

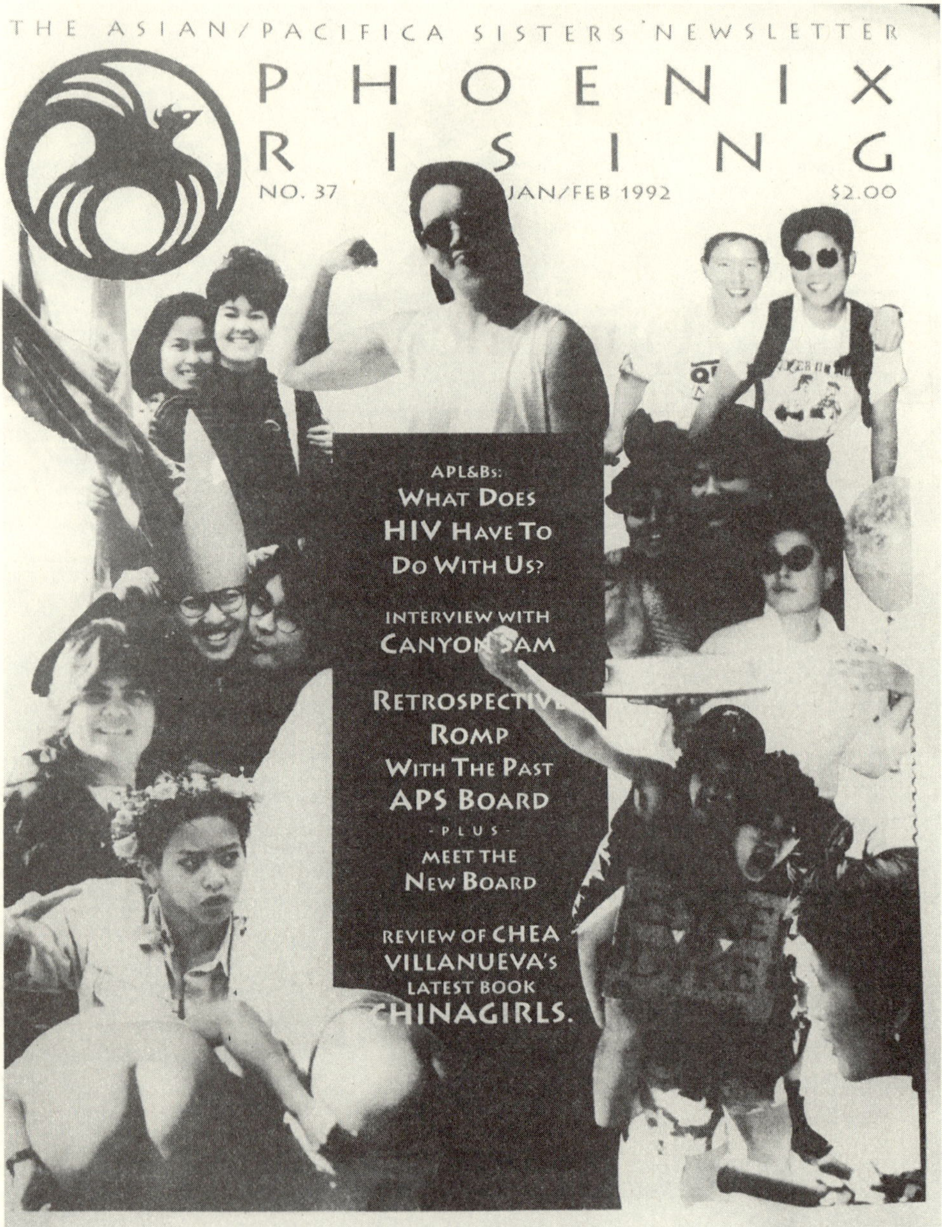

THE ASIAN/PACIFICA SISTERS NEWSLETTER
PHOENIX RISING
NO. 37
JAN/FEB 1992
$2.00
APL&Bs:
WHAT DOES HIV HAVE TO DO WITH US?
INTERVIEW WITH CANYON SAM
RETROSPECTIVE ROMP WITH THE PAST APS BOARD
-PLUS-
MEET THE NEW BOARD
REVIEW OF CHEA VILLANUEVA'S LATEST BOOK CHINAGIRLS.

Cover of *Phoenix Rising: The Asian/Pacifica Sisters Newsletter*, no. 37 (January/February 1992). Image provided by Jaimee A. Swift.

Aché
November/December, 1990 Vol. 2, No. 6 $2 A Journal For Black Lesbians
LA SALA STUDIO
Artwork by Sarita Johnson-Hunt. For more on the artist, see page 4.

Cover of *Aché: A Journal for Black Lesbians* 2, no. 6 (November/December 1990), with artwork by Sarita Johnson-Hunt. Image provided by Jaimee A. Swift.

11.

"Peace and Freedom—Inseparable"

Claudia Jones's Afro-Asian Internationalism

Zifeng Liu

Now widely recognized as a leading light of Black radicalism, organizer, journalist, and intellectual Claudia Jones persisted in linking diverse freedom struggles to challenge interlocking systems of racism, capitalism, heterosexism, and colonialism. The extant scholarship on Jones has redressed her erasure from public memory and a range of academic histories, such as those of antiracism, anticapitalism, feminism, anti-imperialism, and peace advocacy.[1] But the inclusion of North Korean, Japanese, and Chinese revolutionaries in the worldwide revolutionary alliance that she devoted her life to building and accounts of her Afro-Asian solidarity activism are still relatively underexplored. Jones's commitment to national liberation, anticapitalism, and peace prompted her to call for solidarity with East Asian radical movements. It is therefore no wonder that Jones's engagement with that region consisted of campaigning against US nuclear militarism, expressing opposition to the US military intervention in the Korean War, interacting with Japanese peace radicals, and voicing public support for China's nuclear weapons project.[2] In these endeavors, she reimagined peace beyond its dominant definition as the "absence of violence" and emphasized freedom from imperialism and capitalism as its prerequisite.

The East Asian arc of Claudia Jones's internationalism began shortly after the end of World War II. The defeat of the Axis powers did not bring changes to the global order sufficient to ensure long-lasting peace and security. The dropping of an atomic bomb on Hiroshima and Nagasaki, cities inhabited by people of color, seemed to confirm the widely held beliefs among Black activists that white supremacist power pervaded the international system and would continue to be maintained through the deployment of weapons of mass destruction. This fear of nuclear annihilation grew as the United States sought to consolidate its own position as a global hegemon and as Washington's hostility toward Moscow and the communist bloc intensified. The nightmare of nuclear conflagration seemed close to reality when, amid US intervention in the conflict on the Korean Peninsula in the early 1950s, the first hot war of the Cold War, President Harry S. Truman broached the possibility of using nuclear weapons at a press conference.[3] Jones, along with her comrades on the left, spoke out against the United States entering the Korean War.

Rejecting the United States' framing of its involvement in the conflict as an effort -to defend freedom against communism, Jones revealed—in an essay published only three months before the breakout of war—that the continued reproduction of capitalism fueled imperialism and required militarism. Addressing herself to readers primarily committed to left feminist politics, Jones emphasized that US monopoly capitalism's project "only of war and fascism" not only reinforced economic exploitation based on gender, class, and race but also imposed heteropatriarchal values that confined women to domestic spaces and limited women's participation in struggles for peace and social and economic demands.[4] She enthused about the growing momentum of women's peace activism against the Korean War and positioned poor and working Black women at the vanguard of the global struggle against capitalism, imperialism, and militarism.

According to Jones, African American women received letters from their sons and husbands and "are registering alarm, as they become aware that lynching by court martial and wanton shooting of Negro troops in Korea merge with the growth of terrorization of Negro veterans at home." They "see in the bloody massacre of the people of Korea an extension of the foul white supremacy oppression and contempt for the Negro people and the colored people of all of Asia" and were able to link the Black freedom struggle in the United States and the resistance movement against imperialism on the Korean Peninsula. Jones called for the mobilization of women, and in particular Black women, through addressing their concrete needs and "in their specific role as mothers and wives who want peace, so that their children of today and those yet unborn may grow up to manhood and womanhood."[5]

For Jones, women could use maternal and familial strategies to draw their moral authority from the traditional gendered division of labor in the family and their determination to make the world safer for their children and protect their families from violence. This commitment to "fighting for our children" enshrined a pervasive heteronormative logic that views heterosexual reproduction as the end-goal of the global peace movement and thereby reinforces a sexualized hierarchy that pathologizes and oppresses nonreproductive bodies. But Jones also contested the denial of access of Black working women to the fruits of their reproductive labor and positioned motherhood as a radical political subjectivity.[6]

Jones believed her peace activism and Afro-Asian internationalism exposed the co-constitutive relationship between militarism and gendered racial capitalism, which seemingly championed the merits of the Soviet Union's domestic and foreign policy through the ire of Washington.[7] The US state's repressive apparatus imprisoned Jones multiple times, devastating her already fragile health, and deported her to Britain so her political activities could be surveilled and curtailed.[8] But as Carole Boyce Davies argues, Jones's relocation to London did not mean the abandonment of her activist career. Instead, in the contexts of intensifying anticolonial activity in Asia, Africa, and the Americas and the changing dynamics of the political landscape in Britain, Jones reoriented her activism around the interrelated issues of community building and Caribbean and global decolonization.

Moreover, in this leg of her political journey, the advancement of Third World struggles for national liberation and self-determination took priority over the adherence to the Soviet Communist Party's line.[9] Her peace politics radicalized and emphasized to a greater extent the link between the attainment of freedom from war and violence and the waging of militant nationalist struggles.

This emphasis on the inextricability of peace and anticolonial national liberation was threaded throughout Jones's continuing internationalist work regarding East Asia. This was most evident in her participation in the Tenth World Conference against Atomic and Hydrogen Bombs, held in Tokyo in 1964, and her engagement with Mao's China. Attending the antinuclear gathering convening in the only country that ever experienced the ravages of atomic weapons as a vice chairperson of the Conference Drafting Committee, Jones learned about the continuing devastation of the lives of Nagasaki residents wrought by the 1945 bombing. She demanded local and national efforts to prevent further nuclear aggression and, along with other delegates, joined Japanese representatives and activists in fusing the struggles for peace and anticolonial national liberation.[10] This "principled" stance against atomic bombs viewed US imperialism as "the chief enemy of peace" and called for the "concerting of peace and national liberation forces of our globe."[11]

Such a view emphasized the capitalist and imperialist roots of international instability and argued for national self-determination as the prerequisite for global peace, thereby affirming "the right of peoples in the fight for national liberation to use whatever means they choose to defeat the oppressors" and articulating a radical peace politics that did not reject armed struggle, including the development of nuclear weapons, as a liberatory strategy.[12]

Understandably, this perspective was not universally shared. As Jones reported in the *West Indian Gazette and Afro-Asian Caribbean News,* the newspaper she founded in March 1958 in Brixton, London, certain sections of the Japanese Socialist Party—which Jones considered right wing—refused to differentiate between just and unjust wars and called for opposition to nuclear weapons possession by any state. After being barred from serving in leading capacities—a decision Jones emphasized was "unanimously upheld by the delegates"—these Japanese Socialists organized an alternative conference to "rival and confuse the delegates" and promote their prescriptions for world peace. Jones chided the "splitters" for not only disrupting the unity among the conference attendees but also failing to recognize the deeper, structural causes of war and the centrality of anti-imperialism, including its militant forms, as the path to peace. Jones was certainly concerned about the catastrophic consequences of nuclear weapons, but for her, "the mercenaries, the U.S. imperialists, who wield them [nuclear weapons] and threaten peace," were the real danger of security.[13]

The fracture of unity at the Tokyo conference also demonstrates that Jones's radical imagination of peace and security was fraught by Cold War pragmatism. In addition to remaining vigilant against ongoing attempts at colonial and neocolonial violence, she also had to carefully maneuver her way through the thickets of political and ideological tensions between the Soviet Union and China over international revolutionary strategies and visions for the global nuclear order. By the time of Jones's visit to Asia in 1964, the two communist powers had abandoned the pretense of socialist internationalism and become openly antagonistic to each other. The post-Stalinist Soviet policy of peaceful coexistence and competition with capitalism aimed to maintain and stabilize the current nuclear power balance and opposed China's development of atomic weapons, whereas Beijing intensified its efforts to aid Third

World militant struggles against imperialism, colonialism, and capitalism and viewed its recent successful nuclear test as undermining imperialist nuclear blackmail and threats.[14] Two months after the Tokyo gathering, China successfully tested its first atomic bomb. Jones agreed with Beijing's description of the significance of China's nuclear weapons project to the advancement of the global struggle against imperialism. In the *West Indian Gazette and Afro-Asian Caribbean News* and the Chinese Communist Party's mouthpiece *Renmin Ribao,* she celebrated this success of China's socialist construction and policy of self-reliance as a contribution to Third World national liberation movements, the restructuring of the world order, and the creation of the necessary conditions for long-lasting peace.[15]

In an interview that was published in both publications, Jones opined, "The successful Chinese nuclear test has broken the nuclear monopoly and was a rebuff to the US policy of nuclear blackmail." As China's development of atomic bombs "helps the peace forces all over the world for promoting the convening of a world summit conference" against nuclear weapons and "strengthen[s] [China's] defences" against imperialism, she viewed the detonation as a major achievement in the struggle for peace and security.[16]

Additionally, Jones registered her disappointment with the direction Soviet foreign policy had taken in her report of the Tokyo conference. The Soviet delegation attended the parallel conference organized by the Japanese Socialists and supported the vision for peace expressed in the Limited Test Ban Treaty—initiated by Washington, Moscow, and London—that, according to Jones, could not prevent imperialist powers from developing and deploying nuclear powers and aimed to "deny the non-nuclear powers, particularly the People['s] Republic of China, to participate on an equal footing."[17] In voicing her support for Beijing, Jones stressed the importance of the reorganization of the world order around the principles of anti-imperialism and national self-determination. But Jones did not parrot the Chinese stance on its dispute with the Soviet Union. While *Renmin Ribao* was blasting Moscow's "betrayal of the communist cause," she downplayed the implications of the Sino-Soviet split and prioritized forging a global alliance against capitalism and imperialism over engaging in ideological disputes, thereby articulating a relatively independent position.[18]

Immediately following the conclusion of the antinuclear conference, Jones traveled to China on the invitation of the country's official Peace Committee. In China, she observed profound socio-politico-economic transformations under socialism improving ordinary people's lives and met with local and national leaders to discuss the history of the Chinese revolution, the Chinese theory and practice of socialist building, and the common desire for a world without imperialism and for connections and solidarities.[19] In particular, Jones's admiration for the recent Chinese success in detonating an atomic bomb set the tone for her exploration of Chinese socialism. For her, "the great achievement of the Chinese workers, scientists, and technical personnel in China's first nuclear test further proved the correctness and success of the principle of self-reliance of the Chinese people."[20] She sought to learn more about the Chinese policy of self-reliance. In a detailed account of her visit to China, Jones cited agricultural and industrial communes, bumper harvests, and the continuous production of high-quality steel as some of "the great achievements in Socialist Construction in the New China, based on its policy of Self-Reliance in the fields of agriculture and industrialization in light and heavy industry."[21]

Jones's travel narrative certainly idealized the Chinese socialist construction, validated the party-state's claims to ideological superiority, and corresponded to the Chinese Communist Party's geopolitical and domestic aspirations. But such an account also served anti-imperialist and anticapitalist purposes, and the romanticizing tone also reflected her desire for alternatives to racial capitalism and imperialism.

Jones's Afro-Asian internationalism ended when she passed away in her sleep in December 1964. In the November issue of her newspaper, she announced plans to write more about her experiences in China, including her meeting with Mao Zedong, to whet her readers' appetite for news coverage of radical activities in Asia and further forge Afro-Asian solidarity.[22] Since Jones's peace politics radicalized as she increasingly pinned her hope for a more just world order on national liberation movements that were becoming more militant, we can speculate that, at least until the end of the radical phase of China's Cultural Revolution, she would have continued to position Beijing as a central node in the Third World internationalist network she sought to build.

While Jones's Afro-Asian internationalism evolved in the midst of the era's geopolitical shifts, what remained consistent was her unswerving commitment to anti-imperialism, which necessitated linking the struggles for peace and for freedom from all forms of oppression. Jones's formulation of anti-imperialism in internationalist politics is also one of her most important legacies. The headline "Dear Claudia! We Shall Hold High Your Banner of Anti-Imperialism" that appeared in her newspaper when she died serves to encourage us to continue the fight that Jones devoted her entire life to.[23]

12.

At the Intersections of Race, Gender, and Class

Honoring the Revolutionary Feminist Legacy of the Third World Women's Alliance

Karla Méndez

In the 1960s and 1970s, the second wave of feminism was well underway, with organizations advocating for women's rights, lobbying for legislation like Title IX and the approval of the birth control pill. The Civil Rights Movement was contemporaneously happening, fighting for the rights of Black people in the United States. At their convergence was the Third World Women's Alliance (TWWA). Originally initiated as a suggestion by Frances Beal for a women's caucus of the Student Nonviolent Coordinating Committee (SNCC), the revolutionary feminist work of the alliance built a legacy for future radical Black feminists and feminists of color organizations in the United States.

Frances M. Beal's Introduction to Activism and Pan-Africanism

In the 1960s, the feminist movement went through a period commonly referred to as the second wave, which lasted for about two decades. During this time, many feminist groups formed with a mission of working toward equality for women. While middle-class white women fronted many of these mainstream feminist groups, they were often exclusionary of Black women and women of color. However, several organizations were created by and for Black women and women of color that focused on their unique experiences navigating race, gender, capitalism, migration, and more. Among these groups was TWWA in New York City. TWWA also had a San Francisco Bay Area chapter, established by activist Cheryl Johnson in 1971. The Bay Area chapter was founded after Johnson traveled to Cuba with the Venceremos Brigade, an international organization in solidarity with the Cuban Revolution and Cuban workers.[1] The members of the East Coast chapter supported the extension, as it would allow them to recruit more women of color members. TWWA also had a Seattle chapter.[2] Active from 1968 to 1980, TWWA was formed to respond to the need for women's organizations within the antiracist and radical leftist movements.[3]

Prior to the formation of TWWA, the organization was the Black Women's Liberation Committee (BWLC), a faction of SNCC. Founded by civil rights activist Ella Baker in April 1960, SNCC differed from other civil rights organizations as its members did not believe in single leader–centered organizations but instead fostered group-centered leadership.[4] Over time, members of SNCC, such as Frances M. Beal, Mae Jackson, and Gwendolyn Patton, felt injustices against Black women were not being addressed. They wanted to discuss and advocate for reproductive rights, voter registration, political literacy, civil rights legislation, and other issues but continuously came up against misogyny and sexism.

While Black women in SNCC would split from the organization and form BWLC, Beal was essential to the formation of TWWA. As the daughter of a father with African American and Native American ancestry and a Russian-Jewish mother, Beal experienced racism and anti-Semitism early on, which developed her political consciousness and informed her life as an activist.

Beal was born in Binghamton, New York, in 1940, and her family later moved to St. Albans, an integrated neighborhood in Queens.[5] She moved to Paris to study in 1960, and during this time, she underwent politicization due to her interactions with people from francophone colonies, primarily Algeria. The Algerian National Liberation Front (FLN) came to Paris to continue fighting for freedom and were involved in protests that caused tension between the FLN and the police.[6] For Beal, learning from African students from French colonies was the catalyst of her Pan-Africanism and internationalism.

Beal was also part of a group of students who organized to bring Malcolm X to Paris to lead a discussion in 1965.[7] The event was so successful that the group arranged for him to speak again at a bigger venue, as the original location had an overflow of attendees. Malcolm X left for England after the first event, but when he tried to return to Paris, he was prohibited by French authorities.

The Formation of a Radical Group: The Third World Women's Alliance

Like other activists, Beal was influenced by several events to join the Civil Rights Movement. The murder of Emmett Till was a catalyst for her joining SNCC. From 1959 to 1966, although Beal was living in France, she remained involved with SNCC, working with the organization during the summers. During her time with SNCC, Beal was interested in political conversations on abortion and reproductive rights, particularly how both impact the lives of Black women. Although SNCC advocated and fought for racial equality, sexism was present in the organization. Women were relegated to positions that sustained gendered hierarchies. BWLC worked to address the racism and sexism—what we now identify as what feminist scholars Moya Bailey and Trudy aka @thetrudz term "misogynoir"—that Black women experienced in and outside the organization. In the documentary *She's Beautiful When She's Angry,* Beal stated: "I was in the Student Nonviolent Coordinating Committee. You're talking about liberation and freedom half the night on the racial side, and then all of a sudden, men are going to turn around and start talking about putting you in your place."[8]

As SNCC began to close many of its chapters due to changing leadership and the targeting of the organization by the FBI's Counterintelligence Program, the BWLC received new members who had no previous relationship with SNCC.[9] In 1969, the BWLC changed its name to the Black Women's Alliance (BWA). Not only did BWA assert its independence from SNCC as a separate and autonomous organization but it did so politically. According to Ashley Farmer in "The Third World Women's Alliance, Cuba, and the Exchange of Ideas," the ideological leanings of BWA shifted to a more Marxist- and nationalist-oriented framework.[10] As the organization continued to address abortion, reproductive rights, and sterilization abuse in the southern region of the United States, members of BWA were approached by Puerto Rican women who wanted to be part of the organization.

At first, BWA saw African American women's problems as separate and different from those of Puerto Rican women. However, after conversations with Puerto Rican women and other women of color, they began to see that they, too, were dealing with oppressions at the intersections of race, class, gender, capitalism, and imperialism. Just as Black women formed BWA because of the paucity of recognition of their experiences, their ideologies began to expand and shift again when they became aware of the violations women of color were being subjected to—including the forced and nonconsensual sterilization of Puerto Rican women. With the move to accept Puerto Rican women, and later other women of color, into the organization, BWA transformed into TWWA in 1970.[11]

Holding Space for Third World Women and Interlocking Oppressions

Throughout its existence, TWWA experienced pushback from the mainstream white feminist movement, which argued that its explicit focus on women of color took focus from the movement's overall struggle for "all" women. One of the most prominent examples of this was the Women's Strike for Equality on August 26, 1970. Thousands of women gathered on Fifth Avenue in New York City, answering National Organization for Women (NOW) cofounder Betty Friedan's call for a national strike to raise awareness for women's rights and to celebrate the anniversary of the ratification of the Nineteenth Amendment.[12] Yet it's crucial to note the contradictions between a protest commemorating the passage of the right for women to vote and the continual voter suppression of Black women and women of color. How could a march purporting to celebrate suffrage occur when it had not been gained for all women, even fifty years later?

On the day of the strike, TWWA members including Beal made their way to the strike with a banner reading, "Hands Off Angela Davis" in tow. Their banner was a public show of solidarity and support for Davis, who had been arrested for an alleged connection to an attempt to free the Soledad Brothers.[13] TWWA leader Patricia Romney recalls how as they got closer to the crowds, Lucy Komisar, the vice president of NOW and the coordinator of the parade, informed members of TWWA that they would not be able to march because, in her opinion, their banner did not have anything to do with women's liberation.[14] While TWWA was ultimately able to march, the exchange demonstrated the difference between the feminism of TWWA and that of mainstream white feminists.

Not only did TWWA's name change exemplify their commitment to solidarity, but it also echoed their move from "double jeopardy" on sex and race to "triple jeopardy," with a focus on gender, race, and class. According to Beal, the New York City chapter rejected the traditional notions of feminism as they felt they were too narrow.[15]

TWWA pioneered a form of feminism that focused on how US foreign and military policies affect women's lives globally. Its members believed that to achieve liberation, the institutions of racism, capitalism, and imperialism would have to be abolished. TWWA was at the forefront of standing in solidarity with several anti-imperialist and anticolonial struggles globally, including activism against the US war in Vietnam; land struggles in the Chicano movement and Native sovereignty struggles; and campaigns to free Angela Davis, Lolita Lebrón, and other political prisoners.[16]

Among TWWA's many accomplishments was the publication of "Double Jeopardy: To Be Black and Female" in *The Black Woman's Manifesto* in 1969. Written by Beal, "Double Jeopardy" explores the different forms of oppression that African American women contend with in US society. TWWA also published a newspaper titled *Triple Jeopardy,* in which they shared their advocacy and helped raise awareness of the struggles of Third World women. In the first issue of *Triple Jeopardy,* the organization discussed the conditions of racism, classism, and sexism that prompted the formation of TWWA.[17]

TWWA was a critical part of the formation of Black feminist thought and behavior. Their emphasis on how racism and sexism impacted the everyday lives of Black women and their ideological and political movement toward an anticapitalist analysis is one example of a precursor to what we now know as "intersectionality." Coined by legal scholar Kimberlé W. Crenshaw, intersectionality is a framework or lens to view how race, gender, class, and other forms of oppression intersect, interlock, and exacerbate each other.[18] TWWA obviously preceded Crenshaw's conceptualization of intersectionality, and the organization understood early on the material and political impacts of the various identities Black women possess. For example, Beal noted in a 2005 interview that "Black women's liberation is not just the skin analysis. It's not just the class analysis. It's not just the racial analysis. It's how those things operate in the real world in an integrated way, to both understand oppression and exploitation and to understand some methods by which we might kind of try to deal with them."[19]

A Path Forward

Unfortunately, as with other Black and Third World feminist groups of that time, TWWA closed its New York chapter in 1977. The Bay Area chapter continued for a little while longer, organizing committees such as the National Organization to Overturn the Bakke Decision, Coalition to Fight Infant Mortality, Third World Front Against Imperialism, Native American Project, and the Lolita Lebrón Committee.[20] The Bay Area chapter closed in 1979 and evolved into the Alliance Against Women's Oppression (AAWO), which was active until 1989.[21]

In 1990, former members of AAWO, most notably Linda Burnham, founded the Women of Color Resource Center (WCRC) in the Bay Area. A leader in TWWA, Burnham served as the executive director of WCRC for eighteen years. Just like TWWA, WCRC was committed to advancing the rights and needs of women globally and supporting women and girls of color across varying political, social, economic, and cultural backgrounds. In 2008, Burnham stepped down as executive director. After her departure, WCRC endured financial instability and was forced to close its doors in 2010.[22] Though the various chapters of the TWWA are no longer operating, the principles on which it was founded remain in current day feminist of color movements, with other groups taking up the mantle.

TWWA was a place for Black women and women of color to address and advocate for their liberation, and it also paved the way for a more expansive, inclusive, and revolutionary Black feminism. As a result, they carved out their own movement, one that centered their unique experiences and needs.

13.

"We're Here Because You Were There"

On the Organisation of Women of Asian and African Descent

Beverley Bryan and Stella Dadzie interviewed by Jaimee A. Swift

As founding members of the Organisation of Women of Asian and African Descent (OWAAD), a socialist and activist national umbrella organization that emerged as part of the Black British civil rights movement, Beverley Bryan and Stella Dadzie have contributed much to our understanding of radical Black and Asian feminist organizing transnationally.[1] Founded in 1978 in London, OWAAD was formed in response to patriarchal, male-dominated leadership of the African Students Union (ASU) and other local Black activist organizations.[2] While Black women were a part of ASU and other antiracist organizations, they felt their concerns were overlooked and, they were tired of being treated as "minute-takers, typists, and coffee-makers but hardly ever as political and intellectual equals."[3]

OWAAD was formed as an "independent, autonomous, national organization of Black women."[4] Although the original name of the group was the Organisation of Women of Africa and African

Descent, upon realizing the common struggles among Black and Asian women living in Britain, they changed the name to the Organisation of Women of Asian and African Descent.

One of OWAAD's major accomplishments was its first national Black women's conference in March 1979. Held in Brixton, the conference had two hundred attendees and is considered to be the inception of the Black women's movement in the country. OWAAD organized around several key issues, such as immigration and deportation, children's rights in schools, and anti-Black discrimination and policing. Bryan, Dadzie, and members of OWAAD also joined the campaign to end the SUS (stop-and-frisk) laws in England and Wales used against Black youth, whom police could arrest on suspicion they were about to commit a crime. Moreover, OWAAD campaigned and protested for reproductive rights, particularly against the testing of Depo-Provera, a contraceptive drug, on Black, Asian, and other marginalized women. OWAAD also published the newsletter *FOWAAD!*

While OWAAD disbanded in 1983, Bryan and Dadzie continued in their trailblazing activism. I spoke with Bryan and Dadzie in February 2022 about why they started OWAAD, their thoughts on the successes and lessons learned while organizing cross-racially, and the state of solidarity.

Jaimee A. Swift: Given the incredible work you both have done, I am curious to know about your journeys into organizing.

Beverley Bryan (BB): My journey to activism started in my early teens with experiences of what I call casual brutal racism in high school. My parents were the true Windrush generation because they came to Britain in the early fifties and lived in South London.[5] They were supposed to go back to Jamaica in five years, but that didn't happen, as it doesn't happen for many migrants because oftentimes economic plans don't work out. My parents sent for me and my two sisters. I went to school in South London, in Battersea. It was called a secondary modern. I experienced racism, especially from white working-class girls because it was a girls' school. That early experience made me realize I was from another place, even though we were supposed to be welcomed in this country because of our British citizenship. With that, there was a sense of, "This isn't fair, this isn't right."

That sense that these things weren't right also came from the fact that I was quite religious, especially when I was about thirteen or fourteen years old. You know the words of the Sermon on the Mount, that we should love each other? At that time, I was reading a lot and the person that affected me most was James Baldwin. There were two sides of Baldwin: the religious side that came out in *Go Tell It on the Mountain* but also the sense of being a young person growing up in a hostile environment that I saw reflected in *The Fire Next Time*. Those readings had an impact on me. It was also during the mid-sixties and onwards, we were looking at what was happening in America. We weren't just looking at Baldwin—it was also Martin Luther King Jr., Malcolm X, and the Black Power movement.

We had this sense we needed to do more to assert ourselves. We took on the slogans of "Black is beautiful" and "Black Power." We started with owning that we were special, but we had to do something with that specialness. What that meant for me was to join an organization. The first organization I joined was a consciousness raising group, the Black Arts Workshop, where we worked with the West Indian Students' Union. We studied Black literature, Black poetry, Black arts, and Black drama, acted it out, and took it to youth groups in London. The Black Arts Workshop was the way we empowered ourselves. By the time I was eighteen, I decided I wanted to be a teacher. Eventually, I did become a teacher, and I wanted to work somewhere where I felt I would be making a difference. I went to Brixton because my parents had lived there, and I knew it was a Black community. That's where I met up again with Olive [Morris].[6] Olive and I had gone to the same secondary school together. I met up with her during my first months of teaching and she told me about an experience where she had been beaten up by police after being dragged to Brixton Police Station. Because of that experience, she joined the Black Panther Movement.[7] When I heard about what she was doing, I thought, "This is good work." Because the Black Arts Workshop was mostly involved in consciousness raising, I thought if there was an organization that was defending people who were attacked, then I wanted to be a part of that as well. From there, I was in the Panthers for about three years. When the Panthers disintegrated about three years after I joined, we took some of those ideas in those campaigns and started the [Brixton] Black Women's Group (BWG).[8]

Stella Dadzie (SD): The difference for me was that I am of Anglo Ghanaian parentage. I was born to an unmarried mother in the fifties. When people asked me where my activism began, I realized it began subliminally because right through my childhood, I was witnessing or experiencing racism, sexism, and class issues. We lived in poverty when I was a child, well, when I was returned to my mother anyway. When I came to know my father's family, I was about twelve or thirteen years old. I started traveling to Ghana quite regularly. I think that gave me a good grounding, and a good sense of my African identity. My father was involved in the independence struggle in Ghana. There was a lot of talk around the family table of [Kwame] Nkrumah and Pan-Africanism. I was very conscious of the liberation struggles that were being fought on the African continent at that time.

When I went to Germany, I was studying languages, and I was very isolated. There were no other Black women. Later, I came into contact with African students and African refugees, in particular Eritreans who had taken up arms in Eritrea and ended up in Germany. That experience radicalized me because I became aware of how imperialism worked. I began to connect what was happening in Africa with civil rights struggles in the United States. I was also listening to some of the messages coming out of the women's liberation movement, which was very embryonic at the time. Fast forward, I came back to England. I was keen to get involved in some way, and I got involved with some radical journals. One was called *The Black Liberator*, which looked at issues in Britain and across the African diaspora. The other one was the *African Red Family*, a cadre-developing project analyzing what was going on in Africa. Like a lot of women, we were marginalized. We were the minute takers, coffeemakers, and we were often the people who fed ideas to some man who would then stand on his soapbox and speak our truth. That isolation meant that I was drawn to other Black women who shared similar experiences and concerns.

In my fourth year at university, I got involved in the African Students Union. It was through that group that I came to know Olive and other women like Beverley in the Brixton Black Women's Group. I was also teaching at the time. The glaring inequalities in the classroom quickly drew my attention to organizations and groups that were lobbying women around what is now called "decolonizing" the curriculum.

My roots were similar in that those influences—the civil rights movement, Pan-Africanism, the anti-apartheid struggle in South Africa, women's liberation—all of those things were going on at the time. I have to say that to some extent what was happening in the women's movement did not interest me quite as much because it was characterized as a middle-class white women's activity that involved a lot of naval gazing, hatred of men, and that did not really coalesce with the aspirations that I had, which were about race and class equality, as well as gender issues.

BB: Black people in the United Kingdom, we come from different experiences because Britain was an imperial power. We had the slogan "We're here because you were there." To me, that summed up imperialism and colonialism. We all came from different places because of what was done in our individual countries. The Windrush generation is an example of this. They didn't come to Britain simply because they wanted to; they came to Britain because their countries were destroyed. It is because of this past history we could talk of common experiences in the United Kingdom. It is also important to say that it is not just Britain; many European countries have similar history. And we can even extend that internationalist perspective when we come to talk about our Afro-Asian unity.

How did the Organisation of Women of Asian and African Descent form?

SD: In 1978, some African women met each other within the African Students Union in London. It was a group of women of African descent, so we decided to call ourselves the Organisation of Women of Africa and African Descent. When we started to meet regularly, I remember an Asian sister coming to the meeting. The historical context is important here because in the late seventies, there was an influx of Asian people from the [Indian] subcontinent and East Africa migrating to Britain. The Asian sister called Hansa said, "What about us? I'm African, too." It was at that moment we realized we needed to address commonalities and differences between Black and Asian women. I think this reflected the fact that many of us identified as Marxists, believed in internationalism, and that people should unite and offer solidarity across race and continents.

We also shared a common experience of colonialism and racism, especially gendered racism, and racialized sexism in this country, although there were differences. The organization later became the Organisation of Women of Asian and African Descent.

BB: Around that time, I was in the Brixton Black Women's Group.[9] Before the BWG, there was a women's caucus in the Black Panther Movement (BPM), but that caucus was just about how to get more women into the BPM. The women's caucus did not really discuss issues that women felt were important to them, such as women being involved in leadership or dealing with sexual harassment. Those issues were rampant, especially in an organization where women were not seen as vital parts of the leadership. Moving from the BPM into BWG in 1973, it's really significant that out of the Panthers came a women's organization, and that women's organization actually stayed with the issues. That's why we started the bookshop, that's why we continued to work around police harassment, immigration, and also studying and trying to understand ourselves better.

As Stella said, we saw ourselves as Marxists—Marxist feminists—which meant that the issues women wanted to take up were central, but we also understood that race and class were equally important. Addressing class and capitalism was really important to us. That's why, in some cases, we didn't consider what was happening in the women's movement because they did not focus on working-class women. For instance, one of the concerns of organizers in the women's movement was having the choice to work outside the home. We, as working-class Black women, were saying, "We are already in the workforce." For us, it was about better conditions, better pay, and better understanding of the workplace, rather than the right to work.

Stella was working in her group in North London. Stella, yes?

SD: Yes, the United Black Women's Action Group. By the time OWAAD was beginning to form, around 1977, there were Black women's groups and Asian women's groups springing up all over, particularly in London. OWAAD was set up as an umbrella organization. It became a forum for different groups to bring their issues and to seek support and solidarity. I think one of OWAAD's achievements was bringing together such a disparate group of women.

BB: The main idea was that it wasn't about us simply just taking one issue and going back to our chapters and working on it. It came from the other direction—it was from the communities. Our issues came to the center, and we brought it to the forum where it would be discussed. We organized, provided support, and campaigned around issues such as virginity testing.

SD: During that time, they were testing Asian women at the point of entry because of some spurious stereotype that Asian women only came to the country as potential brides. Asian women were stuck in a room with their legs in stirrups and virginity tested.[10] We campaigned and demonstrated outside the airport and got that policy reversed. That was an example of mutual solidarity, but also mutual learning because immigration impacted people of African, Asian, and Caribbean descent, but in different ways. We could see that although we might experience it differently, we had a common enemy.

What are some of the lessons you learned from organizing and founding OWAAD? What were some of the challenges of cross-racial organizing during that time?

SD: We had to learn how to negotiate differences. There were obviously issues of culture, language, and religion, which meant that we didn't always manage to communicate from the same page. There were social events and conferences we organized jointly where there was an ongoing discussion about our differences, and I think we all learned from that. Quite a lot has been made post-OWAAD of the reasons why OWAAD disintegrated. One of the arguments put forward is that we weren't able to manage that interface of African-Asian unity. I would dispute that. I think we managed it quite well. I think a degree of humility in respecting that not everybody experienced racism and sexism in the same way was also key as well.

BB: I would say that certainly in BWG, it was an internationalist organization, so Asian women were also a part of it. There wasn't really a big difference from OWAAD. I know you now talk about political Blackness, but we did not talk about it then. We were organizing from a common history within the context of British colonialism. The idea that anyone would allow cultural differences to prevent you from organizing with each other, whether it was about immigration or police harassment of Black youth in Brixton or Asian youths in Bradford, we didn't have that kind of luxury. Attempts were made to divide us, and some of them were successful, but it was not because the organization itself was crumbling. It was to do with the way the state decided to offer grants. There was a period when they were offering grants within the community—to a particular ethnic group, women from India, Pakistan, e.g., Sikh women or Bengali women. There was that idea that you could offer a grant to a group of women based around their ethnicity. At the same time, there were many Caribbean or even Pan-Africanists who were also following the self-help and welfare route supported by local authorities, but many of the women's groups did not work that way. Some of us worked with the idea that we had common interests and concerns, and gender was what would've held us together. I think OWAAD lived for a period, and it was necessary for a period, but I think—

SD: —It was of its time.

BB: Yes, and it was the weight of our vision. It was too much for one organization without a strong central organizing force. It was a very loose organization, leadership wise. People came, and they looked for support from a central group, and that support was offered in the best way we could offer it. It was a loose arrangement that fulfilled the needs at a particular time.

What does solidarity mean to you? What advice would you give to organizers at this time?

SD: Solidarity involves mutual respect. It involves allyship. It involves learning each other's stories. It's about practical support. It's about taking energy from that collective awareness of our power to make change. You get a lot of mutual energy when you come together with other groups and find that you are speaking with a common voice. Not necessarily about the same issues, but certainly speaking with a common voice, from the same place of indignation about the injustices we face. It's about respecting commonalities as well as differences. It is about grounding unity in a spirit of global sisterhood.

BB: There's nothing there that I would disagree with. I would just underscore the idea that solidarity is recognizing concrete and material practical commonalities that would allow us to work together. Acknowledging there might be differences, which might be cultural, but just because there are differences in culture doesn't mean that the basic realities are not there. Of course, there are those who try to divide you on that basis. One of the lessons that we can take is that we are fighting against a power structure, and power structures do not yield. They will try and divide, and those little issues, what we call little things, are the ways they will try and divide. The most important thing is to organize.

14.

Our Solidarity Is a Lifeline

Pratibha Parmar interviewed by Jaimee A. Swift

A globally recognized and award-winning writer, filmmaker, director, and producer, Pratibha Parmar has committed her life to telling stories of marginalized communities.[1] Her work and activism span the political, cultural, and creative gamut. Her 1991 film *A Place of Rage* featured prominent Black feminist activists and writers such as June Jordan, Angela Davis, and Alice Walker. She also collaborated with Walker on two other documentaries: *Warrior Marks* (1993), which examines the impact of female genital mutilation and cutting, and *Alice Walker: Beauty in Truth*, a feature-length documentary on the life of this Pulitzer Prize–winning author.

Parmar's British short film *Khush* (1991)—which means ecstatic pleasure in Urdu—is one of the first documentaries to bring visibility to the lives, eroticism, and histories of South Asian lesbians and gay men in Britain, North America, and India. Prior to her work as a filmmaker, Parmar was active in antiracist, antifascist, anti-imperialist, and feminist organizing in Britain. Through her moving image work, Parmar embodies a radical politics of solidarity across difference.

In February 2023, I interviewed Parmar about her activism, how Black feminists inspired and radicalized her, and about her thoughts on Black and Asian feminist solidarity.

Jaimee A. Swift: You were born in Nairobi, Kenya, to Indian parents, and you immigrated to the United Kingdom when you were twelve years old. On your website, you note that you've "embraced my outsider status as a gift that opens up pathways to untold stories." Do you mind discussing a little bit about your upbringing and what you mean by "embracing your outsider status?"

Pratibha Parmar: I was born in Nairobi. When Kenya got its independence in the mid-1960s, the Indian communities who lived there had a "choice": either take up Kenyan citizenship (which wasn't encouraged) or leave the country. This was against the historical background of Kenya as a British colony. The Indian community in Kenya had been given British Commonwealth passports by British colonial rulers when large numbers of Indians had arrived on the shores of East Africa, recruited by the British as indentured laborers. There is a massive global Indian diaspora as a direct result of British colonialism, where whole communities were moved as units of labor from different parts of India to work as indentured laborers or to help set up infrastructures in the newly British colonized countries. That's how my grandparents ended up in Kenya, where my mother was born, as part of this movement of labor.

In 1967, my family immigrated to London. We were not one of those rich Indian families leaving East Africa, an image many people have of East African Indians. We were quite a poor family. My father wanted his children to have opportunities and knew that if we went back to India on our limited resources, we would not have the educational opportunities that were possible if we immigrated to the UK. That's why, like many immigrant parents, he decided to go to England, and a year later we followed him on a one-way ticket paid for by a rich Indian family. They did this in return for us taking their quota of money out of the country. We were like money mules for this rich Indian family.

We arrived in England at a time of intense, growing racism, particularly racism toward Asian immigrants. Let me explain this identity/definition imposed on us. It's quite a different definition of Asians than in the United States because if I say I am Asian, people will look at me and think, "What, what do you mean you are Asian? You are Indian." However, in England, we were classified as Asians. There was virulent racism toward us in the media and on the streets. The rhetoric of "hordes of Asians invading our country" was being used as a political football by many right-wing politicians to stir up animosity toward Asian people, as well as Black people from the Caribbean.

My first week on the school playground, I was called a "paki," a "wog," which are derogatory terms for persons of South Asian descent in British slang. I was twelve years old at the time, and I did not understand it. It was a shocking experience. In my late teens, my uncle gave me the book *If They Come for You in the Morning: Voices of Resistance,* edited by Angela Davis. Reading that book was an absolute turning point for me. The book gave me a vocabulary to understand systems of racist and class oppression. It made me realize it was possible to bring about change and that you didn't have to accept things as they were.

The book also gave me a language to understand what was happening to my own family and community in the context of the UK. My mother worked in a sweatshop and was exploited terribly. All these concepts that Angela and other writers in the book put forward so beautifully and passionately set me on this path of politicization. This was the beginning of finding kinship with the civil rights movement, the Black Power Movement, and the struggles for equality and justice that African American people were engaged in.

How did you get involved in activism? Were you affiliated with feminist organizations and initiatives in London?

Like many women of color activists, I was around the Organisation of Women of Asian and African Descent [OWAAD] in the early 1980s. I was also active in Sheba Feminist Publishers, a collective of women of color as well as white women.[2] We were the publishers for Audre Lorde's book *Zami* in the UK. My politicization happened first and foremost around racial injustices. I was active in the antiracist and antifascist movement in the mid- to late 1970s as a student at university. I was also exposed to the women's movement, to feminism, and the LGBTQ+ movement. All of these movements were pivotal to my growth as a political activist. This is reflected in the kind of films I make.

Do you mind sharing more about your experiences organizing cross-racially within these feminist groups, such as OWAAD and Sheba Feminist Publishers?

Before I was involved in the feminist movement, I had been involved as a student in an antiracist and antifascist group at my university in Bradford. Later,

I joined a collective called the Bradford Black Collective. I was the only South Asian person in the group. It was majority Afro-Caribbean men and women. We published a quarterly magazine called *Bradford Black*. One of our biggest campaigns was to secure the release of George Lindo, a Black man who was wrongfully arrested by the police. The campaign to free George Lindo became a national campaign across the UK, and we had solid support from the former Black Power activist Darcus Howe and the Race Today Collective.

Also, it's really important for this anthology and for readers, particularly in the US, to understand that the term "Black" was used as a political term for a specific period of time in Britain to include not just Afro-Caribbean communities but also Asian communities. It was used as an umbrella term to organize across communities experiencing similar kinds of racist oppression from the British state. We had all been subjects of British colonialism in the countries we had come from. Many of the men who had migrated to the UK as workers in factories and in the mills had forged solidarity across these various communities. The ripple effect spread into community organizing and in trade union activities. It was a productive coalition, as we began with what we all had in common, especially the colonial and postcolonial experiences. The umbrella term of "Black," I believe, fizzled out in the mid-1980s.

For me, there was always this natural gravitation toward poets and writers like June Jordan. I read June's book *Civil Wars*, one of her first collections of essays, which the writer Paul Gilroy had given me as a birthday present. The book had a profound impact on me and introduced me to June's work. It was similar to the impact Angela [Davis]'s book had on me as a teenager.

I gravitated toward June's writings because June, at her core, was a global intersectional feminist. She believed in solidarity. She believed in solidarity with Nicaragua—she actually went to Nicaragua, too. She was in solidarity with Palestine before most people spoke out on Palestinian rights. She always believed that none of us can do this alone and that we have to find ways of working together in solidarity to support our struggles for equality and justice. So when I was introduced to June's work, I felt she spoke to me. I also used to teach June's and Angela's writings in an evening course on women, race, and class.

In 1987, June came to London to do a poetry reading. I was asked to interview June for a feminist magazine called *Spare Rib*. When we met, we totally hit it off. She was surprised I knew so much about her work.

I was very specific in my conversation with her, particularly around her work with Buckminster Fuller and her collaboration with him on redesigning

Harlem, a project called Harlem Skyrise. My partner is an architect and was at the time working with a group of Black women to design a Black women's center in London. I was keenly aware of issues around space and who has access, who is denied access, and how this affects the built environment. As women of color, we are often denied being in certain kinds of spaces. We bonded over these stimulating, thought-provoking conversations about architecture, the challenge of essentializing identities, and transnational organizing.

I said to her, "You know, your books should be available in the UK." I offered to help her find a publisher—and I did. I secured publication of two collections of her poetry by the feminist press Virago. That process took about eighteen months, but over that time we wrote to each other and spoke on the phone. Eventually, she came back to London for the publicity tour of her books, and she stayed with my partner and me in our home in North London.

The publication of her books in the UK was really successful. Then she wanted to go to Paris while she was visiting London. Just like with James Baldwin, Paris has a particular kind of resonance for many African American writers and poets. And so we organized a trip to Paris for the weekend. June mentioned that her friend Angela [Davis] was going to be in Paris at the same time too [*laughs*]. We, my partner Shaheen and I, ended up spending time with June and Angela in Paris that weekend. And that is where the idea for my film *A Place of Rage* came to my mind.

Wow, *A Place of Rage*, your award-winning film, the idea came to you when you were in Paris with June Jordan and Angela Davis. What specifically were the creative and political impetuses to directing the film?

The film came together in a really organic way. I decided to make the film partly because of spending time with June and Angela. June was a poet and Angela had been in the Communist Party and was a political prisoner as a result of her involvement in the Black Power movement. Both women came to politics from a different mode of activism. Yet, despite differences in their approaches to political resistance, they were fighting for the same goal, which was the freedom of Black people and all oppressed people around the world. As a filmmaker and storyteller, I was interested in exploring how these two women approached their activist work. Too often, women as shapers of history are left out of official historical narratives. I wanted to pay homage to these women who had had a profound role to play in struggles for the liberation of Black people in the US and their impact and influence outside of the US.

At that time, I had made a few documentaries for Channel Four, a British TV channel, which gave space to what they called "minority voices"—of women filmmakers, people of color, and LGBTQ+ people. I went to them with this idea to make *A Place of Rage,* and they were on board with it instantly. With that support, I approached June and Angela. One of the other important elements to the storytelling was to showcase these women's experiences, their thoughts, and their leadership on discussions on race, class, gender, and sexuality. The Black Power movement had repercussions for movements for liberation across Africa and even India, especially among the Dalit peoples who are deemed as "untouchables."[3] People looked to the strength and the inspiration of the Black Power movement to organize and to resist.

When I was preparing to film, I remembered June's poem "A Poem About Police Violence," especially when she wrote that "every time they kill a Black man, we should kill a cop."[4] That is so resonant right now, especially with the killing of George Floyd. I wanted to get her personal context to that poem. I asked her about her early experiences of activism and politicization, and June shared that her first experience of police brutality was when this young boy, who had lived on the same block as her growing up, was chased by the police to the roof of the building where they lived and brutally beaten. It turned out to be a case of mistaken identity.

June said when she saw this young boy so brutalized for no reason at all, it hardened her. In the film, she points to her heart as her place of rage, which I also think is a metaphor in that the US is rightfully a place of rage for so many people, with the genocide of Indigenous people, the slave trade, and the ongoing incarceration of African American men. I have lived in the US now for a decade and become attuned to how the land and the earth is saturated with the blood and sorrow of so many communities.

A Place of Rage was a celebration for me. It was a celebration of women, like Fannie Lou Hamer, who appears in the film in archival material. It was a celebration of African American women who helped shape the Civil Rights Movement as participants and leaders. I was so incredibly fortunate to know June and to continue to be in community with Angela and Alice Walker. After *A Place of Rage,* Alice asked me if I would partner with her to make *Warrior Marks* (1994), and much later I made *Alice Walker: Beauty in Truth* for the *American Masters* series on PBS.

What does solidarity mean to you? May you please share some reflections specifically on building solidarity with Black feminists?

Being in solidarity means we have a chance at survival. In our current global climate of divisiveness, border fascism, extractive capitalism, and land grabs, solidarity across all our differences is a necessity for life and the future of our planet.

In terms of my solidarity with Black women, it has always been an organic part of my political work. As I mentioned before, Black and Asian communities, as postcolonial citizens living in the UK, shared similar experiences of structural racism in British society. Of course, we cannot deny that there were and are differences, but we used to come out in solidarity for each other's campaigns. I remember the women of the Grunwick Strike of 1976, led by South Asian women.[5] It was one of the biggest strikes of its kind in British trade union history, and it was led by South Asian women who looked like my mother, wearing saris standing on the picket line. The solidarity that was shown to those women came from Black communities, South Asian people, white trade unionists, and feminists. I saw the impact of the coalitions that came together across their differences to support the fight for the rights of these exploited South Asian women workers.

If I were to characterize my solidarity with Black women, it would be that I have used my skills as a storyteller to tell the stories of women who have personally inspired me and shaped my growth in fundamental ways. I am in gratitude to their leadership and friendship. Out of my deep respect for them, I wanted to tell their unique stories and make them accessible and available to everyone.

You know, there is a poem that June Jordan wrote about our weekend in Paris. It is titled "Solidarity." If you have not read it already, please look it up.

You mention that after the premiere of your film *Khush*, several queer folks in the South Asian community thanked you for making the documentary, feeling a sense of belonging. Were there any lesbian or queer Black feminists who encouraged you to feel a sense of belonging, as a South Asian lesbian?

Absolutely. Audre Lorde was a crucial influence on me. Her courage to be out and to be vocal about her sexuality helped me be stronger and more vocal.

I mentioned earlier that through Sheba Feminist Publishers we published Audre's work. Reading her work, meeting her, and spending time with her gave me and many others the strength to speak out as lesbians. I had faced rejection by my own community and family. Her example of speaking your truth was deeply transformative. Audre's warm embrace of women of color lesbians in London was a transformative moment for so many of us.

What are your hopes for the future of Black and Asian feminist solidarities?

Without the stories and poems of Audre Lorde, Cherríe Moraga, Angela Davis, Alice Walker, and June Jordan, I would not have survived as a young woman caught in the cross fires of racism and gender oppression. The example of their lives and art gave shape to my own courage to pursue art in the service of justice and equality. They opened the doors to my imaginary. Like them, I remain an optimist; I remain hopeful. I think our very survival depends on it. Our solidarity is a lifeline for our futures. We have many examples of how different cultural, national, and racial groups have worked together toward a vision of a more just and equitable future. We need to keep creating endless innovative ways of working across our differences and embedding ourselves in our similarities.

15.

Revisiting a Press of Our Own

Barbara Smith interviewed by the Editors

Kitchen Table Press has brought us groundbreaking feminist anthologies by women of color writers, including *This Bridge Called My Back: Writings by Radical Women of Color* (1981) and *Home Girls: A Black Feminist Anthology* (1983), as well as political writing and pamphlets by the Combahee River Collective, Audre Lorde, Merle Woo, Angela Davis, and Barbara Omolade.

When the press started, there was very little interest from mainstream, white-dominated publishing houses for writing by women of color. A catalyzing conversation between Barbara Smith and Audre Lorde sparked the need to try something different. The press was started at Smith's kitchen table, a place symbolic of "grassroots operation" and feminist work and functioned as a way to "determine independently both the content and the conditions of our work" and for women of color to "control the words and images that were produced about us."[1] Now, over forty years later, this writing has shaped and influenced feminist theory and activism across generations. In July 2022, the three coeditors sat down with Barbara Smith to talk about the legacy of Kitchen Table Press and publishing as transformative political work.[2]

Editors: We often describe our collective editorial work as an ongoing relationship and commitment to the practice of solidarity. We're curious about the feminist relationship building at the heart of Kitchen Table Press and what it meant to do feminist work together.

Barbara Smith: In Boston, in early 1979, twelve Black women were murdered in about a four-month period. The Combahee River Collective was central in bringing communities together and also putting out a pamphlet that did a political analysis of what was going on. We asked Audre and Adrienne Rich, who were good friends, if they would come to Boston and do a poetry reading to raise money for the organizing going on, and they did.[3] We also started having Black feminist retreats in the late seventies.

I first met Audre at a Modern Language Association (MLA) convention in 1976.[4] I had been involved with the MLA as an invited member of the Commission on the Status of Women at a time when there were virtually no sessions on African American literature, let alone Black women writers. The MLA commission was important in the formation of women's studies in the United States: some of the people leading women's studies in literature and languages were a part of that commission, such as Florence Howe, the founder of the Feminist Press. Projects that came out of the commission and Feminist Press books included the book I coedited with Akasha Hull and Patricia Bell-Scott, *All the Women Are White, All the Blacks Are Men, But Some of Us Are Brave: Black Women's Studies* (1982). I met Audre because we would have these incredible panels sponsored by the commission.

One day, I was at a bookstore in Boston. I was coming out as a lesbian and picked up a magazine called *Amazon Quarterly*, a new lesbian magazine. I'm looking at the masthead and it said that Audre was a poetry editor. I thought, *Really? Wow. Does that mean she's a lesbian?* That was not part of her reputation nor identity for those of us who knew her through the Black Arts Movement. It was exciting to see.

One of the things I used to wonder about and ask publicly: "Is it possible to be a Black feminist lesbian writer and live to tell about it?"[5] That was a real question for me. It was a question for all of us. I asked Audre that from the audience when we met at the MLA convention. Audre said that one of the reasons that she decided to write *Zami* (1982) is that she thought if people of my age group were asking that question, then it'd be important for them to know about the life of another person who was older and who had gone through some of this already.

I used to talk about the people who were willing to get their hands dirty, and I mean that literally. There were things that we had to do as actual publishers with physical material objects. Going to the post office was one of the things that Audre used to do, because she was one of the few people in Kitchen Table who had a car. It was very inconvenient, as far as getting anything out of the building. It was in this old, very upper-class church between Sixty-Third and Sixty-Fourth on Park Avenue. She'd come and put her blinkers on and whoever was there would bring the boxes down, and she would take them to the Staten Island post office.

It was a really productive friendship. We were actual friends who knew about each other's lives. I knew her children when they were growing up. Kitchen Table was by no means our first project, but it was the most ambitious project.

It seems like in the course of fostering these relationships, one of the sites of your political intervention was transforming the field of literature and also literary publishing. How did that come to be?

I was teaching my first course on Black women writers in the early 1970s. I was familiar with Audre's work and familiar with almost all of the Black writers' work. That was my interest even though I never was able to take a course myself. You couldn't get an advanced degree in Black studies at that time. All the things that people get to do now, we were not able to do that, because we were the people who were making the fields, and that includes ethnic studies, Asian American studies, African American studies. . . . Some departments had African studies, but approached it from a colonial perspective.

There was a press called Broadside Press in Detroit, and they printed broadsides and pamphlet-type books that were very much like the Kitchen Table Press's pamphlet series. They would publish books of poetry, and Audre was one of the Broadside poets. I would use those books in my African American literature classes. I never tried to have a sterling career in the academy. It wasn't like I was pushed out; I pushed myself out. I was much more interested in being a writer and being politically active. Building Black feminism, starting and keeping Kitchen Table: Women of Color Press going. Those were my priorities.

You've described the publishing work of Kitchen Table Press as a "revolutionary tool." To change politics, we have to change culture. How do you see the relationship between media-making and political work? And how have you seen changes to feminist politics over time?

I don't feel that anything's revolutionary unless it's about making economic, political, and social change in the actual world. It's not enough to have good ideas. You have to have a political practice that's going to put those ideas into the real world and see how they work with actual people.

I grew up under Jim Crow. My family had migrated to Cleveland from the post–Civil War South, in Georgia, which had the second-highest number of lynchings of any state in the old Confederacy. The things that people read about in books, I experienced in real time. I didn't read about Emmett Till in a history book. I heard about Emmett Till because my family was talking about him when I was eight years old, how something bad had happened.

The second wave was creating things from scratch at a particular historical moment. We can't reduplicate that. We're living in the hell of post-Roe. Now, some of us lived in the hell of pre-Roe—I would be one of them. This period of history, people talk about how post-Roe is going to be very different from pre-Roe. In some cases, it's going to be not as bad, because we did not have medical abortion at that time, that is nonsurgical abortion that is safe and proven. But then, we also didn't have a right wing laser focused on making sure that it turned back the twentieth century. In 1976, the Hyde Amendment cut off abortion access for recipients of Medicaid, so it's not like we didn't have white patriarchs trying to run and ruin our lives. We did. But what's happening now post-Roe is a different historical period.

What was going on with feminist publishing in that period—just the existence of it had a material effect. Creating an alternative from all-male, cis-heterosexual production, that made a difference. Kitchen Table Press sold a lot of books. I saw the books as having political content and political impact—why wouldn't we want them to get to as many people as possible? *This Bridge Called My Back* was our top-selling book, with nearly one hundred thousand copies sold. *Home Girls* got around thirty thousand sold. These books are still in print; think about that. People are still using them; they're still teaching out of them.

You've written about how your commitment to feminist publishing has made your relations with communities "difficult and even painful." Can you share a bit more about the challenges and lessons learned in the process of creating the press?

I've been very hurt by rejections. During the National Black Writers Conference at Howard University in the late seventies, I was invited to be on the first-ever panel about Black women writers. I presented from my recently written piece "Toward a Black Feminist Criticism" (1977) with some added remarks for a Black audience. After our panel was over, the crowd went wild with casting aspersions. I've also had my car burned up for being a lesbian. Antifeminism and homophobia are very tied to each other, and I don't want to underestimate how much antifeminism there was in the Black community.

There used to be an American Booksellers Association with an annual convention, which was a huge event and book expo. There used to be a feminist and gay publishers aisle, and for many years, Kitchen Table exhibited in that area. However, at a certain point, I decided I'm not dealing with the insensitivity and simple-minded racism that we were getting from some of those white-run women's presses and gay presses. So I said, "Let's start exhibiting with Black presses." That really made a statement. There's only so much mental bandwidth that one has for abuse.

The reason I think people began to see the value of our work is because we remained. The press was in existence for about fifteen years, and our publishing was quite credible. One of the things that's astonishing is now, women of color, specifically queer women of color, their first books are published by mainstream publishers. I think the reason that happens is because of Kitchen Table. We put the writing of women of color on the map. Through our persistence and through the quality of the work that we did, people began to understand dead white men are not the only people who can be great writers.

The right wing in our country wants to shut it all down. They're censoring, banning books, firing teachers, all kinds of horrible things are happening. They're basically destroying our work. I talked about how you couldn't get an advanced degree or even an undergraduate degree in anything that was ethnic studies or Third World studies during my generation. We had to build these fields from scratch. So when they say, "We don't want any of that material in our classrooms," they're basically saying, "We're throwing out all your work."

You've also mentioned that Kitchen Table Press published work not just because it's by a woman of color, but because it consciously examines specific perspectives, experiences, and issues that women of color face. It's clear that we needed feminist of color political analysis. And you've highlighted how the press made a concerted effort to publish across women of color while also navigating some of the constraints of a small press. What was the collective decision-making process behind publishing works that fit with the political vision?

We wanted something that was incisive, that reflected the realities of the lives of various women of color around the world. One of the books that we published was called *A Comrade Is as Precious as a Rice Seedling* by Mila Aguilar, who was in the Philippines during the Marcos regime. While we were producing the book, Mila was thrown into prison. And so, the book had another kind of purpose, which was to publicize her situation as a political prisoner under Marcos. She got out of prison when the Marcos regime fell and was one of the first people to be released.

I hate narrowness, and I hate separatism of all different kinds. People sometimes describe Kitchen Table as a Black press, and I always very quickly tell them, "No, we were not a Black press." Even though most of the people who attended the first press meeting were of African heritage either for a long time in the United States or from the Caribbean, we decided that we would be a press for all women of color. And then we had these wonderful and very nuanced discussions about who do we consider to be a woman of color.

Some of my favorite books that we published were the ones by Mitsuye Yamada and Hisaye Yamamoto. One of them was Mitsuye's *Desert Run*. She's now in her nineties and sends me an annual holiday letter. I met Mitsuye through *This Bridge Called My Back*, and she introduced me to Hisaye, an incredible short story writer. Hisaye had not ever published a book until Kitchen Table because of the anti-Japanese sentiments after World War II. She would have her work included in these incredibly competitive volumes, yet no publisher was reaching out to her. We published her book *Seventeen Syllables* together. Both Mitsuye and Hisaye were in the concentration camps. I had known that those camps existed, but there's such a difference when somebody tells you about the experience and also writes beautifully about those experiences.

They were completely wonderful to work with. They were so kind to me, and they were also a number of years older than me. I always like being around people who are of different ages. Once I was in Los Angeles, and I had never met Hisaye before, and so we went to an art exhibit of Betye and Alison Saar, who are incredible Black women artists. We had a ball.

We also distributed many books that we did not publish and listed them in our catalog. They were books by people of all different backgrounds and sometimes from around the world. We would also get letters from all over. It was always so exciting to me, because I was a secret stamp collector. I loved writing letters, getting letters. And so, going to pick up the Kitchen Table mail, it was always exciting to see interesting stamps and postmarks from Asia, from South Africa.

When Kitchen Table was literally on its last legs and we had less than three dollars in the bank, I refused to let it die. While some people thought it was a waste of our time and money to distribute other people's books, I didn't really care because I knew why we were doing it. It was for solidarity. We weren't a business. We were a network and a resource for people.

Can you share what solidarity means to you and how you use the press to build solidarity among and between women of color?

Solidarity is a political term, and we [women of color in the mid- and late twentieth century] certainly did not invent it. I think what solidarity means is that you understand that other people's struggles absolutely touch you and have an impact on what you think your struggles are.

There were international feminist book fairs, and we went to several of them. This showed what our politics were. For example, two major things that were happening in the 1980s were the struggle to end apartheid in South Africa and the Central America solidarity movement. We were involved with both of those things by signing on or bringing books. There was an annual Asian American Heritage book fair in New York City and a Latin American book fair. We would participate in those because we understood that's where we needed to be.

I think it's hard to have solidarity if you don't really know what's going on with people in other places. Having an international perspective is critical to doing accountable political work. It's very challenging for us who live here in the belly of the beast, because the United States is the root of so many problems globally. The US has a lot of blood on its hands. Even as we speak, there are undeclared wars in many different places. There's a history of exploitation and imperialism that cannot be justified. So, it takes a lot for us here, even as people of color, to be able to be accountable across borders and to take a back seat sometimes because we don't know everything.

The way that we come together is around shared values. Therefore, I have more in common with people whose backgrounds are quite different. As a person who is targeted by oppression, far be it from me not to understand how other people experience similar kinds of things, although by no means identical. And that's what solidarity is about. It hurts me so much when I hear and find out the strife and the violence between different people of color. Let's show the world something different.

16.

Exploring Black and Asian American Lesbian Archives

Aché and *Phoenix Rising*

Jaimee A. Swift

Black feminist scholar Saidiya Hartman in "Venus in Two Acts" writes about the dangers and violence of white supremacist, patriarchal, and cis-heteronormative revisionist histories in the archives.[1] Throughout history, we have seen how Black, Asian, and other communities of color have been excluded and rendered faceless and nameless in the archives. The archives also reflect the continuous anti-Black and anti-Asian state and quotidian violence that impacts our communities.

However, when we interrogate the archives of and by the most marginal in our communities—not as objects or property but as materials written and authored from their own perspectives—what can these archives tell us about the fortitude of Black and Asian American queer women who recognized the urgency to tell their own stories? What about archives that speak to what scholar Tiffany Florvil examines as a politics of queer belonging, but more specifically a Black and Asian American queer belonging?[2] What about archives that speak to Black and Asian American lesbian self-determination and resistance?

The works published by two organizations formerly based in the San Francisco Bay Area—*Phoenix Rising*, a newsletter published by the Asian/

Pacifica Sisters, and *Aché: A Journal for Lesbians of African Descent*—offer critical insights on how Black and Asian American lesbians created community for themselves, in spite of ostracization by mainstream society and the communities they belonged to.[3] *Phoenix Rising* and *Aché* also detail how Black and Asian American lesbian women forged lesbian/queer solidarities and alliances in the United States and in the Asian and African diasporas.[4]

Phoenix Rising: The Asian/Pacifica Sisters Newsletter

The newsletter *Phoenix Rising* emerged in 1984 as a space for Asian and Pacific Island lesbians to build community in the San Francisco Bay Area. The founding editors of *Phoenix Rising*—considered to be the first Asian American lesbian newsletter in the United States—included Lori Lai, May Lee, Susan Lee, Pam Nishikawa, Gisele Pohan, Marie Shim, Doreena Wong, and Zee Wong.[5] According to Amy Sueyoshi, author of "Breathing Fire: Remembering Asian Pacific American Activism in Queer History," the title of the newsletter, *Phoenix Rising*, "referred to these women's resilience and beauty, rising out of the ashes that racism, sexism, and homophobia might otherwise leave behind."[6] Themes and topics discussed in the newsletter included an advice column for Asian and Pacific Island lesbians titled "Ask Miss Maki"; "coming out" stories; news about Asian and Pacific Island lesbians in the diaspora; members participating in the Gay Games; erotica; the HIV/AIDS crisis; and more. *Phoenix Rising* not only curated a space for Asian and Pacific Island bisexual and lesbian women to express pride in themselves and their vibrant community but also "defied stereotypes of quiet Asian women bound by strict families, immigrant values, and submissiveness."[7]

In June 1988, the Asian/Pacifica Sisters (A/PS) was formed out of the originating group publishing *Phoenix Rising*. A/PS was "one of the earliest and largest grassroots organizations at the intersection of lesbian and Asian."[8] Ten Asian and Pacific Island women from San Francisco, San Jose, the East Bay, and Napa formed A/PS after reading the "Butterflies and Dreams" advertisement in *Phoenix Rising*, which was a "calling card and starting point to establish and form an organization that would attempt to speak to the needs and concerns of Asian/Pacific lesbians and bisexuals."[9]

Phoenix Rising and A/PS are a part of a longer legacy of Asian American queer activism and organizing in the Bay Area.[10] For example, Crystal Jang, a Chinese American lesbian activist and cofounder of the Asian Pacific Islander Queer Women & Transgender Community (APIQWTC) and Older Asian Sisters in Solidarity (OASIS), was an outspoken opponent of the 1978

Briggs Initiative, formally known as the California Proposition 6, a ballot proposition authored by conservative state senator John Briggs that would have banned gay and lesbian people from working in schools.[11]

In 1979, Nancy Hom, Genny Lim, Canyon Sam, Kitty Tsui, Nellie Wong, and Merle Woo formed the first Asian American women's performing arts group, Unbound Feet, in the Bay Area.[12] Unbound Feet cofounders Nellie Wong and Merle Woo both contributed to *This Bridge Called My Back: Writings by Radical Women of Color,* edited by Cherríe Moraga and Gloria E. Anzaldúa. *This Bridge Called My Back* was published in 1981 by Persephone Press and later republished in 1983 by Kitchen Table: Women of Color Press.

Prior to being an editor of *Phoenix Rising,* in 1971, Kitty Tsui joined Third World Communications, "a media collective comprised of media people, artists, writers, and poets, cultural workers, and community activists."[13] The media collective published the anthology *Third World Women.* The core group of the collective were Asian, Black, and other women of color artists, educators, and activists, including Janice Mirikitani, Diana Lin, Nina Serrano, Thulani Nkabinde (now Thulani Davis), Geraldine Kutaka, Avotcja Jiltonilro, Penny Williams, Jessica Hagedorn, and Ntozake Shange, best known for her award-winning choreopoem "For Colored Girls Who Have Considered Suicide / When the Rainbow is Enuf."[14] Multiracial collectives that emerged during the second wave of feminism, such as Third World Communications; Poetry for the People, cofounded by Mirikitani and Black feminist poet and activist June Jordan; and the Bay Area chapter of Third World Women's Alliance, sought to challenge racism and sexism within white feminist and predominantly male-led movements from intersectional, anti-imperialist, and class-conscious perspectives.[15]

In the June/July 1987 issue of *Phoenix Rising,* Tsui offered remarks on the Asian/Pacific Lesbian Retreat that took place from May 8 to 10, 1987, in Sonoma County, California. According to the newsletter, this meeting was one of the first of its kind, as almost eighty women congregated to find community as Asian and Pacific Island lesbians. The retreat was dedicated in honor and in memory of Anita Oñang, Tsui's best friend.[16] In "An Open Letter to All of the Retreat Participants," published in *Phoenix Rising,* Tsui shared how the retreat was a transformative experience for her: "The weekend was a very affirming one for me for a number of reasons. When I first came out as a lesbian thirteen years ago, I thought I was the only Asian Lesbian in the world. It was very uplifting to look around our circle and see so many women of all ages and backgrounds together in one place."[17]

The thirtieth issue of *Phoenix Rising*, published in 1989, reviewed events from the second Asian/Pacific Lesbian Retreat, at the University of California, Santa Cruz, from September 1 to 4, 1989. The theme of the retreat was "Coming Together, Moving Forward." Over 175 bisexual and lesbian women of Bangladeshi, Chinese, Fijian, Filipino, CHamoru, Hawaiian, Indian, Indonesian, Japanese, Korean, Malaysian, Pakistani, Singaporean, Sri Lankan, Vietnamese, and other Asian and Pacific Islander backgrounds attended the conference. However, there were tensions and criticisms that arose during the conference, especially when South Asian lesbians brought attention to racism within the Asian/Pacific Islander lesbian community.

V. K. Aruna, one of the South Asian organizers of retreat, wrote in *Phoenix Rising* about how she and other South Asian lesbian women felt ostracized. Aruna's critique was also reprinted in *Shamakami*, a newsletter and organization for South Asian lesbians and bisexuals.[18] Criticisms by South Asian lesbians apparently urged a new editorial direction of *Phoenix Rising*, as the featured story of the 1993 issue was with Indian activist and filmmaker Pratibha Parmar. The interview coincided with the release of Parmar's 1993 award-winning documentary about female genital mutilation and cutting, *Warrior Marks*, which was executive produced by bisexual writer and activist Alice Walker.

Members of the Asian/Pacifica Sisters also organized and participated in the Dynamics of Color Conference that took place November 11 to 12, 1989, in San Francisco. The purpose of the conference provided lesbians of all racial backgrounds "tools to combat racism and focused on addressing racism on three levels: individual, group, and political/theoretical."[19] However, lesbians of color were prioritized at the conference and given the opportunity to share their voices, concerns, and perspectives on racism, "instead of the common racial dynamic that usually 'allows' white lesbians to dominate group discussions." The keynote speaker of the conference was Barbara Smith.

Many members of the A/PS and networks of queer Asians from across the country also participated in the 1993 March on Washington for Lesbian, Gay, and Bi Equal Rights and Liberation. On February 26, 1994, the A/PS and the Gay Asian Pacific Alliance marched in the Chinese New Year Parade in San Francisco, joined by over one hundred marchers, who shouted, "We're queer; we're Asian; and we're all across the nation." The spring/summer 1994 issue of *Phoenix Rising* detailed events of the historic gathering, as it was first time in US history that queer Asians participated in the Chinese New Year Parade in the city.[20]

Aché: A Journal for Lesbians of African Descent

Cofounded in 1989 by archivist and activist Lisbet Tellefsen and storyteller and performance artist Pippa Fleming, *Aché*—known as "the Bay Area's Journal for Black Lesbians"—was a "monthly journal by Black lesbians for the benefit of all Black women."[21] The journal was dedicated in memory of Black lesbian feminist, poet, and activist Pat Parker, who passed away from breast cancer in 1989.[22]

The name of the journal, *Aché*, derives from a Nigerian and, more specifically, Yoruba spiritual and philosophical concept (also written as *Aṣẹ* or *Ashe*), which centers on the life-force, energy, and power that is able to produce change. With members of *Aché* acknowledging how they "experience the power of Black lesbianism on a daily basis," the goals of *Aché* were as follows:

> (1) To celebrate ourselves, our communities, and our accomplishments; (2) to document Black lesbian herstory and culture; (3) to provide a forum where issues impacting our communities can be openly discussed and analyzed; (4) to keep Black lesbians in touch with each other's activities locally, nationally, and globally; (5) to provide a place where Black visual artists and writers can develop and display their skills; and (6) to help organize and empower ourselves; so that we may become more effective allies in the struggle to end the oppression that we, as Black people, women and members of the gay community, face daily.[23]

Themes and topics of the journal spanned the gamut—from creative, fiction, and nonfiction writing to essays on homophobia in the Black community, health care, African spirituality, and a calendar of events about Black and women of color lesbians in the Bay Area and transnationally.

Two years prior to the formation of *Aché*, the Nia Collective, a transgenerational organization created by and for lesbians of African descent, was established during the Black Lesbian Caucus at the Lesbian of Color Conference in San Francisco in 1987.[24] *Aché* was also an extension of the legacy of the *Black Lesbian Newsletter*, later known as *Onyx*, which was published in San Francisco and Berkeley from 1982 to 1984.[25]

Aché was the longest-running journal for Black American lesbians, with twenty-seven issues of the journal published from 1989 to 1993.[26] What started off as Tellefsen and Fleming writing a newsletter for friends and colleagues in the local Bay Area turned into a global network of Black lesbians across the African diaspora, with connections in Barbados, Canada, England, France, Germany, Ghana, St. Croix, South Africa, the US Virgin Islands, and more.[27]

For example, *Aché*'s February/March 1992 issue features a letter from Afro-German activist Ina Röder-Sissako dated October 10, 1991. Röder-Sissako's letter was addressed to Skye Ward, an *Aché* board member who was involved in organizing a cultural and political exchange between members of *Aché* and Afro-German lesbians in Berlin. Röder-Sissako shared details about the sustained anti-Black and racist violence against Black people and people of color in Germany. She also discussed how a network of women of color had come together to repudiate the violent attacks and wrote that "from now on every Monday, we will make manifestations [demonstrations] in all bigger cities with the motto: 'Immigrants, Blacks, and Jewish women and lesbians against FASCIST violence!'"[28]

Audre Lorde, the self-described "Black, lesbian, mother, warrior, poet," who was a key figure in spearheading the Afro-German women's movement, also wrote a letter to the women of *Aché* while living in St. Croix with her partner, Black lesbian feminist scholar-activist Gloria I. Joseph.[29] Lorde's letter, dated November 30, 1989, was published in the February 1990 issue of *Aché*. Sharing about the resiliency of Black, Hispanic, and low-income Crucian people who survived the devastation of Hurricane Hugo, Lorde also thanked the women of *Aché* for sending supplies.[30] At the end of her letter, Lorde wrote: "The existence of *Aché* is a deep and satisfying joy to me. It is important that we encourage and support an organ of communication exploring the potentials of Black Lesbian communities. I have seen *Aché* grow and develop through the hard work of a few committed sisters, and I hope to see even more of our communities and their concerns represented in the future."[31]

The November/December 1990 issue of *Aché* documented I Am Your Sister: Forging Global Connections Across Differences, a conference in honor of Lorde that was held in Boston, Massachusetts, from October 5 to 8, 1990. More than twelve hundred people from twenty-three countries attended the conference.[32] Reatha Fowler wrote about her experience in *Aché* and recalled how Asian women took to the podium to express their grievances of being stereotyped and discriminated against:

> The remainder of the morning was given to women who felt that their voices were not heard. The Asian women were the first to approach the stage. They comprised a group of 12 women, various

> skin hues from cream to brown and countries of origin. They read a poem together and then one-by-one approached the microphone sharing their pain, anger, and joy to the women sitting tensely in the pews. Some of us holding back our tears, others letting them fall freely, but all of us moved. They spoke so deeply from their hearts of their indoctrination to be silent. They wanted to break through our ignorance.
>
> Some of the quotes I was able to dictate through feelings of numbness may give you some idea of the intensity of their pain: "I am not your Oriental ornament to be placed on some narrow shelf in your mind." "Stop telling me to speak English the right way." "You see beauty only in my exoticism." "I'm not your little Indian doll." "Stop telling me to give up my sexist culture. Who are you to tell me what sexism means to me?" The women left the stage free of some tension with the realization they were clearly heard.[33]

Aché also featured artistry, poetry, and writing of more than two hundred writers and visual artists, including works by poet and writer Storme Webber and the founder of the Bay Area Lesbian Archives, Lenn Keller. In 1992, *Aché* became a nonprofit organization, changed its name to the Aché Project, and established a storefront office space on Shattuck Avenue in Berkeley, California, located right next to a former office of the Black Panther Party. While the organization disbanded in 1995, the *Aché* archives are critical to understanding Black lesbian thought, behavior, desire, and belonging.

Learning from the Archives

This chapter on *Phoenix Rising* and *Aché* does not fully showcase the radical work these organizations did to build and instill pride, catalyze community, and create visibility for Black and Asian American lesbians in the Bay Area, across the United States, and in their respective diasporas. The archives of these organizations and journals still have much to be explored, and the connections and community forged inside and outside of their networks is also a much-needed site of investigation. While I showcased some examples of cross-racial Black and Asian American lesbian and queer interactions and ties, these examples do not suggest a utopian relationship between Black and Asian American lesbians. Even within their own organizations and newsletters, *Phoenix Rising* and *Aché* documented some of the tensions that existed among and between their members, in their communities, and in society.

What, then, can we learn from the archives of *Phoenix Rising* and *Aché*? That community matters. That building intraracial and cross-racial solidarities is crucial. That self-determination matters. That tension, naming discomfort, and humility in struggle matter. That centering the most marginalized in our communities matters. That resisting white supremacist, cis-heteronormative, and patriarchal revisionist histories matters. That telling, archiving, and preserving our stories matters.

17.

Reviving the History of Radical Black-Asian Internationalism

Minju Bae and Mark Tseng-Putterman

A version of this piece was originally published in July 2020 in the early months of the COVID-19 pandemic and a resurgent Black Lives Matter movement. As we revisit this piece, we witness the ongoing US-backed genocide of Palestinians in Gaza and the terror of Israeli violence throughout occupied Palestine—calling on us to continue to place anti-imperialism at the center of our political commitments.

Sax Rohmer's 1913 novel, *The Mystery of Dr. Fu Manchu*, captivated readers with its distillation of centuries of Western desire, fear, and fascination of "the East" into a single antagonist: Dr. Fu Manchu, "the yellow peril incarnate."[1] Equipped with both the "cruel cunning of an entire Eastern race" and mastery of the Western sciences, the devious Chinaman thrilled and terrified readers with his spectacular exploits. Fu Manchu crystallized Western associations of Eastern disease, invasion, corruption, and enslavement into a monstrous man to be reviled and vanquished.

The racialization of COVID-19—as the "Chinese virus" or "kung flu"—revives this deeply embedded cultural touchstone. Popular scapegoat narratives that the virus derived from Wuhan's "wet markets" or even escaped from a high-security virology lab highlight the lasting rhetorical uses of the yellow peril trope.[2] As the new Oriental invasion, COVID-19 became a convenient external enemy, necessitating national security and unity in a time of social upheaval, never mind the grossly disproportionate impact of COVID-19 in Black, Indigenous, and Latinx communities. Like the "Chinese Must Go!" labor movements, lynchings, and vigilante violence of the 1870s, recent anti-Asian violence—from a Texas grocery store stabbing to a Brooklyn acid attack—serves to preserve national, economic, and bodily health by violently excising the "alien in our midst."[3]

Yet, as the isolation of social distancing gave way to mass Black Lives Matter mobilizations in the wake of the police murders of George Floyd and Breonna Taylor, another version of yellow peril was revived. Protest signs wielding the slogan "Yellow Peril Supports Black Power" alluded to the oppositional politics of the Asian American movement of the late 1960s and 1970s: one which subverts the nightmare of Oriental invasion into a call for anticolonial revolt. Embedded in this slogan is the spirit of Black-Asian internationalist critiques of global empire and white supremacy that defined the "Third World" idea. The overlapping social upheavals of a pandemic racialized as "Oriental" and Black uprisings against white supremacist policing suture the discourses of anti-Blackness and Orientalism, not as equivalent but as constitutive components of global racial capitalism. Amid the contradictions between an intensifying military "pivot to Asia" and a Black abolitionist vision to divest from carceral institutions, the revolutionary internationalist tradition of Black and Asian anti-imperialists provides a road map for building a different world.

Revulsion or Revolt? Yellow Peril's Competing Discourses

Yellow peril—an imperial discourse—functions as an entity to fear and extinguish; an external enemy around which the idea of the West coheres.[4] The colonial domination of Asia was itself framed as a preemptive measure against the threat of yellow peril. In 1895, as European imperialist powers carved Asia into a series of colonial administrations and concessions, the divine vision of colonial conquest was visualized by a lithograph commissioned by German emperor Wilhelm II.[5] A glowing Buddha floats ominously in the East, as the nations of Europe—personified as angelic Hellenistic warriors—are warned: "Peoples of Europe, Guard Your Most Sacred Possessions." In 1905, when Japan shocked the Western world by defeating a European power in the Russo-Japanese War, Wilhelm's nightmare of an anti-imperial race war seemed imminent.

Yet, for some on the other side of the Atlantic, Japan's victory struck a different chord. Pan-African socialist and sociologist W. E. B. Du Bois heralded what he saw as "the awakening of the yellow race," a movement that the "black and brown" races were sure to follow.[6] "This," Du Bois wrote, "is the problem of the yellow peril and of the color line, and it is the problem of the American Negro."[7] Du Bois's color-line thesis identified the global nature of white supremacy and clarified the power of the world's Black, brown, and yellow majority.[8] Where the Western powers saw a threat to global white supremacy, Du Bois saw yellow peril as a beacon of potential for peoples of color. And while history would prove that Japanese militarism would not challenge but instead would entrench the forces of global imperialism, Du Bois's interpretation demonstrated that yellow peril can be a tool of empire as well as a call to arms against it.

Yellow Peril Supports Black Power

In 1968, when the young members of Berkeley's Asian American Political Alliance showed up to a San Francisco protest to free imprisoned Black Panther Party leader Huey Newton, they carried signs emblazoned with the now-iconic slogan "Yellow Peril Supports Black Power."[9] In Du Boisian fashion, their repurposing of yellow peril became shorthand for a praxis of shared rebellion against racism, imperialism, and capitalism. Asian American radicals—in the midst of the Black Power movement and a US imperialist war in Vietnam—wielded the trope that damned Asians in the United States as "enemy aliens" as a critique of US empire. It clarified a commitment to a revolutionary internationalist order that could undermine the logics of white supremacy, imperialism, and of the United States itself.

"Yellow Peril Supports Black Power" reemerged during the resurgent Black Lives Matter movement, dotting the seas of protest signs at demonstrations as a clarion call for Asian American solidarity. While some have lodged complaints against the "Yellow Peril" slogan on the grounds that it decenters Black struggles, the phrase's internationalist lens was encouraged by leaders of the Black liberation movement themselves.[10] For instance, when Black Panther Party member David Hilliard told the Red Guards, "If you can't relate to China then you can't relate to the Panthers," he was insisting that Asian communist and anti-imperialist movements were crucial complements to the Panthers' struggle against anti-Blackness.[11] To stand with the Panthers, Asian Americans had to look beyond assimilation and instead toward the rising tide of Third World revolution in the East.

Calls for Black-Asian internationalist solidarity ebbed and flowed throughout movements of the twentieth century. In 1943, poet and activist Langston Hughes penned the anticolonial poem "Roar, China!" which called to "smash the revolving doors of the Jim Crow Y.M.C.A."—linking Jim Crow segregation in the US South to white-only businesses in Shanghai's imperialist concessions.[12] In 1964, Malcolm X declared Vietnam the "struggle of the whole Third World." And then, in 1970, the Anti-Imperialist Delegation—headed by Black Panther Party leader Eldridge Cleaver—looked east for revolutionary tactics, leadership, and political ideas to adapt to the belly of the beast and led a "people's diplomacy" tour of the Democratic People's Republic of Korea, North Vietnam, and the People's Republic of China.[13]

Empire was at the heart of this delegation's critiques, noting the ways that racialization was mapped onto the world. As symbols of the Third World idea, Mao Zedong, Ho Chi Minh, and Kim Il Sung represented a different kind of political philosophy, one that could free the masses from capitalist exploitation and colonial trauma. Identifying with the project of the Third World, Black and Asian American radicals forged solidarities based not on equivalence but on the alliances necessary to contest the global color line in an era of decolonization.

Our current crises demonstrate both the longevity of this global arrangement of power and its flexibility. De jure segregation, partitions, and colonial rule have been largely retooled into a contemporary discourse of multicultural inclusion and racial liberalism that celebrates "difference" while retaining racist structures and obscuring ongoing imperialism. In the mid-twentieth century, a new script emerged to incorporate Asian racial difference into the project of empire: the "model minority." In contrast to Black Americans agitating for racial equality and Third World anticolonial, communist national liberation movements, Asian Americans were framed as apolitical, upwardly mobile, and, therefore, proof of the benevolence of US capitalist liberal democracy.[14] Where yellow peril demarcated the global color line through the imagined threat of transgression, the model minority upholds the postracial fantasy of the color line's supposed irrelevance. The model minority narrative domesticates the internationalist spirit of Asian America's radical origins, foreclosing possibilities for oppositional, anti-imperialist politics.

The Counterrevolutionary Functions of the Model Minority

The renewed appeal of "Yellow Peril Supports Black Power" stems from its rejection of the model minority narrative. The historical uses of the model minority myth as a tool to admonish Black-led demands for racial justice have been well documented. William Petersen's 1966 article "Success Story: Japanese American Style," which heralded Japanese American family values, educational achievement, and a culture of diligence amid racial discrimination, is emblematic of the myth's utility in contrasting Asian American "success" with the supposed Black cultural pathology popularized by the Moynihan Report. Then as now, the model minority myth functions as a counterrevolutionary discourse: defanging Black-led calls for an antiracist redistribution and reconstruction of a fundamentally racist US society by pointing to Asian American "success stories" as evidence of US equal opportunity.

What this model minority "origin story" often misses is the myth's other counterrevolutionary function: as imperial propaganda in a Cold War context in which US racism risked derailing the geopolitical project of winning "hearts and minds" across the Third World. Where yellow peril wields the specter of Oriental aggression and poses US imperialism as the shining knight of Western civilization, the model minority subsumes the very existence of empire under a veneer of multicultural harmony. This is visible in the case of multiple US occupations in the Pacific. Scholar Dean Saranillio has written that the representation of Hawaiian statehood as an Asian American civil rights victory provided liberal cover for the entrenchment of settler colonialism over Kanaka Maoli land. The model minority thus gifted US empire both a strategic military foothold in the Pacific and propagandized "proof" of US racial harmony.[15] Likewise, the postwar US occupation of Japan and its molding into a junior partner of the US Cold War agenda in Asia necessitated the racial rehabilitation of Japanese people from their WWII image as "kamikaze" aggressors to that of, as historian Naoko Shibusawa argues, a feminized, docile position as "international model minorities."[16]

Like the model minority's evocation of a "problem" minority, the valorization of model geopolitical allies exists in productive tension with "enemy nations." Through this lens, corporate media's recent portrayal of international pandemic responses could be productively read as a neo–Cold War geography of US agendas in Asia. Where South Korea, Taiwan, and Japan were heralded as models of Asian public health done "the right way," spurious claims about falsified numbers, mass graves, and other markers of "authoritarianism" were weaponized against the governments of China, the Democratic People's Republic of Korea, and Iran. Yellow peril paints an isolated and sanctions-starved DPRK as a belligerent nuclear threat to the American people and justifies US military presence from South Korea to Okinawa, Guam, Hawai'i, and the Philippines as a righteous crusade to "contain" China. Conversely, Japan, South Korea, and others represent "success stories" of Western capitalist modernity. These "model minority" countries act as vindication of US hegemony in Asia in the name of anticommunist containment and capitalist integration. Demarcating Asian "success stories" from "enemy nations," the yellow peril and model minority narratives work in tandem to legitimize US geopolitical supremacy.

Against a Politics of "Claiming America"

The complementary counterrevolutionary functions of the yellow peril and model minority tropes make it difficult to refute one without reifying the other. The pandemic-prompted rise of anti-Asian violence, for instance, has inspired some Asian Americans to attempt to evade the imperial discourse of yellow peril through claims of model minority citizenship. Most notoriously, former presidential candidate Andrew Yang embodied this model minority impulse in his 2020 call for Asian Americans to "show without a shadow of a doubt that we are Americans who will do our part for our country."[17] Despite widespread criticism from the Asian American mainstream, Yang's argument was not too different from the claims that many Asian Americans have long made about safety, inclusion, and belonging. Asian American advocates, politicians, and educators have long insisted that Asian Americans are part of the "fabric of this nation."[18] Pandemic-era declarations that "we belong" likewise deferred a deeper critique of the United States, instead seeking safety from the state discourse of yellow peril in the arms of the state itself. Many have turned to hate crime legislation and police enforcement, legitimizing the role of carceral violence as a salve for rising anti-Asian hate violence. For instance, in May 2020, New York City launched a $100,000 effort to combat anti-Asian discrimination through public outreach, including signs that read "Discrimination and harassment due to COVID-19 are illegal in New York City."[19] Later that year, the New York Police Department formed an Asian Hate Crimes Task Force, a move that was informed by the adoption of a hate crimes framework by many Asian American advocacy organizations.[20] This embrace of the carceral state is part of a longer history of co-opting anti-Asian violence to bolster federal hate crimes legislation—dismissing an anti-imperialist stance that identifies the United States itself as the world's greatest purveyor of violence.[21]

If assimilation has historically mediated the relationship between yellow peril and model minority, then claims of Americanness inevitably swap the imperial nightmare of anticolonial "race war" for the legitimizing imperial fantasy of "postracial" harmony. Instead of resisting the imperial logics of yellow peril, Asian American claims to belonging often function as a simple redirection of imperialist violence. T-shirts proudly stating "I'm Asian but I'm not Chinese" demonstrate this most literally.[22] Merely advocating for expanded parameters to define the American "us" implicitly reifies the dichotomy between "us" and "them."

Despite its ostensible invocation of the specter of Oriental anticolonial revolt, the revival of the "Yellow Peril Supports Black Power" slogan largely obscures this internationalist context in favor of a domesticated version of Asian American solidarity modeled on a template of white allyship.[23] Counterintuitively, the meme-ification of "Yellow Peril Supports Black Power" occurs alongside a brand of Asian American discourse that presumes Asianness is antithetical to the values of social justice on which Asian American support for Black lives is presumably predicated. For instance, the recent "talk to your Asian parents about anti-Blackness" genre poses second-generation, mostly college-educated Asian Americans as the necessary bridges to shepherd their parents into the milieu of recognizing privilege, unpacking colorism, and debunking the model minority myth.[24]

Despite their intent, this genre associates Asianness with ignorance and racism and Asian Americanness with progressivism and solidarity—an assumption that risks excising the anticolonial, anti-imperial, and communist struggles that many of our parents and grandparents lived through as somehow irrelevant to the task of engaging in struggles against anti-Blackness and white supremacy. Rather than limiting Asian American allyship to the same terrain of liberalism and multiculturalism that construct the facade of US postracialism, returning to internationalism enables a fundamental critique of Americanness, where allyship is motivated not by charity or empathy but an analysis of the intertwined systems of anti-Blackness, Orientalism, and global white supremacy.

In spite of the theses that claimed that COVID-19 pulled back the curtain of the model minority to reveal yellow peril, it may be more accurate to say that the pandemic has clarified how instrumental the coexistence of both discourses is to their coherence. In an attempt to reclaim "yellow peril," these efforts unwittingly re-create a new model minority, defanging the radical internationalism at the crux of Asian American identity formation in favor of a model subject of US progressivism and racial liberalism.

The Third World Awaits

As historian Vijay Prashad urges, "The Third World awaits . . . resurrection, not as nostalgia but as a project that matches our contemporary dilemmas."[25] Indeed, the spirit of Third World internationalism is alive and well—if overlooked—in today's Black Lives Matter movement. The stunning 2016 policy platform Vision for Black Lives directly implicated US militarism in its call to divest from carceral structures and invest in Black communities. Citing the "increasing militarization of Africa" under US military programs such as AFRICOM, the document denounced US imperialism as a "direct threat to global Black liberation" and identified demilitarization as a prerequisite for investment in Black communities.[26] Others have identified international police exchanges and the sale of military supplies to police departments as further evidence of the conjoined carceral functions of domestic police occupation and international military hegemony that necessitates an interlinked abolitionist and anti-imperialist movement.[27]

That Black Lives Matter's critical connections to anti-imperialist struggle have been largely silenced in mainstream discussion speaks to a historical truth: Black liberation movements have always posed a particular problem for the maintenance of US empire. In 2020, State Department officials complained that the brutal repression of protesters was undermining the "moral authority" of the United States to projects to advance its geopolitical agenda.[28] Meanwhile, the US embassy of Seoul ostentatiously displayed a Black Lives Matter banner as the US military continues its seventy-year occupation of the Korean Peninsula.[29]

Where Black internationalists have sought to exploit the connections of the Third World by forging strategic alliances with the colonized peoples in Africa, Asia, Latin America, and beyond, US political elites have instead co-opted civil rights progress as "proof" of US democratic values on the world stage. The beneficiaries of today's global color line have an interest in domesticating struggles for racial justice. Domestic rebellions are cordoned off into the same narrative of progressive exceptionalism that in turn necessitate US global leadership.[30]

The first wave of the COVID-19 pandemic prompted an affective crisis for Asian Americans caught between the comfortable invisibility of the model minority and the racialized scrutiny of the yellow peril. Yet the productive contradictions of this emotional turmoil have been largely buried under important but limiting framings of Asian American privilege and allyship in the context of a renewed Black Lives Matter rebellion.

This political crossroads provides an opportunity to understand the crude Orientalism of the "Chinese virus" and the endemic anti-Blackness of our carceral institutions as complementary, constitutive elements of global white supremacy. The intertwined abolitionist and internationalist traditions offer an alternative to imperial hegemony: to center a politics of refusal and commit to dismantling, undoing, unlearning, denying, defunding, and abolishing US imperial rule through internationalist solidarities. As the foundational abolitionist organization Critical Resistance declared in their pandemic policy platform, "This pandemic is not bound by borders. As such, our solidarity and response must be international."[31]

Amid both a global pandemic and a global uprising, the history of Black-Asian internationalism—encapsulated in the slogan "Yellow Peril Supports Black Power"—operates as a critical framework to deconstruct the systems of anti-Blackness and Orientalism, policing and perpetual war, necessary to transform this oppressive world order.

PART 3

Our Liberation

Abolition Feminisms

Illustration honoring the legacy of sex worker organizing in New York City with images of Sylvia Rivera, Marsha P. Johnson, and Mary Jones (top, left to right) and dedicated to Lorena Borjas, Layleen Polanco, and Yang Song (bottom, left to right). Art by Butterflymush.

18.

To My Movement Sister, Ny Nourn

Nate Tan

The following is a letter written to Ny Nourn, a Cambodian refugee and formerly incarcerated domestic violence survivor who was given a life sentence without the possibility of parole in 2003 for the role she played in a murder committed by her abuser. After serving a reduced sixteen-year sentence, Nourn was released and immediately detained by Immigration and Customs Enforcement, which threatened to deport her. Tan and Nourn served together as codirectors of Asian Prisoner Support Committee.

This is not the first letter I've written to you. But this is the first one I've written since you are out of prison and ICE detention. The letters I've written you have been letters of admiration and inspiration. This letter is no different.

When I think about how you've impacted my life, I am reminded of the late James Baldwin and his letter to Angela Davis. He wrote, "If we know, then we must fight for your life as though it were our own." You are always fighting for people's freedom as if it were your own. I remember the stories you used to tell me:

When a judge said you were going to spend the rest of your life in jail, you said: Hell no, I'm not.

You fought for a resentence and were paroled in fifteen years. Still, it was fifteen years too long for a crime you did not commit.

When an immigration judge said you were going to be deported after prison, you said: Hell no, I'm not.

You wrote to an immigration attorney to fight your deportation case.

When an immigration attorney said that you would likely be deported to Cambodia, a country your family escaped as refugees, you said: Hell no, I'm not.

When people underestimated you, you would tell them: I'm going to get free, with or without your help.

Your spirit for freedom was contagious to me. Each story made me believe that freedom was possible. If we were ever to get to a freer world, you'd be one of the leaders to take us there.

I remember crying at your last immigration hearing. When the judge ruled for your release, I was so overwhelmed with immense joy. When I imagine the feeling of freedom—a feeling I'm always chasing—I think of that moment. The moment your release was announced.

I knew when you came home, you were ready to take on the world. And you did.

I was devastated when ICE picked up four of our Cambodian members. This was my hometown. These were people in my neighborhood. The only home they knew was Oakland. I thought, "Can we do this? Can we stop all their deportations?" You looked me dead in the eyes and asked, "How can we keep them home? How can we get them free?"

While I was asking "can," you were asking "how." Those who do not have freedom, have no other option than to believe freedom is possible. Because you believed, hundreds, if not thousands, of us believed.

You influenced organizers, attorneys, impacted family members, and elected officials that we can get our community members free. And we did just that. We got every single one of them free. What I took away from this work with you, Ny, is that we have to have a "why." When the "why" in our life is strong enough, the "how" always becomes clearer.

Ny, without any doubt or hesitation, I am following you to freedom. I will fight alongside you until all people in cages are free. Though the challenge is great, I know the cost of not doing so is even greater. You know better than anyone that none of us are free until all of us are free.

I am a firm believer in what bell hooks shares, "that we would all love better if we used it as a verb." It is most helpful for me to understand that love isn't a moment, it isn't an end point, and it isn't a temporary emotion, but a continuous set of actions and commitments to each other. I only come to this knowledge because of you, Ny.

I did not know what love as a practice looked like before entering this work. Seeing you fight day in and day out for people behind bars showed me what love looks like in action. You taught me that when you love freedom or a person behind bars, you must believe the greatest outcomes are possible. What we do to get there is always rooted in love. Theories, liberatory praxes, and radical politics are pretty on paper, but it is what we practice with each other that will get us free. Thank you, Ny, for teaching me that.

Until we all are free,
Nate Tan

19.

Lessons Learned

Building a Police-Free Future with Abolition Park

VX

George Floyd was murdered on my birthday. The news came to me first from my mother, who sent a reminder to all of her children to be careful and that she loved us more than anything. I remember hearing that George Floyd cried out for his mother with his final breaths. I could relate to him most in that moment. I did not, and still have not, watched the video recording of his death. I'm not able to hold images like that; they get too deep under my skin and make me want to crawl out of it. I might do something dangerous in that state of mind. It honestly didn't even register to me as a significant event in US history. It felt like just another day in America.

Drinking tea at home in the early weeks of quarantine in 2020, friends and I would laugh and joke on Zoom calls about the collapse of the state, which seemed to coincide with the upcoming election. When friends or colleagues would suggest that now we "had to vote for Joe Biden," I found myself inexplicably emotional.

"I won't. We don't have to do that!" I would plead with them, feeling myself near tears.

"What other choice do we have?" they would ask me. "There's no other option."

Tensing my body, I would insist. "We have options!"

"Like what?" they would ask, seemingly unmoved by my pleas for a more imaginative future. The isolation was suffocating. After we would end our calls, I would allow the tears to fall onto my folded hands, a prayer for the end of the world.

A few days later, my partner and I took a road trip to meet up with my closest friend in a cabin in Virginia. On the morning that the Minneapolis precinct was burned to the ground, she burst into my room, beaming from ear to ear.

"They did it! You're gonna love this! Check out Minneapolis, they set fire to the whole precinct!"

Ignited, I was driven to take a detour to Washington, DC, on my way back to New York City. We came immediately upon a massive and militant march circling the White House and allowed ourselves to be swept up in a wave of energy and emotion. I felt a light that I had not even realized was wavering suddenly reignited in my chest. I've been chasing that feeling every night since, moving under the cover of darkness, protecting the flame.

Weeks later in New York City, this energy drove people out into the streets night after night, even as our bodies and voices broke down. The more the police tried to separate people protesting, the closer the crowd grew. The more violently they tried to repress our demands, the more power and conviction we brought in response. The massive scale of the NYPD was revealed in brutal and horrifying displays of force. I couldn't imagine going back to living "peacefully" under the familiar dead weight of oppression. I could not *un*imagine a way out.

On June 23, 2020, someone sent me a message asking, "Can you pull up to City Hall to help set up a camp? We need at least fifteen people to stay the first night." Just a few weeks prior, folks in Seattle had taken control of an entire precinct and effectively pushed the officers out to create an autonomous zone (known as CHAZ) separate from law enforcement. I, like many New Yorkers, was intrigued by the potential of establishing something similar in New York City.

When I arrived at city hall, there were hundreds of people dancing in the street. However, as the night stretched into morning, most people went home. By the end of the first night, about twenty of us remained. We set up camp by sitting on the lawn, resting our heads on our bags or in the grass. At some point in the evening, a notice went out on Instagram asking for supplies to support protestors who were planning to #OccupyCityHall. Within hours people started dropping off blankets, food, and books. As we lay in the dark, one young black woman carrying a Haitian flag and a megaphone spoke to us. Her oratory lifted us to a suspended state, caught between night and day. I remember drifting in and out of consciousness, wrapped in a blanket given by a stranger, carried by her voice. She preached and sang into the sunrise. The thing I remember most was that she sang a slow, languid version of "Happy Birthday" to Tamir Rice on what would have been his eighteenth birthday.

The next day more people came. A library was set up. Then a bodega. By the end of the first week, we had a laundry service, a mental health tent, and a garden. I recall an overwhelming abundance of energy and resources. A black woman with experience in the restaurant industry quickly established a food infrastructure, coordinating meals for everyone. People started to get comfortable.

Being in that space was a deeply moving and immersive educational experience. The park allowed for around-the-clock political education. Innumerable critical dialogues were happening; people were becoming radicalized by walking through the space. I organized a teach-in titled "When Is Reform an Obstacle to Abolition?" because many protestors gathered at City Hall were dissatisfied by the limited call of "Defund the Police" and wanted to mobilize a stronger push for "Abolition Now!" So many people showed up to learn more about abolition that there was not sufficient space for us to gather. Looking around the overcrowded park, I said to everyone, "We can try to fit in here on this small piece of grass, or we can go to the bridge, because f*** it, it's our bridge." Immediately, the crowd responded, "TO THE BRIDGE!!!" and started running toward the entrance, shouting over their shoulders for other comrades in the park to join them. We flowed out into the intersection, stopping traffic. We marched across the bridge, and when we found the police waiting for us at the Brooklyn exit, we climbed the barriers to the opposite lane and marched back to Manhattan against traffic. When we reached the Manhattan base of the bridge, surrounded by agitated police, we sat down on the walkway and continued our teach-in. The police were forced to listen in. We generated so much collective power in that march that it proved to be a key moment of community formation. Most of the people who came for the teach-in and ended up "taking" the bridge that day began organizing toward their political goals as a collective known as Abolition Park.

When we returned to city hall after the teach-in, the original conveners of the encampment were angry. They argued that we did not have consent to take that action, that we brought an increased police presence to the perimeter, and that the action encouraged people to leave the encampment when the intention was to hold the space. This tension caused an immediate split. There was both resentment toward those who didn't follow the more radical movement of the crowd, and from people feeling that we betrayed the original intention of the encampment. It was a real-time role play of how reformist and abolitionist political strategies often don't work hand in hand. That was only the third day of the encampment. By the following day, we realized that we did not have time to fight with each other because we needed to focus our energy on defending ourselves from the police.

Before the city council budget hearing, there were two back-to-back police raids in the early morning hours. Residents of the park moved to form a human chain, linking arms to hold a perimeter while the police literally beat us back. The morning of the first raid, I got a black eye from being hit in the face with the back end of a baton. Although people were injured, pepper-sprayed, and exhausted, the NYPD was not able to enter the park. Footage of their brutal efforts circulated in the news. It looked extreme enough that Mayor Bill de Blasio released a statement telling the NYPD to leave the encampment alone until further notice. This was certainly a victory, but the NYPD remained an ominous and threatening presence.

The night of the city council vote, when the obvious became more obvious (they were not going to cut any money from the police budget), was supposed to be the last night of the encampment. In the morning most of the original organizers took their resources and left, but hundreds of people elected to stay. At that point, a lot of conversations needed to be had. We were strangers gathered in a park, and we didn't really know why yet. We didn't know how we were going to survive in such an unpredictable and volatile space. What we did recognize was that without the resources that we needed, the park would become increasingly dangerous for everyone involved. All the infrastructure around food, donations, and supplies had to be rebuilt from scratch. We were thrown into immediate crisis response.

The most significant shift that happened was the transition of occupants at that time: the composition switched from a group of people who all had another place to live to a majority of folks who had nowhere safe to go. We shifted to an urgent demonstration of why and how the police are a threat to our everyday safety. Instead of speaking for, over, and down to the most vulnerable and disenfranchised people in our city, we welcomed them and enlisted them in the fight for their own liberation. That transition in itself is a victory in my eyes.

I stepped into a role of facilitating daily community meetings. At first, the meetings were very tense gatherings. Once we became more confident in our ability to self-organize, we shifted the meeting to every few days, and then eventually every few weeks. I found my responsibility as a black woman and a feminist to be modeling a radical way of being in relation to others. Some days I was able to provide a consistent, grounded energy to counter the explosive hazards of patriarchy and antiblackness. Other days conflicts erupted into violence. We all had to learn very quickly how to manage our emotions under extreme circumstances. It was a crash course in conflict resolution, community safety, and deescalation.

One of the things that was really helpful in deescalation work was an understanding and compassion for someone else's trauma. It required stepping back and saying, *Yes, I am able to recognize that I've been harmed by this person. But I am also able to find compassion for the trauma that may have brought them to this place. I am going to recognize the root of violence not being here in this immediate interaction. That it's deeper than this moment.*

It was also about self-accountability and recognizing that de-escalating volatile situations is really about my own body and what I can make it do, not what I can make someone else's body do. I can calm my body, my voice. Bring my energy down. Find something centering within myself. Not try to overpower anybody. Taking control of a heightened situation is not about being bigger or stronger than someone. Prioritizing consent was a big part of the conversation.

Another thing we learned that helped was not to be a voyeur to someone else's pain. When someone is in a heightened emotional state in a public place, they start bringing attention to themselves, intentional or not. Typically, people will rush over to see what is happening and escalate that energy, like putting gas on a fire. Alternatively, if you redirect that energy and everyone moves in the opposite direction, a situation is more likely to defuse itself. Moving away also creates a safe space for the necessary expression of the completely reasonable frustrations that so many of us felt. By keeping our distance and allowing a person that autonomy, we provided ten secure square feet for a person to lose their shit. *Don't try to stop it, don't try to control it, don't penalize them for it. If we stay over here, they're not going to hurt anyone. They're going to yell and scream and maybe smash a chair.*

As a community, we agreed that we were not concerned about broken chairs because we could replace them. We kept repeating that we weren't going to police property. If you lost something in the space, then you lost something. It wasn't a thing you could bring to the community seeking punishment for someone else. Do you need a phone? We can get you a new phone. Do you need a new sleeping bag? We have more sleeping bags! We learned to address the violence that comes from scarcity with resources and abundance instead of shame and punishment.

We know that is not how the cops respond. We're watching them watch us. We found that simply inverting police behaviors and the carceral logics that motivated them resolved a lot of our issues. In this way, we were able to keep the park free of police for almost thirty days—until 3:40 a.m. on July 22 when we were raided and violently evicted from the home we had made.

The night of the final raid, the police used a different tactic. Without warning or a sound, they rushed and shook sleeping people from their tents. Within minutes, they had swept us all out of the park. There was no announcement, no opportunity to prepare. Many people living in that park lost everything they had to the NYPD that night. I am referring to poor and unhoused people who lost their legal documents, phones, photographs, family heirlooms, valued possessions—all the precious things an unhoused person might keep with them. The police also seized all of our bikes, medical supplies, generators, coolers, and water.

After they ran us out of the park, we were forced to stay out.

Officers followed us into the street, scattering and arresting people, snatching people for contesting the raid or just standing around too long. We fled with no real sense of direction because there was nowhere to go. We could not have returned to city hall because the NYPD immediately occupied it.

As they pushed us out, they moved in.

We became a displaced community of recently robbed, brutalized, and traumatized unhoused people that needed immediate food and shelter. The people I fled with were a 10-year-old boy and his mother, a man and his wife who hitchhiked from Indiana, and a young black woman who had just been released from jail a few nights prior. While I knew that I could go home eventually, I had no idea where any of the others could safely retreat. We couldn't keep wandering the streets, because the cops were grabbing people. In the immediacy of the raid, where could we go to be safe? The necessary solution required so much of our housed community to open their doors. It was urgent. I started calling people, "Can so-and-so come to your house tonight?" Or just showing up, "We're outside."

That night made the connection between abolition and housing justice painfully clear. Moving forward, housing and ongoing mutual aid became the need we continued to organize around. How could we find safe housing and secure meals, care, and community? How would we continue to sustain networks of care and resources without space to be together?

In the immediate days after the raid, most of our community relocated to Washington Square Park. Miraculously, we had just ordered forty yellow tents, which at the time of the raid were in storage at a nearby office. We started handing tents out to people who lost their homes when we were evicted from city hall.

This was too visible for the cops.

There have always been unhoused people living at Washington Square Park, but if you give them any shelter, it's unacceptable. At city hall, many people had tents or other structures for shelter, but we had the numbers to keep each other safe. At Washington Square, the police were able to quickly and violently break up smaller groups of yellow tents together. They would make daily arrests and confiscate the tents until it was no longer viable for us to be there. The same officers that had been surveilling and threatening us at city hall continued to police our gathering.

Recognizing that small groups of unhoused comrades living in tents was not viable, we started crowdfunding for hotels and Airbnbs to house people. At the same time, community members from the park with housing continued to open up their doors. Some brought multiple people home with them. That wasn't sustainable, but it was an immediate solution. In terms of assessing need, we knew a number of young black girls who did not have access to safe housing, and they were our immediate priority. A large number of our unhoused community members were also older black men, most of whom had already been incarcerated at some point and therefore whose freedom and autonomy under constant police surveillance was very precarious. It was overwhelmingly young women who opened their homes, creating complicated gender dynamics.

When you have one woman who brings three, four, five people home and four of them are men, there are concerns about that kind of intimacy being misread and misinterpreted. It's a big risk for a woman to bring an unfamiliar man into her home. Although I am not aware of any instances of violence or assault that happened in that context, what I know happens is that those women get really fatigued by the burden of caring for everyone. Stepping into this role of provider and caregiver when it cannot be reciprocated always increases the risk of burnout. A woman might not always say it for herself, because there's a lot of guilt around saying, "I don't have this capacity. I'm tired of housing, feeding, and tending to this entire community." You don't want to reproduce harmful gender dynamics in mutual aid but that remains a real challenge.

Meanwhile, we continued to take to the streets every day, engaging in intense standoffs against lines of police in riot gear, publicly demanding the immediate defunding, disarming, and dismantling of the NYPD. We saw the connections between safe housing and abolition in visceral and immediate ways. Without the safety of shelter and community, people are much more exposed to state violence.

At city hall, when we erected structures that offered coverage from sun and rain, the cops used that as a reason to raid us because it is illegal to construct your own shelter. When we gave out tents, the cops arrested people for sleeping in them. Then, as we were renting Airbnbs, paying months in advance, we would check in only to have homeowners cancel the reservations, telling us, "This isn't a homeless shelter."

So you have to not be homeless in order to be eligible to stay in a home?

Such precarity on a day-to-day level makes it much easier for comrades to get caught up in the punitive carceral system. It became increasingly risky for the people who are visibly and vocally protesting the unchecked power of the police to stay on the street because the police terrorized them. We became vocal housing advocates because the police were targeting our most vulnerable community members in an effort to weaken their commitment to fight for their lives.

Police surveillance of protestors continues to increase, and the housing crisis in New York City worsens. Already, there are three empty residences for every unhoused person in the city. Abolition Park continues to strategize around safe housing for our community while publicly demanding safe housing for all New Yorkers. We also extended our network to include community fridges and the distribution of groceries and other resources. These are not supplemental or peripheral activities in our fight for black liberation. The abolitionist principles that we learned from our experiences inside and outside of the camp demand that *care* (not cops) be at the center of any political action we take.

We've become increasingly decentralized, because we get less police surveillance if we keep it moving. Police surveilling a dinner might seem innocuous, but many members of our community have faced arrest, prosecution, and imprisonment. The police are very threatened by our ongoing mutual aid. That's encouraging.

20.

"We Lead the World's Liberation"

A Conversation with Sex Work Activists

Kate Zen and SX Noir

Amid a global pandemic that has reshaped the sex industry, activists Kate Zen and SX Noir met up on Zoom to debrief their work and unpack solidarity between Black and Asian sex workers. Zen and Noir met through their involvement in sex workers' rights organizing and activism—having founded and supported organizations such as Red Canary Song, Red Light Reader, DecrimNY, and Women of Sex Tech, among others. They have collaborated on projects and supported each other's struggles, putting Black and Asian feminist solidarity to work, and their conversations have often blossomed into direct action.

The conversation took place in September 2020, following the Black Sex Worker Liberation March, which was co-led by Noir and took place on August 1, 2020, during a summer of racial justice uprisings and unrest following the murder of George Floyd.[1] They discussed topics including race and immigration at the intersections of sex worker issues past and present and the powerful force of friendship within movements. The following has been edited for length and clarity.[2]

Kate Zen (KZ): I've learned so much from working with you, SX, and it's been an amazing privilege to do different events with you over this past summer—from the sex work decrim teach-in with TS Candii and the Black Sex Worker Liberation March to being part of the work with the Women of Sex Tech.[3]

My activism with sex worker rights has been really shaped by Black activists, in particular Andrea Ritchie. I interned with her when I was in school, when she was in the first few years of building up Streetwise and Safe. We did outreach at shelters and built a cohort of LGBTQ Black and brown youth under the age of twenty-four that were engaged in street economies. Working with Ritchie gave me my political framework for sex worker activism, which is always based in antipolice, antiprison activism—looking at how "broken windows policing" is incredibly racist and how the entire prison system comes out of the institution of slavery in the United States. Ritchie has been so instrumental in reshaping what has been a more white-dominated sex worker activist rhetoric in the US that focused more on pleasure activism, and less on the harms of criminalization and informal labor, or on sexual labor that has been forced because of poverty, exploitative low-wage jobs in formal labor sectors, and immigration laws.

SX Noir (SN): I wrote a manifesto recently for *i-D* mag as one of their revolutionary activists, where I call for the end of using Black femme bodies for profit in digital space.[4] We are no longer your slaves. We are not here to make profit for you. My whole goal is "for us by us," to have Black ownership and sex worker ownership and femme ownership within the digital space.

One of the things I brought up at the Black Sex Worker Liberation March is the demand of an acknowledgment of the Black sex worker impact on culture and having community show up for those who lead the world's liberation. Sex workers lead the world's liberation—this is facts.

One of the things I quote you on from the teach-in—when we were all dancing around and having so much enjoyment in that moment—you said, "It's okay to have personal interest within your activism." I had to really think deeply about how I came to sex work activism, and it truly came from witnessing and navigating the many intersections with criminalization and the prison system in America. I'm the daughter of a formerly incarcerated person, so I am deeply interested in prison abolition and, as a treat, police abolition. But it takes a special person with a particular self-interest to get out there to fight for civil liberties.

KZ: Solidarity means being able to articulate a personal stake in the work and working alongside others to fight against shared oppression.

I worked as an organizer with the Street Vendor Project and learned how to talk to strangers and get people to come to meetings. A lot of the skill sets from organizing I learned from working with other immigrant groups, non–sex workers—first with street vendors and then with domestic workers. There are certain parallels that are definitely applicable to immigrant sex worker outreach, although, oh my God, sex worker outreach is so much harder, because there's just so much more stigma, and people don't want to talk to you. And there's a lot more competitiveness, too. I think the space is harder because we face more oppression. Working with other groups gives a foundation, but it also makes me really aware that sex worker organizing needs to come out of our own space. It may not look like traditional labor organizing or even organizing with other informal workers, and [we need] to be open to what that might need to look like.

SN: It's very interesting, the specific needs of sex workers. My introduction into the sex tech industry came from seeing a lot of discrimination and deletion and ultimately violence happening for sex workers in digital spaces. I was aware of all of these physical elements—street-based workers, poverty-based work, and labor violations—but in the digital space, I'm thinking to myself: "Why do we not talk about this more?" This personal interest and personal navigation of the world definitely impacts how you navigate activism and how you step up and what groups and organizations you work for and support.

KZ: In terms of organizing for the Black Sex Worker Liberation March and going forward, what are ways that you feel that Asian sex workers can be more supportive? Red Canary members, from the June Kink Out rally and the march in Times Square, we've always wanted to find concrete ways to advocate together in solidarity.[5] What are ways that we can help or just be side by side going forward?

SN: I think that's the answer, being side by side. I feel like there needs to be deep support on both levels. One solid way to show up again is at your dinner table, talking to your elders, talking to your family, talking to your community. That's a huge thing. And constantly working on ourselves, doing the readings, doing the shadow work, the work that's on the inside. It starts with teach-ins, and it starts with a conversation like today's. Solidarity means showing up and also attempting to understand and not take up too much space or center yourself in the conversation.

I feel like Asian and Black communities can feel like they're on different ends of the spectrum of the American experience and isolate themselves from each other a lot. There are a lot more intersections in our worlds than meets the eye. I feel like Black sex workers and Asian sex workers have a lot of parallels of stigmas within the sex work industry. There are migrant workers who are also Black sex workers, and there's this idea that they should get paid a lot less than white sex workers. It creates a lot of infighting and scapegoating with both of our communities.

KZ: Historically, sex negativity has been used to exclude Asians from the country. From the passing of the Page Act (1875) to the Chinese Exclusion Act (1882)—Chinese women's "proclivity" for doing sex work was used to pass laws to bar all Chinese people from entering the country. These kinds of stereotypes and persistent cultural ideas definitely still impact the community. In the past people have only addressed the stigma of prostitution on Asian women in a way that looked at media representation, yellow fever, and white fetishization, and as a result blamed sex workers for that negative stereotype. Now I think people are becoming more critical of how complex it is to have economic violence be exerted against you and for people to survive economic violence through sexuality, and how different ideas of prostitution in different countries have such different impact on people's outcomes.

There are so many women in China that are mistresses. There's a stereotype in China that older men, if they reach a certain degree of success, especially in government, have to take on mistresses. It's almost expected, and even their wives expect them to. People both accept it as a reality, and at the same time they support sex work criminalization in the form of reeducation camps, where sex workers have been put into labor camps for two years without trial. People go missing. There's a weird hypocrisy both in China and the US that accepts that prostitution and mistresses exist, and yet if anyone is explicit about that reality, they will be penalized for it, because it's the sort of thing that we have to keep hidden and underground.

Women are certainly not given the same opportunities as men, and sexuality is a weapon that women wield to empower themselves and get capital in a new country. People engage in sex work in the immigrant community because there are no business loans available to immigrants. A lot of women start businesses in laundromats or bakeries or whatever by working as a sex worker for a while. This is an "access to capital" issue. Being up front that this is so common among a lot of new immigrants is something that we need to do culturally, and that's a separate sphere from politics or legislation—just having conversations, being honest about how sex work is so freaking prevalent right now. That's something that would help make lives better in a very gradual but everyday way.

SN: You touched on something really important, which is the need to survive under capitalism in America and how it brings you to sex work. We talk about this within the sex trade, about choice, coercion, and circumstance—and a lot of people are navigating sex work in America under circumstance.

I love that you brought up the historical connections. There's a difference between Asian Americans having a history rooted in immigration and Black Americans having a history rooted in slavery. Historically, Black women have been used not only for labor but to breed the labor force that is the wealth of America today. This involves sex, so Black women were seen as objects and were often raped, abused, and treated as if they were cattle. Sex work as a Black women is an incredibly radical act, any attempt of upward mobility under capitalism.

My personal navigation through the sex trade was one of surviving under capitalism. Black women in America are highly fetishized and hypersexualized. Sex work for Black women is the ultimate form of reparations in my eyes; the redistribution of wealth to me begins with sex workers. That's what I was actively seeing and why I was so drawn to the sex trade, because it was these white men who felt guilty about the excess of wealth they had, and they're having this exchange of services and redistributing that wealth.

When we think about this pipeline of the American "justice" system that criminalizes sex work and feeds people into systems of forced labor, Black sex workers see it all. We come from a history of forced labor, and our future is one of forced labor. Sex workers attempt to break that cycle and redistribute wealth. I think it's beautiful, but I also think that there's a long way to go before sex work is an active choice for most women and is an empowering thing.

KZ: It's interesting you brought up the history of Black women's bodies being used to reproduce slavery, and how within slavery, all women's bodies were forced into sex work. In contrast, a lot of Chinese women were engaging in sex work because immigration laws kept families separated. The men were imported to work on the railroad or to do other labor, but it was very clear that they were supposed to leave—that white America did not want any Asians to permanently settle. Asian women were brought in to keep the laborers happy while they were here, but they were encouraged *not* to have families and to leave the country. The presence of Asian women in sex work was for the opposite reason of reproducing the labor force; rather, it was to keep reproduction from happening and to placate the male labor force.

You see this with militaries, where sex workers surround military encampments. In Flushing, you see immigrant workers—mostly Latino day laborers—sending money home to their families in Mexico or Central America, but they have a fling or make-believe girlfriend relationships with Asian massage workers to sort of bide the time. It's because America doesn't pay a family wage for immigrant workers, because they don't want you to actually have a family here. They don't want you to reproduce, or pay immigrant workers what citizens would be paid. They want you to do work that is exploitative but worth a lot when the money is sent home. When you're tired, they want to ship you back home. Immigration policy is written to extract labor then ship people back, whether in seasonal farmwork or domestic work.

SN: What you just said was so powerful, because it's the truth. One thing I did want to touch on is that we as activists say "sex work," which is what we're talking about today, but there's no such thing as *forced* sex work, right? That's human trafficking and rape. And this is why we have conversations about the sex trade as a whole to incorporate concepts of criminalization, immigration, racist capitalism, et cetera.

KZ: Yes, though it's a blurry line. All work is compelled under economic circumstances of some kind, and generally for most businesses, workers are employed to make a profit for the owners of the business, the managers. Workers are purposefully paid less than the actual profit margins, so that the bulk of the profit can go to someone else.

What's interesting when it comes to sex work is that sexual labor has always existed and it comes alongside unequal gender relations between men and women, where women have traditionally been sold with dowries for marriage and valued for their reproductive capacity. For most of human history in almost every civilization, women have not had property rights, education, or any way of participating in governance. Women have always been doing sex work as a way to reproduce the family unit for men. And what does it mean when women come out of that? What does it mean to trade in a piecemeal way for a little bit of income? Sex work then can only be measured in terms of its labor value compared to marriage, right? You can't understand sex work completely independently of a heteronormative family structure. Until we actually do have a free, queer, polyamorous society, where there is no expectation of women as reproductive units first and foremost. Until every woman is actually paid equal to men, which is not the world we live in, I think the only way to compare sexual labor is to compare it to the historically unwaged work of marriage.

SN: Absolutely, I think every woman has traded sex. That's a controversial statement, but it's the absolute truth. Did you enjoy the drinks and dinner that he bought you? Did you marry for upward mobility?

I'd love to touch on the role of friendship in solidarity and the movement. Kate, I would say that we're growing our friendship, but we are friends, and we met through the activism world. How much do you think our friendship contributes to our activism in solidarity together?

KZ: I have so much respect and love for you as a person, and I want to see you thrive. I'm about ten years older than you, and the sex worker activist world that I've seen has been one with so much conflict, and I just want to see you do well. You are such a natural leader. I just want to make sure that you feel supported and safe within it and that it doesn't eat away at you in a negative way.

SN: You're such a sweet person. You know, I do think that friendship leads to better solidarity in activism. You're standing alongside these people that have the same ideas that you have, that have the same interest, and that means something. I quote Yin Q all the time that "we must celebrate," that that's part of the revolution. We came to sex work activism because we're fucking cool, and when you get together with other people who are also doing the work, it's exciting. I'm looking forward to the day where I do get to know you on a much more personal level.

I think that friendship is something that's important within activism, because we truly care about one another. We don't want our friends to be hurt, to be in pain, to be not welcome, to not be safe. I feel like a lot of the infighting can come from not seeking out friendship and solidarity and not being humble and vulnerable enough to let people see your true colors.

21.

"We Have More in Common Than Not"

8Lives Vigil Speech

Sinnamon Love

On March 16, 2022, Red Canary Song, a grassroots collective of migrant massage workers and sex workers of Asian diaspora, hosted the 8Lives Vigil in honor of the eight victims of a racist, sexist shooting spree targeting three Asian-owned spas in the Atlanta area one year prior. The murderer was a young white man who claimed his "sex addiction" drove him to try to "eliminate" "temptation" with horrific violence—a twisted justification that the police regurgitated.[1] The public vigil included speakers from sex worker and Asian/American organizations and collectives, live performances, and an art memorial and was held in Washington Square Park in New York City. The following is an edited version of the speech delivered at the vigil by BIPOC Adult Industry Collective founder Sinnamon Love.

I have worked in the sex trades since the age of sixteen, when I traded sex for food and shelter as an unhoused youth, and have been a sex worker for twenty-nine years. I am a parent, a grandparent, and the founder of the Black,

Indigenous, and People of Color Collective (BIPOC Collective), providing care for workers in the criminalized and legal sex trades.

After the Atlanta murders, we saw an increase in Asian American and Pacific Islander (AAPI) sex workers seeking financial assistance due to fear of returning to work in person and needing time to mourn and grieve before returning to work online.

I am learning to live with an acquired brain injury, so I ask for grace and compassion as I speak.

Thank you to Red Canary Song for inviting me to take part today as we honor the eight lives murdered a year ago. Today, we say their names: Xiaojie Tan, Daoyou Feng, Delaina Ashley Yaun, Paul Andre Michels, Hyun Jung Grant, Suncha Kim, Soon Chung Park.

Before I proceed, I'd like to acknowledge that today may have been challenging for some. Some of the things I will talk about may be triggering to hear. With that in mind, I'd like to pause for a moment and invite you to join me in taking a few deep, cleansing breaths to ground.

Breathe in through your nose; out of your mouth. Lower your shoulders; unclench your jaw—last one, in through your nose, and out, through your mouth.

As today's vigil nears a close, please take care of your body and spirit for the rest of the day and remember to return to your breath when things become challenging.

Breathing is something we often take for granted until we witness modern-day lynchings on our screens, eight lives cut short by ignorance, stigma, and entitlement; the words, "I can't breathe," etched in our brains over and over again. Or when a respiratory virus threatens the lives of our most vulnerable loved ones. Oxygen is the vital life force that binds us; without it, life ceases to exist. For those of us still among the living, I invite you to appreciate every breath you take.

For the last two years, the thread between AAPI and Black people in the United States has never been more clear. Acts of racial violence against our communities, during an ongoing global health crisis, are a reminder that regardless of whether your ancestors were trafficked, like mine, or came here voluntarily, irrespective of your phenotypical proximity to whiteness, we have more in common than not.

As people of the global majority, and let's be clear, collectively, we *are* the global majority, we often live in multigenerational households, and we value knowledge, culture, and community.[2] We are often told to pull ourselves up from our bootstraps but aren't given access to the boot, or the straps, to do so.[3]

Local, state, and federal governments fail to provide adequate housing, medical care, food, and education for migrant, queer, trans, disabled, poor, working-class, Black, Asian, Latinx, Indigenous, and other communities of color—creating conditions that make the American dream of life, liberty, and the pursuit of happiness nearly impossible.

We have more in common than not. Despite our diversity, many of us engage in informal economies because the dominant white supremacist culture continues to push us out of traditional employment, then criminalizes us for daring to find a way to feed, house, and care for ourselves and our families.

Too often, the best way out is to use the one natural resource we have: our bodies.

Whether we use our bodies on construction sites, harvesting crops, expertly crafting clothing, on football fields and basketball courts, taking care of someone else's children, or on street corners, in hotel rooms, or in massage parlors, we make decisions to survive, every day, by any means necessary.

We have more in common than not. The criminalization of sexual labor and unlicensed massage continues to harm and incarcerate people of the global majority at alarming numbers. Criminalization takes away resources that keep us safe and forces us to operate in the shadows. The conflation of our labor with trafficking erases the horrific realities of genocide, chattel slavery, forced breeding, and false imprisonment endured by people of the global majority who built this country.

We have more in common than not. There are too many states where law enforcement is still legally allowed to sexually assault massage and sex workers to entrap them. Good, hard-working people are subject to arrest and, often, subject to the threat of potential deportation, losing their children, jobs, or housing—all under the guise of saving them from trafficking.

We have more in common than not. The dominant culture wants you to believe that one group of oppressed people has it better than another, or that one group of oppressed people is more morally bankrupt or more violent than another. This tactic of divide and conquer ensures that we cannot stand in solidarity with one another in times of grief, crisis, and pain. This tactic ensures that people of the global majority cannot rise up against tyranny, hatred, and daily violent attacks on our civil liberties.

We have more in common than not. When we begin to look at the common threads between us, we are able to strengthen our communities, fight injustice, overturn destructive legislation, and most importantly, keep one another safe from harm.

We are stronger together. It is time to move past solidarity only in moments of crisis by checking implicit bias and fear-based stereotypes that only prevent us from fighting the real enemy. We have more in common than not.

I invite you to repeat after me:

We Are People of the Global Majority.

Stop Asian Hate.

We Are People of the Global Majority.

Black Lives Matter.

22.

Then, a Palestinian Was Born

Samah Serour Fadil

Cleansing souls to Rome's twisted roads
Paved on stones thrown from Bethlehem
Death came from sin
And he was adorned
It was then that a Palestinian was born

Brown shaded and hairy
Prickly as the fruit
Planted at the root
I search for its name yet
Bloody pulp pursues

A memory I describe to try and remember
Instead, salted earth and fog rubble my brain
Unimaginable if I had grown on the tilth
Of the soil meant to toil the mulch
Of our germinating grains

Ground that begat us
Bespoke, then be gone with us
The mud asks where I am
With the patience of man
And the same sleight of hand, I remember

I remember the Arabic word for patience is sabr
Sabr, the name of fruit I'd forgotten
Sabr I can no longer extend
Sabr grows where European trees wither
Sabr is every checkpoint from West Bank to Rafah

Sabr asks me where I've gone
I don't know where to start
My parents played in its shadow
Holding hands with its stem
Withstanding Occupation out of scorn

In those moments, a Palestinian was born
When even our flag unbearable for settlers to see
They denied us the pride of a culture's dignity
When sabr left,
we planted watermelon seeds

Grew symbols and ate them piece by peace
A juicy flesh beneath thin layers of green
Digging out an escape
For those meant to be free
Our politics, a spoon carved out of stone

It is with a rock in hand that a Palestinian is born

23.

Searching for Care and Justice

Antiviolence Organizing and Theories of Survival

Salonee Bhaman

Mandeep Kaur took her own life in the summer of 2022, leaving an emotional farewell video detailing nearly a decade of living with the violence of her husband and in-laws. Kaur's family and advocates soon released further evidence of what the 30-year-old mother of two had endured over the course of her eight-year marriage, including graphic CCTV footage of Kaur being brutalized by her husband and the berating voicemails left for her by in-laws overseas. Individuals moved by Kaur's story reposted the recordings, along with the hashtag #JusticeforMandeep on a variety of social media accounts. And so, Mandeep Kaur's story quickly spread across the South Asian diaspora. Among organizers fighting gender-based violence, her death was emblematic of a shadow epidemic of intimate partner violence that had grown rapidly during the first months of the COVID-19 pandemic.[1] For others, Kaur's story was resonant because it was a particularly brutal example of a widespread community secret about the prevalence of gender-based violence in South Asian families.

The attention to Kaur's death invited many responses from those grappling with the complex social reality of intimate partner violence. In Kaur's neighborhood of Richmond Hill, Queens, friends and neighbors planned and hosted a memorial service for her. Leaders from the gurdwara where she frequently worshiped began a campaign to take custody of Kaur's two daughters, who remained with their father weeks after her death. As the hashtag spread beyond Kaur's immediate community, calls for Kaur's husband, Ranjodbheer Singh Sandhu, to be arrested began to grow. Social media accounts shared his picture, alongside his name and occupation. Family members, neighbors, and concerned strangers called upon the New York Police Department to investigate the case as a homicide, rather than a suicide. In India, Kaur's parents filed a criminal complaint against Sandhu's family. Kaur's viral videos had attracted the kind of public attention that could not be swept under the rug. The immediacy of video evidence rendered Kaur's particular case a public crisis.

In response, three gender justice organizations working within Kaur's community—Sakhi, Manavi, and the Jahajee Sisters—released a statement in memory of Kaur that noted how intimate partner violence had been a long-standing issue that required a continued commitment to building community ties and tackling the root causes of familial violence.[2] Striking a different tone, during a keynote speech at a mayor's office roundtable on domestic violence in the South Asian diaspora, New York State Assembly member Jenifer Rajkumar also announced a new investigative task force to assist police and declared her office a "sanctuary for immigrant women fleeing abuse."[3] Characterizing those who committed intimate partner violence as "morally depraved," Rajkumar's office insisted that perpetrators of violence "must face the full consequences of our criminal justice system."[4]

On its face, Rajkumar's call for police intervention and prosecution doesn't contradict or occlude the enduring nature of the problem. However, each response hinted at fractures and compromises within contemporary antiviolence work negotiated over decades of addressing a crisis rooted in patriarchy, violence, and capitalism with solutions located within an expanding criminal-legal system. While both statements reflect a desire for justice, acknowledgement, and accountability, they diverge in their diagnosis of the nature of the problem itself.

Kaur's story made its way to me in a WhatsApp group for volunteer staff of the hotline operated by Sakhi, a New York City gender justice and antiviolence organization dedicated to serving the South Asian community. I had begun volunteering for the hotline in 2021, as part of an initiative to resurrect the organization's volunteer program as COVID-19 lockdowns increased demand for hotline services among survivors in their homes and created unique challenges for staff advocates attempting to maintain contact with those at risk. Nonprofit service providers like Sakhi had revived a strategy from the organization's movement roots to address these changes: community power.

The crisis hotline itself is, after all, part of a feminist tradition of mutual aid. A service like the hotline represents a promise made between members of a community: between the hours of 9:00 a.m. and 10:00 p.m., someone would answer the phone if you needed help and called. Volunteers for the hotline are trained in some basic crisis management techniques: how to create a safety plan, provide basic psychological first aid, and address emotional distress with validation and empathy. Though many of the staff members who worked the hotline were professional social workers or mental health professionals, volunteer staff came from all walks of life. In our first training session, we shared our respective backgrounds as students, business professionals, lawyers, and full-time caregivers. During Zoom training, we practiced identifying a caller's immediate needs; creating action plans for future contact; and preparing a list of resources to refer callers to in emergencies. Along the way, we also become keenly aware of the system's limitations: it is useless to try to do a shelter intake after 5:00 p.m.; translation services are clunky and often ineffective; and our callers may not like the answers we have to give them. Perhaps the most important thing we all learned, however, is that the caller is the expert on their own life. While they may need assistance navigating systems or planning for the unexpected, they are ultimately the best arbiters of their own safety.

This is an especially crucial point, as callers frequently find themselves navigating multiple outcomes that may be less than ideal. The hotline's promise to help is fundamentally limited by the state-sanctioned vulnerability that callers find themselves navigating. Callers must weigh a series of risks against each other: Will calling the police end violence or create more? If they call the police, will they be believed? If the police arrest their abuser, will they be able to afford the rent? Will they jeopardize their immigration status? Will child protective services remove their children from the home?

Volunteers do not have the answer to these questions. We can only support our callers in thinking through each of their options, presenting them with an honest representation of what might happen should they dial 911 or get in touch with a domestic violence shelter. Unfortunately, many callers face the choice between two forms of violence: one is public and the other private.

My cohort of hotline volunteers were deeply affected by news of Mandeep Kaur's death. As the details emerged that Kaur had stayed in an abusive situation because she feared being unable to raise her two daughters alone, I wondered just how many options she had. Given the intense stigma associated with openly discussing familial violence, I imagined that Kaur might have faced the double isolation that many immigrant survivors of abuse experience when community and state spaces are unwilling or unable to support them.

The first South Asian women's organizations were founded to serve immigrant communities that weren't being served by mainstream gender justice organizations while also raising consciousness about the prevalence of violence within our communities. Manavi, for example, was born when a group of South Asian organizers in eastern New Jersey began to organize around the 1981 trial of Amita Vadlamudi, an Indian American woman accused of murdering her husband. Vadlamudi argued that she had acted in response to years of physical abuse. Sakhi was founded in 1989 as part of an effort to encourage public accountability for Mohammad Mohsin, a computer technician who had attempted to murder his wife, Syeda Sufian. In addition to providing Sufian with emotional and financial support, the first Sakhi organizers protested outside Mohsin's home and workplace.[5] Though some of the protestors were calling for the state to take action against Mohsin, they were engaging in a community accountability process (naming the perpetrator of violence and demanding his actions be publicly acknowledged) that existed outside of the criminal legal system. These groups and many others across the country organized consciousness-raising meetings, recruited volunteers, and established networks with which to provide battered women with resources that ran the gamut from legal aid to food assistance.[6]

Groups like Manavi and Sakhi grew in size and scope in an era when feminists were engaged in a serious debate about what kind of relationship gender justice groups should maintain with the state. In search of resources to provide shelter, cash assistance, and other support, some groups and organizations accepted state funding despite initial misgivings, while others resisted such institutional alliances as ultimately harmful. These questions came to a head in 1994, when congress passed the Violence Against Women Act (VAWA). The bill made funds available to a host of organizations under the umbrella of the broader 1994 Violent Crime Control and Law Enforcement Act. As a result, resources were often predicated on an organization or agency's willingness to participate in the criminal-legal system to the fullest extent possible. Some feminists, often termed "carceral feminists," embraced institutions of policing and punishment as vehicles for redress and accountability. Others accepted the terms of state largesse more begrudgingly, noting that valuable social welfare resources remain at stake.[7]

Over more than forty years, the same South Asian women's organizations that once met in living rooms and conducted radical actions against alleged perpetrators of violence have grown into major nonprofit organizations. While many remain ambivalent about their relationship to carceral institutions, they have largely embraced state funding and continue courting private philanthropy as a means of expansion. Indeed, these groups are now able to hire professional social workers, attorneys, and agency staff and provide a host of crisis response services in a variety of languages.

This compromise comes at intellectual and political costs that sever the struggles of intimate violence survivors from broader struggles for racial equity and freedom from state-sponsored violence and oppression. Formations like INCITE! Women of Color Against Violence and Survived & Punished offer feminist organizers a more expansive vision for what justice will require by highlighting the ways that survivors themselves are criminalized within the carceral system and tying together the impacts of police and state violence against survivors of color and the consequences of punitive immigration policies, settler colonialism, disruptive family law statutes, and US militarism.[8]

The urgency of an analysis that critiques state violence when imagining "survivorship" is essential for antiviolence organizations serving immigrant communities navigating systems of organized vulnerability produced by a hostile criminal-legal system. For example, many individuals who lack legal immigration status or who are economically dependent on an abusive family member are placed between a rock and a hard place when considering deportation or child separation as a consequence of seeking help. After all, it is an undeniable reality that state policing agencies—from child protective services to Immigration and Customs Enforcement—function to make individual lives more precarious, dangerous, and immiserated.[9]

Those providing direct services from within antiviolence organizations during the COVID-19 lockdowns identified areas where existing frameworks continue to fall short, including the need for programming that acknowledged different types of gender-based violence beyond what is covered in legislation like the VAWA—resources that would work for queer clients, elderly clients, and youth affected by violence within their homes. They dreamt of a system that prevented violence before it happened by engaging parents and children in constructive dialogue. Many had come to understand the roots of violence not in individual perpetrators but in the broader social conditions that produced intense vulnerability, isolation, and stress.[10]

Mandeep Kaur's death in the summer of 2022 came on the heels of another tragedy: in July, popular blogger and TikTok creator Sania Khan was murdered by her ex-husband. Khan had built a following by sharing parts of her life—including the shame and stigma that accompanies divorce within her Pakistani community. The case catalyzed a public conversation about a usually private matter, raising important questions about culture, patriarchy, coercion, and violence.

My fellow volunteers and I sometimes share our experiences on the hotline in a WhatsApp group. On occasion, we have gathered virtually for a check-in via Zoom. We share news stories and decompress after hotline shifts. We are all largely frustrated by the unsatisfying options we are able to offer those in need, by how broken the system seems to be. According to a 2021 survey of workers at organizations serving South Asian survivors, many frontline staff reflected that they feel that their organizations are "starved of sufficient funding, resources, and capacity to meaningfully invest in upstream and prevention work."[11] They also note that the same survivors they serve are often harmed by the criminal legal system that they are referred to—leaving some workers with the feeling that they are contributing to harm rather than alleviating it.[12]

Many of us also discuss the discomfort expressed by our respective communities when we share our choice to volunteer at the hotline, or even at the mention of intimate violence. Given that almost all of us have experienced or witnessed such violence, these reactions defy belief: intimate violence is a pervasive, if often secret, problem. These reactions, it seems, serve to uphold the categories that have been created as a way to sow division among communities with fundamentally linked interests—welfare recipients, incarcerated women, survivors of violence, sex workers, home health aides, and domestic workers, to name just a few. These are categories that include "deserving" and "undeserving" migrants, "good" and "bad" women, "hardworking" and "habitually" poor people, "modern" and "backward" religions.

By failing to interrogate the sites where state surveillance, punitive policy, and social stigma overlap to produce vulnerability, we allow the intimate space of family, cultural mandates of respectability, and economic exploitation to be levied as tools in maintaining the status quo.

24.

Beyond Gilded Cages

South Asians for Abolition

Mon M.

In the summer of 2019, a delegation with Desis Rising Up and Moving (DRUM), a New York City base-building organization focused on strengthening South Asian working-class power, attended a city council hearing on land use with a delegation of community members. The hearing pertained to land use for four proposed new jails, specifically whether the sites slated for new construction were environmentally safe and had sufficient structural integrity to withstand construction. I watched as a young member of DRUM provided her testimony. She was Nepali and had a translator sitting next to her. As she spoke, she cried. She described enduring domestic violence at home, and how, upon gathering the courage to leave, she had struggled to find language support to access resources like shelters and counseling. Why was the city considering a multibillion-dollar jail construction plan when there weren't even enough translators for women forced into living on the street, for the very circumstances which left people vulnerable to arrest?

I found myself there after an email from the prison abolitionist organization Critical Resistance in 2017 featured a call to action, letting readers know about a community board meeting in Brooklyn regarding a new jail. I was shocked. Why would a city that had enabled the deaths of Kalief Browder, Eric Garner, Eleanor Bumpurs, Kyam Livingston, and Akai Gurley, and that continued to empower police to terrorize neighborhoods, be left unopposed in what felt like a blatantly antihuman, antirelational project?

At these hearings, you could pick up a glossy brochure printed by the Mayor's Office of Criminal Justice about the jail plan.[1] Jails could be "a good neighbor," they promised, citing concerns about parking, traffic, and property values as central to "architecture and design that minimizes street level impact." Pro-jail nonprofits also justified the proposed jail expansion by saying building new jails would lead to closure of Rikers, New York City's notorious penal colony. Politicians seized on the opportunity to align themselves with the faux progressive aim of criminal justice reform. Against all these and more, swathes of anticonstruction organizers emerged, many of whom joined No New Jails New York City (NNJ NYC), an explicitly abolitionist campaign that demanded that Rikers be shut down without new jail construction.

We did not win this campaign. The New York City Council voted to build four new jails in October 2019. Writing this, now six years later, little has changed. Despite the testimonies of people like that DRUM member, New York City's carceral capacity has only grown. As criminalized people have known and argued for decades, innovating at the point of incarceration is always a failure, because imprisonment is the *consequence* of an anti-Black, murderous, extractive, ableist, and depraved political economy. As No New Jails NYC wrote, "Predictably those who support the status quo of jails and prisons are never forced to justify their continued reliance on these institutions of state violence, even as abolitionists are constantly asked to 'prove' that alternatives work."

Several months later, in 2020, No New Jails NYC splintered for a variety of reasons, including, but not limited to, misogynoir within the internal organizing formation; differences over strategy, tactics, and timeline; disillusionment about the result of the campaign; interpersonal conflicts related to organizational partners; and, most significantly, abuse experienced by members of the collective and dismissed by others.

My time in No New Jails NYC overlapped in part with the time I spent in the South Asian Diaspora Artist Collective (SADAC). The group, while formed with best intentions, was slowly beginning to implode as community members were confronted by their abusers at the collectives' events and as different levels of interpersonal harm continued to hurt members of the collective. Incidents included events with a poet who recited poetry that had anti-Black elements; misgendering of trans members; and anger over Indo-centric, Hindi-centric discussions within the meeting spaces.

A lack of political education and community accountability skills meant that the collective lacked cohesive, rigorous political analysis around the many topics that divide and unite South Asians. Some participants believed the group could be apolitical, where all art and culture were received without context. Others rejected such atomistic approaches. These antagonisms threatened the group's existence, but SADAC had few formal conflict response and accountability mechanisms—an oversight.

The simultaneous experiences within the No New Jails NYC movement and SADAC moved me politically as I, twenty-three years old at the time, was in an incredible moment of radicalization. While the former at times reached thousands of people around the United States, and the latter was specific to South Asian artists of a certain age, the schisms that occurred in both collectives had roots in casteism, transphobia, and anti-Blackness. In both spaces, I observed the impact of conflict avoidance rooted in white supremacy culture, and I felt how relational norms give us few choices in meaningfully responding to violence, harm, and abuse. Neither ideological unity nor identity-based connections had been sufficient to prevent intracommunity, intragroup resentment and violence. Confronting these layers of principled conflict that crossed borders and generations, while I was becoming more self-aware about my own positionality in these spaces, felt incredibly urgent but disorienting. The fallouts throughout these spaces were serious and manifested serious questions about accountability, generational harm and interpersonal violence, which remain at the center of how we participate in social movements.

In the year after both of these groups came to their troubled end, the world entered the COVID-19 lockdown, and then an uprising. Medical apartheid during the first two years of a debilitating and genocidal pandemic was animated by anti-Asian racism, yet community responses to the new "yellow peril" elevated carceral and equally racist solutions.[2] Like the other social movements of the past decade, efforts to #FreeThemAllForPublicHealth and Abolish the Police demanded investments into social provisioning. Relief checks and global protests caused many people to identify connections between police violence and poverty even more deeply. Momentary pauses in the gears of neoliberalism created opportunities for us to organize against occupation and austerity, in ways that continue to bear fruit.

Attempting to catalyze these experiences, I began to wonder: What does it actually mean to be a South Asian abolitionist organizing in this settler state at this time on the clock of the world? What commitments and accountabilities might it compel? What guidance could it produce for the future? Solidarity could not be assumed on the basis of culture nor organizing purpose, as I learned through NNJ NYC and SADAC. I reached for an embodied solidarity practice that has Black liberation, caste abolition, and anticapitalism at its core. These values have continued to inform my organizing, particularly at the intersections of pathology, criminalization, and settler violence. In the years since both groups were operational, I've been grateful to learn from people in campaigns that have successfully fought jail construction, closed detention centers, created inside-outside publications, coordinated mass actions, and more.

I see three areas of critical work, storytelling, and action for South Asian abolitionists in the United States to take up in co-conspiracy with Black, Dalit, and working-class liberation struggles. These are critical for me as someone who was not born on the lands of the so-called United States and who comes from a caste-oppressor background.

1. Building decolonial and **cross-border connections** between movements and being in solidarity with the margins of the Global South, from antisettler efforts in Kashmir, Hawai'i, American Samoa, and Palestine to anti-imperialist struggles in Guam and Iraq to global workers and peasants movements.
2. Resourcing, supporting, and organizing for **community self-determination** and healing, especially to respond to violence without necessarily relying on carceral systems, particularly for caste-oppressed, poor, queer, migrant, disabled, trans, and non-Indian South Asians.
3. Recognizing and **organizing against false solutions**—"gilded cages"—when they are presented to us, from fascist collaborations sold as cultural exchange and "representation"-based concessions, to casteist narratives and reformist solutions, by centering rebellion and freedom. Doing so through a multitude of strategies, including strategies that critically engage the archive and preserve insurrectionary cultural histories, as well as strategies that are grounded in rigorous political study. We need social transformation that will address our communities' issues at the roots.

Progressive and radically identified Indians in the United States, as well as South Asians and other Asian diasporic communities, must orient toward the dismantling of all systems of entrapment, control, coercion, and punishment as part of an antiracist politics of solidarity. We must be prepared to challenge and diminish elitist, Brahmanical, and anti-Black sentiments in our community networks. At the personal or local level, this might look like working with friends to support a person who is incarcerated or fighting charges placed on them; publicly opposing settler violence and organizing for a free Kashmir; fundraising for mask and test distribution with a community group; refusing to engage with media that celebrate Brahmanical and white supremacy; participating in an antiwar or abolitionist study group, and so much more.

Decolonial Cross-Border Connections

While people outside of the United States have vastly different relationships and experiences of policing, decolonial cross-border solidarity and international abolitionist struggle is critical. South Asian abolitionists in the United States, especially those who are North Indian, dominant caste, cis, or straight, need to recognize the interdependency of struggles and look beyond the United States toward communities undertaking their own uprisings against casteist, extractive, and anti-Black systems. Our communities can engage in a politics of refusal by refusing to work with police at their houses of faith; refusing to labor for the production of carceral technologies; refusing to accept abject working conditions for ourselves and others.

From my Brooklyn neighborhood, I've looked to Delhi, where hundreds of farmers resisted intense police repression while protesting predatory agricultural reform. And to Colombo, where anticorruption protesters have criticized the imperialist status quo imposed by the International Monetary Fund despite the threat of enforced disappearances. To Pakistan, where the first Afro-Sheedi parliamentarian, Tanzeela Qambrani, pushed for a resolution in the Pakistani parliament condemning the murder of George Floyd and expressed the oppression that people of African descent face around the world. And to Guyana, where police killed three people during a series of protests in 2020. Custodial deaths, which have become common business in New York City's Rikers Island prison and Los Angeles's Central Jail, play out similarly for dissidents like Stan Swamy, jailed under India's Unlawful Activities (Prevention) Act (UAPA), an antiterrorism act used by Indian police to cast a wide carceral net. Everywhere, people are resisting police repression, political imprisonment, and censorship designed to concentrate power among a few.

In 2020, thousands of people in India, led by Dalit women, protested the brutal gang rape and forced cremation of a young woman in Hathras, Uttar Pradesh, India. Police conducted the forced cremation and refused to provide information, protecting the dominant caste abusers of the case. Dalit communities have widely decried the impunity of Indian police as purveyors of caste apartheid. The Southall Black Sisters, who organized in the UK to demand freedom for Zoora, a Pakistani survivor of patriarchal violence, offer yet another example for transformative global solidarity. Ceyenne Doroshow, a Black trans activist, worked with Guyanese trans activist Twinkle Paul to provide COVID-19 rent assistance for trans sex workers in Guyana and Suriname. Across the United States, groups such as Equality Labs, an anticaste South Asian power-building organization, and Alliance of South Asians Taking Action (ASATA), a Bay Area–based collective, have modeled cross-border solidarity by building relationships with activists living and working in South Asia, working to send mutual aid to Dalit communities impacted by COVID-19.

In 2023, when Indian prime minister Narendra Modi visited the United States, South Asian organizations across the country criticized the move and staged a series of creative actions to criticize the "crime minister," urging US lawmakers to consider how his government has encouraged systematic violence against Dalit people, Muslims, and Adivasi groups. Modi, overseeing the construction of some of the largest detention centers in Indian history and the widely condemned genocidal Citizenship Amendment Bill, has also ushered in a new era of Indian violence in Kashmir. Through the work of organizations like the Dalit Solidarity Network, dominant caste Indian Hindus can recognize the networks of caste privilege that allowed their families to migrate to the United States. Instead of reifying toxic and anti-Black "model minority" archetypes, we can understand these tropes to be what they truly are: a means of obscuring historic and ongoing systemic violence.[3] Rather than idolizing figures like Gandhi, who was actively anti-Black and casteist, we can unlearn Brahmanical supremacy and do community education to uplift leaders like Dr. B. R. Ambedkar and Savitribai Phule. We can challenge the occupation of Palestine and Kashmir in the same breath, knowing that India and Israel increasingly share an autocratic playbook.

A South Asian–American cross-border struggle for abolition must seek solidarities that materially empower people oppressed at the intersections of class, caste, race, religion, gender, and ancestry. To be clear, this is not the farcical decolonialism of strongmen like Modi and Netanyahu, which co-opts indigeneity to promote a genocidal agenda. Rather, being against the continued sprawl of empires and the relentless theft of ancestral land requires us to have a clear-eyed understanding of how the concepts that motivate us remain vulnerable to co-optation. Our loyalty, therefore, is to each other, not to one particular concept.

Community Self-Determination

From support for substance abuse to reproductive justice to free housing to freedom from occupation and to freedom of movement, South Asian abolitionists must demand community self-determination. We must expand our analysis of caging to include many kinds of caging and control, many levels of local and global violence, while holding the critical tensions and nuances within our communities and developing skills to process and respond to violence in non-carceral and careful ways.

There are nuances related to power beyond the scope of what I will write about here, but it's critical that 'South Asian' be understood as anything but a monolith. Bengali, Nepali, Tamil, and Indo-Caribbean immigrants can be some of the most economically depressed demographics in US cities, particularly if they're undocumented, even as many South Asians thrive in high-earning industries like those in the tech sectors. In places like New York City and San Francisco, Indian American communities directly benefit from the massive displacement produced by the expansion of companies like Meta and Google, while other South Asian communities face the consequences. Some communities hold the memory and generational trauma of surviving war, while others benefit from the spoils of the warfare and genocide. These vast differences and antagonisms within this arbitrary and reductive classification of "South Asian" and "Desi" are rooted in capitalism's disunifying effects. The erasure of our complicated intracommunity dynamics through this flattening hinders our ability to be in solidarity with one another. Although our ancestors may have shared a region of the world, we cannot take our connections for granted and need to be in consistent, communal study about one another's histories.

Like many people from caste-oppressor backgrounds, I grew up in a home where Brahmanical patriarchy was the norm, and domestic violence was our reality. I also had close relationships with disabled and mad people. These experiences would go on to inform my understanding of what transformative self-determination and autonomy might look like. In that environment, I recognized how circumstances leave people without the tools to leave harmful situations. Instead, they endure the isolation that occurs as a result of social structures that are not concerned with stopping violence, only making it invisible or commodifying it.

South Asians, particularly Bangladeshi, Indo-Caribbean, Nepali, and Dalit people of all genders, have spent decades protesting and addressing patriarchal violence and abuse within their communities. They have also created robust intergenerational organizations to advance Third World feminist demands, provide services to survivors and refugees, and strengthen labor protections for domestic workers, sex workers, and others in marginal economies dominated by immigrant women. Yet, South Asian antiviolence organizing in the United States has been plagued by a malignant combination of Savarna and carceral feminisms that continue to collaborate with the police or erase the labor of working-class, non-Indian, and trans activists in their efforts.

South Asians SOAR and API Chaya are two organizations focusing on survivor-centered storytelling and non-carceral skills development, as well as support for South Asian survivors in the United States. In practice, this looks like archiving and sharing survivors' stories, creating multilingual Know Your Rights resources, offering support with finding housing or work, and hosting spaces to support survivors interested in transformative responses to harm. Resourcing, supporting, and organizing for community self-determination requires understanding that this will look different for all of us as well as building awareness and responding to structural power.

I think back to what took place while I organized with SADAC. We were a loose formation, and while we never relied on police, having the skills to respond to harm would have helped us keep more people safer for longer. Our communities must develop the tools we need to keep each other safe without systems of punishment, but with accountability and consequences. We must also be ready to acknowledge and respond to those who perpetuate contradictions, harms, and historically rooted violence within our communities through strategies like removal, accountability, and reparations for those harmed.

Rejecting False Solutions and Manifesting Solidarities

For a certain number of South Asians in the United States, obtaining mainstream acceptance and rights-based protections has been the crux of their political engagements in the United States. Visas, green cards, and citizenship are coveted, while the growing popularity of cultural practices such as yoga and Vedic astrology have been a thing of uncritical casteist pride. Culturally, often, economic success and intellectual achievement are a major sign of success. While Savarna, class-privileged, cis, and straight South Asians have pursued wins on the basis of "rights" and political inclusion, undocumented, incarcerated, and climate-displaced South Asians have been left to fend for themselves.

Dominant caste Indians, for example, have fought for expanded-access H-1B visas (a special category of immigration) for those with an Indian passport, even as Sri Lankan Tamil organizers have advocated for the abolition of Immigration and Customs Enforcement and Nepali organizers have struggled to win even Temporary Protected Status for themselves. Emerging alliances between white supremacist conservatives and South Asian conservatives have supported mass incarceration in the United States, killed net neutrality, excused violent anti-Muslim pogroms, and chummed it up with Hindu fascists.

This desire for political incorporation into dominant systems has also looked like so-called political representation from liberal prosecutors like Kamala Harris, who, as California attorney general, was proudly "tough on crime," essentially code for deeply carceral and anti-Black politics, despite her Black and Tamil multiracial identity. It has looked like "Brown Girl Solidarity," appropriating the concept of "Black Girl Magic," to celebrate representations by any "brown" South Asian woman, no matter their problematic political views. It has looked like Indian American politicians and police officers embracing the "hate crime" framework to explain white supremacist violence targeted at South Asians, despite the ways this frame is weaponized to fund more policing.[4]

Discerning between opportunities for liberatory demands and opportunities that are merely detours into liberal reforms creates pathways for genuine solidarity. The so-called United States has long relied on counterinsurgency to confuse those interested in fighting for a better, different world. This was evident in the borough-based jails plan in New York City, where jails were rebranded as humane and rehabilitative. It is the logic at the center of bipartisan efforts to entrap migrants in endless cycles of surveillance and deportation, at the heart of mass imprisonment of political dissidents, and at the core of DEI-driven activism.

Rather than look to these gilded cages as false solutions, South Asian abolitionists can do better and demand more. Groups like DRUM, Believers

Bail Out, Justice for Muslims Collective, South Asian Solidarity Initiative, and CAAAV: Organizing Asian Communities have worked hard to reject pro-police narratives within our communities by offering abolitionist interventions. Other tactics have included counter-recruitment to stop the scapegoating of their communities by the police, participatory defense campaigns to demand freedom for incarcerated and detained people, translation services for those vulnerable to reproductive criminalization, door-knocking conversations with people about police, and correctional defunding.

The suggestions in this essay are hopefully a starting point for deepening study and practicing transformative solidarity. I am still finding my place among the abolitionist movements of the world and strengthening my political commitments. We are on the threshold of a historic shift in the political context for abolition, thanks to countless generations of disabled, trans, and poor radicals before us. The notion of going beyond gilded cages is both about real cages—jails, prisons, detention centers, foster homes, psych wards—and the glittering lies used to weld them. It is also about the metaphorical cages: the lackluster politics of representation, fantasies of multiracial unity, and callous dismissals of past failure, which degrade our humility and infuse our organizing with self-interest. By rejecting these false solutions, engaging in cross-border struggles, and creating necessary antiviolence resources within our communities, we can destroy the power relations that entrench injustice and oppression.

PART 4

Our Interconnections

From the Transnational to the Interpersonal

Real Girl's Talk (Per Nina Simone) **by Mon M.**

Yuri Kochiyama, Angela Davis, and Akemi Kochiyama-Ladson
African/Asian Roundtable at San Francisco State University, October 1997
Photo credit: Bob Hsiang

25.

Not Victims

On Global Sex Worker Organizing

TD Tso

In the spring of 2021, people in the United States and across the world grappled with mass violence committed against Asian women after eight people, including six immigrant Chinese and Korean massage workers, were killed at Asian spas in the Atlanta area. The murderer, a white man, admitted to targeting Asian sex workers because of his own shame and guilt around "sex addiction," at odds with the antisex beliefs of his conservative Christian upbringing. While March 16, 2021, is framed as a horrific one-time tragedy caused by a "lone gunman," we cannot separate these events from the fact that Asian spas and massage parlors remain systematic targets of patriarchal violence, whether from antiprostitution police stings under the guise of white saviorism or antitrafficking organizations that frame all workers as victims.

The Atlanta shootings shattered the illusion many in this country have about Asian women's model minority status by prompting a recognition of Asian women who are working-class migrant sex workers, fetishized and victimized by white patriarchy. Personally, Asian femmes like myself have understood that our place in the American imagination, since the foundation of this country, has been informed by the ways American soldiers treat Asian women abroad at military bases and during wartime; how migrant Asian workers are treated here in the United States; how Asian femmes are depicted in Western media and movies; and even how we are written into law.[1] To the American imagination, we are the Lotus Blossoms, Dragon Ladies, and Yellow Peril, all in need of saving and extinguishing.[2] Disposable.

Long before the Atlanta tragedies, so-called radical feminists have debated how to situate the experiences of migrant Asian massage workers and sex workers, often claiming they are all victims of human trafficking. Those pushing for the decriminalization of sex work have been called privileged and the "pimp lobby" and been accused of glamorizing prostitution at the expense of women and girls in the Global South.[3]

"We thought Asian massage workers and sex workers would be treated differently after the shooting," wrote Elene Lam, the executive director of Butterfly, a support network for Asian and migrant sex workers, in a statement for the 8Lives Vigil hosted by Red Canary Song one year after the shootings. "However, they continue being targeted by the hate, violence, laws, and law enforcement, particularly the racist and anti–sex work organizations. They are silencing the Asian workers by calling them ignorant trafficked victims."

To add to the tragedy of losing eight lives to racialized, gendered violence that year in Atlanta, the victims are now unable to speak for themselves. They are unable to define their own relationship to their work and their identities. We must now call them "victims" because they succumbed to their injuries, not because of their jobs, ethnicities, or immigration statuses.

The ideological arguments that frame all sex workers as trafficked victims strip away agency from migrant sex workers and sex workers in the Global South. "I am not a trafficked victim. I use my hand to support myself and my family," says massage worker Ching Li, through a message shared by Butterfly. "Please stop imposing your moralistic, colonial, and religious ideas on me."[4] From my experience listening to migrant sex workers and sex workers in the Global South, they, like their North American counterparts, also want decriminalization, rights (not rescue), and believe sex work is work.[5] Based on current material conditions and needs, these workers do not want to "end prostitution" even if they do want opportunities to exit the trade at their own volition.

Much of the global sex worker movement has been driven by and inspired by workers in the Global South. One prime example is the establishment of International Sex Workers Rights Day, an international holiday that sprung out of a sex worker collective in West Bengal, India. On March 3, 2001, Durbar Mahila Samanwaya Committee (দুর্বার মহিলা সমন্বয় সমিতি), often referred to as Durbar or DMSC, hosted a festival for twenty-five thousand sex workers in Kolkata. On the same day the next year, Durbar invited sex worker organizations from across the world to commemorate the day together. The holiday is now celebrated annually on March 3.[6]

"We all came under the same umbrella," Bharati Dey, mentor for Durbar, said during a Sex Work in a Transnational Context panel in 2021.[7] "We raise our voices on the same day. Sex work is work. We want our rights as sex workers."[8]

Durbar has been a ground-breaking organization since its formation in 1995. Initially, its founding members came together under the shared goal of HIV/STI prevention, but they soon began organizing on a number of other issues, including police harassment, access to financial services, their children's education, and other sex workers' rights. By August 1995, the collective formed the largest and first-ever sex worker–owned banking co-op in South Asia, USHA Multipurpose Cooperative Society, providing members with nondiscriminatory banking as well as financial security and mobility. In November 1997, Durbar hosted the first National Conference of Sex Workers in India; its rallying slogan was "sex work is legitimate work, we want workers' rights."[9]

"Earlier, when we used to advocate for ourselves, we rebranded ourselves as HIV/AIDS advocates, an intervention program we have," Dey shared. "When we used to approach people for this intervention work, they wouldn't believe us. They used to think, 'This is a sex worker, how can she do health work? She isn't educated, she's illiterate, she has no knowledge of this work.'"[10]

Sex workers are continually being underestimated and left out. In 2012, after immigration restrictions prevented sex workers from attending the XIX International AIDS Conference in Washington, DC, Dey, with Durbar, organized the Sex Worker Freedom Festival in Kolkata.[11] The five-day festival was held at the same time as the AIDS conference, and more than 667 participants—including sex worker organizers, allies, gay men, and people who use drugs—from over forty countries across the globe attended.[12] Extensive visa regulations for sex workers and people who use drugs prevented those who are most impacted and often on the front lines of disease prevention and harm reduction from attending the global AIDS conference. But Indian sex workers refused to be left out of the conversation. They created space for themselves and other workers, including sex workers from countries across Africa, who in turn took what they learned from Indian organizers to create their own curriculum.

Sex worker organizing has ripple effects across the Global South—workers universally want to be liberated, safe, and in community. After the Freedom Festival, sex workers from Botswana, Kenya, Uganda, and Zimbabwe visited two Indian sex worker collectives, VAMP in Sangli and Ashodaya Samithi in Mysore, to collect organizing strategies to implement within their own communities. As Grace Kamau, regional coordinator for African Sex Workers Alliance, has recalled, the sex workers who traveled to India "learned about the model sex workers were using in India and how sex workers are implementing [that model]. Sex workers from Africa, we took the learning. We took it and put in the context as Africans, and from there we get the African Sex Workers Academy. The Academy is a program that brings together sex workers from Africa."[13]

The academy launched in 2015 and is held several times a year over the course of one week with different national cohorts from across Africa.[14] It hosts workshops and art advocacy sessions to develop organizing skills, share best practices, strengthen national sex worker movements, and build networks across the continent.

Predating all of these groups is a Thai sex worker organization, EMPOWER (Education Means Protection of Women Engaged in Recreation), which was founded in 1984. The formation of EMPOWER is especially noteworthy given the particular stereotyping sex workers in Thailand experience due in part to the country's massive sex tourism industry, which grew rapidly during the American war in Vietnam to meet the demands of US servicemen.[15] As a result, Thai sex workers are portrayed as exploited victims of war in Western media. In *Bad Girls Dictionary,* a book released by the organization in 2007, EMPOWER directly responds to these portrayals with its definition of the term "documentaries" as "sneaky-cam footage of sex workers, bars, brothels and sometimes customers; interview with sex worker filming her in dark or blurred face or just her hands for her sad story; film her poor rural home village and interview with greedy or stupid or tragic family member."[16]

Since 2005, the organization has run Empower University, which has nine centers in four provinces in Thailand and educates sex workers on topics such as political strategy, labor rights, migration, business, and health. "Sex workers have been organizing against criminalization as EMPOWER for thirty-six years," Mai Junta, an organizer with EMPOWER, shared during an Asia Pacific Social Forum panel on sex work criminalization in South and Southeast Asia in 2022. "Criminalization keeps us outside the labor law. It means we cannot access financial services for credit cards or loans. A criminal history means we cannot get visas to travel to some countries. We cannot access other rights, for example social security, labor rights protection, and justice before the law."[17]

EMPOWER also made history by opening up the first and possibly only bar owned and run by a sex worker collective, Can Do, in Chiang Mai, northern Thailand. Established in 2006, Can Do provides a way for sex workers to respond to exploitative working conditions in bars. In a bar owned by sex workers for sex workers, they are able to build a space with fair pay and labor expectations, rights and protections, and safe practices and facilities. "Most sex workers are women and mothers, all are family providers who work to raise the quality of life for the family," Junta said of her peers. "We have done many jobs before sex work and are not doing sex work for survival alone."[18]

These initiatives rising out of sex worker organizing from across the globe demonstrate how the people we were meant to view as trafficked, as victims of pimps and imperialism, and as lacking any agency are in fact the ones speaking up the loudest and advocating for themselves. They are also the ones working hardest to ensure workers *aren't* being exploited or trafficked.

26.

Taking Up Each Other's Cause

A Conversation on Tigray and Kashmir

"Tsinia't" and "Bint Ali" interviewed by Simi Kadirgamar

One of the more insidious aspects of state violence and genocide lies in the lengths perpetrators go to silence and ignore victims. Worse still is that survivors must contend with the obstinate indifference of the wider world even as they speak out.

This edited conversation, held in the fall of 2021, between a Tigrayan survivor of war, a Kashmiri scholar-activist evading Indian state surveillance, and myself, a Sri Lankan Tamil trans woman and journalist who grew up in the United States—attempts to challenge these dynamics. The Ethiopian and Eritrean armed forces have perpetrated atrocities in Tigray, including mass killings and weaponized rape, not unlike their Indian counterparts occupying Kashmir. By discussing their experiences, both interviewees demand recognition and solidarity for their communities' struggles.

Located on the border between Ethiopia and Eritrea, Tigray has been caught in a vicious pincer assault by both countries' armed forces. Ethiopia's prime minister, Abiy Ahmed, spearheaded this attack in hopes of crushing the region's historic calls for self-determination and keeping the Ethiopian state consolidated under the supremacy of the Amhara ethnic group. "Tsinia't" (*to persevere* in Tigrigna), a writer from Tigray who has repeatedly had to conceal his name, joined this conversation after witnessing this gruesome endeavor firsthand. Under the Amharic pseudonym Mistir Sew, he documented how the groundwork was laid for a manufactured famine (a brutal repressive tactic used throughout Ethiopia's history) and how even burying loved ones killed by Eritrean and Ethiopian soldiers has become grounds for extrajudicial execution.

The Indian military has occupied the Himalayan state of Jammu and Kashmir for more than seventy years. Despite having their territory divided between rivals India and Pakistan, and later on, China, Kashmiris have long demanded respect for their right to self-determination. Following armed uprisings in the 1990s, India's response to Kashmiri aspirations became especially brutal. The state of constant siege has made Kashmir one of the most militarized places on earth. Indian soldiers in Kashmir have total impunity to abuse the population. Below, "Bint Ali,"—a scholar-activist from Jammu and Kashmir who is also using a pseudonym to protect herself from the Indian government—explains that the military presence, the New Delhi government's repeal of the territory's limited autonomy, and the laws enabling settler colonialism represent a mandate to seize Kashmiris' land and wipe away their identity.

Simi Kadirgamar: While Tigray and Kashmir are geographically distant from each other, they both face settler colonial violence. Could you explain the broader history of the violence Tigrayans are facing now?

Tsinia't (T): It goes all the way back to the way the Ethiopian state was made. The Ethiopian state is an empire and also a colony—not a white colony, a Black colony. The current borders of the Ethiopian state were made by colonizing the people in the southern part of Ethiopia, for instance the Oromos, and the people from the Southern Nations, Nationalities, and People's (SNNPR) region who make up about one-third of Ethiopia and the more than fifty ethnicities in that region.

Abyssinia, or the highlands of Ethiopia, has a long history. The lowlands, the other southern parts of Ethiopia, have their own civilization and their own history as well. Ethiopia as we know it today was established by Emperor Menelik II in the nineteenth century and the Neftenya system was introduced, where the people from the highlands, specifically from the areas of the Amhara, would establish themselves as landlords and would basically enslave the native people in the southern parts of Ethiopia to do their work. The native people would till the land and give the landlords the whole yield. Tigray was part of the highlands, part of the former Abyssinia. It's not one of the regions that was subjugated by the Neftenya system, but Tigray, despite being in this part of Abyssinia, recognizes the right of self-determination or the right to rule oneself, because Tigray has been an independent state for close to three thousand years.

This is where the clash with the Ethiopian colonizers comes because the colonizers want an Ethiopia that is in the image of them, that speaks the Amharic language, that has Ethiopian culture. Tigray's strong sense of self-rule was considered a setback to the formation of Ethiopia as a nation-state with one language and one culture. This is the root cause of the conflict.

How has the government of Abiy Ahmed continued this agenda of creating a consolidated Ethiopia under the auspices of Amhara supremacy?

T: Abiy Ahmed is actually Amhara. His mother is from Amhara. His father is from Oromia. But more than his ethnicity is his actual line of thinking—Abiy Ahmed is infatuated with the idea of becoming an emperor and he wants to be a king. He doesn't want nations that want self-rule, that want classification of power between federal and regional states. If it was about ethnicity, the Oromos would have accepted him. Most Oromo intellectuals are against him because Abiy Ahmed represents everything that they fought against, everything that was undone by the 1974 revolution. The student movement in the late 1960s and 1970s had two fundamental questions. The first one was the land to the tiller—they wanted to undo the Neftenya system so there would not be any landlords and the tiller should own the land. The second one was the question of nations and nationalities. Nations and nationalities should be recognized and should have the right to express themselves in their own language, express their culture and rule themselves. Abiy Ahmed wants to roll this back, all these gains, and take us back to 1974, which is why the Oromos are also against him. His ideology is more in line with the empire of Ethiopia than an Ethiopia that recognizes its citizens, that recognizes that there are eighty-plus nations and nationalities inside Ethiopia now.

Do you see parallels between the story of Tigray and the story of Kashmir's refusal to be incorporated into the Indian Republic, and also its history of fighting for self-determination that goes back to resisting British colonialism in the nineteenth century and beyond?

Bint Ali (BA): Kashmir wasn't ever directly ruled by the British. The British did, however, sell us to the Dogra dynasty. But, of course, there are a lot of similarities. What really hit me was when Tsinia't was talking about land to the tiller in Tigray because, in Kashmir, we have something similar. The "land-to-the-tiller act" was brought into place around the 1950s, and everybody in Kashmir owns some kind of land now because of that act.

First and foremost, it's not just the land that India wants to take away. They want to change the names of our places. They want to turn us into something that we are not. They want us to forget our language. They want Kashmiri land, but they don't want Kashmiri people. It's an assault and an attack on our very ethnic and indigenous identity.

Looking at the things that keep changing in Kashmir every single day and the level of oppression that people are under, I have to refresh my social media feeds to see if any news is coming out officially, if any Kashmiri is posting anything. There is hardly anything at all, because all of us have been silenced. As much as I feel hopeless, I know that one day, very soon, this silence is going to be so deadly, and people will not be able to carry its weight anymore. They are going to burst. That's where resistance comes in.

One very striking similarity between the war in Tigray and India's state violence in Kashmir is the use of information blockades and communications shutdowns. I was wondering if the two of you could comment on how you have navigated those restrictions and how they have affected your political activity.

(BA): When people think about internet and communication blackouts in Kashmir, 2019 immediately comes to their minds, but blackouts have been happening ever since we had telecommunication. And, ever since the internet became common in Kashmir, internet blackouts also became common.

In 2008, when this discourse of Kashmir wanting freedom and Kashmiri people resisting came into online public spheres and people started organizing on these platforms, somebody would be killed somewhere, and there would be a call on Facebook—"Assemble here, there's a protest." And you would see huge protests. For example, if a local rebel would get killed in an army fight, thousands of people would attend the funeral.

There was a little bit of space for that kind of dissent and protest, and a little bit of space for at least mourning and expressing your grief. That was completely, completely taken away from us in August 2019. India basically monitored everything—how Kashmiris breathe and eat and sleep, they monitored it, and they came up with ways to stifle Kashmiris in each and every possible way.

It's interesting what technology does and how it makes you feel. I was in Kashmir that August. I remember waking up into this kind of absurdity and hollowness. I suddenly felt like I was thrown into some kind of a black hole. I couldn't locate myself, I couldn't map myself, where I was and what I was supposed to do. And there was absolute silence everywhere because it was not just the communication, it was that there was a complete curfew. You couldn't go outside your home. You didn't know what was happening just one mile away in your friend's or relative's home. People died, and their relatives and immediate family wouldn't even know. In that time I even had to leave my home and go abroad and study. And for months to come I had no idea if my family was alive.

Internet bans still happen in Kashmir. This is heartbreaking. We didn't have the internet to download directions and guidelines for what we were supposed to do in the COVID pandemic. What is the pandemic, how are we supposed to keep ourselves safe? There were no resources. The pandemic, as well as the existing lockdown in Kashmir, was a deadly combination.

The worst part is the level of censorship we face. We really don't have platforms and avenues to go and tell our story and say these things. Many places don't want to publish anything about this. In spite of all this violence and this intense censorship that we are going through, no one else is speaking. We have to take up each other's cause! Only then can we sort of achieve this ideal and this future of global justice where we imagine communities not living under occupation and war anymore.

What about the impact of the Ethiopian state's information ban around Tigray?

(T): Tigray was in a communication blackout for more than one hundred days now in retaliation for Tigrayan victories in June 2021. When they started the war in November 2020, they blocked the power. They turned off the internet. They turned off communication like telephone and everything. Because of this, most people don't have enough batteries on their phones to record atrocities. This deliberate strategy was part of the genocidal act.

Rape was used as a weapon of war, where soldiers were, in an institutionalized manner, encouraged to rape women. More than 22,500 women, according to the United Nations, were raped. You know that if one woman said that she was raped, there are at least twenty that aren't in the report, so we can multiply the numbers. Besides that, there are atrocities. More than 250 massacre sites and 250 massacres have been recorded so far by the University of Ghent, even with all these communication blackouts.

There is also now a manmade famine in Tigray. All the yields of the farmers were deliberately destroyed. Anyone that was found farming was shot. Now they have closed Tigray, put it under a Gaza-like siege, and are not allowing humanitarian aid to go into Tigray. In the last eighty-six days, there were 900,000 people under famine-like conditions. Only 5 percent of the food that was needed for this 900,000 to survive was allowed to come in . . . basically, 5 percent of 900,000 were allowed to survive. The other 95 percent were doomed and condemned to be killed by starvation.

What is making this worse is the communication blackout. There is no internet, there is no telephone, and even the United Nations cannot move food because fuel is not allowed either. People are killed in darkness by starvation and dying a very slow, excruciating, painful death. This is what the genocide has come to.

The world cannot see this because the world cannot see Tigray. It's in complete blackout. Not only internet, not only telephone, but also power, banking, fuel, everything. Places that were lively are now quiet. Even if you have one million birr in the bank, you can't use it. You will starve to death because there is no banking service. All the money is locked by the Ethiopian government.

In relation to the communication blackout, you can't even speak about this because you are blocked. You're in darkness. The world only gets to hear about this cruelty through information that's trickling out.

You've also written before that people were being killed for trying to bury the dead.[1] I was wondering if you could comment on the impact of this sort of disruption of grief as well.

(T): This is not accidental, where a disgruntled soldier wouldn't allow you to bury, for instance, your daughter who was killed or your father who was killed. This was actually a policy, especially by the Eritrean government—they wanted to break the morale of the people, they wanted to subjugate them—that if they killed someone inside your house, they wouldn't allow you to bury them. You're supposed to live with the body that's smelling for days, and they come daily and check whether you buried it or not.

It's institutionalized. They want you to live with that body because they want to traumatize you. And they want to subjugate you. You are not allowed to mourn. You are not allowed to bury your dead. They make sure that they leave someone to live, to be traumatized.

But it didn't actually subjugate the people of Tigray. It made them much more resilient, much stronger to fight back. In the recent agriculture study from the University of Ghent, they found out that the number of people that joined the resistance corresponds to the amount of cruelty that was committed in a given village. They tried to subjugate us, but the more savagery that they showed, the more atrocities that they committed, the stronger the resistance became.

The detail is sickening, but I also think about what you're describing, Bint Ali. Obviously, there are many mass graves in Kashmir. I wonder if this at all reminded you of the Indian state confiscating the body of Syed Ali Shah Geelani and the use of enforced disappearances?

(BA): Honestly, I'm still processing the details. I wish these awful and horrendous things were not happening. But it's also heartwarming that people are resisting and not just bending down to what's coming their way.

In Kashmir, sexual violence has been used against men and woman. Men have been tortured, sodomized, and forced to masturbate in front of each other. And then women have been raped. Entire villages have been raped, like Kunan Poshpora in the nineties. The men were rounded up outside and all the women were raped, from 8-year-olds to 80-year-olds. And they are still seeking justice! India, in fact, never acknowledged that the Indian Army did this.

Another thing in Kashmir is, of course, enforced disappearances, which leave behind families, half-widows (women whose husbands are disappeared and missing), children, or parents. It's absolutely disturbing. Then people end up in these mass graves. Two years back, an organization in Kashmir called Jammu Kashmir Coalition for Civil Society came out with a study that found that there were so many hundreds and hundreds of mass graves where unidentified people were buried. Families literally live the rest of their lives in trauma and go in search of these people who have been disappeared, hoping they'll find them somewhere. Another thing is how India controls bodies that are dead. This year, teenagers who were killed by the Indian Army, their bodies were not returned. They were not rebels. They were taken away from their home and then killed. . . . And then India says, "Oh, they were militants. That's why we killed them." Or, "We don't know how they got killed, et cetera, et cetera," to label civilians as militants and all these things. They were juveniles, and their families were mourning.

Not that the families expected any justice—they just wanted the dead bodies. They just wanted closure, to bury the dead themselves. The right of mourning, the right of burying bodies has been taken away from Kashmiris. And recently we saw it in the case of Syed Ali Shah Geelani, may Allah have mercy on him. But it has been happening all along with the bodies of so many other Kashmiris. They get buried in very, very remote areas of Kashmir so that the families can't even reach there.

Is there a way you can see Kashmiris and Tigrayans developing bonds of solidarity? What would you say for people outside of these respective communities who are interested in seeing justice done for those who have been violated and in supporting liberation from these oppressions?

(BA): People who come out for different causes, whether it's Black Lives Matter or Palestine's liberation, can also come out for lesser-known causes like Kashmir, like Tigray, because there cannot be peace in the world unless there is peace in these regions. I pray for Palestine every single day and Inshallah, I hope Palestine will be free. One good thing about talking about issues and bringing different people together is that it does help. We start these conversations among ourselves. As much as we need solidarity from the rest of the world, we need solidarity from each other. Because we would understand each other's pain way better than somebody who has not actually lived it. And there are so many of us, so if we join hands, we can actually change the course of action, we can actually change our present. It's very important for all of us to have solidarity between each other and then the rest of the world to have solidarity with us.

Each successive year since this conversation occurred has revealed new contours of violence. In fall 2023, significant sections of global media hailed "peace" in Tigray as an achievement for Abiy Ahmed's "fractured" Ethiopia.[2] Nearly all of Tigray's medical centers lay in ruins. Banking and communications infrastructure, devastated as part of the siege, was slowly being revived. Furthermore, Amhara militias continued their occupation of Western Tigray and welcomed a contingent of special forces to join their cause.[3] Amhara nationalism remained ascendent, even if some of its excesses drew Abiy's ire, reflected in his brutal campaign to discipline his erstwhile allies and culminating in mass killings of civilians.[4] If there had been a peace, "pyrrhic" would have been the way to describe it. As 2024 unfolded, kidnappings by the Oromo Liberation Army, which initially targeted police and state agents, became a lucrative enterprise. As for Tigray, picking up the pieces after genocide is the basis for myriad generational scars.

There is no cause for celebration in Kashmir either. Tsinia't and Bint Ali shared a common experience in having been silenced by internet shutdowns and media blackouts. The Indian settlers destined for compounds and smart cities in Kashmir are unlikely to relate.[5] These additions to India's colonial presence do not merely represent a form of digital segregation. Rather, they create a reality for Kashmiris that closely mirrors the experience of surveillance and control by Palestinians in the West Bank.[6]

Palestine is present in the minds of people living in the aftermath of Western Empire as well as for those living under other forms of sanctioned oppression, from Sudan to Congo and beyond. The events mentioned above were all roughly coterminous with Israel's genocidal rampage through Gaza. The opening days of 2024 serve as a stark reminder of how our world is geographically divided into killing fields, borderlands, and zones of hyper-exploitation. As atrocities compound, it remains imperative that we be prepared to take up each other's cause.

27.

con flama

(excerpt)

Sharon Bridgforth

A child of the African American Great Migration, I came of age during assassinations, riots, the civil rights and Black Power movements, and soul music.† I strive to queerly/embody the unbending dignity, commitment to community, self-determination, and love of Black cultures that was modeled for me.

From age nine to sixteen, I used public transportation to get from my home in Black, working-class South Central Los Angeles to school (and anywhere else I needed to go). Since my high school was located near Echo Park, I was blessed with the experience of cross-cultural travel every day. I feel that I became a citizen of the world through the experience of witnessing changing languages, smells, music, style, and protocol as part of the everyday journey. During the course of a simple bus ride, communities intersected

† *Con flama* is a blues-based jazz performance script. It is blues in its sensibility and history. It is jazz in its composition, communal telling, and nonlinear exploration of time. Set in Los Angeles in the 1940s to 1970s, *con flama* gives glimpses of a Black gurl's coming of age, via her family history. The gurl's story unfolds as she makes her way through the cultural landscape of Los Angeles on the bus.

and shifted many times. This is the trip that I was thinking of when I wrote *con flama.*‡

With language as the vehicle/I wanted to explore the cultural landscapes of American life/within the context of my family's migration story.

Setting:

The bus, Los Angeles. 1940s–1970s

Leads (all African American):§

GURL. Should be played by an adult. She is sometimes a wo'mn/exists in different time periods/ages and places throughout the piece. She is queer.

GRANDMOTHER. From the Delta South.

MOTHER. A Southerner who has moved to the big city.

i saw my Ancestors in the eyes of strangers/sitting on the bus. i collected their stories on the bus/in the creased faces the bent backs the blistered hands the pieces of memory

flickering neath the blackbrowntanyellowredwhitebeige flow of skin the lilt and curve of languages spoken and silence the music blasting hair wavy kinky straight

curly shaved gone doors swinging open laughter strutting broken yelling fists crumpled smells somebody's dinner rushing in from streets we passed closed curtains weeping silence and smiles stepping aboard/i saw myself. who do they look out the window for/wait to return home from work who are their Ancestors i wondered.

---

‡ *Con flama* means confusion, frustration, and drama (Black gay slang). In Spanish *con flama* means "with flame."

§ There are a community of voices that appear throughout the piece, in the life and memory of the little girl. They are part of the communal/layered telling of her story. Text should be layered throughout the piece so that language becomes a part of the music and environment in the world of the piece. A majority of cast members should be singers.

i saw my Ancestors in the eyes of strangers/sitting on the bus i collected their stories/created my story proudly.

western

1965

(There are some specific [Los Angeles] streets referenced, which could be interpreted as "bus stops." These "stops" should be announced.)

tommy nakamura was the coolest drink of water to ever

get on the number 84 northbound.

i never missed my 6:30 a.m. bus

cause at 7:15 when we pulled up to olympic avenue

tommy nakamura would step aboard

black shades black silk shirt black slacks

shiny black ankle boots no jewelry no smiling tommy would stroll down the aisle like a cool breeze.

by the time the bus pulled off i'd smile into a sweet sleep having just seen beauty.

see/i know how to get them good fifteen minute/no head knocking the window/no neck snapping/no drooling on your neighbor/no stop missing/ you bet not mess with me naps/cause i know how to ride the bus!

and i knew that one day i'd get to know tommy a little bit better.

i just never imagined

that it would be at my bus stop/at dusk.

when i asked him what the heck he was doing on century boulevard about to transfer towards watts/tommy said

i was born in prison.

may 16, 1942 i came screaming into the world

and twenty three years later i am still screaming/inside.

high barbed-wired fences with armed soldiers

and guard towers—strategically located surrounding/504 barracks

made of quarter-inch boards over wooden frames covered with

tar paper /with batten boards

steel framed cots with straw mattresses six of us

living in a 20 x 24 ft. space with dust

always dust

in the midst of a man-made desert created by the united states government president roosevelt's executive order 9066!

my birthplace was

manzanar

one of ten

internment camps

that held 120,000 of my people

77,000 of us/ u.s. citizens.

no one had committed a crime.

they called us evacuees/voluntary but we were

not

free to leave

and the guns were pointed inside not out.

so i say

we were prisoners.

my parents were Nisei

second generation Japanese american. american born

american raised

american educated

american loyal

u.s. american citizen/PRISONERS!

my earliest memory

is a dream

of burning my birth place to the ground.

so when i read that your people were burning this place down i chanted with you burn baby burn.

and i just had to come see/as close as possible cause maybe your fire

will release

the scream in me.

also

i like the way you sleep.

i was hoping to get a clearer picture of where you lay your head at night when you're not bopping on the number 84.

well

i didn't give tommy no clear nothing that night but eventually i did.

and we been sleeping together ever since.

vermont

1972

papi's granda is Korean/his granna too

granda came over first to work on the sugar plantations in hawai'i/they called it contract labor but papi says the Koreans were made to slave like the first-there-Islanders and the Africans the Chinese the Japanese and the Puerto Ricans who all also worked them same sugar plantations over the years.

granna came over and her and granda moved to los angeles just before the hate laws prevented Asian people from buying land in california.

granda's american nickname for papi is lucky

cause he was the first grandchild born on the hong family manor/which was really a tiny farmhouse surrounded by land granda granna and their children worked magic from. they sent all the hong grandchildren to college

which is where papi met mami/who he said he fell deeply in love with at first look in her eyes.

papi said he recognized the still water of tears buried by the sorrow of missing home. i saw my own heart he said.

mami always said

lucky hong/don't you keep telling these children your mentiras

it ain't sorrow buried in my belly

no no es tristeza es

rabia/baby. rabia/to the bone.

when my abuelo's people have control of their own affairs

cuando isla querida de mi abuela is no longer a testing site

a dumping ground una base militar for killing/when Borinquen is sovereign and independent then/i will have time for tears

hasta entonces

rabia es lo que tengo moving me to action!

mami's a trip.

papi always winks at me when she gets like this cause we both know that his favorite pastime is to get mami going/which ain't hard to do especially on the subject of home/cause her grand-daddy

moved from puerto rico to hawai'i the same as granda/to work the sugar plantation

and like papi/mami was born in los angeles but her great-uncles never made it cause after they got off the ship from puerto rico onto the train in new york/trying to get to jobs/to make a better life for their families

one died of sickness and the other two froze to death—no clothes for the winter/in route to the ship that would have taken them to hawai'i.

mami says that every night she dreams/she is sitting with her mami and papi on her grand-daddy's island watching the sky from her grand-mami's porch swing crying the loss of her dead tios.

i carry those tears too. i call them exile blues/which is what you have/ when home is a place you feel but have never seen.

sadness burns in you

a hole that can't be filled.

my friends have it too

but we keep ourselves too busy to think about it most days.

there is alofa momoli/she's Samoan

we call her queenie cause every time we say

i

she pinches us and says

i

is from palagi

i'ma teach you faasamoa

cause the word *i* means *we* in the Samoan way

and queenie wants us to understand the full benefits of family.

there is eloisa coloma who is Filipina and who is so tuff she ain't even never had to fight

all she have to do is look at you/and you been beat

and there is alberta davis who is from alabama/whose daddy is papi's best friend who we been begging to please don't take papi to no more movies

cause every time he see me and queenie and eloisa and alberta together/ papi say *you some baddmatha shutyomouths!*

he just tickle hisself silly/laughing and we really are sick of it by now.

but together we are quite something.

we do do family like queenie teach us

and we do have all each other's houses to be family in

which helps a lot/especially last summer when we each lost a brother to the war. queenie's brother came back in a box.

eloisa's brother came back on heroin.

my brother came back without a heart

cause he left it with his left hand and his woman and baby in vietnam. alberta's brother came back in his body but not in his head

and every time somebody light a incense he start to fighting that war all over again and usually ends up in jail or the hospital.

so mami and alberta's mami have to pray every week-end

please don't let tonk jr. go to no party lawd help him lawd help him now lawd Jesus!

los angeles

home/back in the day

i remember

running through my neighborhood on rooftops/jumping on the abandoned mattress from the hole in the top of the last house/then racing round the block to start all over. throwing baseballs at each other against somebody's garage door.

playing tackle with the boys until they decided i was a girl and barred me from the game. stealing plastic puppets from the oscar mayer hot dog packages at the liquor store eating cereal out the box at the grocery store.

sneaking in the movie theatre to watch cleopatra jones/again

riding the bus the length of the city/just cause/asking strangers on the other side of town for change so we could eat hamburgers and catch the bus back home before midnight. city rats/playing games. resisting urban planning and economic restraints. walking down hollywood blvd/before it got deserted/after the glamour faded in the noise of male prostitutes psychedelic funk and drunken teenagers

dancing in the park after curfew/to the isley brothers and santana

driving friends to the drive-in in my mama's hooptie/two in the trunk two on the floor in the back three sitting upright/and nonchalant using fake id's to party till dawn

with beautiful Arab men in westwood discotheques

soul brothers at the red onion on wilshire

hippie cats at bahama mama's on venice

pimps and pushers at the place with no name

across the street from the 24 hour pastrami joint on adams

places we didn't need no id's like catherine's and charlynne's off vine and vivian's backyard in echo park where her big sister served us beer and taught us

how to use peripheral vision to admire the cholas/so we wouldn't get caught staring like the love starved puppies that we were

home.

parliament funkadellic and the mother ship landed on crenshaw blvd.

dancing in bars filled with girls dancing with girls/me dancing with girls/me enjoying heels tall skirts small/laughter and sexy dj's house mix

griffin park filled with drummers and dancers and families out in the sun/on saturdays under the moon concerts with sheila and pete escovedo roy ayers gill scott-heron willie bobo tania marie war tower of power sly and the family stone earth wind and fire

jose feliano los lobos and too many others to name

knowing every short cut scenic route real eatery and swapmeet never having to explain myself

never feeling like a stranger

never forming the question

where do i belong

i remember knowing where

home was

the beach

all-times/cherished

this is the land of the Tongva

my offerings go to their Mother. pieces of skin

and blood.

i have dropped myself

into the cultural landscape of this place

sacrificed/deeply planted memories

in this place

now called

the city of Angels

my dreams

have been released here

dreams carefully placed/each one

broken each one shattered each one

denied stepped on and crushed

my dreams i put them neatly down/used

the rage in my heart to light the stack

salve for the wounds/the flame

will stop the weeping.

my dreams have gone home now

carried by the smoke

my dreams light the sky

leaving their ashes

in the sand

i emerge

having shed the pain/i

stand

and

dream

anew.

28.

Celebrating a Hundred Years of Yuri Kochiyama

Akemi Kochiyama-Ladson interviewed by Jaimee A. Swift

> *My priority would be to fight against polarization. Because this whole society is so polarized. I think there are so many issues that all people of color should come together on, and there are forces in this country who want this polarization to take place.*
>
> —Yuri Kochiyama

On May 19, 1921, in San Pedro, California, Mary Yuriko Nakahara—popularly known as Yuri Kochiyama—was born. A formidable Japanese American civil rights activist who was a staunch ally and champion for the rights and freedom of Black, Asian, and communities of color, Kochiyama left an indelible mark in history as a radical leader, organizer, and educator. She was—and still is—a profound example of what cross-racial solidarity and activism can and should look like.

Kochiyama was a survivor of the Japanese American incarceration camps during World War II, during which the US government, enacted by President Franklin D. Roosevelt's Executive Order 9066, forcibly imprisoned Japanese Americans after the attack on Pearl Harbor.[1] She later met her husband, Bill Kochiyama, who served on the 442nd Infantry US Regiment, the segregated all-Japanese regiment that fought on the front lines of World War II.[2] The couple relocated to New York City and lived in Manhattanville, a low-income public housing project in Harlem, alongside Black and Latino communities. In 1963, Yuri Kochiyama met Malcolm X, and her encounter with him radicalized her. A subsequent friendship between them blossomed. Both she and Malcom share the same birthday, May 19, on which Kochiyama was born in 1921 and Malcolm was born in 1925. In 1964, she hosted a reception for three Japanese writers and a cohort of Hiroshima and Nagasaki atomic bomb survivors who were a part of a World Peace Study Mission to meet and speak with Malcolm X in her apartment.[3]

A member of Malcolm X's Organization for Afro-American Unity, Kochiyama was at the Audubon Ballroom (which is now the Malcolm X and Dr. Betty Shabazz Memorial and Educational Center) where Malcolm X was assassinated on February 21, 1965. A *Life* magazine photo shows Kochiyama cradling him in her arms as he lay lifeless on the ground. In a 1972 radio interview, Kochiyama stated that Malcolm "certainly changed my life. I was heading in one direction, integration, and he was going in another, total liberation, and he opened my eyes."

Her activism for Black, Asian, and Third World liberation spanned the gamut—she joined the Young Lords party, was active in the Harlem Committee for Self-Defense, and was an opponent of the Vietnam War. She invited and hosted countless activists in her home, with her political meetings being affectionately known as "Grand Central Station" or the "Revolutionary Salon."[4] Kochiyama was the founder of Asian Americans for Action, an organization with a mission to catalyze Asian American political movement building in solidarity with Black liberation struggles. In 1977, she was part of a protest with Puerto Rican activists who took over the Statue of Liberty to raise awareness about Puerto Rican independence.[5]

Fighting for reparations for Japanese Americans, she was also on the front lines to free political prisoners. Kochiyama and Chinese American activist and organizer Gloria Lum cofounded Asians for Mumia, an organization that sought to bring together Asians and Asian Americans to collectively organize for the release of former Black Panther and radio journalist Mumia Abu-Jamal, who was accused of murdering a police officer in 1981.[6] She was also a friend and ally to former Black Panther and ex-political prisoner Assata Shakur. Kochiyama was also part of the New York Justice for Vincent Chin Coalition, a collective that demanded justice for Vincent Chin, a Chinese American man who was beaten to death by two white men in Detroit, Michigan, in 1982. A Nobel Peace Prize nominee, Kochiyama was featured alongside Dr. Angela Y. Davis in the 2009 documentary *Mountains That Take Wing*, in which the two powerhouse activists discussed their individual, collective, and overlapping experiences for human and civil rights.

After decades of activism and organizing, Yuri Kochiyama passed away on June 1, 2014. On her one hundredth birthday, scholar-activist and community builder Akemi Kochiyama-Ladson shared her thoughts on her grandmother's life, legacy, and leadership and gave insights to the radical organizer and activist who was, is, and will always be Yuri Kochiyama.

Jaimee A. Swift: Do you mind sharing your favorite memories of your grandmother? What did she teach you personally, politically, and spiritually?

Akemi Kochiyama: I remember her very fondly interacting with people—in our neighborhood in Harlem, on the streets, in the community, at public events, and especially at performances. She was always so supportive. I had the opportunity to accompany her on her college speaking circuit when I was older. I watched both my grandmother and grandfather so graciously and generously host others in their home. They were so warm and open to everyone who walked through their door—and there were a lot of people who walked through there. For a couple of decades, they would host an open house party on Saturday night where everybody was welcome. I witnessed the last ten or so years of their hosting. I think as a kid it was a tremendous opportunity to see your family do that over and over again. It teaches you how to be a human being.

Seeing my grandmother interact with so many people—whether it was a random person on the street or a student meeting her for the first time at a college—she was so enthusiastic about every person she met. She wanted to know their life story, where they were from, and how they got where they are. She would take little notes, take their address, and stay in touch with them [*laughs*]. She would take all that information home and in a very disciplined way, I watched her every night put that information into her address book and organize it. She organized your information by name but also by where you are from and your background so that when she was mailing or inviting people to an event, she could easily find you. It was incredible to watch her graciousness and the respect she had for everyone around her. I saw her interact with well-known people in the political world, celebrities, and everyday people. She treated everyone the same. For me, that was an amazing experience and that experience of her continues to impact me now.

Do you recall your grandmother sharing stories about her friendship with Malcolm X? If so, what stood out to you the most about what she said about him? How did Malcolm X shape your politics?

Yuri talked about Malcolm constantly during my childhood and throughout my life. He was a part of the culture of the Kochiyama family. Prior to Yuri's passing, May 19 was always about celebrating and honoring Malcolm. Sometimes, I went to three or four events with Yuri in Harlem to celebrate Malcolm's birthday on May 19. If you were hanging with Yuri that day, that is what we were doing. At some point throughout the day, we would try to do something privately as a family for her birthday, but it was always about honoring Malcolm. And she honored Malcolm not only on his birthday but all the time. She met Malcolm a couple of years before he died. She always said meeting him was the beginning of her radical consciousness. He had a profound impact on her and because of him, she started thinking more broadly in terms of having an internationalist and anti-imperialist scope. She really started to understand what was happening in Africa, Asia, and in the United States because of Malcolm. She also began to have a more historical view of certain inequities. That impact resonated throughout my family, including my mother and her siblings. If you look at our letters and family communication back then, we were always talking about Malcolm. We often talked about his radical love for his people and for all people of color.

Because of her and Malcolm's closeness, Attallah [Malcolm X's and Dr. Betty Shabazz's eldest daughter] was always in the Kochiyama household, as well as her sisters. We were always interacting with Betty and the Shabazz family, so there was always this constant presence of him. Our relationship with the Shabazz family is important to the Kochiyama family. In terms of my politics, Malcolm also influenced me to have a more internationalist view. As someone of Black and Japanese descent, the internationalist view made a lot of sense to me, and it connects very neatly with my family's understandings of antiracism, anti-imperialism, anticapitalism, and antisexism. My family was already really steeped in Malcolm's teachings before I was even born. I was born in the midst of Black nationalism, which was a really radical time period.[7] My father was a Black Panther and so was my stepfather. Malcolm's presence and teachings were always so seamlessly tied throughout my life.

I think what is really interesting is that my grandparents hosted Japanese writers and a group of atomic bomb survivors who really wanted to meet Malcolm. They were on a world peace tour and study mission, and they were really interested in Malcolm and believed what he said was relevant to them. Yuri said that more than anyone else, they wanted to meet Malcolm. I think those connections show broader international contexts.

What does solidarity mean to you? In what ways did your grandmother teach you about solidarity?

I had the benefit of growing up in an extremely multicultural, multiracial, and multigenerational radical and anti-imperialist family and broader community. I had many layers in which I was exposed to understanding my identity and the world around me. I am Japanese and Black, and I grew up in Harlem, but my Japanese family is from public housing. Being in that context made it really easy for me to understand all the connections between capitalism, sexism, racism, imperialism, colonialism, and all the systems that are very purposeful in oppressing various groups of people. In my own experience as a Black Nikkei (a person of African and Japanese descent), I see how these oppressions are very common experiences of Black and Japanese Americans. It is very interesting to see in the media that the current presentation of Black and Asian relations is on anti-Asian violence. However, statistically, if you look at the reported anti-Asian incidents of violence, most of the perpetrators are actually not Black.[8] It is very interesting and not surprising to me that what is being presented is Black-on-Asian violence and that is a part of a larger narrative and purposeful reinforcement of the "model minority" versus Black people. I think that is very destructive. All of that informs my desire to really work against that and to put a longer history and personal context to alternative narratives.

My story is one of many stories. I used to think my story was an anomaly that my family—the Kochiyamas—ended up in public housing. I felt that was only particular to our family history. However, I learned later on about Japanese families living in Manhattanville also. I also learned that a lot of Japanese families coming out of internment camps ended up relocating to predominantly Black communities because of the purposeful disenfranchisement they faced under Executive Order 9066. They lost everything. After they were released from the internment camps, not only did they have to rebuild their lives, but they also had the negative stamp of being an enemy of the state. It was actually very common for Japanese communities to be with Black communities during that time period.

Also, another commonality between Black and Asian communities was the GI Bill. My grandfather was a part of the 442nd Infantry Regiment, which was the all-Japanese regiment that fought on the front lines of World War II.[9] They were highly decorated because they lost so many lives. My grandfather was from Harlem and grew up on 126th Street in a predominately white orphanage. At the age of eighteen, he moved to California, and he started to see what it was like to be an Asian American, and then Executive Order 9066 happened. He ended up in Topaz, Utah, at an internment camp. He jumped at a chance to join the army and to get out of the internment camp to prove his patriotism. He ended up in Hattiesburg, Mississippi, at the Camp Shelby army base, where there were only Black and Japanese soldiers.

Ironically, my grandparents met in Hattiesburg because [my grandmother] was at an internment camp in Jerome, Arkansas. At the time, she and other young women were given the opportunity to work at an all-Japanese United Service Organization. My grandmother volunteered so she could get out of the internment camp. She arrived at Hattiesburg, and she met my grandfather. It was love at first sight. They wrote letters to each other all during the war and they were married right afterward. They eventually moved to New York City, where my grandfather is from.

However, in all of those instances, my grandmother said that when she arrived in Hattiesburg was the first time she experienced Jim Crow segregation. She was from California, so she had never experienced segregation like that until then. She told me that years later she ended up working at Chock Full o'Nuts in Harlem with all these Black people from Hattiesburg, and they provided her with more context for her experience. She said it was so incredibly useful for her to have context of what was going on in Hattiesburg because at the time she did not understand.

It is so interesting to know all the ways in which Black and Japanese Americans have had these parallel experiences since World War II that are sort of unspoken or people are unaware of. It is really important to document those stories. I am currently working on my grandmother's archive right now. Archiving and documenting are really important parts of radical interventions to fight against these narratives that oppress us and try to disrupt Black, Asian, Indigenous, and people of color solidarity.

What has the process been like to ensure that your grandmother's legacy of radical activism and organizing is known to current and future generations?

It has been a long process [*laughs*]. My aunt and I are codirectors of the Yuri Kochiyama Archives Project. About twelve or thirteen years ago, when my grandmother was still alive, we all agreed we should start thinking about her legacy. We all were very aware of her papers because it was a family joke that as her children started to move out of her apartment, the rooms were replaced by all her papers [*laughs*]. We realized that with all her papers and newspaper clippings, we had to do something about them. Later on, we actually had to move my grandmother out to California in 1999 because she became physically unable to stay in Manhattanville independently and she needed more support. When we had to empty that four-bedroom apartment that she and my grandfather had lived in for almost fifty years, we had all these materials that had to be organized.

It was an incredible process, and I have to thank all my family members who helped. People flew in from California and all over the United States to help with my grandmother's archives. We were able to organize her archives into categories. We had teams of people working on Yuri's archives on Black nationalism, Black arts, Asian American politics, and so much more. We were also able to track down some of her work she previously donated. Over the course of her life, she donated hundreds of boxes of her work to UCLA's Asian American Studies Department, Medgar Evers College, the Schomburg Center for Research in Black Culture, and the University of Connecticut. There was also a lot of Yuri's work in my home, my aunt's home in California, and a family friend's home in Brooklyn. We were very concerned about protecting her work.

There were a lot of different processes in terms of archiving her work. We met with archival brokers, which was a new term for me at the time. We went through many iterations of this to find the right type of relationship and we ended up working with Columbia University. It was a long process, and it took almost ten years before we came to an agreement. We ended up selling and donating parts of Yuri's archive to Columbia University, but there are significant parts of the archive already at UCLA. One of the most important goals as a family in looking for the right partners, people, and institutions to work with was working with an institution that could provide the freest public access. However, it has been a long process. I've learned the importance of protecting materials and being cognizant of where one's materials go and who has access.

Being that you are Black Nikkei, how did your family teach you about the importance of honoring and embracing your Black and Japanese heritages and traditions? Were you ever made to feel that you had to "choose" one identity over the other?

I am very lucky with how I grew up. I was able to study classical Japanese dance and karate as a child at a Buddhist temple. My cousin Zulu—who is also Black Nikkei—and I, we studied there and felt very welcomed. I learned so much about Japanese culture. I also worked at the Japan Society. I was in all these spaces of Japanese-ness and also Blackness. I grew up in Harlem. I am from the Manhattanville Project, and I grew up in Sugar Hill. I went to public school then to private school and then back to public. Then I went to Spelman College. I felt comfortable with myself in all those spaces in every single way.

One of the first instances I had where my Blackness was questioned was when I was at Spelman. Although it was only in one particular class, it was a really interesting experience. There was a debate in a social science class I was in about what makes people "more Black." There was an argument that a person that looked like me could be less Black than a person who had blonde hair and blue eyes. It was an interesting conversation and debate to have for the first time in my life about my Blackness at the age of nineteen. Being that I was from Harlem, it was interesting to me that I didn't encounter that type of questioning until I went to Georgia. In retrospect, now that I understand the dynamics of Georgia as opposed to New York, I understand why this came up in that context. I saw for the first time how Blackness and Asianness were defined and how often they were defined in conflict with each other in certain contexts.

What are your hopes for the future of Black and Asian solidarities, especially at this political juncture?

It is so important right now—it has always been important. I live in Harlem and there was an incident where an elderly Asian man—who collected cans because he lost his job in the restaurant industry due to the pandemic—was brutally beaten by a Black man, who was probably mentally ill. It was so disturbing this took place near where I live. For me to know the larger context and the history, it is painful and so wrong. I really feel that if people had more context, education, and understanding of where Black and Asian histories overlap, intersect, and where we have common oppression, we can truly be in solidarity. It is so shocking to see violence escalate especially in a place like New York City. How could that happen here? But it keeps happening here, which says a lot. We can see how the impacts of racism are affecting all of us, and it seems like it is getting worse each day in America. I think Black and Asian conflict is something that people need to really understand, deconstruct, and move on from, and I am doing everything I can to help inform that process. Why would we not be concerned as people of color seeing violence happen to other people of color? It is very basic, and it does impact us all.

29.

Meditations on Black/Asian Locations

Julie Ae Kim

When you look up my parents' now closed fish store, Mr. Fish Market, on Google, there are fifty reviews with an average of a four-star rating. One particular review tickled me, "Fish sandwich was great. . . . They have a woman of color frying the fish and it was so good!!" by a "Local Guide." To think of my immigrant Korean mom as a woman of color kind of shocked me, even though it is technically true. My mother would never have self-identified as a woman of color. She would think of herself as Korean. But I do and have identified as a woman of color. There is a conscious choice in aligning yourself as part of a larger group beyond the prebuilt identifiers offered to you—like ones built on race, nationality, ethnicity, religion. To claim an identity built on solidarities requires a larger view outside of oneself and interrogates the functions of "identity." I didn't think of myself as a woman of color prior to my mid-twenties, likely because I was focused on myself, finding her, being her. And it took the places that I was located to sharpen my own thoughts around how identity, and in turn, solidarity, can shift.

Mr. Fish Market was located in Rochdale Village, a self-contained housing cooperative in South Queens, New York City, with its own library, two shopping malls, and twenty-five thousand residents. Its population is 98 percent nonwhite residents and mostly Black people. When it was built, it was pitched as a model of integration, white and Black people living together during the civil rights era. However, much of the white population moved out to live in the suburbs. The fish market existed like a portal to another world I didn't know, and my parents by default represented the "Asian shopkeeper." An entire area of Queens that I only knew through this small market.

My family moved into Bayside, in North Queens, when I was five, in 1996. This area was predominantly "ethnic white," made up of Italian, Irish, and Greek immigrants until Korean immigrants also started moving into the neighborhood in the mid-1990s. Korean churches speckled the neighborhood, some just basements in someone's home. They functioned as religious institutions, day care, and Korean language schools, providing access to organized sports and entertainment and fellowship. I think about the safety in enclaves that enabled my parents to thrive even when they spoke no English and had no safety nets because they refused to use public benefits or welfare for fear that "someone" was keeping track and would use that to deny them something in the future. My parents were paranoid of even a single dollar on my Queens public library card. Once, we had an illegal cable box in our home. My brother, as a latchkey kid, let some cable person into the house to see it when nobody was home. When my dad found out, he took the entire box, drove to the nearby park, and chucked the whole thing into the lake.

Where one lives and where one works. We were in the middle of two worlds in a borough. North and South Queens.

How does one end up where they are?

2018. Sarang 콜택시. Love Taxi.

I had just visited my parents in Bayside and was going back to where I now lived in Prospect Lefferts Garden, Brooklyn. "Julie, call Sarang Taxi and ask them how much it'll cost to take you there." Uber was quoting me $75. Sarang Taxi said they'd take me for $50. Still using a call dispatcher, the black car showed up, and I used my fifth-grade-level Korean to say hello. As he pulled up to my apartment, he says, "You live in Flatbush? This place used to be so dangerous back then. Lots of gang activity. Take care of yourself, 아가씨 (miss)."

Flatbush is made up of predominantly Caribbean and West African immigrants, specifically Haitians. The switch from a majority white population to Black population happened between 1980 and 1990. I moved there, to what I knew at the time as Prospect Lefferts Garden (PLG) to follow my then partner. I couldn't afford an apartment on my own after all. What do you call that? A love gentrifier? I understood the desire to point at the gentrifiers (me), for catharsis, however brief, to identify in a person a problem that felt too big to tackle. What is the limit to individual responsibility? Or is there one? How does one end up where they are? What makes me uncomfortable is when the language of nativism comes through even in innocuous ways. *I'm a third-generation New Yorker, or "born and raised" New Yorker. Native New Yorker.* What other language can be used to signify belonging, which is at the core of the statements? I liked calling myself a "Queens girl," letting the place define, modify, represent me. But where does one belong when one doesn't have a stable place to call home or is forced to be mobile or stateless?

There were stickers on the telephone poles: "FLATBUSH not PLG." My then partner, F, and I would walk to PLG Coffee House in the mornings for $6 breakfast croissant sandwiches. As a child growing up in Queens, I imagined myself escaping to Manhattan, "The City." F lived on Parkside Avenue, and we'd walk past the McDonald's on the corner, the Korean-owned laundromat, the fish fry place, the West African restaurant with its minimalist white walls, the Popeye's, the beef patty takeout, the Dominican buffet restaurant, Errol's Caribbean Delights. F had lived there for six years before the coffee shops, the sexy-lighting Italian restaurant where they swirl your wine to taste. They say that the first signs of gentrification are bookstores and coffee shops coming into the neighborhood. I always joked how much I loved both those things.

1823 Church Avenue. That's the site of Family Red Apple store and the boycott. I didn't realize or even think about how close I was to the site of the yearlong boycott of 1990 when I moved to PLG. How am I the same or different from my parents or how is my generation different from the previous one and isn't that also an important relationship to consider in context to revived conversations around Black/Asian solidarities, Black Lives Matter movements, and anti-Asian violence? Living in Flatbush, the location has a history that its people circulate, and if we're conscientious, can transform.

There are times where I find that pointing to white supremacy as the problem feels too abstract—like asking a person to look at the big picture when a person who has physically, psychologically, materially harmed them is in front of their face. I find that to point at a larger system during a moment of pain and trauma doesn't alleviate the personal, specific, intimate pain that a person may endure. What does the history of places and locations we are a part of offer us?

Without history, we're left grasping at what's put in front of us. The myopic nature of conflict is what makes it so difficult. With any conflict, between lovers, family, friends, a blowup isn't just what that one fight was about. Usually it's a long history—of resentment, neglect, disappointments—that one day is blown up into view. The irony being that much of interpersonal conflict stems from a shared intimacy, a relationship that exists. Isn't that why I mostly end up fighting with the people I love or wish to love?

Black-Korean conflict is a term that is associated with events like the Family Red Apple boycott in New York City, the LA rebellions in 1992, or as Koreans called "Sa-i-gu."[1] These events were often heralded as examples of Black-Asian conflict. These were also events that, when I came across them, I immediately felt both implicated and curious. Implicated because I felt *I* was those Korean Americans. While I was growing up, my parents owned a fish market in a predominantly Black neighborhood, and we could've been, are, those Korean Americans. But also curious, because I wanted to dig deeper, I wanted to find some kind of truth beyond a generalized Black-Asian conflict. To categorize the relationship with conflict felt to me an obfuscation of the "intimacies," associations that had to have already existed.

In graduate school, I read Lisa Lowe's *Intimacies of the Four Continents*, which shares specific examples of racialization as a way to differentiate, generate, and sustain conflict between Asian and Black people.[2] I started to see the ways that identity categories, even in instances that feel innocuous, like Asian American studies, can keep ourselves sectioned off from thinking across differences and intertwined histories. Lowe starkly lays bare some of the theoretical concepts that I've come across in ethnic and Asian American studies, such as the model minority myth and racial triangulation, by utilizing the memos written by British colonial officers detailing the strategies they used to structure racial hierarchy and to administrate intimate conflict. These documents were related to the design of introducing Chinese laborers to West Indian plantations. While she refers here to classifications in the archive, I found it useful to apply it to this term of Black-Asian conflict. In the book, Lowe explains how colonial divisions were sowed through the figure of the indentured servant representing the progressive myth of free labor and the replacement for slavery, where the import of Chinese contract laborers would "be a barrier between us and the Negroes with whom they do not associate; and consequently to whom they will always offer formidable opposition."[3] Further, she talks about how the divided boundaries and racial classifications were a part of the colonial strategy to prevent intimacies among people. These "intimacies" refer to the shared goal of survival under colonial rule, proximity, and affinity that are inevitable when people share a location together, to imagine the various collaborations that "include the political, sexual, and intellectual." A handshake across the counter, the everyday hellos at the park, the relationships that occur against dominant societal norms, the "subaltern revolts and uprisings."[4]

I Love Dance Studio is in a basement along a row of small businesses in Murray Hill, Queens. There's a *phở* place next door, a yoga studio, and a sneaker store. Murray Hill has a place called 먹자골목 (Tasty Corner), which is a street lined with a plethora of restaurants. I walked past Tasty Corner from my new apartment to the dance studio, which was about a mile away from me. Eight months into the pandemic, I moved back to Flushing, Queens, where I grew up and went to middle school. My parents were now only a ten- to fifteen-minute drive away and I was surrounded by predominantly East Asians. The shift in demographic changed me psychologically—I wasn't the only or one of few East Asian faces in a crowd. Place shapes identity, and I'm finding it impossible not to write about place when I think about Black/Asian intimacies. While Flushing for as long as I could remember had a predominantly Asian population, I remember learning the fact that the Bowne House, which I would pass by from time to time, likely served as a stop on the Underground Railroad. How does place shape how we dis/connect with each other and how we approach how we view each other?

While I knew about the studio for a few years, I started going to I Love Dance studio when I moved back. It's a K-pop/street-style dance studio where one can learn the actual choreography of the K-pop and hip-hop stars on YouTube channels and TV. While I had taken a few years of tap and jazz dance as a child, I hadn't moved my body in an intentional dance class outside of dancing at weddings or a club for many years. Each song is given one month (four classes once a week), unless you take a beginner's class, which dedicates two classes to one song.

I'm like yeah she fine
Wonder when She'll be mine
She walk past I press rewind

I fold my hips, stick out my chest, drop my knees, focusing on my dance instructor, Ness, as he glides through the moves. I feel my brain sending instructions to my body, but it's consistently a beat too slow and I feel the effort of trying. Fetty Wap taking over my entire body, bringing back the summer of 2014 when it had only been a year after graduating college, still dancing every Friday night with my high school best friends. I think of the article by Hanif Abdurraqib proclaiming "Trap Queen" as our generation's greatest love song and I think of joy.[5] And in another class, I'm jumping up and down to "Dun Dun Dance" by Oh My Girl. As I go every week, I start to notice how diverse my classes are, Black and Latinx students dancing alongside the Korean American and Asian American kids of the neighborhoods and the way that there are no white dance instructors. It reminds me of when I used to work the cash register at my parents' fish market and their Black women customers would ask me if I had watched "Boys Over Flowers" or various K-dramas that were popular at the time. Imagining us, a class, dancing, learning, together.

Like my mom doesn't see herself as part of a larger coalition of 'woman of color,' I am reminded that ultimately solidarity may require multiple strategies—from the individual to the interpersonal, which can foster personal relationships, to larger ideological ideas of coalition building. Less and less I feel I have the answer to solidarity building besides desiring it like one desires world liberation—idealistically, earnestly. But am I ready for what relationships and solidarity requires? A digging into those parts that I'd rather turn away from but also a dedication to truly understand the places that I am in, the history of it, and where I stand.

I can try.

30.

Academia and Activism

Inside and Outside the Ivory Tower

Shreerekha Pillai, Eunsong Kim, Demita Frazier, and Moya Bailey

Dear reader, how do you know someone is truly down? When do you know you fuck with someone? We—Shreerekha, Eunsong, Demita, and Moya—discuss when that moment of knowing occurred in our respective friendships. It's not easy, and this conversation only begins to touch the surface and set the stage. We are excited for you to bear witness and hope it fosters conversations within your own relationships. This conversation is an excerpt from an episode of *The Gathering Table,* a podcast series with Moya Bailey and Demita Frazier. The transcript has been edited and adapted for clarity.

Shreerekha Pillai (SP): I finally met Demita in person in Baltimore at the 2017 National Women's Studies Association's annual conference themed "Forty Years After Combahee." I had known Demita because her voice charted the solidarity that I sought in my friends to give me light in moments of darkness. So much of Demita informed the person I became. Radical Black feminist thought has framed my life and helped me survive.

Demita Frazier (DF): Shreerekha and I were talking at the conference, and her eyes were all sparkly. She said, "Have you eaten? You need some food."

It was that kind of incantatory thing that someone says to you that vibrates inside of you a certain way.

Moya Bailey (MB): Eunsong and I were in Boston at Northeastern, which for both of us was really difficult 'cause there are ways that New England imagines itself as more progressive than it actually is. We connected out of a real desire to talk about things that weren't working.

Eunsong Kim (EK): Moya was so welcoming in terms of inviting me to things. We just talked about life, television, and food most of the time. Then there were different things that came up at the university that deepened our connection. When did you know that you were comrades, Demita and Shreerekha?

DF: It was the pajama party for me. Shreerekha and I have been to two conferences, and she invited me to the pajama party in her room.

SP: I usually open up my room 'cause conferences are very costly, and a lot of the people have a hard time getting there.

DF: One of the things that I found very powerful about Shreerekha is she gave me permission to be vulnerable and to talk about real life, not just academia. When you can have a conversation where you really open up to another person and what you get back is what you've longed for with other people, that intimacy, the absolute daringness of it, also deepened our relationship.

MB: One of my favorites is this moment where we realized that we could commit crimes together. I'm hypervisible as a dark-skinned Black woman moving through the world, and Eunsong is virtually invisible. We had this moment where we realized we could really do some things.

EK: I should be really clear that Claire Jean Kim says invisibility is as good as it's going to get in the racial order.[1] There's a kind of way in which a liberal East Asian politics revolves around wanting a kind of visibility within the racial order that is akin to whiteness. When invisibility is as good as it's going to get, that's a call to rupture the racial order, not to affirm it. My navigation through the university is essentially under the umbrella of invisibility, and we were thinking we could weaponize this against institutions.

As I was finishing my PhD, a university I was interviewing at took a picture from the internet of somebody who has my name but is an economist in Korea. They made a job talk poster with this other person, and I didn't really know how to tell this white woman, who I had met earlier, that the person in the photo wasn't me. I sent her my picture and asked her to please use this instead, without correcting her. She responded and said, "Oh, I just used the picture in the flyer that we made." And I didn't say anything beyond this. I know how white people sometimes punish you for pointing out racism, so I didn't. When they say employment is humiliation, it's tactical, and visceral. When I first told Moya, she said, "We have to figure out a way to commit crime."

DF: I'm thinking about this scheme that allowed me to do some work at Shreerekha's university with her committee on cultural competence and diversity. You find out pretty quickly in white academia, certain things only go so far. I knew we were going to be friends for life when she called a person who's on that committee a fucking asshole. I was like, *Heck yes. He is!* For me it's always a bellwether for something good when somebody can just put it out there.

SP: Demita doesn't hold back. I had been navigating through the eggshells of administrative work in chairing my department, while at the same time trying to remain true to what I believe in. I feel part of the work I do in the classroom is to undo this supreme reign of white feminism. We need to give centrality to radical Black feminism, but also feminisms from Asia and other parts of the world. You think of Sojourner Truth, her speech in 1851. In that year you have activists in India teaching hundreds of women who are from the lower caste, the outcast community, being able to receive education. And those stories don't get exemplified or talked about. Finding those moments in history are very meaningful to link the work being done in the margins of North America and South Asia.

MB: What you were talking about, Shreerekha, reminds me of something that's happening right now in my and Eunsong's friendship. Eunsong is in the archive looking at Pat Parker's and June Jordan's work and discovering all of these connections that they have to other women of color, including Asian feminists.

EK: I've loved Pat Parker's poetry for so long and spent the summer of 2022 reading her papers and the papers of June Jordan. Pat had a lengthy correspondence with Audre Lorde and was organizing with women transnationally, and she kept flyers for Unbound Feet—a socialist Asian American feminist collective, and documentation on the firing of Merle Woo by UC Berkeley for being openly queer and socialist. Pat gave speeches on organizing transnationally against the rise of fascism and was incredibly connected to different Asian American and women of color activists in the Bay. Knowing her as a poet and then engaging with her deeper as an activist has been exciting for me.

MB: I think about the solidarities throughout history because there is a way that the names we hear are the same names. What you shared with me today, Eunsong, those were names that I didn't know, but now I do and they're part of my larger understanding of the women of color doing that work.

DF: Not enough of the stories of when we connect and build together get told and that's purposeful. There is an undercurrent within white supremacist thinking that definitely pushes against us doing any of that. When I think about the different waves of interaction and encounter, I have to tell you that the work that we're all doing together now feels the richest to me.

SP: Usually, the way the structure of power works is that we are all isolated. They keep us separate because if we come together, we'll make trouble.

MB: What do we risk by forging friendship and feminist solidarity across these lines? What do we gain?

DF: I grew up in Chicago, in a very segregated Black neighborhood. There was a Chinese family that was running the last laundry on Seventy-First Street. My mother had me take the sheets there and they wouldn't talk to me. It wasn't until several years later, when I was fourteen and went to this fancy high school, my friend Lily, who I will remember forever, said, "They're not talking to you because you're not encouraged as a Chinese person to get to know Black people. You can sell to them, you can have commerce with them, but they are not to be invited to your house. They are not to be included in your family." I went to Lily's house with her, and it caused a big brouhaha. She almost got kicked out of her house just for having a friend over who was Black. She was the first person I met that was truly brutally honest about her own culture. And she cried because she said, "There's something so wrong with the way they teach us, and we end up trusting these stupid white people who end up not really even recognizing us." From that point on, I realized the reasons why people act the way they act is really about acculturation to white supremacist society.

SP: I'm a first-generation immigrant and reached New York City at fourteen. I came equipped with a lot of privilege. I grew up in the capital of India. I was fluent in English. My struggle had to do with colorism in India. I grew up with a lot of that pain of children telling me, we can't touch you, we can't play with you. Your color is going to rub off on us. And that always connected me to a different generation of elder African American friends who grew up with that too.

As immigrants, we are given that sort of ladder that you can climb and be adjacent to whiteness. And for some of us, depending on where you are on the color spectrum, it's easier than others to pass. For me the passing game was never going to work, so I found women of color to link arms with.

DF: If we're going to think about this bridge-building activity we want to be involved in, we have to tell people the entire story about the losses. About being exiled in your own community.

I've noticed that so often you get pushback from your own culture about wanting to step across those lines. There are many ways we punch one another for contributing to the dominant paradigm. I also think we don't do enough sharing with one another about the mechanics of what it means to step across those lines and what it takes in terms of being strong when we fail. Oftentimes, I feel we go through these phases of trying to connect. Maybe we do projects together, but in reality, there's still a kind of not knowing one another.

SP: When I went to Baltimore at twenty-one, which at that point was mostly a Black city, that's the first time I had kids tell me, "You're all right. We accept you. We got all different kinds here and they're all part of the Black community." There was a way of acceptance. I felt that was the first time I felt at home. And as an immigrant, there was no sense of feeling stable, I always felt I didn't belong.

When I would travel back to my immigrant communities, the anti-Blackness was so out there. It was so pronounced in the various languages I spoke. And immigrants took refuge that they're not articulating their anti-Blackness in English, they're saying it in other languages. So, you could actually just be out there and be bold and brazen and absolutely unchecked. I kept having conversations with my immigrant community, asking, "Why do you say these things? The people who have been the kindest for many of us are people in the Black community. The white people are not accepting you."

MB: You know, this also has me thinking about some of Eunsong's writing about beauty and why certain things like eyelid surgery exist. I'm also thinking about it in the context of the story of hair and nails, of the gas station, of that interaction between Black folks and Asian folks, and the tensions there that are unspoken. How whiteness is operating even though there are no white people in that space at all. It's impacting what is considered desirable, what is beautiful, and that we're participating in this transaction. White supremacy has us missing the moments of where we could actually build and fortify a kind of community connection at this border crossing, and what would we risk if we had a different understanding of beauty and desirability.

EK: There's a way in which white feminists and the white media sensationalized plastic surgery in Korea or Asia, particularly the double eyelid surgery. They cited it as internal colonization, which is a surface reading. I wrote this short poem about the first time the double eyelid surgery was performed was during the Korean War, which figures like Paul Robeson and other activists protested. It was performed during the war by a US military surgeon on prostituted Korean women to make the women have eyes less like the enemies. The layers of that are just so painful, because it's that part of the military history that becomes normalized into an aesthetic ideal. What will it take for us to actually have different kinds of desires? I don't want the imagination of the US military surgeon to uphold the ideal for desirability.

DF: You know what's interesting, all of us come from cultures where issues of colorism are there. When I look back historically at people who have been the first judge, the first professor, the first this or that, there's a curious unanimity of how they look. They're all light and bright and white. When my sister, who happens to be half-white, walks into a classroom, she's going to get a level of respect that I don't get as a dark-skinned Black woman. The struggle between dark-skinned Black women and light-skinned Black women is a quiet phenomenon.

SP: How do we recognize the way our desires and our imaginations can be affected by the white imagination and how do we disrupt that? That's really hard work and the hardest work is with our families and with our very intimate communities. It happens in our bedrooms, in our kitchens. That's a really hard job and it makes us very difficult companions for everybody.

DF: In the absence of whiteness, how can we dream of what we would be? Poetry can help with this because poetry can leave doors open for people to peek through. I feel bridges can be built upon if we're willing to be honest with one another and really cop to the fact there's been a lot of interruptions that keep us from our earthly purpose.

EK: I feel often imagination is brought up as just the closing word and then everyone just sort of ends there and exits when there's labor and work. As you imagine, you continue to unlearn and interrogate and critique as part of the process. I was thinking about Moya's question of what do we risk? And something that I really think a lot about is Christina Sharpe's idea of distributed risk.[2] What it might mean to have less or take on certain kinds of risks. In the immigrant dream, you buy a house. But, you partake in settler colonial activity, which is still an ongoing process. What could it be that not owning land, not owning property, what might it mean to have a different relationship to this thing called the dream?

DF: When I was twenty, we started this women's collective and lived together, I thought, *Let's try this whole socialism thing, what does it really mean? How will we do it?* It was through that experience that I learned what creatures of our own past we really are. It can be a great thing to have five women living together. We pooled all our money together, we bought groceries, a car. We were able to do a lot with a little bit of money 'cause we pooled it. In the end, we went our separate ways, and it was not a model that could be repeated. I was still very much interested in how we will make this work if we're talking about creating a world that's equitable, knowing that the American dream is to own a little bit of Indigenous people's land and that takes them to the next thing. We are talking about this house, this building that sits on this land. It's bittersweet. Cause when are you going to give it back? It's another one of those performative moments when we can say, we are recognizing where we are and what we're doing, but that recognition is meaningless to Indigenous people.

What does it mean for people of color to have that relationship with other people of color? What does that mean when we say, in Mississippi, this is Choctaw land. Well, my great-grandfather was an African American Indigenous slave child to the Choctaw. So, whose land is that? It's a very complicated thing. So, as we imagine what's possible and we try to experiment with it, our survival's going to depend on our interdependence. And what does it mean when you're not interested in money under late-stage capitalism? I have to relearn all over again. Sometimes, dreaming has to be in a group. Sometimes you're alone in your head and you reach the limits of your imagination. How about dreaming together?

MB: I'm thinking about that language of land acknowledgements and saying the traditional stewards of the land as opposed to using that language of this land belongs to. Because that's the other thing about white supremacy and capitalism—it'll have you replicating that same problematic structure. The point wasn't that this was their land, the point is that they had a different relationship to the land. And that has me thinking about Eunsong's question about property. What does it mean to try to imagine what a collective cooperative housing situation can be, where we're not having to participate in the thing that we're trying to undo? Because the other reality too is that it's Black women who are getting evicted at a rate that is unparalleled. Renting can be so dangerous, but at the same time, owning property puts you back into this system and also makes you beholden to the law in a different way.

I'm still thinking about how Eunsong and I want to commit crimes. There's some potential for criminality in renting that feels less possible when you own a house. The deeper you get embedded into the system, the more likely you are to defend it. I just feel there's so much possibility when we work together.

SP: There's a writer that I really adored, Meena Alexander, who wrote poetry about her immigration journey from India to Africa to the US. She was teaching in New York City, where she put together a panel with Kamala Das, Claribel Alegria, and Audre Lorde. That sounds really amazing to many of us now, but they never put it on the program. So, Meena, who has now passed away, was talking about the ways in which when one attempts to do this solidarity work across color lines, it gets rendered invisible. I had always glorified that gathering. I had no idea that the panel was just left off the program. They had to share it through pamphlets. Our solidarity work needs to happen, and it needs to be rendered visible.

DF: When we have better control of the narrative, we can make that happen. I think that's really interesting and amazing to even think about the fact that Audre was involved with that. That was very close to the time when she was dying.

EK: I think that the question of solidarity and the question of friction sit together. Oftentimes I feel there's a liberal move with solidarity, where you're with each other so that you gain something, because there's some upward mobility, rather than you're with each other because you care about each other. Maybe a different word needs to be there, because it's not necessarily about this kind of consumptive understanding of gain. If you're really with each other, then I think that the difficult conversations are going to happen. I sent this to Moya the other day, but the last thing I'll share is a page from one of Pat Parker's poetry journals.

She writes, "I'll march for abortion rights and take back the night. I'll protest at any hour for Black, brown, yellow, and red power. I'll struggle to be free, but I want to see you standing right next to me. So please don't call me sister unless you mean it."

31.

What Ethical Non-monogamy, Queer Platonic Intimacy, and Parenthood Taught Us About Community and the Movement

Jamy Drapeza and Shaé Smith

Queer as not about who you're having sex with, that can be a dimension of it, but queer as being about the self that is at odds with everything around it and has to invent and create and find a place to speak and to thrive and to live.

—bell hooks

Defining Terms

ethical non-monogamy (ENM)—In which a person gives and receives romantic and/or sexual intimacy with a commitment to ethical conduct at all times. ENM does not lean on assumptions, instead operating on a craving for communication, transparency, and radical honesty for mutual pleasure. Discipline, attention to detail, and maintenance are all rooted in care and consent.

queer platonic intimacy (QPI)—Actively resisting the Western societal notion that soft, poetic, abundant, and unabashed expressions of love are ones to be reserved exclusively for romantic exploration and partnership. QPI affirms and holds space for what oneself as well as what members of one's chosen family may need to feel affirmed, held, and cared for. It assesses one's own capacity and creates realities where one can flow, move, and shift with their (platonic) loves again and again until things feel most aligned.

Shaé Smith (SS): At last summer's peak, I thought often about the ways in which life's ebbs, flows, and energy of transition would impact my relationship to queerness and queer kin. At this time, I was nine months pregnant, melting into the sand, the salty ocean currents. Prior to this point in my journey, I spoke with intention and shared my plan for bringing new life into the world with members of my chosen family. Immediately, they shared the ways they'd hoped to hold us: teachings and wisdom they wished to impart—new iterations of love for us and baby. Days after, my partner and I would join community space in honor of Pride. Organizers would ask us what we would need in order to feel safe. Partygoers would share soft sentiments. Ask permission to freeze this moment in time. New friends would offer care directly following.

Jamy Drapeza (JD): ethical non-monogamy—I give and receive romantic intimacy with a responsibility to honor boundaries and limits of all and myself, navigating and agreeing on expectations together. I build and sustain relationships with full awareness of each other's capacity and needs, nurturing and understanding as needed to tend to our connection.

queer platonic intimacy—We are so deeply rooted to each other and this relationship, yet any romantic, sensual, or erotic energy is barely there, if not absent entirely. Our capacity for closeness is informed by our queerness, and it is safe to be here.

Let me disclaim, I was not a great organizer and have certainly fumbled with many mistakes and insecurities of being a baby queer, unprincipled activist, and newly non-monogamous person—even with my professional training as a licensed therapist. And also, finding grace and the option of radical acceptance to access when I'm ready has been such a transformative form of love and justice to hold on to.

I was drawn to activism as a way to explore my roots as a Filipino American and the issues that defined the country my parents left behind with equal parts sadness and relief.

In my brief time with a mass organizing group, I witness the political become personal in the collective care aspect of the work. Exploring the practice of "criticism, self-criticism" based on Mao Zedong's Five Golden Rays, this experience of laying my face bare to others and receiving that same naked vulnerability was the type of intimacy previously accessed by lovers and confidants after time and effort. (See exercise 1.) Instead, that level of closeness was part of the package deal in comrade spaces.

What I've come to understand is the interconnectedness of movement work and healing work. Movement work is like healing work in that the goal is to make our roles obsolete. Our calling is to build a society in which values of collective care, healing, and anti-oppression are normative, ordinary, sacred, and systemic. In building political awareness to advance movement work, the personal must also follow. Societies are built on relationships and perspectives before they are built on policies and laws. Ethical non-monogamy and queer platonic intimacy celebrate a principled practice of love, acceptance, and closeness via platonic, romantic, erotic, and communal relationships.

Like ethical non-monogamy, there is a leap of giddiness, fear, and awe when consciously practicing mutually assumed vulnerability with someone attracted to the same values and actions as you. There's something about being so visible in a lifestyle, a set of principles, a creed that is radical by existence in comparison with the capitalist, monogamous, cis, and hetero norms of how we're *supposed to* relate to others and accomplish pleasure.

SS: So much of what many of us have come to understand surrounding kinship (i.e., bonds created, maintained, and nurtured between given and chosen family, as well as intimate/platonic love) and the literal building of (intergenerational) community has been revealed through a cis- heteronormative lens. As queer and trans folks looking to form deep, intentional connectedness through the intersections of Blackness, Asian-ness, and, for a portion of us, immigrant and first-generation statuses, it is imperative that we unearth, unlearn, and ultimately transform the ways in which we have been taught to *be* in community with one another. This will aid in our ability to achieve *liberatory love,* or a love in which we are able to honor, nurture, protect, and care for one another. (See exercise 2.)

I found it strange, the stark comparison between the culture of celebration and coming together between those I had grown up with—sisters and cousins who looked like me yet felt distant in most other ways—and that of my chosen family, nurturing the identities at the intersections of Blackness, Brownness, queerness, transness. Among the sisters and cousins, specific life moments and milestones called for expressive, grandiose outpourings of love and communal intimacy. When they wed their monogamous partners, folks witnessed and basked in their love. They shared tender sentiments and set intentions for the couple as they transitioned into a new unfolding of their journeys. When they became pregnant, folks showed up differently: softer, more lovingly, more generously. With wisdom, with stories, with food, bearing gifts. Outside of the moments, lengthy conversations, life check-ins, and flowers *just because* were few and far between.

I learned quickly how easy it is for these ideals to seep into the ways we show up in organizing with one another. While folks welcomed the possibility for newness in our vision and approach to intergenerational movement building and radical healing, there was a premature mourning of the dynamics and expectations we'd grown to know. We took time to explore what showing up in new capacities could look like as I entered this space of parenthood and care work. Similar to conversations that may take place in ethical non-monogamous and queer platonic relationships, I learned that when new community members enter into an existing and established dynamic, managing and renegotiating expectations is imperative.

" . . . ethical non-monogamy as not about. . ."	**". . . that can be a dimension of it, but ethical non-monogamy as in. . ."**
falling in love	**rising in the ways that decolonial love can take form**
freedom	
accessibility	*holding space for the multiplicities of ourselves, partners, metamours (partners of partners), as we undergo cycles of death + rebirth*
safety	
feelings of joy + feelings of grief, simultaneously	acknowledging dynamics of power, shared + individual traumas; accountability; comradeship
	inner-child nurturing

When we allow space to dream, harvest, and manifest, we imagine queer platonic intimacy as...

deepening our understanding to relationship needs + boundaries

creating room for "friend dates," cuddles, soft expressions of love, affirmation, adoration...

<u>challenging hierarchies between platonic + romantic intimacies</u>

communicating comfort zones as we move through seasons of transition + personal growth

healthy relationship endings

In community, many meaningful queer platonic moments began on dating apps and cruising pages; through six-hour friend dates in Prospect Park; sharing injera at a place we once frequented with lovers past; cuddled up on couches, tending to all of the post-Pride-month feels; through artistry; mutual aid; mutual mess; the necessary discomfort of accountability processes. As we move through changing life tides, we have the ability to revisit (over and over again) and redefine (over and over again) what kinship could look and feel like in the midst of collective pain, trauma, and unknowing. In the midst of deep vulnerability, belly laughs, joy, and fullness. As we explore different iterations of ourselves and chosen family, we learn what it means to love and care for one another within and between functions, kickbacks, circles, virtual spaces, and ones IRL.

What we learn as queer folks, as trans folks, as Black folks, as Brown folks, and as children of immigrants is that we can create capacity for love beyond and outside of monogamous partnership. For us, *survival* looks like and depends on our ability to create tenderness and care out of the mundane. A "text me when you get home" follow-through from your chosen kin is reason to rejoice because, for many of us, a moment closer to elderhood feels sweet, fleeting, unpromised.

"We must never throw anyone away."

—Cynthia Brown

References, Resources, and Tools for Liberation

1 ***Exercise: Criticism, Self-Criticism***

Goal: To practice listening, receiving, and being perceived in a principled, transparent structure that encourages closeness and action.

1. Set a nice environment: comfy places to sit, access to water, a good time of day where everyone is in a generally positive, if not receiving, mood. Share what you hope to get out of this exercise, and make agreements on how to respect yourself and others in the space. Decide whether all attendees can afford to make time after the listening phase to stay and discuss feelings and next steps further, or if that needs to be another meeting. Agree on how to take breaks and how you want to leave the space after the exercise.
2. Set aside about 15 minutes per person joining the exercise
3. There are four active roles, three of which need to be held by one person if this is a pair exercise
   a. Speaker—The person sharing their self-criticisms during this round
   b. Timekeeper—If not a timepiece shared between two people, a third person
   c. Note Taker—Someone documenting what is shared during the round
   d. Listener—Everyone that is not the Speaker is invited to actively listen
4. **Round 1**: Speaker shares their self-criticisms—strengths and challenges—for 5 minutes
5. **Round 2**: If a paired activity, partner gets 5 minutes to respond to what the Speaker shared. If 3+ people are involved, gauge about 1–2 minutes per person.
6. **Round 3**: Speaker gets 5 minutes to reflect on their Listeners' responses

7. Repeat rounds 1–3 for each person present, the Timekeeper and Note Taker role will need to change when it's that person's turn to be Speaker.

2 *Liberatory Love—Finding Your Enthusiastic Yes*

Boundaries are the distance at which I can love me and you simultaneously.

—Prentiss Hemphill

Exercise: I can see the future, and it looks like you and I . . .

Goal: Invite your heart, mind, body, and soul to play in this potential future so you can set clearer intentions and desires at present

1. Your phone buzzes, and you know it's them. A smile spreads across your face before you even open the message. What is this person sending you to make you feel so giddy?
2. It's a cozy morning, before you open your eyes, you feel the warmth of their body near yours. How does it feel to wake up next to them?
3. It was a bad day, you're sad/upset/angry and don't know what you want or need next to feel better. This is the first person you want to hear from. What do they do for you that's so important?
4. It happened. An old emotional trigger flared up, and they're seeing it on you for the first time. How is their reaction different? How are you different?
5. You just met someone through a safe space/group and feel connected to them. Knowing that they have comrade energy and will be safe to say anything to, what do you say next to shoot your shot?
6. You have to share space with someone you broke ties with. What do you need to be in loving community while also protecting your own peace and sense of self?

Guidance from Us, the Therapists

- Look to commit to the person, not the idea of the person.
- Chemistry doesn't mean you're on the same page.

- Make an emotional safety plan with 1–2 people you trust to "pull you back" and ground you.
- How do you balance openness and vulnerability, while still remaining aware of red flags?
- Differentiate when you are operating from a place of self-preservation and care versus from a place of trauma.
- Recognize who has shown up for you and has shown love for you; take the time to express gratitude and care back.

3 *Movement Work—Resentment, Burnout, and Tenderness*

> *When we sacrifice taking the time necessary to exercise wisdom, intuition, spirituality, and embodiment, we reinforce power hierarchies and reward systems that prioritize expediency and highly visible results instead of what is good for the whole.*
>
> —Tema Okun

Overheard in queer and movement spaces:

"We are comrades in the struggle, we share social political views; what do you mean I can't take more of your time outside committee meetings?"

Spaces like these simultaneously serve as places to belong, places to be seen, places where voices and lived experiences are synonymous to advancing the cause. What then when relationships break down, tensions arise, when people are tired and cannot pour into those around them on a given day? Keeping in mind that perfectionism is a white supremacy cultural tool; healing invokes the opposite.

Survival can look like the passage above, but can also look like inviting interaction, communication, and radical tenderness, rather than perpetuating internalized capitalist values such as "what can you give me" or "if you do not contribute in how I want you to, you are not valuable." To meet people where they are at, we must also exercise reaching out for care and normalizing statements such as:

- "I don't have it today."
- "I need . . ."
- "This is all I have to give right now, and no more."

When Carol Hanisch popularized the phrase "the personal is political," she recalls how her group responds to political issues with personal anecdotes of their lived experiences to find "collective action for a collective solution." She also calls into question the importance of analysis, of asking "why the action is necessary" when considering why people don't join their cause. To combat the internalized imperialism of "you have to think like us and live like us," this is where personhood and relationships are more vital than ever. When we make room for messiness and discomfort and for adjusting the boundaries and expectations in each relationship we hold, we dismantle the binaries of what is "in" and "out" into "what is possible," "what is needed," and "what can we achieve together?"

32.

From the Other Coast, with Love

Zuri Gordon and Cecile A

Z

Under an autumn
chill around four, we were born,
doctors said it's a —

poem! We will be a problem,
us, both nonwhite and women,[1]

spinning gold out of
words, tearing oneself in two,
pretend to daughter.

You were given family.
Girls like us, we get to choose.

—

C

Sifting through static
of life during the latest
apocalypse, my

earthquake kit mocks me. What use
are beans and flashlights? In case

of emergency,
call my best friend. She's lighthouse
and life raft, spinning

hope out of despair. Girls like
us, we'll survive together.

—

Z

I can't complain but
I'm going to. When the coast
clears, you're invited

to my vision, the home I've
been building. We always start

from scratch, carry our
own water. If I don't build
it, I can't live there.

I want to be sustained by
a world that we create.

—

C

We *chop wood, carry*
water.[2] The translation in
my bloodstream is a

directive, but I return
to the root: action without

doer simply is
not done. The future belongs
to us, we're making

it in our image, all those
that history left behind.

—

Z

Coming from a line
of women who look like me
and men who left sun

for snow, I am familiar
with want. I tanned in the heat

til my skin was warm
and black like the earth's inside.[3]
Now I'm looking to

light this expiring candle.
Before it burns out, or in.

—

C

Grief into ash, dust
to dust. Is that how it goes?
I was never taught.

But there's mountain provinces
all round the world, all rock and

pine and fire. I'm at
home anywhere above tree-
line, surrounded by

the horizon. A temple
built for the world, and of it.

—

Z

On the other side,
I check the time. It's mourning,
and I wish I could

reach across the grief to you.
Years ago, we were neighbors

crying on campus.
In our room starting trouble.
And what do I know

of home? If I'm looking for
safety I know it will be

—

C

everywhere, for all
of us. You and I, the ones
that we love, and the

ones that they love, all gathered
under a very blue sky

near to flowering
trees.[4] Turning grief into green,
the earth loves us back.

She'll always give us joy and
roses, wherever we are.

—

Z

I didn't know I
could keep anything alive
after the jade died

under my care, in my room.
In another country you

are tending to your
garden. I am filling my
glass with water, too.

Every day we do the work
and then reap what we have grown.

—

C

In every day
is the possibility
for a small, quiet

revolution. We save seeds
to cultivate an Eden:

No cops, no borders,
no conquests. No distractions.
The sun rises and

our future exhales, peaceful
in the tender morning light.

PART 5

Our Joy

Centering Pleasure, Care, and Love in the Movement

Finding solidarity and survival within a transnational, intergenerational Zoom dance party. Art by Angel Trazo.

33.

The Breadfruit Does Not Float Far from the Tree

Rosa Bordallo

On a late winter day, I was with my friend Joanie in my kitchen about to deep fry a sticky dough that I had blended with my hands. The scent and sound of batter sizzling in oil sends me right back to childhood. It's the sweet anticipation of a warm and loving embrace on my taste buds. That day our experiment was a success. For the first time since leaving my homeland in the Mariana Islands, I successfully made breadfruit doughnuts, known in my native language as *buñelos lemmai*.

As a CHamoru child, I knew breadfruit (*lemmai*) intimately.[1] It wasn't sold in the store. We had to import milk and meat and cereal and apples and broccoli, and pretty much everything else we ate. But a few foods came from our land and waters, and it connected us to our ancestors and everything they went through in the past centuries of colonization. Of course I didn't think about it in these terms as a kid. But I knew of breadfruit as being a local thing, a family thing, a CHamoru thing—it was *ours*. As a colonized person, this is no small thing.

Being CHamoru means being native to the Mariana Islands, an archipelago in the Pacific region known geographically as Micronesia. The largest and most populated island is Guam (Guåhan), and that's where I was born and raised before I moved to New York City for college. Two decades have passed and yet that moment of my leaving still feels raw. Nearly a third of the island is still under military occupation. The cost of living is high, and good jobs are scarce. I didn't feel like I had a choice, but I also feel guilty for having *made* that choice.

My ancestral history goes back four thousand years and is literally carved into stone. The megalithic *latte* stones throughout our islands are reminders of a society that thrived long before Magellan's arrival—and his men's raping and pillaging—in 1521. The latte stone's iconic shape of capstone and pillar has come to signify cultural pride among CHamoru people, both at home and throughout the diaspora in the "mainland" United States. Being CHamoru is complicated. We don't even agree on a spelling. For many, we are "Chamorro." For others, like myself, who reclaim a distinctly non-Western identity, we are "CHamoru."

But back to breadfruit. We had a grove of *trunkon lemmai* on our land, and any year it evaded a destructive typhoon season long enough to bear fruit, we felt lucky. One of my earliest memories is the scent of it ripening in a big bowl in my family's kitchen. My *mom's* kitchen, really. She was a busy woman. She raised four kids while helping my father run his business. And like my father, she was woven into the grassroots politics of our island, often volunteering for various campaigns and fundraisers. But she showed her deepest passion through her recipes, and cooking was her favorite way to unwind. Like many moms across America, she owned a tattered copy of that *Better Homes and Gardens* cookbook. The one with the gingham cover. She was just as comfortable cooking mainstream recipes as she was making something local and traditional. Come Christmastime, it was my mother who grated our native yam into a wet batter so that it could be deep fried into *buñelos dågu* and served at the family holiday party. The crispy ball of fried soft dough was served with a side of pancake syrup. I have a photo of her handling the dough, with toddler-size me standing beside her. She looks unamused and a bit bored, like she could do this in her sleep. But have you tried to grate a raw yam? It's a workout! And it can make your hands itchy, if you're sensitive.

Back to breadfruit—for real this time!

The *lemmai* that I remember from childhood was a seedless variety endemic to the Marianas. The scent of it ripening would fill the front half of our house, where the kitchen, living room, and dining area were laid out in one large room. Other than my mom's doughnuts, my favorite way to eat breadfruit was as *gollai åppan lemmai*, a common side dish at village fiestas. It's simply breadfruit simmered in fresh coconut milk long enough for a thick layer of coconut cream to coat the breadfruit. The starchy breadfruit morphs into warm, gooey, coconut-y sweetness.

After the breadfruit was harvested, my mom would let it overripen close to the point of it being just shy of rotten. But this was key to making a doughnut that was sweet enough. There was no added sugar and barely any wheat flour in her recipe. The batter was thick and tacky to the touch, and she would shape it into rings and deep-fry them in a stockpot.

Her doughnuts were so enjoyable that it became a signature dish for the restaurant she built, owned, and operated on our land for over a decade, starting in the early 2000s. The restaurant was called the Lemai Cafe after the family breadfruit grove right beside it. The trees still stand today, though the restaurant has since shuttered.

These are the memories that inspired me to make my own breadfruit doughnuts in 2022, for the first time, as a middle-aged adult and assimilated Amerikånu. My mom and most of my family still lived on Guam, so I was lucky that I could call her and ask for tips. But it seems to be a rule among busy mothers and grandmothers not to do the sensible thing of writing recipes down. So my mother would tell me in her off-handed way that you just put this and that together. A handful of flour, maybe a teaspoon (or three) of baking powder? In short, I was on my own.

Except that's not true at all. I had Joanie! There in my kitchen was a CHamoru woman the same age as me. We had met the summer before, and we had both studied, lived, and worked in New York City for most of our adult lives. Our main difference was that Joanie grew up in Virginia and Texas, the daughter of a CHamoru man who had left the island when he enlisted in the armed forces. Her CHamoru grandmother and aunts eventually followed, and they loomed large in her upbringing, for they ruled the roost with a specific brand of totalitarianism most CHamoru kids recognize. The traditions of our matrilineal society survived centuries of Western colonization—they could certainly survive a generational uprooting across the ocean.

For many CHamoru people, the military presents a path to success, promising a stable career and a middle-class life. In other words, a path to being "American." For Joanie, a military brat raised by a CHamoru matriarch, cooking CHamoru food came fraught with a sense of obedience. She was making good progress learning traditional recipes, but she was sometimes afraid to share them at the big family gatherings and risk facing her aunts' scrutiny and criticism.

My friendship with Joanie was fortunate because we both felt like the black sheep of our respective CHamoru families. I had created a far-flung life. I chose to raise my son as a single mom in the big city, rather than stay back home—a place I found challenging, so much so that all I ever wanted as a kid was to escape. But it would have been arguably easier for me to raise a child there. People say, "It takes a village . . ." and as a CHamoru from Guam, I know exactly *which* village.

For Joanie, being the black sheep meant that she did not share the political views of her conservative family members. Like me, she also did not support the American military occupation of Guåhan. We supported decolonization, self-determination, and the sovereignty of the CHamoru people. To say these things aloud was to invite the disdain of both natives and nonnatives, for there is a prevailing attitude in the Marianas that America is a boon to our islands. That we should be so lucky, basically. But Joanie was insistent and knew in her heart how to heal the intergenerational trauma that befell us. She was part of an online community of diasporic CHamorus who were helping each other learn our native language, our suppressed history, and the political challenges that plague our homelands today. Like the weaving of a *talåya* fishing net, we were strengthening the bonds of our splintered identity and community.

The reason I have to bring Joanie into the picture is because I have her to thank for finally making my breadfruit doughnuts. We had already planned to have Sunday brunch at my apartment when I mentioned I was going to Chinatown, and did she want me to look out for anything? And she said she was craving breadfruit. In all my years of living in New York City, I still had never found breadfruit in a grocery store. It's not jackfruit, and it's not durian. I had gone to great lengths to find this fruit. Once I felt so lucky because I found a Caribbean grocery store that accepted online orders. But both times I tried, the order was canceled due to it being out of stock. I even sent emails to organizations and companies, hoping someone could give me a good lead. One such lead was fruitful: it provided the name and phone number of a breadfruit wholesaler in the Bronx. But his business hours were exclusively at night. Traveling to the Bronx from Sheepshead Bay at night had proven unsurmountable.

When Joanie asked, I figured I should just search Google Maps for Caribbean grocery stores and start calling people up. Lo and behold, the second market I called had fresh breadfruit in stock! Not only did they have fresh breadfruit, but they also had it frozen, and roasted, and ground up as a flour. . . . I was beside myself.

I looked up the address to this grocery store. No way. It was right next door to my new job. I started working at a boutique wine and liquor store in a Brooklyn neighborhood known as Little Caribbean, and I was still getting acclimated to the area. But I have since been eating my way through its incredible array of lunch food options, while picking up history lessons in the process. As it turns out, breadfruit was brought from Polynesia to the Caribbean by English colonizers as a way to cheaply feed the people they had enslaved to work the plantations.[2] It's a staple in many Caribbean and Central American cuisines.

Here I was, a conflicted CHamoru, struggling to feel connected to home after years of assimilation as part of an exodus that brought many Pacific Islanders to the contingent United States. I cannot discount the privilege that has enabled me to move and reside for years in New York. Being a citizen and having a US passport is just one way my path was clear of obstacles. But the longing (*mahålang*) for home never ends, and breadfruit had become my consolation prize.

What I did not foresee was that breadfruit had also gone through a transoceanic migration at the hands of imperial forces. For years I was just trying to keep my head above water. I did not see the benevolent tide had carried me to safety among my community. The breadfruit tree now has roots in the so-called Americas that are deep and long-lasting. With a history that speaks to pain and suffering as equally as it speaks to resilience and liberation, it's a reminder that within one's heavy heart, a new joy can be cultivated.

34.

Finding Solidarity and Survival Within a Transnational, Intergenerational Zoom Dance Party

TD Tso

As feminists of color, we often find ourselves united by our pain, our struggles, and the perpetual violence we suffer at the hands of white supremacy, colonialism, and sexism. This sentiment has certainly rung true following the Atlanta spa shootings, which claimed the lives of eight people, including six Asian women. It remains true in the aftermath of the mass shooting at a FedEx facility in Indianapolis, where eight were killed, including four Sikh community members.[1] Tragedy has long united us, igniting intraracial and cross-racial alliances in the face of violence enacted against us by racist and patriarchal individuals and a white supremacist state.

Pain as a uniting force can be useful. It has the power to bring people into the struggle. When we are able to name the harms against us, we can then band together to protect ourselves against them. Our disappointment, grief, and righteous anger drives us to fight back and to imagine a better world in which we can thrive. But more and more I've found myself curious about the opposite: How can we unite based on our shared love, joy, and humanity?

This is the code I've been trying to crack throughout this pandemic, during a time period that has been defined by violence and negligence so ubiquitous I won't even name it all. It's been particularly difficult to see beauty, spark joy, and feel loved in this atmosphere of anxiety, cruelty, and death. But I had to try because, ultimately, I am committed to my own survival. I was grateful when I began to find the answers within an intergenerational, transnational virtual dance party on Zoom hosted by feminist scholar and activist Dr. Margo Okazawa-Rey, aka DJ MOR Love and Joy, who has also contributed generously to this project of ours.[2]

> *I learned a lot about the importance of connecting through joy. Of course, what we share in this space often is not only joy—so many horrible things happened in this last year—but we kept dancing together, checking in with each other, trying to be there for each other, and smiling at each other. Seeing the joy in people's faces (especially in BIPoC) gives me life.*
>
> —Sushi, 45, Vienna, Austria

The ongoing dance party, which in its short history has been titled "TRANSNATIONAL Feminist Dance Party for Life and Love" or "Listen and Dance Party for HOPE, Life and Love," began in April 2020, soon after the country went into lockdown. However, I didn't find my way to the space until late November 2020, following an invitation from Dr. Okazawa-Rey during an Asia Society book club.[3] Ever since, it's become part of my weekly routine to log in on Thursday afternoons, dance around alone in my apartment, and connect with warmhearted strangers (now friends) from across the globe.

I sought the space out during a particularly depressed and despondent period in my life. I was intentionally trying to bolster my energy and open my heart when I found myself gravitating toward Dr. Okazawa-Rey's spirit and her messages on embracing love and joy. While I've been unemployed and perpetually self-quarantining, oftentimes the dance parties are the first or only time during the day (or week) where I move my body freely, shaking it out of its usual slouched, slumped, and supine state. By being present enough in my body to dance for that one hour, I'm gently reminded of my own humanity—I am a person in a body that moves in these different ways. And watching windows of other people across continents, ages, and body types do the same thing reminds me of our collective humanity.

The parties are fairly simple: DJ MOR Love and Joy shares her audio and plays an hour of music from an international playlist with songs like "Djadja" by French Malian artist Aya Nakamura; "I Will Survive" by Gloria Gaynor; "Enjoy Enjaami" by Tamil artists Dhee, Arivu, and Santhosh Narayanan; and other songs submitted by attendees. She sends the emails out in English, Spanish, and Arabic. The invite list has been built through her personal connections, though she has seeded out invitations in various virtual learning spaces she's taken part in. Folks from across the United States, South Africa, Palestine, Austria, Switzerland, and more join in every week—each one responding to an invitation from Dr. Okazawa-Rey.

> *It's been a reminder of the importance of radical love, which DJ MOR just embodies and evokes. We absorb so much cynicism and fear, the release is necessary. Almost like a detox.*
>
> —Saaret, 35, Washington, DC, USA

"I just invite people when I feel like there's a good vibe," she tells me. "That's how other people have come in, basically really through word of mouth."

The party initially began as a two-person dance party. Dr. Okazawa-Rey used to take walks with her friend Dr. Paola Bacchetta in Berkeley. But when COVID-19 hit, they started talking on the phone instead. Chatting on the phone turned into sharing music back and forth, which became the two of them dancing together virtually. Then they decided to invite their friends from across different time zones, which is how the party ended up happening in the morning for West Coasters. A core group of around twelve usually show up, with people coming and going as they please. "The boundaries are really loose: you can come any time; come as you are; you don't have to turn on your camera," Dr. Okazawa-Rey says. "It feels like a safe space. Nobody's performing anything; nobody has to prove anything. It's relaxation, and it's fun. And that's what I want."

"In academic settings, all we do is talk, talk, talk. But with dancing, there's no talk, there's no language barrier," she says. But DJ MOR Love and Joy didn't always embrace her inner dancing queen, and it's only been within the last four years that she's felt herself reconnecting with joy and love—often through the language of music and dancing. She recalls a time period in 2018 when her friend Miye, a student at Pitzer College, turned her on to Shakira and Spotify and reignited her love of music and dance. That year, she began to be known as the dancing professor or the "ethnic studies dancing queen" at Mills College, because she always insisted on playing music in classes and in the plaza. "This is who I've come back to," she tells me, sharing a photo of herself as an eight year old with a giant grin on her face. "After an elliptical journey of going far from it and coming back to it, this has been my character, who I am, from very early on."

A reconnection with our inner children, that's what we're all looking for when we nurture ourselves, when we try to heal from a lifetime of wounds. Within that reconnection, we can embrace laughter, joy, self-care, love, creativity, and imagination more readily. Through dancing and the connection I felt with all these new faces, I recognize the importance of physical movement and togetherness in our movement work, especially in a time of deep isolation, disconnection, and dehumanization. This is why protests, collective meetings, and talk circles are all such powerful spaces to be in, because of that sense of being physically united by the same cause. So when we come together with a commitment to fostering more love and joy, we open up a world of infinite possibilities and a world of beauty. The parties have reminded me that the work isn't just about dismantling harmful institutions and systems; it's also about loving and supporting one another so that we can all make it through to the other side of liberation. I no longer self-censor my tenderness, sentimentality, or vulnerability.

Yes, "the dancing is dancing," Dr. Okazawa-Rey says, "and it's also rooted in a serious commitment to deepening relationships with other people across time and space." Reorienting her focus on love has been "about becoming more human," she tells me. "It's been an antidote to countering all the dehumanization that happens all around us."

As a group, we've celebrated eightieth birthdays, sent condolences to members who've lost loved ones, and mourned global tragedies such as the Atlanta mass shooting, the military coup in Myanmar, and all the COVID-19 losses.[4] After Derek Chauvin's murder conviction, we listened to protest anthems, including Mavis Staples's "We Shall Not Be Moved" and Edwin Starr's "War."[5] For Lunar New Year, we danced to songs from Asia, including the Chinese New Year anthem "Gong Xi Gong Xi."

> *It's really special to have this space where you can just show up as is, and cultivate joy. Especially during the past few months when my home country [Myanmar] has been under political terror, the virtual space has allowed me to find community, solace, and healing. Just to be present in the space and knowing that this community is also present brings a sort of comfort to me.*
>
> —Edna, 26, Los Angeles, California, USA

The Thursday following the mass shooting at Asian spas in Atlanta, I found myself logging into the weekly dance party out of habit. Halfway through the playlist, DJ MOR Love and Joy played "I'm Alive" by Celine Dion. The song, a celebration of being alive by the grace of someone else's love, hit me hard. The lyrics "When you bless the day / I just drift away / All my worries die / I'm glad that I'm alive" brought me to tears, even as I swayed my body along to the music. It reminded me that my own survival is rooted in love—in my openness to receiving love and my desire to share love with others.

Writing this, I'm reminded of this sentence from the Combahee River Collective statement: "Our politics evolve from a healthy love for ourselves, our sisters and our community which allows us to continue our struggle and work."[6] This quote from 1977 still rings true because our work as feminist organizers and activists is deeply rooted in love and care for ourselves, our people, and the earth. This is how movements survive.

> *The space has taught me that limitations and boundaries have no place in my feminism, and I can reach out not only for the struggles we wage but for the enrichment and loving that sisters share. It's wonderful to come together as we are, when we are with no pressure to deliver or "change the world," as we do it in our own way, time, and methods.*
>
> —Thoko Matshe, 65, Johannesburg, South Africa

"I think more than ever, we have to infuse everything we do with love," Dr. Okazawa-Rey tells me. "And love in the big sense—a commitment to being alive, a commitment to justice, looking out for other people, recognition that we're all interconnected and interdependent. It's urgent." It is urgent. This is why, as a practice in sharing and spreading love, I want to gift everyone with a Black and Asian Feminist Solidarity playlist made in collaboration with DJ MOR Love and Joy, as well as a DIY guide to starting your own feminist dance parties on Zoom.[7] Please help spread love and joy.

Do It Yourself: Feminist Zoom Dance Parties

1. Create an email list of friends, family, colleagues, and co-conspirators you'd like to invite. Make sure your invite list reflects the safe space you'd like to create.
2. Establish a day of the week and a time that potentially works for all invitees' time zones and schedules.

3. Begin making a playlist on Spotify, Apple Music, iTunes, or music player of your choice. This playlist may be selected by you or created collaboratively with friends. Feel free to use my Black and Asian Feminist Solidarity playlist on Spotify as a starter!
4. Using a Zoom Pro account (or another video call platform), schedule a recurring meeting for the established time and copy the meeting link.
5. Send out this meeting invitation by email or a Google Calendar invitation. Allow people to come as they are; keep the boundaries loose and pressure-free. (Note: If your invite list is large and not everyone knows each other, it may be best to send out weekly emails with all invitees BCC'd.)
6. When the party starts and attendees join, share your audio. (On Zoom: utilize the "Share Screen" function on the bottom of the window, toggle over to "Advanced" settings at the top of the pop up, and select "Music or Computer Sound Only" to begin sharing your device's audio.)
7. Start the music and start dancing (or just listening—no pressure or requirement to move)!

35.

A Black Feminist Perspective on the Politics of Care

Monaye Johnson

Black women are socialized to assume the role of omnipotent caregiver. . . . Our passive acceptance of this role is a critical barrier to our self-recovery.
—bell hooks, *Sisters of the Yam*

I am no stranger to pain.
I am no stranger to care or caretaking.
And I am no stranger to love either.

In my life, those were the three ingredients most familiar to me. Growing up as the eldest daughter, the question of "care" has always been important to me. Many girls and people socialized as girls are inundated daily with messages about serving others as early as they can remember. More specifically, they are socialized into ignoring their desires, needs, and wants for the family's sake, upward mobility, love, and more. It is critical to note that modes of violence also maintain this forgoing of the self.

When I use the word "love," I do not mean agape or any Christian-based idea pushing us to love our enemies. I mean a love and care ethic rooted in Black feminist principles—it acknowledges that the world is awful and wants you to hate yourself and Blackness. Still, you instead practice refusal of patriarchy, capitalism, and white supremacy.

One of my favorite definitions of love is from the poem Resolution #1,003 by June Jordan:

I will love who loves me
I will love as much as I am loved
I will hate who hates me
I will feel nothing for everyone oblivious to me
I will stay indifferent to indifference
I will live hostile to hostility
I will make myself a passionate and eager lover
in response to passionate and eager love

I will be nobody's fool.

I ground my work in this poem because it speaks to a care ethic and love practice that does not force people into denial about their experiences or the world. I am not pushing people to meet acts of violence with love. But, when you can become passionate and eager to love, do you have the skills to do so? Are you grounded in discernment and able to move beyond your pain enough to give and receive love when hostility, indifference, and hate are absent? And on the opposite end, can you retract your care and love when hostility, indifference, and contempt are present?

We must define care, love, and intimacy for ourselves outside of capitalist logic and abandon the grammar of patriarchy. I believe love requires care, but care does not require love. You can care for someone or be caring, but that does not mean you are loving. Like bell hooks, I view care and care ethics as something we do and show praxis. I am not invested in making people love each other. My care ethic says I do not need to love you, and I don't exactly need to know you. Still, I understand our fundamental interdependence, and I am clear about what the stakes against capitalism and patriarchy are.

Care, care work, care economy, and care ethics have long been theorized and researched. Care, in general, has been subject to feminist debate and critique on the individual, collective, and global scale. An ethic of care and love is embedded in Black feminist praxis and modes of relation. Black writers such as Toni Morrison, James Baldwin, Maya Angelou, and Lorraine Hansberry speak about a love and care ethic in their novels, poems, and interviews. The groundbreaking Combahee River Collective Statement named their politics "evolve from a healthy love for ourselves, our sisters and our community, which allows us to continue our struggle and work. We have arrived at the necessity for developing an understanding of class relationships that considers the specific class position of Black women who are generally marginal in the labor force."[1] Their statement highlights a theme of movement between the personal and the political. The personal is political, yes—but it also moves from the self to the community to an understanding of our class relationships or a relationship to systems of power. The movement can happen one by one, simultaneously, forward or backward. The point is that one's capacity to care deepens and expands.

Over the last few years, I have tracked themes of love and care in Black women's writings: how they receive, give, and retract it. In her essay, "Practicing Love: Black Feminism, Love-Politics, and Post-Intersectionality," Jennifer Nash noted, "Black feminism's plea for love as a significant call for ordering the self and transcending the self, a strategy for remaking the self and for moving beyond the limitations of selfhood."[2] We move beyond the limitations of selfhood and individualism when we evolve into radical politics and collectivist approaches. But, when Black feminism is simply an identity marker for someone or a lifestyle, they stay in the "reordering the self" stage, and very few people ever move beyond the limits of selfhood. I would argue that the majority of people never even make it to the reordering stage at all. "Self-care" has been co-opted into capitalist indulgence, liberalism, and offsetting of suffering onto more vulnerable power. When Audre Lorde was grappling with the idea of self-care, she was on her second battle with breast cancer. In *A Burst of Light,* Lorde writes,

> I had to examine, in my dreams as well as in my immune-function tests, the devastating effects of overextension. Overextending myself is not stretching myself. I had to accept how difficult it is to monitor the difference. Necessary for me as cutting down on sugar. Crucial. Physically. Psychically. Caring for myself is not self-indulgence, it is self-preservation, and that is an act of political warfare.[3]

Contending with the structures of power that force Black women into such physical, emotional, and psychological overextension, Lorde was writing at the intersection of disability, labor, interpersonal reflection, and systemic critique. But popular culture and liberal feminists have completely divorced much of this work from its context and left the "political warfare" out of their frameworks by design. Social media platforms and pop culture have oriented people around "luxury-based" approaches to self-care. Self-care has become outsourcing domestic labor and overall consumerism. The capitalist and self-aggrandizing marketplace of love and care are expansive, with new routines, books, products, and content entering our lives daily. There is a lack of consideration for our relationships with service providers, workers, and vulnerable communities, only coded language for neoliberal extraction and exploitation guised as self-help or self-care. However, this is not to say that Black women and gender-expansive people are not making genuine personal and material shifts toward caring for themselves and others.

What self-care and community care should look like has been under rigorous debate from disability, socialist, feminist, afro-pessimists, and abolitionist frameworks. One point of contention critical to my work on this topic recognizes how care ethics and efforts stabilize the state. Care work and a care ethic tend to place the burden of doing onto the same vulnerable groups of people. In "The Womb of Western Theory: Trauma, Time Theft, and the Captive Maternal," Joy James argued that "the captive maternal is one who is tied to the state's violence through the non-transferable agency they have to care for another."[4] A captive maternal is not an identity but a relation to the state and a function. The caretaking, self-sacrificing, and labor of Black women, mainly, is used to restabilize the state.[5] This leads me back to my question above: *What does it mean to retract care?*

This life-sustaining practice that everyone relies on for survival is also death work. I often think about the amount of famous Black women writers who died from (breast) cancer: Lorde, Toni Cade Bambara, Lucille Clifton, Pat Parker, Barbara Christian, Bebe Moore Campbell, and countless others. So many of these women speak to the same kind of "overextension" that Lorde faced in her final days. These overextensions are why I say every Black Death is premature: we are robbed of our health, wellness, agency, and sovereignty daily. We also have to contend with "non-care," a term Nash provided in *Birthing Black Mothers*.[6] Non-care refers to the obstetric violence Black women and birthing people experience. Non-care can also be applied to medical experiences more broadly. In the United States, Black women are three times more likely to die in childbirth than any other racial group of women.[7] The maternal mortality rates of other gender-marginalized people are ignored. Another critical point Nash makes is that white people predetermine the quality or type of care Black people receive. While central to a critique of the medical-industrial complex, one can also argue that forms of non-care permeate the lives of Black women, girls, and gender-expansive people.

How do we navigate a world and systems pricing us out of essential resources and promising ecological disaster, militarized police violence, chronic illnesses, and patriarchal violence? How do we resist becoming or being omnipotent caregivers while also understanding that care is still a generative power necessary for our survival?

I struggle to answer these questions across all the areas mentioned above. What I believe is that no one can opt out of care entirely. We must always understand our relationship to care because it relates to shifting power. Reordering the self gives us new grammar and language to govern our internal scripts and capture our evolving politics. We have to abandon market language such as "luxury apartments" and "luxury Black girls" and maintain a discourse of collectivist and materialist approaches. Rather than assign receiving care or practicing self-care as a "reward" that we have earned from overextension, we must hold that everyone should have access to care and resources.

On the other hand, we must practice refusal and refuse the role of an omnipotent caregiver. But, most importantly, we have to know when care is being used as a stand-in for violence or that care itself can be a form of violence. Black people have and can have their agency and lives taken from them in the name of being cared for.

On the individual and interpersonal level, I want Black women and gender-expansive people to undertake reordering themselves. I want them to sit and define and redefine love and care and ground themselves in the ideologies and frameworks they need to live out their lives. What definition and praxis will bring you closer to the community and allow you to move without feeling that everyone's survival is on your shoulders? How do you handle the stress and weight of having no one else to care for you? We must resist the people who make us invulnerable heroes, servants, and political saviors and deepen relationships with those who can hold us. The capacity to care and love is a skill we must build and learn daily. If you wake up one day and have no idea who you are outside of caring for everyone else, know you can always meet yourself again. And if you feel the sentiment of "If I don't do it, no one will," then it is time to assess the situation and find out where retraction is possible.

Nothing about this essay should be romanticized. Much of this work can create hostility, isolation, and violence in your life. And still refusing omnipotent caregiver status is a personal and political necessity. It is hard but a worthy task for us all.

36.

On Healing Through Nature, Kink, and Communion

A Conversation

Yin Q and J Wortham

Yin Q is a kink practitioner, writer, and community organizer with Kink Out and Red Canary Song. J Wortham is a sound healer, reiki practitioner, staff writer for the *New York Times Magazine*, and cohost of the podcast *Still Processing*. The pair met for the first time in 2018 at a book event at the Museum of Sex, developed a mutual admiration for each other's work, and arranged a coffee date shortly after. The relationship evolved into the two of them doing energy exchanges: rope bondage for reiki.

In September 2022, we gathered Wortham and Q virtually to talk about their relationship, their healing modalities, and safe spaces. The following conversation has been edited for clarity and flow.[1]

Healing Through Nature

J Wortham: I was trying to do some research to figure out how long we've known each other, but at least in the course of the last couple of years that I've known you, I feel like being in the country and being in nature, you have blossomed. You're in bloom because you're in the country, and I love hearing about it.

Yin Q: I don't know if I would have chosen this for myself. I really thought that I needed to stay in the city because of the work that I was doing, my communities. I really held off finding space outside of the city to call home base, but it was really a choice for my children. I think about self-care in ways of how I grew through being a dominatrix and sex work, and then having children, so many of the things that I chose—to be healthier, to take hiatuses from drinking—was really for my children. But it also was such a healing process to even have the baby inside of me, of understanding that *this is truly your inner child that you are healing.*

I see you just diving into all different kinds of wildness out there from all over the country, right?

JW: I never really imagined that being a writer could also allow spaciousness for creativity and a slower pace of life. I really only knew one way of writing as a younger reporter. I think the disruptions over the last couple of years have helped me really reconnect to an earliest version of myself that remembers running through fields and biking and falling off my bike and climbing trees and swimming in bodies of water in the world. Someone who follows more of a flow of the day, like, "What does today need to hold?" And finally being in a place in my career where I can arrange things that way. I actually never knew that I could get to a place where I could prioritize care and rest and still have an incredibly productive and fruitful career. I thought those two things were in competition with each other.

I think something that inspires me when I listen to your life transitions is how much you're able to fill up yourself so that you can give back, so you can pour into all these organizations and pour into all these things that you want to do.

YQ: I feel like with the work that we're doing in the world, sometimes it can feel so urgent. We're talking about this idea of anti-urgency. To be anticapitalist is to be anti-urgency. When you're actually in nature and planting a garden, it is such long work because it's learning about what the particular soil that you are actually living on is going to be fruitful with. You can't just expect things to be put into the earth and to produce. You really have to see: What are the animals going to eat? What is this particular sunshine going to bring? What is this moisture and the soil nutrients going to give to what you want to plant? You have to have that conversation with the land.

It's a much slower conversation than emails are and text messages and social media. The way that we think about organizing work is like, "We've got to get to every event. We've got to get to every rally. We've got to make sure we make these connections, get to the panel, get onto the Zoom." To be able to take that step back and say—calling upon a lot of organizers who have already said this—that we are not on their timeline. Our timeline is much broader. We are only going to see a section of the movements that we are planting, and we are still sowing and tilling from others. That's what the woods and the river have given me.

I feel like we should back up for a moment though just to talk about how long we have known each other. Through little seeds of conversations back and forth, from people in community and how we were introduced, and our story together, because it does tie in on all of these topics of healing and my kink and your healing practices as well, since we do exchange, which I think no one else really knows about.

Healing Through Kink

JW: No. It's the best kept secret. I mean, our community knows about it, but it is this really lovely thing.

YQ: I'd been listening to your podcast, and I think your podcast had gotten me through a hard winter, so it was really fantastic to meet for coffee. I think we were talking about kink and how to get into spaces of kink. I was hosting Kink Out events. I've always wanted to center BIPOC queers, and that was my community who I was centering for my smaller private gatherings.

JW: I remember, too, you were so kind because we had made an episode of the podcast about the disappearance of the Craigslist personal ads, and I didn't fully understand the implications of the FOSTA-SESTA laws and how much they would impact sex workers. You sent me such wonderful feedback and we incorporated it into the next episode, because it was really important to be really careful and not fall into media clichés or tropes or mischaracterize the impact of those laws. I remember being so impacted by that generosity.

That was an incredible moment of solidarity. But yeah, we were having coffee, and Yin looks at me and goes, "Would you ever be interested in rope play?" Do you remember that?

YQ: I don't know if I remember saying, "Would you be interested in rope play?"

I'm blushing to think that I would be so forward, but that's good for me. I'm very shy about asking people to play unless they approach me. I do remember saying, "How about we do an exchange of healing? Let's see what an exchange would look like." I remember offering rope play and saying, "If this would be an interest, let's see if we can actually create something where I would come to you for reiki, and you would come to me for a meditative ritual."

I am always offering my community rope work, rope workshops, whatever it is, and offering as barter so that way I can really give back to people in the community who are doing a lot of work. It felt so good to be able to do an energy exchange barter.

JW: You were so gentle and generous and kind. It was a really beautiful exchange, and we were able to participate in that pretty much until the pandemic started. We were able to find time every couple of weeks at various locations.

When we met, I was at the beginning of figuring out how to write about dissociation, which is this book project that I'm working on. I didn't really ever fully feel embodied or I was in my body, and I didn't know how to get back into my body. It was such a long process. And that's why I have been initiated and trained in so many different healing modalities, because it's just been such a lifelong search to figure out how to heal myself, essentially, and how to stuff myself back into myself.

And that practice between us—there was something about being tightly bound up that allowed me to feel the edges of myself, and I always knew where I was in space and time. It was so unexpected that that was one of the ways that I would be able to counter some of the out-of-bodiedness that I, at that time, was always feeling and not even really aware that I was feeling, if I'm totally honest. I just was a little cloud floating through NYC all the time, like a little glittery gold cloud, and I had no idea.

That was the beginning of learning how to have these exchanges of energy and also vulnerability and trust and that being part of a healing, reembodying process too.

YQ: I do remember this coming up, this idea of dissociation, and that's likely why I brought up bondage right away as opposed to any other type of kink play, because rope bondage is such a great way for one to get in touch with the outer perimeters of one's body and bringing the psyche back into those spaces. But then also being able to float out and come back in and learning what it means to actually float out of one's skin and then feel that process so that when you're doing it without the bondage on, you can recognize it and learn techniques of breathing or movement to come back in.

Certainly for me, there's always been different modalities of kink that can address different areas of where I feel like I need to heal from trauma. Being able to share that with you was really fantastic. It's been written about how yoga has been healing for people with PTSD, but we haven't gotten a lot of literature just yet about how kink can do the same thing. That's something that I'm really interested in writing about, and talking to you and to people about, and sharing with others. Along with your practices of sound healing and reiki, has there been anything surprising to you, in terms of that journey, of what you've learned and how you practice it with others?

JW: I think I've always needed this healing work, but I had entered into this process in a very Western-oriented way where I sort of assumed I would identify the problem and solve it, like there was a solution. And it's been really paradigm shifting to understand there really isn't a solution, that I do find moments of absolute clarity and absolute sobriety and absolute embodiment. And when I'm in them, the ability to recognize it and feel gratitude is the ultimate gift of presence and consciousness and awareness.

And it's not forever. I was just in a period of deep embodiment when I saw you upstate. I had been coming through this period of being in nature, feeling a slower pace of life, being in my flow writing, feeling really present. And then now, with the tidal wave of fall feeling like it has just fully landed at my doorstep and all of the urgencies of living in a place like New York and everyone else's anxieties and concerns about time and efficiency and money hitting me, I feel really disembodied.

Before, that shift would have really startled me and been really disorienting, but I know that this is also temporary, this will pass, and I will move back into that embodiment phase. I don't know when, but I have more clues about the how. I received an invitation to meet with my BIPOC group of reiki healers, and that is a very quick way to land back in myself. Just knowing that's on the horizon is so helpful.

A lot of people want to know if there's an upside to dissociation. A lot of people use it as a coping strategy . . . like W. E. B. Du Bois's theory of double consciousness.[2] It's a strategy. This is a specific strategy of being able to bifurcate yourself.

I think that's also really meaningful to people at this moment in time and understanding that they maybe don't have a ton of power and agency over their circumstances or surroundings, but they can choose what to tune in and tune out for, when it is a voluntary process. Maybe there is this kind of radical possibility of untethering from this late-stage capitalist disaster-riddled moment that can feel really powerless to be a part of, and that pressing a personal eject button for some people is very liberatory. That kind of blows my mind. I didn't expect to find that out. And there is some comfort in that being a shared experience too.

YQ: Actually, this is something that I talk about to anyone who's going to visit family whom they may not see eye-to-eye with or have a lot of personal turmoil with, to whom they still feel obligated. As well as from my own experience of being in sex work, too, that was my experience with being with lots of clients. Often I would be very much in the scene with them, because I was on and creating this curated scene. There's this line that Glenn Close has in *Dangerous Liaisons* where she talks about sitting at a dinner table and stabbing her hand with a fork. I would literally be in dinners with clients and playing the part that I needed to play to ensure that I could survive in New York City with the income that was coming in from this client, and be pressing my nails into my palms to get myself through or to give myself that distance of actual dissociation so that I can get through what I'm doing. And this is not uncommon with sex workers.

Also, as you said before, we're not always aware of it. When we're not aware of it, then a loss of control can really get out of hand in terms of going for more and more dissociation and losing ourselves into that—not just being the glittery cloud, but becoming this toxic atmosphere all around us and melding into that. But we have those conversations insularly, because there's so much that is at stake right now in terms of sex worker politics. Sharing too much of our vulnerabilities or our tricks of the trade can pollute the conversations that need to be had about the rest of our movement.

Healing Through Communion

JW: I think what you've highlighted there about being mindful of certain conversations that are held publicly to not interfere with larger progressive and political goals of a movement, that dance is really interesting. It always, for me, raises the need and importance of sacred, private inner space within communities, within organizing groups, even if those conversations can't break through. Because they might be too nuanced for mainstream digestion.

I've just come back from this Black trans gender-nonconforming retreat in Georgia that was run by Prentis Hemphill and a couple other facilitators. There were these incredibly intimate and personal and deep conversations about bodies and bodily experiences and needs and things that can't be held in a larger debate because the climate is so volatile right now about trans health care and safety. I guess I wanted to bring that up on the record, because it's really important for the most vulnerable among us to figure out how to find spaces to release and celebrate and to do it in a way that is not always up for public consumption.

Because there is so much public curiosity and fascination about us so-called deviants. I love Cathy Cohen, who's this Black feminist scholar who talks a lot about the queer radical power of being a "deviant" outside of the "norms of society" and the power that can live within that.[3] I feel like thinking about joy and pleasure and healing, I've been gravitating more towards having that in these very secret semi-private, semi-public spaces.

YQ: I feel most important for sex worker (especially BIPOC, queer, trans sex worker) gatherings is privacy, because there's so much at risk when we are out in public. Doing rallies is also necessary, but we need so many more allies to be able to come to our aid to be together. Because to be in public on a constant basis, to teach from the most marginalized corner is just exhausting.

I feel like my part in both Red Canary Song and Kink Out is I'm a gatherer; I'm not a leader in these organizations. I really feel that I'm a person who can gather people and then I get to feed people. That's my other joy: to be sure that there's food around, there's dance music, and that we can do movement.

Recently, I had a Red Canary Song visit, and I hired a masseuse who was doing Thai massage. It was a queer cis male who was massaging these Asian migrant massage worker women who have never gotten a massage at a "higher end" spa where there might be white people working. For them to get a massage and to be able to actually think about how massage for themselves can be seen as healing as opposed to the quickness of the work they do. To be able to slow it down and to offer them, the workers. To say, "You are a healer. You can own that as one part of your identity," I think is a great way to flip that conversation within work and healing and thinking towards joy and pleasure too. How do we create radical rest and radical joy for the people who are most at risk of systemic violence at this time?

JW: You're doing it. You're hosting these retreats. You're bringing these women into a space where they can rest and feel safe and free on this beautiful parcel of land that you now steward next to water and to receive a massage by someone who's caring and also someone who flips a power paradigm. I mean, who knows what that somatic experience feels like? It sounds so radical to me. In the last couple of years, there's been a lot of talk about what it means to start thinking about building these BIPOC communes and communities, and there are a few examples of people who've been able to do it successfully, because these things require a lot of time and energy and money and patience and capacity.

Your existing and sharing stories about the women that you're bringing in through Red Canary Song and wanting to both offer a place of rest but also have these exchanges and do some oral history work to get these stories down is really inspiring to me. And it helps concretize something that for me kind of still feels like a fantasy.

YQ: I feel very grateful and blessed to have the privilege of having a space up in the countryside, of being a property owner, which comes in conflict with a lot of ideas from the past. But at the same time, we have to understand what are the values of owning spaces now where we can create community. I do live on the lands of Lenape. They were never owned. Nobody believed in property ownership or land ownership. You staked out lands and were nomadic and lived off the lands, but it was for your tribe, not for just a single person. That's something that I really wanted to constantly remind myself, that what I'm doing up here is to create space for my "tribe" and to bring the people who have been tilling our earth and creating spaces for so long and yet not being able to profit from that work up here to enjoy the land as well.

I will say too just to give reverence to my land: As a sex worker, I became an adoptive family with a client who came to me and was an elder, and then as they had no family, I started to take care of them in their older years. They had dementia; it was me and my leather family taking care of this person. After they'd passed away, they were able to allow me to create space. So it is also space that has been earned in sex work and caretaking work, which is about the body. When we think about sex workers, body workers, massage workers, reiki healers, and energy healers, it all comes down to care work, right? And how do we care for the body and the spirit the same?

The Moon Festival is coming up this weekend. That's a big ritual for giving thanks to not only our families but also giving thanks to the moon, which I'm very closely tied to being a moon child, Cancer. There is the organizational work of us creating food through Red Canary Song. We do mutual aid. We create food packages to give out to massage workers in Flushing. Charlotte, one of the members of RCS, has this incredible kimchi that she makes, and we do vats of them where we're all standing next to each other creating these vats of kimchi for our community.

37.

On Dalit Dreaming and Rebellious Joy

Shaista Aziz Patel and Vijeta Kumar

This conversation between Vijeta Kumar and Shaista Aziz Patel was commissioned for *The Funambulist*'s special issue, "Decentering the US," which asked why so many people outside the settler colony called the United States of America are so deeply influenced by and interpret their own contexts through the political "software" created by US-based academics and activists. "On Dalit Dreaming and Rebellious Joy" addresses one significant gap of this US epistemology: caste. In an issue dedicated to the pluriversal imaginaries often prevented by US influence, Vijeta and Shaista exchanged letters about their perspectives on Dalit resistance from the two distinct geographies of the Indian subcontinent and the diaspora in the United States.

Dear Vijeta,
We are two caste-oppressed women, coming from different contexts. To be able to come together to share our thoughts on caste and casteism in this very unkind world somehow feels like an act of rebellious joy.

This opportunity is quite precious for me. I am excited to see what we can tell here in words; I am even more excited about the silences we are collaborating on in our writing. All the ellipses, all the words that trail off into nothingness. This is the bond we are forming here through writing and refusing to write.

As I write this, Black feminist scholar Katherine McKittrick's words ring loud in my ears: "The story asks that we live with the difficult and frustrating ways of knowing differentially. (And some things we keep to ourselves. They cannot have everything. Stop her autopsy.) They cannot have everything."[1]

We won't tear open our flesh or that of our kin so that the reader can understand how genocidal caste violence has been for centuries. Let them Google things. They have cheered over and probed at our decaying and burnt flesh long enough.

But to you, I say what you already know: no matter how intent the Brahmanical and white supremacist world order is on erasing us in all our forms, how much it wants to erase our histories, we are here, and we are the future ancestors of those whose arrival into the world has been challenged for millennia. Every act of ours towards addressing caste violence, even this act of coming together, I see as welcoming them into a world where they can live wholeheartedly.

Vijeta, I will be grateful to hear some reflections on your work as an educator in India. It's a context I am somewhat unfamiliar with as a diasporic Pakistani.

Dear Shaista,

I've been thinking about what it means to "get" an education. I am considering the word "get" (c. 1200, "to obtain, reach; to be able to; to beget; to learn"). The word is dependent on the act of obtaining. As in not something that is already there for you to take but relies on your ability to "get" it.

Last week I spoke to a student sitting across from me at my table in college, who could have very well not been sitting there—not because of fate or chance, but because of caste. He told me that he believed he was a weak student. At parent-teacher meetings, his parents were told to take him back because he didn't have the capacity to learn anything.

His mother, a sweeper, was once asked by a neighbor what the point of sending him to school was. "It's not like he's going to do anything great. What can a sweeper's son do?" When the exam results were announced that year, his mother was sweeping the street outside his school and discovered that her son's photo was displayed on the school gate for having topped the exam. She called him from someone's phone and made him come to the school. They stood outside for a long time looking at his photo. Later, his mother bought a box of sweets and went to the neighbor to also casually ask where her son's photo was. He laughed as he told me this and the joy in his face stunned my need to break down.

It reminded me of the late Kannada Dalit writer Siddalingaiah, who recollected a story about being invited for a talk at a hostel and going up on stage to be felicitated. He was surprised to see his cheering mother, a sweeper in the hostel, holding a broom in one hand and waving at him from the other.

These are stories of mothers and the brooms they hold in one hand and the joy they hold for their children with the other.

We may never learn a lot of what those who come before us sacrifice. There is so much about education this country takes for granted that I am afraid that I may take it for granted too. When the student finished telling me this story, we both scrambled for other words to fill the silence. He hadn't talked in class for a long time until one day he saw a picture of Dr. B. R. Ambedkar on my window and, since then, every time he came to see me, he came with more stories. It scares me sometimes to think what would have happened if he had never seen that picture or, worse, if that picture was never there.

I am thinking what it means to get an education when there's so little for Dalit students on campus to want to continue. There is more of an active pursuit to keep them off campuses than there is to keep them in. Especially when it takes so little for them to feel like they belong. And as teachers who were once students like them, when there are students carrying caste on their shoulders, what do we do with ours?

Sometimes, when I am reading an essay or a poem for class, I have the gall to be inspired by a beautiful line and I want to remain with that sentence for the rest of the day and leave my caste outside.

I am not always able to do that because as the saying goes, you may not follow caste, but other people do. Something in my body or its memory or that of a student's will take control of my day and I give up and return to being the scared and weak student I once was.

Toni Morrison speaks of race as a distraction in her 1975 keynote address at Portland State University: "The function, the very serious function of racism is distraction. It keeps you from doing your work. It keeps you explaining, over and over again, your reason for being."

This is true of caste as well. It is a distraction. It is exhausting to have to think of different ways to say the same thing over and over again.

"It keeps us from doing our work."

This was just a small glimpse into my workday. What is yours like, Shaista?

Hi Vijeta,

What you've shared is so powerful. There are places where I have left comments on your reflection, asking for references or dates, all in an effort to make some of the words, some of the people you've mentioned more legible to Western readers. I now wonder whether I should have done that. . . . Refusing to become legible is refusal to be devoured by them. So, I apologize for my earlier comments, Vijeta.

Your desire to leave caste outside your classroom is a concrete example of that otherwise dubious-for-me conception of building a different kind of a world—an otherwise world. What you said reminded me of a line from the formidable Dr. Kumud Pawde's autobiography, where she notes, "What comes by birth, but can't be cast off by dying—that is caste."[2] I have read this line many times, but hearing your desire to "leave caste outside" while reveling in the generosity of beautiful words, is making me feel so many things. I do have fleeting images of unfleshing myself. . . . Like that would let one leave their caste or race at the threshold.

I wonder if there are Dalit genomic scientists examining our DNA sequencing and if they can find that our centuries of survival, of living in the face of most brutal humiliation and genocides can teach the world something about humanity, about reliance, about willing our way out of apocalypses.

I just finished reading Métis novelist Cherie Dimaline's book *The Marrow Thieves*. This young adult fiction is about a futuristic world—maybe it's the world we live in right now? My tenses are all confused and I laugh and chock it up to English being my second language but, really, that is so not the case. In the novel, white people have lost their ability to dream and so they hunt down Indigenous people for their bone marrow since it holds the cure for this fatal calamity of dreamlessness. I kept thinking about what the power of Dalit dreaming might also be able to teach the world.

Everything you have shared above is, for me, an intentional practice of living with dignity, of building communities outside of a world order made meaningful through caste hierarchies. I just want to take a moment to appreciate all that you are sharing with me. My writing of a "response" is shifting and I keep going back to my sentences, and erasing them. I hope what I write can be read as a continuing engagement with your reflections. This way, I would find some peace in knowing that readers understand that my thoughts in this moment are insignificant and a "bad draft" in relation to what I might have written tomorrow or the day after . . .

I was going to talk to you about casteism in the US academy. But I genuinely don't know what to share. I feel like an unfeeling robot some days, constantly trying to make caste legible in Western academia, constantly reminding students, colleagues, and all the administration people that caste, as a 2,500-year-old structure of violence, as one of the oldest forms of incarceration, is older than that of white supremacy.

I am forced to make those equivalences to give some credence to my world ordered by not only white supremacy but also by intense anti-Muslimness and casteism.

Here I am, wanting to talk about Dalitness as recalcitrant, as rebellious, as an errant, as a refusal of and challenge to the very ways in which life is organized in our world, but the utterances from my mouth at meetings and in emails to my department are requests to include/recognize caste in my university's antidiscrimination policy. All my thoughts about Dalit dreaming and its teachings get reduced to requests for inclusion. This diversity work forces me to sometimes engulf caste violence, and I stay there, waiting for my turn to bring up anti-Muslimness and casteism.

Sometimes, after meetings, I ask myself, What does it mean to be present in ways that you do not even recognize yourself? I move around my office, walk around my campus and in the world, feeling disengaged and alienated from myself. It's like I am the shadow walking with that other [redacted] body. I have an analysis of caste and race and what it means to think about caste in a department like Ethnic Studies. Or even what it is to keep doing anticaste work at my school with its Brahman cis man [redacted]. But instead, here I am, stuck in all the affect and all the sensations, miserably failing to write in a scripted, "professional" form that I am expected to deliver my writing in . . . [redacted] or myself, feeling completely isolated.

[These redactions are an unseeing of my words because I mean to refuse (1) more information and (2) let you revel in my misery. I am grateful to Christina Sharpe, Billy-Ray Belcourt, and Eve Tuck (forever) for teaching me this practice.[3]]

Were I to speak, I'd look
like a cracked windshield.
My two hundred and six lonely bones
    have each acquired a type of consciousness.
    ↓
    Sometimes a body is that which happens to you.[4]

Vijeta, that quote from the wonderful Toni Morrison is so powerful. We are alienated from our being, from our kin, all in an effort to make our humanity legible to these systems of domination in the first place. In that effort, our ability to love ourselves and each other is compromised.

What I have been saying about Dalit dreaming is something, I think, even my bone marrow probably doesn't hold anymore after centuries of so many dispossessions that I have even forgotten what it is that I have forgotten.

Where caste is rejected as vestigial in a casteism-like-genocide world order, what futurity can even be afforded to those whose lives are marked as completely disposable? As I was writing this, I was reminded of how somebody shared a news story in a WhatsApp group on how they, that is, genocidal, anti-Muslim, casteist, and heteropatriarchal Bollywood, are now making a biopic on that Thakur man who shot and killed our revolutionary warrior elder, Phoolan Devi. That man is now a politician, which is not an aberration. We know that they become leaders only through our massacres and genocides. Every day, the casteist and anti-Muslim violence feels so intense. I am enraged every single day. But even then I want to hold on to this sense of futurity because, look, I am so privileged. Caste is not a site of genocide in Pakistan or its diaspora, so I feel like I need to be quiet. But here I am, all weepy and excited because I get to write these letters to you in all my incoherence and with all these tangential-to-the-script disruptions. These words . . . *futurity, otherwise worlds, joy, liberation* . . . do not come easily to me. But as our sister Thenmozhi Soundararajan reminds me, our ancestors did not fight and live the lives they did just so we can be sad. So it's a constant dance between terror, hope, living, refusals, escaping death. . . . As a Dalit woman in India, you know better than I ever can.

Dear Shaista,

"Dalit dreaming" is a phrase I have never heard before and feel all too overwhelmed by the possibilities it holds. And to hear of it for the first time from you, like this, makes these possibilities all too touchable, reachable. I am wondering what it means for you, me, and others like us to dream. I am thinking what it must be like for you to carry around these dreams in your eyes, your body, and mind every day and to have them "reduced to requests for inclusion" in meetings. What you've said with such deliberation is at the heart of what I wasn't able to articulate and what I have struggled with in the past, and continue to struggle with even now.

Sometimes when I talk about caste in my classroom, a part of the energy goes into proving to a caste-ignorant student that caste is alive and thriving. After having gone through every excruciating detail from history, lived experience, anecdotes (those of mine, and others), I see a look of absolute disgust on the student's face. That's a look I know well, and regardless of how familiar this look is, it always unsettles me. It's the belittling look of someone asking, "If indeed things are as bad as you say they are, how did you end up here?" Nothing prepares me for the way I want to abandon myself for the rest of the day.

That student is merely mimicking what they have picked up from home, the street, friends, but I hate that in that moment, I am allowing someone to consume me. I worry that my defensiveness, eagerness to prove the student wrong, or more importantly, to prove myself right, gets in the way of their learning.

Classrooms are meant to be learning spaces after all. How is any kind of learning possible for them or for me if I am constantly protecting myself and being vulnerable at the same time? It is easy to borrow the manufactured rage from Twitter and unleash it on students, to drop words like "entitled," "savarna" (dominant caste), "spoilt," etc., but as a teacher, my job demands that I leave that rage and rely on something more surgical, cold, unyielding like logic to defeat them.

On some days, my bitterness scares me; my own capacity to rely on bitterness as an excuse to not work hard scares me more.

It's true, bitterness is useless in the struggle against caste. But what I am terrified of is losing kindness. It would be comical to lose kindness in this whole process of learning to be human.

So when you say, what does it mean to be present in ways that you do not even recognize yourself, Shaista, I was able to see you, and I was able to see me.

Dalit History Month, for me, is a constant reminder of kindness. I don't know if I have it in me to return to kindness every day, but I want to try. What is your Dalit History Month like?

Hi Vijeta,
We are exchanging these messages in April, which is indeed Dalit History Month. I don't really know how (widely) it is celebrated in India, and if there are discussions on themes for the month, and how it disrupts the Brahmanical supremacy of Indian institutions. But I genuinely appreciate this reminder of kindness from you. I am going to hold on to it.

Here, in the US, I sit in terror during this month, waiting for event announcements on social media from casteist Indian scholars who never engaged with caste in their analyses, but have now learned that caste is a profitable site of career building. These academics have, through hard work of Dalit, Bahujan, and Adivasi theorists/organizers, realized their "caste complicity" and purport to design research projects (with funds, of course) and write on the matter, and yet can never be honest about their very willful participation in upholding the caste-based and anti-Muslim genocidal world order. You can never make them speak about the particularities of their own families' participation in this dehumanizing-for-us structure of Brahmanical patriarchy.

In Western academia, brown-skinned South Asians are flattened into the Diversity, Equity, Inclusion (DEI) categorization of "brown" or "Asian." We then circulate as being the same kind of people coming from similar histories and political locations, as if there isn't a centuries-old caste apartheid in place. In North America, Brahmans, presenting themselves as injured subjects of white supremacist universities and touting postcolonial and subaltern theories, pretend to present seemingly "alternative" archives of history from that of the colonizers. There is much respect for Subaltern and Postcolonial Studies in South Asia and in the West. However, as done by caste-dominant South Asian academics, these fields have always been led by Brahman and other caste-privileged Indian academics and yet . . . I am untenured, Vijeta. There is so much I want to say and have said, but in the face of genociding caste powers, sometimes my knees shake. . . . I dream of Savitribai Phule, Mohtarma Fatima Sheikh, Nangeli devi, Jhalkaribai, all of them forever generating vengeance and haunting these academics. The rage in my body for them makes me hope that these pretentious "subalterns" are actually silenced through sheer terror of being haunted.

I'm so clearly reminded here of this quote by Eve Tuck and Christine Ree: "Haunting does not hope to change people's perceptions, nor does it hope for reconciliation. Haunting lies precisely in its refusal to stop."[5] I am exasperated. See how a celebratory month for me also becomes about all this bitterness.

In my department of Ethnic Studies, I wrote and released an anticaste statement. It went relatively easy for me, with people either staying silent (a majority) or emailing to support this statement. The administration is Brahmanical and white supremacist, but I don't think I am on their radar as yet, which is the reason for all this happening smoothly. I think about the experiences of Dalit and allied savarna students and alumni who had to fight so hard to get caste included in California State universities; the things we heard at the Santa Clara Commission for Human Rights hearing on caste in 2021; the notorious case of caste apartheid at Cisco and in all workplaces in the US where Indians are; the BAPS mandir in New Jersey, which used Dalits for coerced labor . . . all of these tell you caste violence is very well alive in diaspora. As Babasaheb (Ambedkar) said, "If Hindus migrate to other regions on earth, Indian caste would become a world problem."[6]

I end my message with a hollowness in my stomach but still holding on to this practice of Dalit dreaming and my special gratitude to Indigenous scholars for teaching me that we can dream different futurities for people written off as dying.

While these dominant caste people continue to steal our lands, bones, flesh, souls, futurities, I am going to continue my refusal to give in and continue to do my work and think through how our (Dalit and Muslim) acts of meaning making can serve our ancestors, our people, our future generations.

They can't steal the sacred from us. We will continue to dream different lives. *Insha'Allah. Jai Bhim. Jai Savitri. Jai Fatima.*

38.

Reimagining the Autistic Mother Tongue

Jane Shi

For most of my life, I attributed my needs and the fact that others frequently didn't understand them to an inherent lack.

I was bad at communicating. I was bad at chores. I was bad at being in groups. The worst part, the unspoken shame of meltdowns, before I had a name for them, was that I felt like I was fundamentally a bad person—manipulative and spoiled, aggressive and violent, unable to control my temper. My anger made me feel out of control. Sometimes, I felt and then acted like I needed to be controlled.

The problem was me, the problem was me, the problem was me.

But my disabled friends and community, including and especially disabled QTIBIPOC (Queer Transgender Intersex Black, Indigenous, People of Color), weren't going to let me believe that for long. Over the course of the pandemic, letting myself fully confront the ableism of the world around me—yes, the world that let hundreds of thousands of people die for the economy—and in turn, the respect I deserve as a human being, I realized I was autistic.

I was nervous. I wasn't just making this up, was I? I watched TikToks, QTIBIPOC autistic public speakers' speeches on YouTube, and documentaries; listened to interviews in podcasts; and read disability justice books, poetry, and blog posts. I got to know people in the community, asked questions, and did research. One of my closest friends told me that they thought I was autistic this entire time. What?!

I loved researching this new-to-me identity. I had always been so good at putting myself last, that giving a name to something that I was, am, and will be my entire life felt liberating. I also knew I couldn't stop there. In "Cinderella's Stepsisters," a speech for Barnard College's 1979 graduation in New York City, Toni Morrison said that "the function of freedom is to free somebody else."

Realizing I was autistic made me feel powerful. As a poet, I felt like I could write into the depths of neurodivergence and offer new outlines of previously hidden truths about the world we live in. I felt like I could release the shame of ableist violence I experienced throughout my life. And that also meant the responsibility of making space for others, to imagine beyond myself, to consider the future, to free someone else.

A New Chinese Name for Autism?

Within a few months of realizing I was autistic, the world found out about a boy named Huxley.[1] Huxley is an autistic Chinese boy who was adopted by white American parents who had put his meltdowns all on display on YouTube, and then, one day, after not vlogging about him for months, these parents revealed that they had decided to "rehome" him. Like a coffee table on Facebook Marketplace.

The thing I couldn't stop thinking about, as a 1.5 generation Chinese settler who isn't an adoptee, was that Huxley must have had a Chinese name.

Is it wrong for me to wonder? Why did his white adoptive parents, or perhaps the adoption agency, name him after an English dystopian author?

After the white supremacist and misogynistic shootings in Atlanta, when a white man killed six Asian women, and after people attacked and even killed Asian elders in the United States, many in the East Asian diaspora on Twitter began putting their Asian names on their accounts. It was in response to the mainstream media wrongly abbreviating many of the women killed in Atlanta. It was in response to their English, Korean, and Chinese names placed side by side throughout our social media eulogies. It was in response to the violence that Asian elders were experiencing throughout North America, of centuries of white supremacy. It was in response to the shame we have been made to feel for so long, and yearning to finally—collectively—let it go.

My own Chinese name on Twitter isn't my real one: it's a homonym of "pipagao" the herbal cough syrup also known as Pei Poa Goa, or the brand name Nin Jiom, made from loquat. The homonym roughly translates to high crawling skin—it's silly, goth, and doesn't make a lot of sense. But it makes me happy that I can protect my privacy online while also proudly displaying my heritage at the same time.

Names are complicated. They're sacred and beautiful. And they're also hidden away, stolen, forced on a person, made up, and subject to change. Sometimes, names are like keys we use to open and close a room. Other times, they are like coats you take on and take off, a hat that others can recognize you by in a crowd full of masks, a playful tattoo on your collar bone. Sometimes we don't share our given names in public because of surveillance from our country of origin. Other times we change them to better fit our gender. Sometimes our names are considered difficult to pronounce, and in turn, we are considered difficult.

A lot of the time, we are given names to assimilate into a dominant culture. That is one of the reasons I go by Jane, the English name I was given in grade one in English class in a Shanghainese elementary school. But unlike Huxley, I have the privilege of knowing my Chinese name.

The two current names for autism in Chinese are 自症 /自閉症 (zìbì zhèng) or 孤独症/孤獨症 (gūdú zhèng). The first set of characters means self, shut-in, and disease, respectively; the second means loneliness, disease. It's funny—they remind me of quarantine, a hermit who wants to keep safe from a pandemic, an aching loneliness of the moment we're in, an aching isolation of being excluded from public health decisions.

But these names also remind me that autists are still largely misunderstood and pathologized in the motherland and around the world. Ableist insults in Chinese like 笨蛋 (bèn dàn), which means idiot or fool and can be transliterated as "dumb egg" or "stupid melon," sometimes even said affectionately to one's closest loves, pervaded my upbringing. Terms like 白痴 (báichī) paint innocence as idiotic, and lack of intelligence as a flaw. Global capitalist, Western, and ableist pressure push Chinese parents to create ill-researched institutions for their developmentally autistic children that are not about accommodation and care but about conformity; on YouTube, when you look up "autism" and "China," media shows weeping mothers expressing the challenges they face as parents, while their child is restrained.

Such context urges me to reimagine cultural reclamation as one that must involve disabled people—speaking for ourselves.

What would a better name be for autism in Chinese? After all, language is malleable—like putty, like water, like the walls of prisons crumbling (because we made them crumble) to make way for a better society. Slang emerges constantly from Hong Kong, Chinese, and Taiwanese internets. The character for biangbiang noodles, a popular dish, uses one of the most complex Chinese characters that cannot be typed on a computer. Biang is an elaborate amalgamation of multiple characters, including the characters for moon, horse, speak, heart, eight, roof, knife, and walk.

The creation of the gender-neutral Chinese "X也" reminds us of the Western, colonial roots of the gender binary itself, and that "他" had originally applied to all genders.

The problem with the Chinese word for autism—a problem that all autistic people face today—is that the history of autism is inextricably tied to the history of eugenics. It is a European history of studying people, speaking for people, mis-categorizing people, confining people, torturing and killing people.

It is a history of violence and force and stripping people of their autonomy and real identities. Applied Behavioral Analysis (ABA) was a method of interventionist treatment of autistic children created by Dr. Ole Ivar Lovaas, the same doctor who created gay conversion therapy, which targeted autistic behaviors. Such frameworks follow the logic of sex addiction therapy, the misogynist shame that led the killer in the Atlanta spa shooting to murder. By extension, "treatments" rooted in stigma follow the logic of substance use disorder treatment that shames people who use drugs out of healing. It prevents the implementation of harm reduction services that save lives in a poisoning crisis.

This violent web of historical and present associations is why many in the autistic community have decided that Asperger's is no longer a good term for us, why many of us reject "low-" and "high-functioning" labels, and why we constantly discuss what words and language we want to use for ourselves. All told, if we view autism from the perspective of those who had originally coined it, and not of contemporary autistic people, we would never live in a just society where everyone could survive and thrive.

Finding Language to Love Ourselves

One night, I couldn't sleep. I thought, why not come up with a new Chinese word for autism? Being a heritage speaker, my vocabulary is small. All I could think of was the words for "cute person"—可爱的人 (kě'ài de rén)—which involves the characters for "can"—可 (kě)—and the character for "love"—爱 (ài). That is, those who allow themselves to be loved. Then, I got out my pink pen and put the character for love inside the "口" (ku—i.e., mouth, opening, entrance) of the character for can (可). It was like putting love inside of one's mouth, protected and held, but still present. Then, when I put the character for "self"—自(zì)—beside this new word, I got the meaning, "those who allow themselves to love themselves." This new word reminded

The Chinese character for self (自/zì) and the character in can (可/kě) with the traditional Chinese character for love (愛/*ài*) inside the character for mouth (口/ kǒu). The letters are black and are centered on a translucent white inset rectangular background in front of a background of an abundant bush of leaves and pink-white roses. Image created by Jane Shi.

me that we do not have to tell each other we love each other to express love. It reminded me that speaking is not the only way to communicate.

I was mostly joking and playing around when I posted this neologism on Twitter. I was also trying to imagine ourselves as autistic people as loveable, as loveable to ourselves, not to others. Not as shut-ins but as those who have boundaries and are protective of the love we give. Not as inherently lonely but made lonely by a world that has chosen to isolate us.

Sianne Ngai's theory of cute culture, as it applies to avant-garde art, fascinates me. She argues that cuteness in our capitalist society is about consumption.[2] It would be wrong to call autistic people cute as a whole—we are not trinkets to buy and throw away, a plaything you only want around when soft and cuddly, never sharp or hard. But my speculative linguistic reimagining makes me ask: Why do we choose to marginalize autistic people—infantilized and perceived as cute or consumable in one moment, and then violent and aggressive in another—in the first place?

In Rotem Anna Diamant's 2017 review of Ngai's theory, she argues that cuteness can be subversive for people reclaiming it through physical appearance: "Cuteness can be a layer of artifice that signals to someone else what we desire to communicate; it can enable us to appear how we want to appear; it is a conversation about who we are that we do not need to speak out loud." When I reclaim cuteness as a small, short, East Asian, queer, and autistic person—who is always already perceived as cute—and when I use the word for cute to reimagine autism in Chinese, I expose the powerlessness that autistic people have endured throughout time. I ask, is others' perception of my cuteness permission to harm me? Does it let others love me like the Chinese word for cute suggests? Is it better to be lonely, shut-in, or consumed? Why are these the only categories available?

A lot of us autists keep adorable plushies by our sides. Though we are adults, we get treated like children, which only shows how badly our society treats children. But really, our special interests and stim toys are how we practice self-care and self-love—much wiser and compassionate lessons for children and adults alike than punishment and deprivation.

Language is a playground; words are stim toys. It doesn't make sense for only me to play with them. Whether it's better to reclaim the current Chinese word for autism, to destigmatize it, or come up with a new word is up to the community. I don't imagine there to be a single answer that fits everyone.

Dear reader: If you are autistic and have a relationship to the Chinese language—whether it is because you grew up with it, are fluent in it, are a heritage speaker, want to reconnect with it, or live under its imperial rule, what do you want the word for autism to be?

I live on the occupied ancestral, unceded, and traditional homelands of the Musqueam, Squamish, and Tsleil-Waututh peoples. What are the words for neurodivergence and autism (just as it exists in Cree) in Sḵwx̱wú7mesh sníchim and hən̓q̓əmin̓əm̓?

How do you say autism in your language? Do you think it should be something else?

These questions are not merely rhetorical. I want the broader autistic community to be free enough for us multilingual racialized people to express and remix our respective heritages. I want the Chinese diaspora to be a place where I can live freely as an autistic person. Through reimagining language, I want to imagine that we can undo the colonial and ableist violence around us, too.

Diaspora has the agency to remake culture and tradition, just like those in the homeland, just like autistic people in the diaspora. The point isn't only who or where.

The point is that it frees us.

39.

Claiming My Power

Simone Devi Jhingoor

I want to raise my voice
to decibels so high
it causes oceans to quiver
like jello and return to stillness.

I want to take up so much space
on this earth; be expansive
with arms reaching wide
to hug the Rocky Mountains.

I want to love myself so deep
there won't be an ounce of room
left for doubt about my abilities.
Instead, I will own my power
soaring like a fiery Phoenix.

I am stardust sparkling the night's sky.
Not bound by any limitations.
Free to be seen, free to be heard
in all of my beauty.

I am a glorious Devi!

Fears of living in my fullness
no longer force me to shrink.
Don't question my worth,
douse my fire, dim my shine
break me down at dusk.

I burn down outdated worldviews
like a ferocious Khaleesi riding my dragon.
I spark controversy, shatter conventions.

Dusting off old-fashioned norms,
I am found—FREE!
Unbound by any limitations
I heal into my most magical, liberated self.

Can you see me? Can you hear me?
Can you behold . . . me?

I am a glorious Devi!

40.

Unapologetic Agreements

Sonya Renee Taylor

Moving from a radical self-love that transforms you to a radical love that creates justice and equity in the world may feel like a tall order, but you are already on your way.[1] As we cultivate new ways of being in our own bodies, we develop new ways of *being* on this planet with other bodies. A return to radical self-love requires our commitment to building shame-free, inclusive communities that uplift one another while honestly addressing body terrorism and all the ways it manifests as oppression based on age, race, gender, size, ability, sexual orientation, mental health status, and all other human attributes. Some will deride our efforts with charges of playing to "identity politics." We should remind those people that they, too, have identities that are informed by their bodies. Their lack of awareness about those identities generally means their body falls into a multiplicity of default identities that uphold the social hierarchy of bodies. The luxury of not having to think about one's body always comes at another body's expense. We should, with compassion, remind them that oppression oppresses us all, even those who are default. Not even they will always have a body at the top of the ladder. No one wins in a world of body terrorism.

At this very moment, someone is wringing their hands in worry. "But what if I make a mistake, Sonya? What if I say or do the wrong thing?" If it is you who is worrying, let me calm your precious nerves by assuring you that you *will* make a mistake . . . and then reminding you to revisit pillar 4 (collective compassion).[2] Creating a radical self-love world requires our willingness to have challenging conversations about privilege, power, history, culture, inequality, pain, and injustice. We will mess up and say something in French.

That doesn't mean we quit. It also doesn't mean we become defensive and retreat to judgment and blame. It means we apologize and try again, holding fast to our intention to connect with other humans in different bodies from a place of compassion and shared humanity. As you move the conversation of radical self-love from an internal dialogue out into your family, community, and world, try on the Unapologetic Agreements that appear below. Commit to engaging in the type of radical self-love communication that grows our understanding of ourselves and one another—the type of communication that fosters global change.

1. **Be a body-shame-free friend.** Eliminate language that disparages bodies based on race, age, size, gender, ability, sexual orientation, religion, mental health status, or any other attribute. Compassionately challenge others you hear using body-shame language to describe themselves or others. This includes health or concern trolling (making unsolicited comments about a person's health based on their physical appearance).
2. **Engage and encourage curiosity-driven *dialogue,* not debate or arguing.** Practice the value of sharing and listening to the perspectives of others. The goal of dialogue need not be to change anyone's mind, but to *offer* and *receive* a perspective for consideration and curiosity.
3. **Embrace multiple perspectives.** Avoid having conversations from the assumption of right and wrong. Even if every cell in your body disagrees with someone's perspective, remember that making people "bad" and "wrong" will never build connection and understanding. People who feel judged and attacked often only become further entrenched in their ideas.[3]
4. **Have compassion for and honor people's varied journeys.** Not everyone has read the books you've read or had the experiences you've had. There was a time when you had not had them either. Our journeys are unique and varied. Compassion births patience.
5. **Expect and accept discomfort.** Conversations about centuries-old oppressions are *hard*! If they were not, the world would be rid of body terrorism and oppression by now. Honor how we all have been indoctrinated into systems of oppression that we each must unlearn. Unlearning is challenging. Do not expect neat, tidy resolutions or assume that we will instantly fix the world's

ills in a single dialogue. We can, however, get closer to those goals if we are willing to be uncomfortable. Remember, fear is not necessarily danger.

6. **Acknowledge intent while addressing impact.** It is possible to be well meaning and still cause harm. No matter our intention, we practice accountability when we are willing to acknowledge the impact of our words and actions on others. Likewise, people's words and behaviors may have an impact on us, but they are rarely actually about us. The way we respond to situations is most often a reflection of our own journey. Refraining from personalization makes accepting discomfort easier.
7. **Take breaks for self-care.** Talking with friends, family, and community about radical self-love, body terrorism, and body shame can be joyous and eye opening. It can also be challenging and triggering. These conversations often involve issues that have caused great trauma in the world—and in our own lives. Some dialogues may bring up painful memories, old wounds, present hurts, and current resentments. We place a premium on self-care as a tool of radical self-love! Do what you need to do to navigate your mental, emotional, and physical well-being. Step away from conversations when needed. Focus on yourself and come back when you are recentered. Radical self-love dialogue depends on your wellness.
8. **Interrupt attempts to derail.** Oftentimes, conversations about body terrorism and oppression bring up such discomfort that we immediately attempt to change the conversations to something that feels more comfortable. Before you know it, the conversation turns to pickle farmers in Europe when we started out talking about fat shaming. Work to keep the focus on the subject being addressed and avoid the desire to derail.
9. **Remember that personal attacks, name-calling, heavy sarcasm, and general unkindness are unhelpful.** The fastest way to devolve a dialogue is to turn to mean or hurtful language. Our anger need not be expressed as cruelty. We should work to speak from our "inside voice."
10. **Practice unapologetic inquiry.** Part of helping people sort through their ideas and beliefs is to ask questions about those ideas. That includes asking *ourselves* hard questions: "Why do I believe this? What am I afraid of? What am I gaining or losing

by trying on a new perspective?" The answers that stick with us over time are the answers we come up with ourselves. Good questions get us to good answers.

11. **Have conversations based on what was actually said.** Often our translations of people's ideas are not accurate depictions of what they were sharing. Be sure to engage with people based on their actual words and not what you assume those words meant. If you are unsure, ask for clarity.
12. **Assume the best about one another.** It is exceptionally painful to be dismissed, called a liar, or accused of making up your experiences. Start from the assumption that people's experiences are *real* and that they are the expert on their experience. We *may* have shared experiences, but this is not always true. Ask to learn more about other people's truths, rather than erasing them. Start from the assumption that we are all doing our best at any given moment with the tools we have.
13. **Celebrate difference.** Identifying difference is a way to embrace how we can all show up as our fullest, most authentic selves without shame. Acknowledge and embrace those things that are varied in us. Notice when difference is absent and investigate why. Ask who is not in the room. Our love of difference translates into creating a movement that welcomes everybody and every body.
14. **Make the goal of the conversation radical, unapologetic love.** The desire for a world free of body terrorism is a desire born out of love. Activist Che Guevara once said, "At the risk of seeming ridiculous, let me say that the true revolutionary is guided by a great feeling of love."[4] Allow your conversations to be guided by the primary principle of love.

"Sonya, will following these agreements keep me from arguing with my racist, fatphobic Aunt Martha during Thanksgiving dinner?" Listen, love, I cannot promise that you will never again storm out of the house and be forced to have your holiday meal of a bag of stale potato chips in your car. However, I can tell you that I have seen the Unapologetic Agreements transform hostility into human connection and acrimony into camaraderie. Like all radical self-love principles, they will take time and effort to master. But keep working at it. "You will be amazed before you are even halfway through."[5]

PART 6

Our Futures

Imagining and Building Feminist Worlds

An Iranian childhood Siyah.black. Image by Priscillia Kounkou-Hoveyda.

the stamp was my grandfather's.

اصفهان، شهری که او در آن بزرگ ش

Isfahan the city he grew up in.

با اتوبوس از تهران به اصفهان می رفتیم

We'd take the bus from Tehran to Isfahan.

41.

Dreaming Is Our Radical Inheritance and "radical imagiNation"

Kai Naima Williams

These remarks were originally delivered at the Abolition Is virtual concert on May 8, 2021, to accompany a performance of the poem "radical imagiNation." Created by and for students of abolition, Abolition Is is "a multimedia platform dedicated to amplifying the tools we need to build the world we deserve: one in which the violences of prisons, policing, and surveillance are obsolete."[1]

The poem "radical imagiNation" was initially written for Densho, an organization that seeks to preserve, educate, and share stories about the World War II Japanese American incarceration camps.

My family was incarcerated in Japanese American concentration camps. My great-grandmother was twenty years old at the time of her imprisonment, and she later went on to become a revolutionary by the name of Yuri Kochiyama. Yuri was incarcerated with her siblings and her mother, and her father's life was stolen by FBI agents. On December 7th, 1941, mere hours after Japanese soldiers bombed Pearl Harbor, Yuri's father was forcibly taken from his home on suspicions of being a Japanese spy after having just returned from the hospital for ulcer surgery. He was interrogated and presumably tortured for weeks, and when he was brought home to my family, he had been denied his medicine for the entire duration of the interrogation. He could not speak nor recognize any of his family members and he died the next day.

Systems of incarceration, punishment, and policing are foundationally rooted in racism. My family became aware of this when they were profiled, displaced, and imprisoned by the US government. Generations prior, on my father's other side of the family, my African ancestors were captured and sold into chattel slavery in the American South. Like many of us, my lineage and existence in America has been bound in struggle against captivity and carceral punishment.

In the wake of the killings in Atlanta and violence against Asians during the pandemic, many people are calling for increased policing in Asian neighborhoods and for hate crime legislation. They are calling on the state to protect and defend their people and to recognize this violence as racism. And yet, the women who were murdered were among groups of people most targeted, criminalized, and violated by the police: low-wage, migrant, perhaps undocumented women, massage parlor workers, and potentially sex workers. These women were likely survivors of police violence, as massage parlor workers and sex workers often are. In spite of these identifying factors, the nuances of their experiences, of their intersectionality, get erased in the conflation of all anti-Asian violence. And they are rendered irrelevant when people name law enforcement, the most prominent and empowered perpetrator of violence against women working in their industries, as the solution to the problem. As Dr. Connie Wun, a brilliant abolitionist, puts it, "When you conflate and decide to name solutions for the most vulnerable you leave them susceptible to violence that you didn't consider."[2]

We cannot seek protection against racist violence from a state that refuses to implicate itself in the creation of that violence. It is crucial that we look to a history of US imperialism and wars in countries like Korea, Vietnam, and the Philippines as a legacy of racist and misogynistic violence against Asian people. When we point the finger at one another, when we center interpersonal violence, when we look to define the violence as individualized acts of hate, we ignore the actual and active cause of our oppressions: the state. We must accept that we cannot work with the state, reform it, or ask it for help. We have to find alternatives.

The beautiful thing is that the alternatives already exist. They are already enacted, enabled, documented, shared, and prepared to direct us. The alternatives are abolition.

Ruth Wilson Gilmore has said, "Abolition is not absence, it is presence. What the world will become already exists in fragments and pieces, experiments, and possibilities. . . . Abolition is building the future from the present, in all of the ways we can."[3] We already know that building transformative futures requires great imagination, but what I've come to love most about looking forward is that there are blueprints for dreaming available to us whenever we look back. What critics and skeptics who react fearfully to the idea of abolition aren't recognizing is that alternatives for protection, health, and caretaking have existed in communities of color in the United States since their inceptions.

I open this poem with a quote from Mumia Abu-Jamal, a political prisoner and activist. Mumia was my grandma Yuri's dear friend. She began their relationship by writing to him while he was imprisoned, and they maintained contact until she died in 2014. Mumia was one among hundreds of incarcerated activists that Yuri wrote to every single day of her life. Correspondence, letter writing—that was their way of fighting the carceral system through sustained communication and community building. The letters—again, Yuri wrote thousands of them—disseminated information from the outside in. She sent books and newspapers, and in response, comrades passed her names of other imprisoned people who needed channels of aid. These actions were intended to sustain the lives, health, and dignity of those incarcerated people—to remind them that they were never forgotten or discarded and that even inside the darkest, loneliest, most evil constructions of the criminal-industrial complex, struggle and hope persisted.

Correspondence wasn't Yuri's only method of alternative care. She also embodied the concept of mutual aid by opening her home to anyone, literally anyone, who needed shelter or food, a place to hide or a place to sleep or a place to organize. When there were no more beds, she slept in the bathtub or in the crib with the baby. Every Saturday night, she and her husband, Bill, opened their home for a gathering of everyone imaginable: activists, artists, teachers, entertainers, neighbors, comrades, strangers, and everyone was welcome. This was Harlem in the sixties, in a housing project on 126th Street, in an apartment that could not house the amount of folks that passed through it but did. The door was always open. Yuri and Bill created the conditions for safety and mutual trust and exchange. I think about this act of construction, and it seems remarkable to me that the work of her life was in building and expanding communities that were accountable to one another, in which everyone had a person and a place to go for help.

I see many connections between the practices of racial solidarity and abolition, particularly in the ways that people perceive these practices and regard them with weariness and distrust. Some people hear the word "abolition" and decide it can't or doesn't exist. They cannot envision or imagine the possibilities it suggests. They don't see the long history of abolition in application that is as old as the systems it challenges. Some people hear the word "solidarity" and decide that it cannot exist. That it is a myth, a false promise, or an optimistic delusion. When we are conditioned to maintain divisions between one another, we fail to understand that alliances between people of color are and have been as real, frequent, and continuous as conflicts between them.

As a person who is both Black and Asian, I see instances of interpersonal violence between Black and Asian people be upheld, centered, and pointed at in so many narratives about our communities. It is far more rare to hear the true and persistent stories of solidarity between folks, coalitional solidarity that enabled movements. These stories are absent not because these events are less critical or less worthy of being documented but because they threaten the forces that benefit from our division. The myth that our communities are inherently incapable of working together, as well as the myth of our need for oppressive systems, only serve and protect a state that wants to keep us complacent and sick. So, when people regard abolition or solidarity as futurist fantasies that are impossible to realize, I think about all the ways these alternatives of care and justice and love have already been initiated. As organizers, the act of dreaming and daring to do so is our radical inheritance. We inherit the dreams of those who struggled before us and develop them and continue them. Acknowledging the ancestry of those dreams helps us reinforce our belief that they are not only achievable, but pragmatic and real.

The dreams I inherited are not limited by immobility or lies about what we can't change. They are full of tools and lessons. I take comfort in knowing that these dreams are not fallacies or unchecked fantasies but imagined realities that are as true as the daily functions and interactions of our communities, who have been denied and invisibilized for so long, and persisted still.

In 1964, Malcolm X visited Yuri's apartment in Harlem. She was hosting survivors of the Hiroshima bombing, but when people heard Malcolm might be in attendance, the whole neighborhood came out to hear him. When Malcolm spoke to the survivors, he drew a connection. He said, "You were bombed and are physically scarred. We too were bombed, and you saw some of the scars in our neighborhood. We are constantly hit by the bombs of racism."[4]

Then he made a prophetic pronouncement; this was before the US incursion into Southeast Asia. Malcolm gave a warning. He told them, "If America sends troops to Vietnam, you should protest. The struggle of the Vietnamese is the struggle of the whole Third World, the struggle against colonialism, Neo-colonialism and imperialism."[5] Yuri would later point to Harlem's early participation in the antiwar movement and attribute it to Malcolm's vision.

When I am told stories about Malcolm and Yuri, I think about how their friendship was contingent upon a shared vision of the future that was viable for all people scarred by racism. As I was writing the poem, I asked myself what a future like that might look like. For a long time, I couldn't move past the first stanza, because the visions I tried to conjure in my mind's eye looked blurry and unclear.

Then one day I asked my ancestors the same question, "What does this future look like?" And they started to speak. The words I received and translated through my own language are constructions of other dreams, and mine.

radical imagiNation

> *Conventional wisdom would have one believe that it is insane to resist this, the mightiest of empires, but what history really shows us is that today's empire is tomorrow's ashes; that nothing lasts forever.*
>
> —Mumia Abu-Jamal

In this, our new country, I gather my children
Say,

How lucky you are, to grow up
out of ashes

We have buried all the emperors for you
to play with your cousins on the grass
their bodies give.

The only thing they had to offer
the earth, in the end

For you to run free
thru prairies, hills

forests and fields
that belong to none of us

because in this country, we sidestepped the grave
error of etching our names onto everything

with its own language, instead, we let the land
break our tongues over its own pronunciation

this time, the land tells us how we can be of use
and we train our ears to receive

and that was just the first decree, in this, our new country,
where it is not a crime to come from somewhere else

and citizenship is granted upon re-enactment
of one's most beloved proverb,

since every "other" is part of one, another
blended harmony standing out in a national anthem
and you can be a bended knee or raised fist or palm over heart

since, in this country, we mind our business,
don't tell no body how to move against the swell of song

In the old empire,

They labeled us poison while leading
the life out of water
isolated us like illness in the body
they drew us into, a body they invaded first
and claimed to have
came to consciousness inside.

They constellated the land with confinements,
cut fences and clamped circles round whole demographics,

from the knowingest grandmother
to the freshest son, who never got the chance to be alive

and young enough not to be hated by his country

They shut us into camps, concentrated their eyes on our entire
lives, registered our birthdays, they took fishermen for spies

then handed them back to our families broken
into scales. they swiped our language and left
only the bare skeletons of folktales

They closed us into prisons while plantations stayed open
for white people to throw weddings on

they closed in at the protests and beat us open
as if to batter their obsession, bloodtaste for blackness
out on all the bodies their batons could touch

and I know,
I know

it may be irresponsible to use the word "We"

presumptuous pronoun "Us," in a poem,

but *This* is a country. (!)

and we made "Us," a possibility,

an even plane.
a wilderness of differences
with the same height,
the same healthcare,
the same rights,
the same blood,
the same children

And I am an "Us,"

a mixture of countries and blood

that met as comrades   and created the same children

My ancestors come to my candle, whisper,

"We suffered different beneath the same rule
but our resistances rubbed shoulders
and the shared muscle is you—"

They told me that so I could tell you,
my children,

We have burned it all down for you !

There are NO PRISONS, ONLY GARDENS,
NO WARDENS, ONLY WOMEN
with an eye on your progress
as you make it home late at night,
there are NO COPS. JUST YOUR GIRLS
running up to form a chain,
just witches twitching to twist up a perp's name
with their tongues, there are no reservations,
only free feast programs running from coast to coast,
no cages, only open bars for boarders
to mingle with hosts, we have every reason
to toast the grand old guardsmen of convention,
because they were SO WRONG

we, the natives, survived the end they promised would never come
and we marched on. at some point with our backs turned

the past   entombed itself in glass   re-named itself history

We thought their war on Us
would always last
but here you are

Blessed progeny of protest
Anointed with ash
Uprising every dawn

42.

Nā Wāhine Noho Mauna

Leadership, Solidarity, and Gender on Maunakea

Noelani Goodyear-Kaʻōpua

In 2019, Kanaka Maoli and our allies engaged in the largest outpouring of activism to protect Hawaiian lands and waters in our modern history. Thousands upon thousands gathered on Maunakea, the tallest mountain in Hawaiʻi. From seafloor to summit, it is also the tallest mountain in Oceania. Since the early 2000s, Native Hawaiian kiaʻi (guardians/protectors) had been leading the protection of this sacred summit against the proposed construction of a massive complex housing, the Thirty-Meter Telescope, or TMT.

The struggle to protect Maunakea against the construction of the TMT, an eighteen-story building occupying over five acres of conservation land, takes place amid the backdrop of an existing footprint of astronomy observatories that have already been found to have caused "substantial, significant, and adverse" cultural and environmental impacts over the past sixty years.

The struggle has been filled with profound expressions of mana wāhine and mana māhū: the power of womxn, trans, and gender-expansive folx.[1]

Construction of the TMT was scheduled to begin on July 15, 2019. About two hundred people gathered on the mountain over the weekend. On Sunday night, a group of eight decided that the construction vehicles would only pass onto the Mauna Kea Access Road if they were willing to drive over our bodies. That evening, the kūpuna, or elders, established a front line that became the center point of a camp that eventully swelled to thousands and thousands of protectors.

On July 17, hundreds of us stood as police declared that they would begin arresting these elders. Rows and rows of officers from multiple law enforcement divisions lined the access road. In a hypermasculine spectacle of the settler state's capacity for violence, riot police were fully armed as they prepared to face off with peaceful folks, who were outfitted with little more than hats, lei, and sunscreen.

The kūpuna commanded us to be quiet. They told us they would be the first to face arrest, and that we could give the police no excuse to use violence. So, we stood in tortured silence. We cried. We bit our tongues. We raised our hands to signal our love for our elders: these artists, teachers, knowledge keepers, business owners, community leaders who were arrested and slowly taken one by one.[2]

Eighty-one-year-old Maxine Kahaulelio fearlessly cried out, "As a wāhine koa, I'm gonna stand firm. You wanna arrest me? Arrest me!" About three hours into the arrest process, police got impatient about how slowly it was moving. So, the commanding officer approached the dozens more kūpuna who were still sitting ready to be carried off. We could all see the LRAD (Long Range Acoustic Device), or "sound cannon," directly facing the elders' tent. The officer announced: "I'm giving you folks notice: we are going to come harder, faster, and with more force if you don't disperse immediately."

The wāhine who had been slowly gathering behind the kūpuna immediately responded, reforming into a line in front of the elders. First twenty. Then forty. Then three lines, then four, five, swelling to over one hundred womxn, locked arm-in-arm in front of the elders. Then our men came and sat down behind us, another human barrier between the police and our kūpuna.

For the next hour, we chanted together, sang together, as police marched into their own ranks facing us. So close we could almost feel each other breathing. Yet, many bore no names on their uniforms. Many wore sunglasses so we could not see their eyes. I called out to them,

> We are the educators who teach your children. We are the doctors, nurses, and healers who care for your families. We are the counselors who help our people work through the cultural traumas we carry. We are farmers, fishers, technicians, accountants. We are

filmmakers, writers, storytellers, students. We are your sisters, your mothers, your daughters, your aunties. Before you arrest us, know who we are!

We readied ourselves for pepper spray and for worse.

Then, as the standoff reached an almost unbearable intensity, someone called out from the sideline just off the road. A call from Oahu, five islands away. There, a convoy of vehicles organized by māhū leaders had stopped traffic on the largest highway in Honolulu. Leading the convoy was Kumu Hinaleimoana Wong, a revered Hawaiian teacher, cultural practitioner, and leader who has taught so many about the importance of māhū in Hawaiian history and in our lives today.

"Mana māhū!" we yelled from the wāhine line in jubilation! Māhū power! In that moment, the police realized that their violence on Maunakea would trigger other shutdowns in the major economic centers of Oʻahu and Maui, the police withdrew and did not arrest a single other elder.

Then, few months later, māhū members of our Native Hawaiian community led the organizing and execution of what was the largest protest/unity march in Hawaiʻi ever. More than twenty-five thousand people marched through Waikiki, and at the very front were massive black-and-white banners that proclaimed "Mana Māhū."[3]

Wāhine (womxn) have been protecting Mauna a Wākea, also known as Maunakea, since time immemorial. Many deities who are embodied as forms of water—snow, mist, lake, springs, storms—reside on and give life to the mountain. Poliʻahu, Lilinoe, Waiau, Kahoupokāne. Kanaka Maoli recognize these elements as female. Among the kūpuna wāhine arrested on July 17 were womxn who have for years been leading seasonal ceremonies on Maunakea to honor these and other deities on the mountain.

Throughout the 2019 standoff, womxn played major leadership roles in the puʻuhonua (sanctuary) that was established and consecrated three days before the first confrontation with law enforcement in July.

Womxn organized and ran various parts of the camp. The check-in tent, the kitchen, the kūpuna council, the childcare tent, and the organic university that has sprung up on the lava fields at the base of Puʻu Huluhulu. Coordinating medics, media, donations, and childcare. All of these are organized and led primarily by womxn. People of all genders were critical to the functioning of this place of refuge that hosted thousands over several months. Yet the important responsibilities that wāhine and māhū carried within this movement was not widely covered in mainstream news media.

It took a tremendous amount of labor to sustain a community expanding and contracting, like lungs breathing the crisp air, around a tiny parking lot on the slopes of a mountain. This is "ea," a Hawaiian word that refers all at once to life, breath, and sovereignty.

Wāhine like Kumu Hula (hula master teachers) Pualani Kanakaʻole, Pua Case, and Kekuhi Kealiʻikanakaʻoleohaililani led ceremonial protocols three times a day, to focus protectors on the reason we gathered and to remind us to conduct ourselves in kapu aloha (collective code for protecting sacred spaces) while on the Mauna. Wāhine like Uʻi Chong—who ran the kitchen—inventoried food supplies, planned menus, organized volunteers, and maintained commercial kitchen-level standards for food safety, all while providing free meals for everyone in the puʻuhonua. Wāhine like Ruth Aloua, who had been a heart of the movement since 2015, tended crops and fishponds off-site, to remind us that the boundaries of this puʻuhonua are not the boundaries of this movement. Wāhine like ʻIlima Long wrote press releases, greeted news reporters, directed media requests, and helped build the story-based strategies of the movement. Wāhine like Marie Alohalani Brown received and redistributed donations of clothing, blankets, and other supplies to ensure that people who are camping can safely face the alternating blazing sun and bitter cold. Educator Presley Keʻalaanuhea Ah Mook Sang—founder of Puʻuhuluhulu University—coordinated daily classes and workshops so that people could learn and grow while protecting the Mauna. Wāhine like Kalama Niheu, Maile Wong, and Noelani Ahia coordinated free medical care and culture-based healing at the Mauna medics tent around the clock. Wāhine like Yvonne Mahelona, Makanalani Gomes, Keano Davis, and Tia Masaniai welcomed visiting protectors and tourists who arrived at the check-in booth. They educated foreigners and locals about the histories of Maunakea, of telescopes on the Mauna, and of the longer genealogies of Hawaiian resistance in which the current movement sits. They directed volunteers to stations needing help. They received and sorted donations. They deescalated tense situations, especially when tourists were upset about not being allowed to ascend the summit.

Elders, youth, wāhine, kāne, māhū folx working together—there is still no TMT on Maunakea.

Mauna protectors reinvested our own governing authority through a kapu aloha, reaffirmed with ceremonies of chant and dance three times a day. A kapu can be a prohibition. Typically kapu regulate human behavior in the face of that which is sacred—mountain summits, water supplies, fisheries, blood, great leaders, and other sources of life. Kapu remind us how to act, in light of our place in the more-than-human family that is our world. Historically oral pronouncements, kapu can be seen as enactments of Kanaka jurisdiction, on the Mauna and beyond.[4]

What happened on and around Maunakea in 2019 was much more than a struggle to stop the TMT from being built on our sacred summit. It was a rebirth of Kanaka Maoli jurisdiction on a scale we had not seen for two centuries. By asserting our own forms of jurisdiction, Kānaka destabilized the self-proclaimed sovereignty of the occupying settler state.

The year 2019 marked exactly two hundred years since the breaking of the ʻai kapu—a historical set of rules related to food preparation, eating, and gender that structured relations between humans and deities and between men and women. In her book *The Kingdom and the Republic*, Noelani Arista explains that "the end of the ʻai kapu took along with it the schedule of rituals regulating the pace of people's agricultural lives . . . the lives of Hawaiians were no longer structured by the ritual calendar. Lives were marked to a different time." In short, Kānaka began to transition from ceremonies focused on rhythms of the natural/spiritual world to rituals and social events focused on markets, on chronological and biblical time.

What provoked the nineteenth-century shift from oral kapu to written law was that Hawaiian political leaders were confronted with white male foreigners who were violently demanding sexual access to Hawaiian women's bodies. When we consider this historical fact, then it is all the more significant that wāhine and māhū, along with kāne, were so central in leading assertions of Kanaka jurisdiction on Maunakea.

In light of historical and ongoing heteropatriarchal machinations of the US occupation of Hawaiʻi, it is incredibly significant that mana māhū and mana wāhine—as assertions of Hawaiian juridical and sovereign power—have been central in the Kū Kiaʻi Mauna movement. This is a key to why the movement was so successful. We were celebrating and embracing (once again) the political leadership of Native Hawaiian people as a collective organizing beyond a Western binary gender system. As Heoli Osorio taught on the mauna: "Our aloha is not straight," because we love one another through honoring how we are connected by our lands and waters.

Oceanic and trans-Indigenous solidarities were also critical to the success of this movement. One vibrant example occured on the tenth day of the blockade, when a Tongan delegation of over a hundred people visited the Mauna. Families, elders, and people of various ages, rocking red dresses, ta'ovala, and Tonga rugby jerseys processed down the Saddle Road. A red river of kainga flowed onto Ke Ala Hulu Kūpuna (The Way of the Beloved Elders, also known as the Mauna Kea Access Road). They sang in harmony, with Tonga flags flying high and wrapped around their bodies. Kumu Hinaleimoana Wong has poured years of her life into building relationships between Kanaka Maoli and Tongan communities in both our archipelagos. In turn, Tongan community leaders in Hawai'i, like Ulise Funaki and Tevita Ka'ili, also became key players in a parallel struggle on O'ahu to protect the Kahuku community against the siting of massive wind turbines only five hundred meters from homes and schools.

Decades earlier, Tongan scholar 'Epeli Hau'ofa found inspiration for a new vision of our region as he drove on the Saddle Road between Mauna Loa and Maunakea: "As I watched the Big Island of Hawai'i expanding into and rising from the depths," he wrote, "I saw in it the future for Oceania, our sea of islands." This framing of "our sea of islands" contrasts the imperial view of our Pacific region as tiny islands in a far sea. Hau'ofa reminds us that

> [our] future lies in the hands of our own people, and not of those who would prescribe [it] for us. . . . Oceania is vast, Oceania is expanding, Oceania is hospitable and generous, Oceania is humanity rising from the depths of brine and regions of fire deeper still, Oceania is us. We are the sea, we are the ocean, we must wake up to this ancient truth and together use it to overturn all hegemonic views that aim ultimately to confine us again, physically and psychologically.[5]

His vision was not only prophetic. His words helped bring the solidarities that animated the Kū Kia'i Mauna movement into being. Many of our fellow Oceanians made the pilgrimage to Maunakea or expressed their solidarity from across the sea that connects us.

On August 16, 2019, when a pan-Micronesian delegation traveled along the Saddle Road and then turned onto Ke Ala Hulu Kūpuna, Mauna protector Pua Case called out to them in a speech that resonated with Hauʻofa's words:

we are the hoaloha, we are the friends, the comrades, the allies,
we are kākou apau, and we are here to aloha ʻāina, love this land . . .
we are the guardians who stand strong as mountains; we are these rocks standing.
we are the ground, the foundation under our feet.
we are protectors of the waters of Mauna a Wakea, of waters around the world
. . . and we rise like a mighty wave . . . E hū e! Hū!"

At the feet of Kanaka Maoli elders, our Oceanic relatives from various Micronesian islands presented offerings and expressions of support, and they reminded everyone gathered that the protection of Maunakea is also connected to the protection of Litekyan, Pågan, and Tinian from further imperialist military expansion.

They embodied the term "hoawelo like," which kiaʻi Pua Case coined in the chant "Oli Kukulu," which she composed and taught to countless groups in the Kū Kiaʻi Mauna uprising. The chant calls out to those who would join the kiaʻi in protection of waters and lands: "E nā hoaʻāina ē / E nā hoawelo like ē / E nā hoapili ē." With these three lines, she offers three possible positions to inhabit in relation to the ʻāina and their protectors. The root word "hoa" can refer to an associate, a peer, or even an antagonist, depending on the modifier that follows. Hoaʻāina are the people of that place, the Kanaka Maoli in the case of Hawaiʻi. While similar to terms like ally or accomplice or comrade that have been used to designate supporters in movements, *hoawelo like* captures a distinctly Hawaiian cultural viewpoint, where "welo" conjures imagery like the ways leaves or a cape flutter when blown by the wind; the setting of the sun; a star by which whose movements a sailor can navigate. Hoawelo like are those with whom there is both an ancestral connection *and* who are inspired to move together with you. Hoapili are the close friends, which can include anyone who joins in the struggle, who offers their mutual care, respect, and aloha.

By continuing to assert our own forms of jurisdiction, the Kānaka Maoli who are hoaʻāina to Maunakea, along with their hoawelo like and hoapili, destabilized the self-proclaimed sovereignty of the occupying settler state. Instead we reinvested in own governing authority. Expressions of mana wāhine and mana māhū were central to these jurisdictional practices of collective care and collective authority, because such mana is manifest in the lands and waters that give us life.

At the Puʻuhonua o Puʻuhuluhulu on Maunakea, a noncapitalist community grounded in living Hawaiian cultural practice and Oceanic solidarity rose like the kupukupu ferns that grow from cracks in the black lava rock and unfurl toward the sun.

43.

Toward Transnational Feminist Futures

Loretta J. Ross interviewed by the Editors

The reproductive justice movement is rooted in Black feminist thought and women of color coalitions built in the late twentieth century; thus, it is often referenced in discussions of cross-racial feminist solidarity. One of the twelve Black women who created the reproductive justice framework is Loretta J. Ross, a cofounder of SisterSong Women of Color Reproductive Justice Collective, which helped define the three core values of reproductive justice: the right to have a child, the right to not have a child, and the right to parent a child or children in safe and healthy environments.[1] Her lifelong activism and scholarship informs our own work and understandings as Black and Asian feminists working in solidarity with one another.

In June 2022, we sat down with Ross to talk about her learnings as a leader in the reproductive justice movement, transnational solidarities, longevity in activism, and more. The following conversation has been edited for clarity and flow.[2]

Editors: Why are solidarities crucial to the reproductive justice movement?

Loretta Ross: I can't imagine any form of reproductive oppression that can be solved by only the group targeted for that time because like any other form of oppression, it takes solidarity to address it. I think it takes all identities, all generations, and many political perspectives to solve problems of oppression. I'm not sure if any one group, however they're targeted, can solve the problem. If Black people could get rid of anti-Black racism by ourselves, it would've been long gone. Obviously, we can't, and it ain't, so all oppressions take a team to work on.

What have been political frameworks that have been useful in building relationships of solidarity?

When I was much younger, I was a Marxist-Leninist, so I thought that everybody who agreed on the class struggle, I could work with in solidarity. Then I found people who were so devoted to the class struggle that they ignored race and gender, and I had to find people who could work on those intersections in a way that people who were straight up a Marxist or Leninist couldn't do.

Then solidarity was built based on what issues we worked on, particularly transnational solidarity. Back in the eighties and the nineties, I spent a lot more time working internationally than I did domestically sometimes, because there was so much imperialist aggression by the United States against other countries. As a radical activist, we did a lot of work in the Philippines fighting the Marcos dictatorship, or in Nicaragua fighting the Contras, or in El Salvador fighting the US government, or in South Africa fighting apartheid.

I'm not seeing activists go to other countries as much as when I was younger and actually spend time in those countries doing solidarity work. It seems to be exceedingly rare nowadays for that to happen. I don't know if people think that because they can get information through the internet, they don't have to go anywhere. It's very disappointing that we don't do as many of what we call exposure trips, where you go immerse yourself in a country so that you can come back and describe the reality of what US tax dollars are doing to people overseas.

In terms of your transnational solidarity work, we'd love to hear you expand a little bit on that. What did you learn, and how did that bring you into the reproductive justice movement?

Once I started doing international work, we started with the UN World Decade for Women, going to conferences in Copenhagen, Kenya, and Beijing. When you meet with feminists from other countries, they tell you, "We could solve all of our problems if you would get the United States's foot off of our neck." They always interpreted to me that the role of US feminists was to stop US imperialism: "Don't come over here thinking you're going to save us when you can't even save yourself from your own government."

That was always the rationale that I took toward doing solidarity work. It wasn't about what I could do for other people; it's what I needed to learn to have an impact here domestically on my government. It's not like the Peace Corps.[3] It's not like going over there and helping these poor brown people learn how to eat or plant seeds. It's about changing our country's policies toward these other countries, particularly with what they call low-intensity conflicts. Because we would not actually have wars with these countries, it was low-intensity oppression against the countries that stifled their development and stifled their ability to make independent financial or economic relationships.

To use as an example, I've been to the Philippines three or four times. We always went at the invitation of GABRIELA, which is a coalition of women's organizations in the Philippines. They're the ones who created that famous phrase "women's rights are human rights." Most people don't even know where it started, but they started it in opposition to the Marcos dictatorship.[4] The Philippines is a Catholic country, but we learned that nuns in Luzon were assisting women achieve reproductive autonomy under the radar of the Catholic Church, which was mind-blowing. I was quite surprised to find these very bold nuns who distributed information about underground abortion kits that they would obtain from feminists in the US because they were committed to not letting people die from unsafe abortions. That's just one story of reproductive oppression.

How have you seen Black and Asian feminists utilize, organize, and expand on reproductive justice as a theory and praxis?

Well, very specifically here in the United States: Reproductive justice was created in 1994 by twelve Black women. SisterSong was founded in 1997, and one of our founding member organizations was called Asian Pacific Islanders for Reproductive Health, or APIRH, founded before as Asians and Pacific Islanders for Choice (APIC). They're one of the sixteen founding members of SisterSong.

When we embraced using reproductive justice as our framework, APIRH renamed themselves Asian Communities for Reproductive Justice (ACRJ). I think they were the first women of color group to incorporate "reproductive justice" into their name. We cowrote a paper together called *A New Vision.*[5] They expanded the framework and refined it. Sujatha Jesudason worked with them at the time and is the one who did the analysis identifying the distinction between reproductive health, reproductive rights, and reproductive justice. Then maybe a few years after that they renamed themselves Forward Together. They keep rebranding themselves as they see their mission shifting.

Our Asian Pacific Islander mini-community within SisterSong represented seventeen countries, and these seventeen countries didn't all get along with each other. It was a misnomer to think that they could all just peacefully be together and that there weren't tensions within the group. The API community was always complicated by the large number of countries represented, many of which had been invaded by Japan and had very uneasy relationships with Japan. That was hard to navigate.

That didn't even deal with the fact that we still had to learn to be culturally competent across races and ethnic groups, so that we could say, "What do Black women know about Asian American women?" and "What do Latinos know about Black women?"

What are the movement histories that you draw upon in your own movement building?

In 1985, I was told by the president of the National Organization for Women (NOW) that I needed to organize women of color to attend the first abortion rights march scheduled for April 9, 1986. I had to go to my Black feminist elders and ask them how in the world am I supposed to talk to communities about abortion when we are still calling it "the A word?" Nobody was actually talking about abortion in the Black community in particular, but as far as I could tell in no other community of color, really. Fortunately, there were a couple of older Black women, not the least of whom was Shirley Chisholm, who was the first Black woman to head up NARAL's [now renamed Reproductive Freedom for All] board of directors.[6] Donna Brazile, Jewel Jackson McCabe, Faye Wattleton, and Dorothy Height, and others who had been fighting the fight for a long, long time helped me understand that the history was there. It just wasn't well known.

I started doing research on that early activism of Black women around abortion, and I wrote "African-American Women and Abortion" based on that.[7] That writing project was born out of an organizing need. I had to pull people together over and over again for our marches, so I had to produce evidence that we had this history of working on these issues as a way of persuading the groups that they needed to pick up the mantle and do as their ancestors had done.

My scholarship was born out of organizing, because I had to prove to people we had this history—and the same with Indigenous women, the same with Latinas, and the same with API women. I would have to do a lot of research about what took place before and present arguments for why people need to be engaged now.

When you were organizing the march, what were some initial reactions from community members when you were discussing abortion, given that they didn't know about those histories?

First of all, they said, "We don't have abortions." That was the popular myth, except that you could look at the Guttmacher Institute statistics.[8] One-third of the abortions obtained in America are obtained by Black women, so "we don't have abortions" is a myth. Coupled with the rising HIV/AIDS crisis, not talking about sex was a death sentence in our community. We had to point that out to people. Not talking about sex is not a survival strategy. We had to come at it through HIV/AIDS and through reproductive oppression to have these conversations.

We would just be rude and insistent, no matter how embarrassed the sorority was, or the church was. If you call yourself representing Black women and you aren't noticing that one-third of your congregation has probably had an abortion, you ain't serving your people if you can't talk about this. If you can't notice that your Black children are at risk of HIV/AIDS at X times the rate of white kids, you ain't serving your people very well. We had to be pretty aggressive to get these conversations going.

What have been political contradictions and tensions in movement-building spaces that you've been a part of?

I think the biggest contradiction is internalized oppression, that master's voice that ends up affecting how you work with others who are also oppressed. The problem is that the work we do is very attractive to people who are traumatized, so they bring their trauma into the movement, into the work. We have to learn not to be surprised when that trauma shows up because that's who our base is. People who are having great lives and don't feel any stress, they're not the ones who are drawn to human rights work. It's the people who life has been fucked over in some kind of way that are drawn to this work, and so it's not unexpected that that's going to show up in the work.

The thing that we have to focus on is how to manage that trauma showing up because the goal of the movement is not to address your trauma but to end the reasons for that trauma. We have to spend a lot of time persuading people that the movement is not a therapy space. Some people need to go get therapy instead of a keyboard because they act out their trauma through the internet and social media. That ain't going to help anything. All they do is blow up our organizations and a lot of relationships, and they still don't feel better about themselves. That's why I promote "calling in" instead of the "calling out/cancel culture" negative behaviors in our human rights movement.

There are a lot of tensions between Black and Asian communities. How does a movement move forward when people come into a movement with trauma, but those traumas also have roots and connections to each other's communities and histories?

I was too young to remember the Korean War. The war I remember was the Vietnam War because that was when I was conscious enough to know that my classmates were going there, and they were dying. I first saw Asian American and African American solidarity happen within the antiwar movement against the Vietnam War.

We saw an immediate impact on the Black community with the relocation of Vietnamese refugees. That was the beginning of the whole Vietnamese nail shop industry in the Black community. To this day, I've been going to this one shop for thirty or forty years. That's where we saw a lot of contact and communication start taking place. But you can never talk about relationships between the Black and the Asian American community without talking about the imperialist wars that our country was involved in.

It was really sad, because during the height of the Rodney King protests in 1992, that's when we had a real fracturing of the Black-Asian relationship because a Korean store owner killed a Black girl.[9] She accused her of shoplifting in a store in Los Angeles. That set relationships backward because it highlighted the fact that what had happened in the Black community was that the little mom-and-pop stores that Jewish people used to run were now being bought out by Asian Americans. What was consistent through all of that was that the Black people were denied loans to operate these stores themselves. It was almost like Asian Americans started occupying the economic niche that Jewish Americans had occupied within the Black community as store owners and landlords. That produces a certain amount of tension. But even within that, there were always conscious people trying to work on Black-Asian alliances.

What's happening that is a concern to me is that more and more of our immigrant communities are tilting toward the right and not leftist or progressive like you would expect them to be. Particularly I think that there's a real risk of high-income Asian Americans soon being read as white.[10]

What other shifts and transformations are you seeing within movement spaces you're part of?

I started out by saying that the biggest shift that I've seen, and the most disappointing one, is the lack of transnational solidarity. When I was younger, you did as much international work as you did domestic. Now I don't see that happening as much.

The other shift I see is, I hate to say it without sounding condemnatory, a lot more "me" focused and not "we" focus in the work. Like I said, this expectation that a movement is supposed to fulfill you, supposed make you feel safe, comforted, and accepted. You don't join this work because you need friends and a womb, you join this work because you want to end oppression. We call it the navel-gazing stage. "If it isn't happening in my body, it ain't important."

One of the ways that manifests itself is a bad interpretation of relational organizing. When relational organizing is misinterpreted, there's a lot of emphasis on you getting to know people and people getting to know you, but then you only develop a circle of concern for the people you know or those who know you. That's a very limited way of feeling compassion. You should feel compassion for people in Yemen if you've never met a Yemeni person in your life. With relational organizing, they attach all these big words to it, but when it's reduced to its essence, it's the same old white supremacist kith-and-kin and system, just with radical language wrapped around it. It's not nearly as original as people think it is. To me, the best use of relational organizing is the relationship you establish with your integrity, that you care about bombs being dropped in Syria because of who you are, not whether you know a Syrian. I think the whole concept of relational organizing has gone astray. That's a shift that I would like us to correct.

With the overturning of *Roe v. Wade*, we would love to get your thoughts on reproductive justice at this political juncture.

I think the right's obsession with abortion is around trying to compel white women to have more babies. I don't think they want more brown and Black babies to be born. I don't think they want more API babies to be born. Let's be clear, all of us who are people of color, we're like roadkill in the struggles for abortion rights, because if they could restrict abortion to people of color, they'd send Cadillacs to take us to the clinics. We know that for a fact. If you don't have a racial analysis attached to your gender analysis around abortion, you're missing half the story.

Certainly when you look at how low-income women of color have been treated, they never really enjoyed the full privileges of *Roe* in the first place, particularly with the passage of the Hyde Amendment, so they've always dealt with restrictions on abortion, at least since 1976.[11] In many ways, things will change very little for them, because abortion was never quite accessible for them in the first place.

We're going to have to keep low-income women at the center of our lens and make sure that we provide whatever services we can—whether it's an underground railroad taking them to other states, smuggling in the abortion pills, or setting up a couple of hundred Jane Collectives around the country where we're doing D&E abortions.[12] And we need the pro-choice movement to stand as the lawyers to get us out of jail in case we get arrested and prosecuted for doing what we need to do.

The reproductive rights/pro-choice wing of our movement is going to continue the legal fight, but meanwhile, we have to make sure that the direct services component is emphasized. I think the midwives and doulas of the world are going to be the heroes of our movement because they're going to be standing on the front lines to make sure people don't die.

What advice would you give organizers today? Especially in terms of achieving longevity in activism and movement spaces, how do we continue this work without burning out or selling out?

I can share with y'all what someone told me when I was sixteen: "You party as hard as you work." Somebody said that to me after getting tear-gassed at my first demonstration, and I've never lost that.

You must have a toggle switch where you can turn your consciousness on and off. Sometimes you turn that consciousness off so you can watch *Twilight* without a feminist critique or shake your booty to some totally inappropriate music without saying, "I feel bad about myself because I like this beat." Then when it's time to do the work, you toggle your consciousness back on, and you do the work. You accept that you're a complicated person, and that you will burn out if you're *on* all the time. Not only that, you'll piss everybody off because you're a Debbie Downer. Everybody's trying to have fun, and you're trying to tell them why they shouldn't be having fun.

A few years later, one of my mentors, Leonard Zeskind, put it differently. We had just come back from Blakely, Georgia, where the fire department was run by the Ku Klux Klan. A 5-year-old Black kid had perished in a house fire with the fire station only two blocks from his house because the Klan fire chief called a Black home on fire "neighborhood beautification," so they let this kid die.[13] No one, of course, was ever prosecuted. When I was coming back from Blakely with Leonard, he told me, "Loretta, you need to lighten up. You take everything too seriously. You take everything to heart. Fighting Nazis should be fun. It's being a Nazi that sucks." I say that all the time. If you're not having fun doing this work, you need to examine what you can do better to embrace more of the joy of the work as opposed to the horror.

Toni Cade said this in her book, "Our job is to make the revolution irresistible."[14] What makes it irresistible is showing how much joy, fun, and fulfillment you get out of doing this work, even as you're looking at the vomit of the world. That's my sustainability plant. You ain't never seen a party until Loretta turns up and starts partying.

44.

Collective Reproductive Freedom Is Racial Justice

Senti Sojwal

The first time I had a pregnancy scare, I was twenty years old on a study abroad program in Havana, Cuba. I felt young and alive spending evenings dancing until the sun rose and gave in, easily, to everything around me. I had a brief fling. We weren't safe. My period was late, and one night, two friends and I gathered in a circle around my pregnancy test like witches performing a seance. I knew then, as I know now, that the decision to terminate a pregnancy is mine and mine alone. That my future and body belongs to no one else but me. At the same time, women of color feminism also taught me that reproductive freedom is more than my individual choice, and that a liberated world is one in which all of us have the power to determine our lives for ourselves.

I am lucky to have called the reproductive justice movement my political home for over a decade, since those days as a young college student thirsty for meaning, organizing for gender equity, and having my world opened up by brilliant feminist thinkers like Loretta Ross, Audre Lorde, Chandra Talpade Mohanty, and many others for the first time. The Black feminist–led reproductive justice movement teaches us that we can only achieve reproductive justice through an intersectional lens: by analyzing power systems, centering the most marginalized, and joining together in solidarity, as all our struggles are connected.

In a historic decision on June 24, 2022, the US Supreme Court reversed *Roe v. Wade*, the landmark 1973 legislation that made access to abortion a federal right. With this decision, abortion access as an essential health service became unavailable and rendered criminal in large swaths of the United States. The implications of the ruling were immediate and devastating: mass chaos, implementation of "trigger bans" in thirteen states that banned abortion immediately after the court decision, clinic shutdowns, and a widespread threat to bodily autonomy and self-determination.

Mass protests swelled in city streets, municipal centers, and parks from small towns to major cities. Many protestors, largely organized by mainstream reproductive rights organizations, wore green (a symbolic homage to Latin American abortion freedom fighters), while also waving homemade signs with long-standing reproductive rights slogans from white-led feminism: "bans off our bodies," "abortion is health care," and the ever-present "my body, my choice." While the sentiments behind these statements clearly beg repeating in our current political moment, its focus on individual rights versus a resounding demand for our collective liberation rings hollow—especially for people of color, who have long experienced attacks on our bodies and livelihood at the hands of white supremacy. Solely "rights-based" frameworks are clearly failing our communities, especially the most marginalized.

While fear and outrage permeated the general political sentiment from historically white reproductive rights and women's organizations like Planned Parenthood, Reproductive Freedom for All (formerly NARAL Pro-choice America), and the National Organization for Women (NOW), the sentiment from reproductive justice organizers of color was decidedly different. No less aghast, but unshocked: "We are not surprised. The courts have never served our communities," said Lupe M. Rodríguez, executive director of the National Latina Institute for Reproductive Justice to CNN. "Once again, the Supreme Court has gone against the will of the people."[1] People who have long lived within the violence of state-sanctioned reproductive control in this country, including Black, brown, Asian, Indigenous, and queer people, have known that this nation is built on the control and punishment of racialized people. In the emergence of a post-Roe nation, the mainstream political and social analysis of what this ruling means for our futures continues to be largely absent of intersectionality and an understanding of the long-standing struggles of people of color and queer and trans communities. The individualism behind the statement "my body, my choice" represents a white feminist politic that has no place in the collective imagining of the future that marginalized people require to live with true autonomy.

The reproductive justice organizing framework, founded by Black women in the nineties, upholds that the three tenets of reproductive justice are: the right to have a child, to not have a child, and to raise the children we do have in safe and healthy communities. A far cry from the abortion-centric narrative of mainstream reproductive rights organizations, this framework calls on us to analyze power systems, address intersecting oppressions, center the most marginalized, and join together across issues and identities—only then will we achieve reproductive justice. Where the dominant narrative says that the right to abortion is the only way to measure our right to control our reproductive lives, a reproductive justice analysis understands that our reproductive destinies are deeply tied to our economic realities, our gender presentation and experience, our family structure, and more.

One of the most ludicrous arguments made by the court and our national leadership as they overturned *Roe* and steadily rolled back our reproductive access state by state is that today, forced pregnancy and parenthood are no longer the "hardship" they once were. The line of thinking is that in the United States today, women (to them, of course, women are the singular entity requiring reproductive health care) can balance career and family, and those who wish not to parent can simply give up their children for adoption. The idea is we have achieved gender equality due to policies prohibiting discrimination on the basis of sex and requiring equal opportunity, and we now live in a golden age of "women's empowerment." Never mind our complete lack of a social safety net for working and immigrant families, a global public health crisis that has upended our education system and pushed millions of women out of the workforce, the rising cost of childcare and lack of support for care workers, devastating maternal mortality rates for women of color, a trauma-inducing child welfare state, and our broken health care system that has created widespread racial health disparities.

White women are angry because their government has told them their bodies are not their own. However, this has long been the reality for many. The consequences of overturning *Roe* are not new to us. History has shown us time and time again that white women will be comfortable clinging to sexism as a signifier of their oppression while upholding and perpetuating systems of violence that deny and punish autonomy and self-determination to people of color, especially Black people. From the white suffragettes who left women of color out of their fight and Carolyn Bryant falsely accusing the teenage Emmett Till of whistling at her in a Mississippi grocery store, leading to his gruesome lynching, to the modern-day "Karens" who call the police on Black people simply living their lives, white women have shown they are content with state violence that protects them and secures their position of power and privilege through the cost of ongoing violence and harm against others.

People of color have long lived under the violence of state-sanctioned misogyny—with our bodily autonomy constantly criminalized and under siege, we must break from white feminist epistemologies to make way for the radical vision of reproductive justice. In a post-Roe America, achieving reproductive justice for all feels farther away than ever. With this devastating attack on abortion rights, it's people of color, the working class, disabled folks, immigrants, queer and trans people, and others on the margins that continue to suffer the most. Reproductive justice is racial justice—and we're in the fight for our future.

Reproductive Control as a Tool of White Supremacy

The United States' long history of reproductive coercion is cruel, devastating, and intimately tied to race. Many know that the roots of gynecological practice are entrenched in harrowing racism. J. Marion Sims, the "father of modern gynecology," conducted medical experiments on enslaved Black women without anesthesia before perfecting his techniques and using them on white women who were sedated.[2] In the 1950s, the first large-scale human trial of contraceptive pills was conducted in a public housing project in Puerto Rico.[3] The eugenics movement advocated for the compulsory sterilization of the "feeble-minded," poor people, and people of color. In the 1970s, thousands of Native women were sterilized without their consent. These abuses go on throughout history and continue, in many forms, today.

As an Asian American, I have seen racist and sexist false stereotypes used to criminalize abortions and justify abortion bans and excuse the racial profiling of our communities, and we remain critically underserved when it comes to reproductive health-care access and education.[4]

For example, cultural stereotypes about Asian preferences for sons are often cited by legislators as reasons for banning sex-selective abortions in the United States. This is an anti-immigrant myth that supports efforts of our right-wing political leadership to undermine reproductive rights and justice while sinisterly co-opting the language of gender equity. Similar to the justifications used for sex-selective abortion bans like "protecting women," patronizing women also justified continued colonial rule in parts of Asia and is part of a much longer history of cultural misrepresentation used to disempower and attack women. Today, nearly one-third of low-income Asian women live in states with limited abortion access. Like other marginalized groups, Asian Americans' access to health care is complicated by several intersecting barriers, including affordability, immigration status, language accessibility, and insurance. Abortion bans based on race selection or fetal diagnosis target the moral "reason" behind a person's decision to end a pregnancy.[5] However, there are no "good" or "bad" reasons to have an abortion, and politicians have no place interrogating or criminalizing our decision-making when it comes to our health, families, and futures.

Throughout our country's history, the reproduction and fertility of people of color have been utilized and manipulated to benefit a narrow white patriarchal ableist political agenda hell-bent on diminishing the power of others.[6] The overturning of *Roe* is another step in the harrowing playbook of advancing white supremacy through reproductive control and diminishing self-determination.

Abortion and Reproductive Justice Are Critical Racial and Economic Justice Issues

People of color have more abortions in the United States than do white people, which has been linked to systemic barriers to health care and health education. Antiabortion actors often stigmatize abortion as an "irresponsible" choice, a racist and classist claim that further marginalizes those who already experience barriers to care. Research shows that when abortion access is banned or restricted, maternal mortality rates rise and access to other critical reproductive health care like natal support and birth control becomes even more limited.[7] The health of women of color, especially Black women, is an ongoing and appalling crisis in this country. According to a 2014 World Health Organization report, the maternal mortality rate in the United States grew by a whopping 136 percent in the years between 1990 and 2013—one of the worst rates in the so-called developed world.[8] Poor people of color experience the brunt of this devastation and preventable death; in 2021, the Centers for Disease Control found that Black women face a maternal mortality rate three times that of white women.[9]

Abortion access is a critical mental health issue, too. The landmark Turnaway Study, led by demographer Diana Greene Foster, found that denying women wanted abortions worsened anxiety and lowered self-esteem.[10] The Turnaway Study also found that women denied abortions were four times more likely to live in poverty four years later, and were three times more likely to be unemployed than those who were able to obtain an abortion.[11] Forced pregnancy has often led to loss of job and education opportunities and higher debt rates. In a misogynistic and white supremacist country that fails to support mothers, birthing people, and families, this comes as no surprise. With a majority of workers having little to no access to paid family leave, the sky-high costs of childcare, and lack of pay equity to give birth in this country is to be punished economically, especially as a person of color.[12] When we can control if, when, and how we reproduce and also provide social infrastructure to support reproductive access, we create a society where bodily autonomy is honored. It's clear that investing in the well-being of our communities means investing in and expanding abortion access and reproductive health.

Where Do We Go from Here?

In *Against White Feminism: Notes on Disruption*, author Rafia Zakaria defines a white feminist as "someone who refuses to consider the role that whiteness and the racial privilege attached to it have played and continue to play in universalizing white feminist concerns, agendas, and beliefs as being those of all feminism and all feminists."[13] White feminists, who took up abortion rights as the central pillar of their movement, have failed us. White feminist models of organizing for individual rights have not used their power to truly join forces with women of color and present a collective, organized front in the battle for our reproductive lives. As people of color, we are uniquely positioned in this moment to carry forward a powerful, visible, and charged reproductive justice movement and truly "pro-life" message—one that fights for the autonomy and livelihood of everyone.

According to a 2022 Pew research study, a majority of Americans want to safeguard our abortion access. Yet our elected leadership and Supreme Court sides with an extreme right-wing minority and puts our health and lives at risk. Yes, while we must fight tooth and nail to ensure that abortion access is protected and strategically organize to expand the court; we must also think beyond passing laws and winning elections.

All those years ago, sitting in a circle with my friends, I breathed a sigh of relief when only one stripe appeared: I wasn't pregnant. Many years later, in the spring of 2024, I did have an unplanned pregnancy, at thirty-three. I was in a very different place in my life. Still, I wasn't yet ready for parenthood, and with the support of my partner, I chose to have an abortion. It was not a difficult decision, and one I made with a sense of love and care for myself.

Living in New York City, with a stable job where I had PTO and health insurance, I was privileged to schedule my abortion without hurdles. The week of my procedure, hundreds of miles away, Florida's six-week abortion ban went into effect. Had I lived there, I would have had to travel out of state for my care. The complete cruelty and shattering injustice of this ban, prohibiting bodily autonomy before most people know they are pregnant, filled me with rage and resolve. I want to live in a world where every person has the safety of knowing they will have access to the care they need, whatever it may be, on demand, without apology. Our future belongs to us.

The reproductive justice framework implores us to imagine a world that reflects the values and the needs of our communities and where our communities can live with dignity, joy, and opportunity—where our identities and experiences are honored, where reproductive justice is understood as environmental justice, economic justice, and racial justice. Achieving this is a process of deep love and creativity—an exercise in expanding our belief in what's possible. We are not just fighting for abortion access. We are fighting for collective liberation.

45.

Síyah, Hypervisible in Silence Is Violence

Priscillia Kounkou-Hoveyda

At the end of April, my mother unfailingly came to my school, nestled between the towers of the projects in the Parisian suburbs, and negotiated with the director for an early dismissal. A single working mother, she needed me to go live with my grandparents every year so she could "have some space." Since I was always top of my class, the director relented unconcerned, and I'd fly to Iran until September.

I'd begin then to mentally prepare myself for something I was not allowed to discuss with my family. Something that I couldn't even bear bringing up to myself without my stomach churning with fear.

At night, *maman* says I scream in my sleep. She took me to the psychiatrist, who prescribed some capsules to help with that and my sleepwalking.

"What if she goes outside on the balcony one night and jumps?" She anxiously presses the doctor.

"Why would your ten-year-old even subconsciously commit such an act?" He leans in my direction expecting a response.

I didn't know what they were referring to, but what I knew was that I was going to bring my Game Boy and Super Mario World and that those worlds would be the ones I exist in.

"Why can't you sleep well, child?" my mother whispers, curling my hand into hers on our way on the bus to the tall French towers, only staring at the skies they thought they were promised.

"It doesn't feel as if I sleep bad, maman," I whisper back as we push the broken glass door of our tower open.

15 June 1992, Tehran, Iran

Episode 120—I'd choose a title of the episode at the end of my day since I didn't know what grandma had planned for me: more errands at the bazaar, another *mehmooni*, or the busy park where I could never disappear.[1]

The knock on my door has me pause my gaming with Mario's fist up in the air about to jump to another hill. I've already made it to Level 3, and I know to slow down if I want this game to last me the four months left.

"*Papar,* come put your *manteau* and *roussari* on, we're going out."[2] Grandma's voice is traveling from the main door. She must be ready to go.

I've already used up all the excuses to avoid going out this week, even managed to skip one of my great aunt's many *mehmooni.*

I'm just hoping it's not the Grand Bazaar.

It's the supermarket down the street, Grandma explains, pushing her other foot in the beige orthopedic shoes her favorite son got her from America. I flatten the frizz of my curls against my scalp the best I can, although I know my hair always ends up rising like a riot under my *roussari.*

Grandma walks her usual nonchalant pace, one hand carrying her bag, the other dug in the pocket of her manteau. Her flowery roussari perfectly set on her faux blonde faux curls. The sidewalk is wet; I imagine neighbors watering the pavement to make the streets cooler.

Salam khanoom, an old woman stops us as we are about to finally make the turn. She nods in my direction and through her teeth gripping at the hem of her flowery chador asks the questions most people ask when they see a *siyah,* black, as a reference to the color black and the color of my skin, me.

I wish I could disappear into one of the worlds in Super Mario, the one with multiple rainbows in the sky.

Yes, I look really *bamazeh,* and no, it's not the sun and it doesn't wash off and never will.[3]

It must be this woman's first time seeing a siyah.

Even the big woman at the hammam maman I used to love being washed by when we were living in Iran hadn't managed to make me lighter, despite rubbing the *kisse* on my skin with more vigor than on my mother's.[4]

The heat has already caused some of my curls to rebel under the roussari. I'm only hoping this won't attract more inquisitions. I had seen a siyah on rare occurrences in Tehran, an occurrence that I could count on one hand only, despite me being called *siyah* every day.

Siyah was my other name around here.

"*Siyah!*" The car screeches by as we enter the supermarket.

We stop at the house cleaning aisle. I thought Grandma had already cleaned our two-story house all the way to the basement.

She crouches down, selects a detergent, gets back up, and as I'm about to trail down the aisle, a man hisses, "*Soosk! Soosk e siyah.*"

I turn.

"Black roach" is another one of my nicknames here. The man, mid-twenties, wearing a fitted cap, is already spraying soosk repellant all over my face. I flap the fumes away and see him walk away through my coughing spree.

Grandma is gently placing the detergent on the checkout counter.

We didn't talk about what happened that day. She never acknowledged any of it even happening.

Grandpa was home early from his game of *takhteh*, with warm *nan sangaak*, already claiming that if I prayed more, he'd love me more, his furry eyebrows carved into his wrinkled skin like writings.[5]

Allah never heard my prayers, not even the time I prayed not to have someone offer me work again in front of the other kids at the park.

"All of this is in your head, my child," Grandma said that time I came back from the park with a nosebleed and a swollen cheek, as I search for words to explain how I felt.

"Why can't you keep clean when you play?! I'm going to have to wash you again!" She pushes cotton pads inside my nostril. They had also called me *kaka siyah*, but I wasn't sure if my feelings were hurt because of it.[6]

I turn on the knob of the old television in my room. Pass on the prayer channel, some static footage about Iran-Iraq martyrs, and then the screen smoothens to a Persian-dubbed American cartoon, *The Adventures of Huckleberry Finn*.

Jim, a formerly enslaved African American man, got in trouble again in today's episode. Always slow to understand what's happening, the 10-year-old white American boy, Huck, is the one saving him. I loved Jim, although it made me uncomfortable to know other kids were also watching this cartoon.

Ali, who lived across the street and acted like Captain Tsubasa in the Persian dubbed Japanese football anime that was showing next, was the one who had started calling me Jim.

I didn't dare go down to watch the game, cherishing my loneliness as the only safe space from the mockeries that being *siyah* entailed. So, I pushed open the mosquito mesh door to my balcony and observed the game from up there.

Every day, I'd imagine my life being that of another person, an unlucky girl who did not have the words to even describe how she was terribly unlucky. But I wasn't her and she wasn't me and the acting was impressive.

Closing my eyes that night I gave the day's episode the title:

"Soosk-e-siyah
black roach"

I hope tomorrow I get to stay in my bedroom or on the rooftop playing shadow or down in the basement playing with my uncle's old toy cars. I always have enough time to put them back on the mantle before Grandma gets down.

Credits roll.

June 1987, Tehran, Iran

I'm about to turn six, so my grandpa decided nobody would mind me starting first grade.

"This is your granddaughter, you're saying?" The shop owner asks somewhere between shock and disgust. My grandpa didn't like explaining how his grandchild turned siyah.

School was still in session the next day when Grandpa hurried his pace back home. The instructions were clear: if there are any bombings during school days, we are to hide under our desks.[7]

If I close my eyes really strongly, can they make me disappear?

It was ash that rained from the ceilings of the classroom onto the floors where all of us were curled up under our tables. Even the teacher's eyes are shut hard.

The first time she saw me, she had dragged me to the bathroom.

"Khoda, why are you so dirty??"[8]

I stare at my own reflection, my face wet from all the water she has poured on it, even on the hem of my maghnae, the compulsory veil reserved for pupils and students. The teacher is staring ahead at me, in the mirror. Her eyes round with stupor that none of her efforts had made the siyah go away.

The chuckles are what remind me of the presence of the other children. She turns off the water, flips me around:

"We are all children of Khoda, even a siyah," she says in a tone I aim to take for empathy.

Race isn't real in Iran. Racism is a product of my imagination and my existence as a result cannot be real.

I looked forward to existing in the suspended realms of the dreams I escaped to. There, I became Mitra, who looked much more like what my grandma's grandchild should have looked like: green eyes, soft hair, and rosy cheeks like the black-and-white wedding portrait of my grandma, which hung on her otherwise bare bedroom's wall.

It took me years before I came upon the words of Audre Lorde that taught me that "I feel, therefore I can be free."[9] Otherwise, I would have continued testifying against my feelings.

It took me years to research the few available historical records on the Persian Gulf slave trade and the story of Khyzran, born in Zanzibar in 1834 and trafficked into slavery in Southern Iran in 1856, where she fought for her freedom.

The Persian Gulf slave trade was abolished only in 1929. Grandpa was nine.

Yet conversations around the consequences of such histories, the communities formed and relationships that exist, are not allowed. To this day, the Islamic Republic is enforcing a dictate of identity that is devoid of any lived diversity that should inform points of view and society at large. Instead, a dictate of censorship and further systems of oppression against minoritized populations have been perpetrated for well over forty years.

Languages such as Bandari or Khargi that derive from populations of African and Arab descent and that are a mix of languages like Swahili, Persian, Arabic, and more are not taught at school. Visuals associated with Black folks—the very rare times there are any—are forced to exist through the "Abadani or Bandari lens," rich with folklore but devoid of any intellectual agency.[10]

Hossein's dad used to shave his head as soon as the first growth.

Kids would call me sheep and beat me up at recess, but the teachers were the worst.

Hossein dropped out of school at ten.

Then in his late twenties, he was arrested by the Bassiji, the Islamic police. The reason for his arrest was his hair: the locks he had grown were judged un-Islamic.

They shaved my locks in court and then I had to attend Islamic classes so I can understand why my hair is un-Islamic.

In 2023, following the death of Jina Mahsa Amin, who was arrested for allegedly showing "too much hair," Saba joined protests on the streets of her neighborhood. Despite Saba being from a city in the south where most populations of African descent live, in the neighborhood called *mahale-e-siyahan*, her sight stood out, especially in the context of widespread protests in the country.[11]

When Saba was ID'd on the streets by the police for protesting, she started coming home to find a large piece of coal with a COVID-19 mask wrapped around it at her doorstep.

Coal is another derogatory term used for Black folks in Iranian society. Saba's grandmother was eight years old when she was trafficked from Zanzibar into Iran with her parents, right before abolition.

One piece of coal per day every day, until Saba, fearful for her life, decided to go into hiding.

Despite harmful patterns of erasing it, race and racism have always been part of Iranian making and society. I founded the Collective for Black Iranians to think critically about who we are and to produce a variety of points of view that look into our society. The collective produces stories past and present of being Black and Iranian, from those of Khyzran and Wallade to those of Hossein and Saba, or mine, so that these histories and stories can contribute to furthering our understanding of who we are and to a more critical understanding of what is happening to us because of *who* and *where* we are.

Being Black and Iranian, Black and Middle Eastern, Black and Asian, has never been mutually exclusive. On the contrary, Blackness and Iranian identity is an inclusive reality that has been forming diverse points of view—despite little to no collective consciousness as to our existences and despite an environment that insists on national hegemony. It is beyond time to include the diversity of our points of view in the larger understanding of Iran and Iranian identity.

Credits roll.

46.

Black Feminist Solidarity and Palestine

Beverly Guy-Sheftall

This brief excerpt is from remarks given by Dr. Beverly Guy-Sheftall during the Black Women Radicals event Black Feminist Writers and Palestine, held on October 22, 2023. The moderator and panelists for the event also included Clarissa Brooks, Angela Y. Davis, Monaye Johnson, Briona Simone Jones, and Jaimee A. Swift. During her remarks, Dr. Guy-Sheftall reflects on her experience being a part of a delegation of Indigenous and women of color feminists to Palestine in June 2011. The excerpt has been edited for clarity.

My serious involvement with Palestine came as a result of my friendship with radical Black feminist historian Barbara Ransby. She was the one who organized us—eleven Indigenous and women of color—to go to Palestine in 2011. That week we were in Palestine was the most transformative week of my life. We were Palestinian, we were African American, we were South Asian, we were Indigenous. Some of us had grown up in South Africa. Some of us had grown up in the Jim and Jane Crow South, one of us grew up on a reservation.

I thought having grown up in the Jim Crow South in Memphis, Tennessee, that I really understood some of the worst aspects of oppression. Since 2011, I have not been able to get this trip out of my mind. I remember when we were on the buses, we were stopped. Israeli soldiers brought German shepherd dogs on the bus, and it reminded me of protesting in the sixties in the South. We also met a Palestinian family who was expelled from their house. When we came to visit the family, the young Jewish kids who were in the front of the house actually shouted obscenities at us. I remember going through checkpoints and we were not always treated with fairness and dignity. One of the things that I remember was meeting with Palestinian queers. There's the assumption that queer people are just in the West or in the US.

I want to read a little bit from the statement that Angela Davis insisted upon us writing, "A Call to Action from Indigenous and Women of Color Feminists":

> We reject the argument that to criticize the State of Israel is anti-Semitic. We stand with Palestinians, an increasing number of Jews, and other human rights activists all over the world in condemning the flagrant injustices of the Israeli occupation. We call upon all of our academic and activist colleagues in the US and elsewhere to join us by endorsing the BDS (boycott, divestment, and sanctions) campaign and by working to end US financial support, at $8.2 million daily, for the Israeli state and its occupation. We call upon all people of conscience to engage in serious dialogue about Palestine and to acknowledge connections between the Palestinian cause and other struggles for justice. Injustice anywhere is a threat to justice everywhere.

47.

"Commitment Is the Key"

Grace Lee Boggs and the Rigor of Revolution

Rachel Kuo

In historical recoveries of Black and Asian solidarities, Grace Lee Boggs is often propped up as a feminist icon. Her activism has demonstrated ways to reimagine political identifications and alignments, and her work has brought people into rigorous political relationship with one another, into struggle, and toward revolution. Through her lifetime, she has given us a tremendous body of writing about social movements, generating theory through her organizing praxis and through her speeches, correspondences, and newsletters. She offers us an imagination of revolution as longer, iterative processes, rather than as a singular, penultimate moment.[1]

Her 1971 essay "Organization Means Commitment (Commitment Is the Key)" offers us a set of ideas and practices toward understanding the rigor of solidarity and movement organizing, particularly what it means to maintain and build political relationships.[2] For Boggs, an ongoing commitment to collective learning and reflection alongside other people was a requirement for collective struggle. Sustaining political solidarity, Boggs writes, takes "time and patience" and "a lot of hard work." In the essay, Boggs outlines different elements for building revolutionary cadre organizations premised on practices for disciplined commitment: building a shared ideology, program, structure, standards, and methods. Cadres, originally meaning framework, are the basis for revolution—to build political alignment in order to transform people to transform the world. Building a revolutionary cadre requires both theoretical rigor through political education and methodological rigor through relationship building, including working through conflict.

Maintaining, building, and expanding relationships around a shared vision takes work, including developing structures for membership and participation aligned with political values. Throughout the document, she offers granular details about how to practice commitment, including how to create a schedule for regular meetings with a clearly organized agenda and keeping minutes. She also discusses the importance of ongoing critical evaluation of all political projects rooted in principled practice. At the end of the essay, Boggs emphasizes the importance of study to prepare people for collective struggle. She writes, "Without revolutionary theory, there can be no revolutionary practice, and without commitment to collective and protracted struggle, there can be no successful revolution." For Boggs, engaging in rigorous study and analysis of the dynamics of revolution and political struggle enable new understandings and applicability of revolutionary theory in local organizing and brings disciplined methods for political work. Solidarity is a long-haul commitment, and organizing solidarity also requires *organization*.

Guidelines for a Revolutionary Study Group

Setting Up the Group

1. Requirements for participation should be clearly established.
2. Be clear about your program.
3. At the first meeting, establish program, methods, ground rules together: conditions for participation, work expected, attendance expected, time and place.

Program Purpose

1. To study twentieth-century revolutions and political struggles that have taken place in the world for the purpose of developing our own understanding of the dynamics of revolution, our ability to analyze the social forces in the United States, and our

understanding of the importance and responsibilities of revolutionary theory and leadership.

2. To develop and practice the ability to analyze revolutions; to develop disciplined methods of work; to carry on political discussions together; to practice political criticism and self-criticism.
3. To select those persons who possess the dedication, commitment, discipline, patience, and willingness to build a revolutionary organization and to eliminate those who do not meet the required standards.

Methods

1. Select participants carefully.
2. Carry on a carefully organized study of revolutions in colonial or semi-colonial countries as a background to understand the dynamics of the struggle for Black Revolutionary Power in the U.S.A.
3. Each person is to assume responsibility for leading one or more discussions.
4. Each person is to assume responsibility for summing up a previous discussion.
5. Meetings are to take place regularly at a set time and place, once a week or once every two weeks.
6. Programs and procedures are to be agreed upon by all participants in advance.

From Grace Lee Boggs (1971) Organization Means Commitment. Reprinted with permission from the James and Grace Lee Boggs Papers (UP001342), Walter P. Reuther Library, Archives of Labor and Urban Affairs, Wayne State University, Detroit, MI, United States.

48.

On How

Franny Choi

After Nate Marshall

we wrote new chants
& bailed folks out
& plate-scooped meals
& healed old wounds
& walked cold blocks
& drummed up, stumped
& "stole" back land
& claimed back facts
& sewed loud flags
& sowed right crops
& cut cops' cash
& heaved gold rot
& let go ghosts
& surged, rode crests
& spread wealth flat
& clawed down walls
& ex-learned harm
& nixed cruel laws
& crowdsourced grace
& ground teeth down
& laid cards flat
& dug toward hope

& sang off-key
& worked through shit
& took sweet time
& pre-lived worlds
& strode past doom
& walked, fell, walked,
fell, walked, fell, walked.

AFTERWORD

Tough Love

Margo Okazawa-Rey

As an African American and Japanese woman born in post–World War II occupied Japan, I was not meant to exist.[1] My parents transgressed strictly drawn cultural, political, national, class, race, and gender boundaries. Their union was simultaneously deeply loving and defiant, as well as sometimes problematic. Because of cultural taboos and expectations, as expected, my grandfather officially removed his daughter, his oldest surviving offspring, from the family registry, *koseki*. Nonetheless, he and all the family members remained connected and never abandoned her. My brother and I were welcomed as the first grandchildren, and I developed a deep emotional and spiritual connection to my *ojii chan*, grandfather.

In my mother and father's spirit of love and defiance of convention and my own understandings of the critical importance of moving through and beyond existing boundaries, my love of exploration and adventure, and my joy in connectedness, I identify as a transnational feminist. Since what I experienced as a Fulbright Researcher in South Korea in 1994, I've been learning and thinking about the feeling, experience, concept, and practice of solidarity, individually and as a member of various collectives. Especially significant and complex for me has been understanding the meanings, responsibilities, and accountabilities in practice to be in solidarity as a member of the globally dominant US state who benefits in various ways from its dominance, irrespective of my experiences of marginalization in the United States and of anti-US, anti-imperialist, anticapitalist, and antimilitarist politics and commitments.

Solidarities of any kind are never easy. Yet, they are necessary for the survival of us all and the natural world.

Every group that seeks to be in solidarity with another bears the burden of conflictual histories, within itself and across groups with whom they aspire to bond, to build relationships, and to create societal changes. Most often, the conflicts are not of their own making, and the groups are positioned as "opposites." Nonetheless, the burdens and scars of intentional and forced divisions shape the values, intentions, and relational practices of the actors, not to mention the groups' collective memories.

So, how do groups become opposites? Through systematic and systemic characterization, discrimination, and exclusion, including by law enforcement, state violence, and popular culture. African American people always and consistently have been labeled, judged, and stereotyped as "lazy," "shiftless," "dangerous," "immoral," "disruptive," "angry," and more. This characterization persisted even as they were forcibly made to toil, often to their deaths in one form or another, as enslaved Black folks to enrich individual slavers and to build the material wealth of what eventually became the United States of America. Although not enslaved like African peoples, Asian immigrants, mostly Chinese men, the first to come "voluntarily" in significant numbers, labored in the goldmines and to build the continental railroad in the first half of the nineteenth century, among other toils. These men were similarly characterized as "dangerous," "predatory," and stealing gold and work from white men. Asian immigrants became the "yellow peril," and Chinese laborers were prohibited by the Chinese Exclusion Act in 1882 from immigrating to the United States, the first group to be prohibited based on race. The infamous Executive Order 9066 issued by President Franklin D. Roosevelt in 1942 forcibly removed people of Japanese descent from their homes and incarcerated them in detention centers located in several states under the banner of "national security."[2] Other groups have been excluded and maltreated in various ways by state and civil society actors.

Although the demonization of African American people persists, by the early 1960s, Asian immigrants and their Asian American offspring, especially Chinese and Japanese, were cast as "the model minority"—"virtuous," "hardworking," "quiet" (i.e., did not rock the political boat), "industrious," "studious," economically successful, and more. Thus, in some sense, they were given the status of "honorary white," as were all Japanese people during apartheid South Africa, and as were the "Five Civilized Tribes" in the southeastern United States in the 1800s because they were judged as most closely approximating dominant white, Eurocentric, masculinist values. Asian and Asian American people have been held up to people of color, especially immigrants, as the model to emulate.[3] Their "opposites," African American descendants of enslaved African peoples, were to be avoided at all costs. For example, women were admonished that, if you must marry out, don't ever marry an African American man. Therefore, relations between these communities have been mixed at best. In some ways, the Los Angeles rebellion of 1992, according to some and known as "Sa I Gu" by some Korean people, was one of the most visible and explicit manifestations of the tension and alleged hatred between the communities and exploited by the media.

The characterizations described above, however, historically have shape-shifted. Prevailing political and economic conditions at any given moment or in specific contexts redraw and give rise to new stereotypes. The "rebellious" enslaved people were characterized as docile and happy in their condition to justify slavery. Although the "model minority," Asian people generally were declared by the sitting US president as the carriers of "Kung Flu" and the "Chinese virus" at the onset of the coronavirus pandemic in 2020 that incited violence against them.

If we base possibilities for Black-Asian solidarity on only stereotypes and the "official" history, this anthology most likely will not have ever seen the light of day. The editors of the book and its contributors know a different, much less-known history. Frederick Douglass actively opposed the Chinese Exclusion Act; Black folks supported Filipinos in the Philippine–American War; Black folks and Asian Americans stood side by side to oppose the US war in Vietnam; Third World Liberation at San Francisco State University and antiwar strikes on college campuses brought communities together. [4]

Black-Asian solidarities were formed globally as well. In 1955, the global Asian-Black solidarity united countries at the Bandung Conference.[5] In distant Okinawa, a group of Black (and antiracist white) servicemen stationed at US bases there united with activists among the Okinawan people, colonized by the Japanese and occupied at the time by the United States, in their struggle for Black liberation and reversion of Okinawa in the early 1970s.[6] And largely overlooked is the Afro-Asian solidarity movement of a loose coalition of Japanese activists who organized the Japan Anti-Apartheid Committee, a segment of the global anti-apartheid movement.[7]

For decades, our foremothers Yuri Kochiyama and Grace Lee Boggs were longtime allies in the Black Freedom struggle beginning in the early 1960s. Some of the contributors to this volume are makers of the history of

Black-Asian/Asian-Black solidarity. Mari Matsuda is one of the legal scholars who laid the foundation of critical race theory (alongside Black feminist scholars Patricia Williams and Kimberlé Crenshaw), and Barbara Smith was a founding member of the Combahee River Collective that framed and promoted Black, lesbian, anti-imperialist, and anticapitalist feminism. The present collection builds on these early foundations.

This anthology, however, furthers our thinking and notions of the possible because feminism pushes the boundaries of race-based, nationalist, and predominantly intellectual and theoretical understandings of issues. The collection enables the readers to reimagine and to reframe fundamentally the nature of alliances, first of all. Feminism demands that we pay attention to the personal, to the process, and to the interconnectedness of issues, of body-mind-spirit, of nature and humans. Ultimately, the collection compels and inspires us to recognize our common destiny as inhabitants of planet Earth. All these transcend, and are rooted in, our respective identities and social locations.

Alongside Black-Asian solidarity explored by the contributors in this collection, I insist that, as Black and Asian feminists (indeed as any feminist) committed to being in solidarity of any kind, we must face and address the question of interpersonal and structural power and how they shape and manifest in all our interactions and in the spaces we occupy. I have come to understand, at the core of my being, its critical importance. How do we, often in marginalized and excluded positions, come to recognize our simultaneously dominant position? How do we come to understand the related dynamics, given that being in a dominant position means we do not have to see the category that places us in that position? What must we understand about our emotional relationships to power? Being in dominant positions, how do we face the associated guilt and shame that often accompanies our becoming more conscious? Ultimately, how do we confront the core of the dominance—the US state in all our activist and movement work?

These questions are at their most crucial, indeed a matter of life and death for thousands and thousands, as we witness the unfolding genocide in Gaza directly, which is unequivocally supported militarily, ideologically, politically, and more, by the US state. As we understand the role of the United States in the humanitarian crises in DRC, Haiti, Sudan, and Yemen. As we observe the military buildup in the Asia Pacific with the United States easing toward first-strike nuclear capabilities in its war against China. As students on college campuses across the country are being assaulted by police and campus security, facing suspension, being expelled, being "blacklisted" by alumni for their antigenocide, anti-Zionist, pro-Palestinian, antiwar activism.

Tough love? Tough love as solidarity is learning about our true, complex histories and acknowledging what must be acknowledged: "the good, the bad, and the ugly," to quote a popular 1966 film title. It's recognizing the limitations of our own understanding. Identifying and somehow addressing our respective structural contradictions of being in solidarity. Feeling our vulnerability and uncertainty. Shifting our hearts from individualistic orientation and presence to collectivist. Saying "no" when necessary so our "yes" is true and meaningful. Given the current moral and political crises confronting us, what are we saying yes! and no! to? What does Black-Asian solidarity mean and look like? How do we move beyond "Black-Asian" to a truly transnational feminist solidarity and a movement that transcends particular identities and social categories and instead reaches deep into the roots of the interlocking humanitarian and moral crises we are facing: global capitalism undergirded by militarism and armed conflict; imperialism; patriarchy and misogyny; racism and ethnocentrism; caste oppression; and more? What kinds of solidarities and movements will enable us to transform the current, dominant culture of killing into a culture of life?

Like my ojiichan taught us through his practice over seventy years ago, we never give up on our loved ones. Loretta Ross teaches us now: "Call in!" Loved ones for me extend far beyond family as ojiichan understood us. Loved ones, for me, include life itself.

The readings in this collection teach us these lessons and much more. Most of all, they remind us of what June Jordan inspired: "We are the ones we have been waiting for!"[8]

Margo Okazawa-Rey
Claremont, California
Spring 2024

ACKNOWLEDGMENTS

We often discuss how solidarity is an ongoing relationship and commitment. Feminist frameworks of care and community have made it possible to create this anthology together.

We would like to thank Róisín Davis, Maria Isabelle Carlos, Katy O'Donnell, and the team at Haymarket for believing in this project, as well as Rachel Cohen and Dao Tran for the support at the finish line. We are grateful to Jyothi Natarajan for reaching out to Black Women Radicals (BWR) and the Asian American Feminist Collective (AAFC) to provide a home at the Asian American Writer's Workshop's *The Margins* for the Black and Asian Feminist Solidarities project, and to Dana Isokawa and the AAWW team for their editorial support. We are thankful to the co-leaders of the AAFC—Salonee Bhaman, Julie Ae Kim, and Senti Sojwal—for the loving support and guidance they have offered in the duration of this project. Additionally, we appreciate all the contributors who have written for our editorial project at *The Margins,* who have shaped our thinking and built the foundations on which this anthology emerges.

While housed at AAWW and *The Margins,* the project received support from the Henry Luce Foundation and the Art for Justice Fund, a sponsored project of Rockefeller Philanthropy Advisors. We are also thankful to the Asian Women Giving Circle, which has materially supported this anthology by allowing us to pay contributors, and also the Asian American Arts Alliance and the Museum of Contemporary African Diasporan Art, which supported TD through the Bandung Residency.

We also acknowledge and honor our feminist elders and ancestors, who paved the way for us to do this work. Thank you to Ericka Huggins, Denise Oliver-Velez, and Barbara Smith for encouraging Jaimee to connect with AAFC and for demonstrating the importance of building cross-racial solidarities.

We are thankful to our friends, mentors, and co-conspirators for the many conversations that enabled us to explore, practice, and experiment on questions of feminist solidarity: Minju Bae, TS Candii, Courtney M. Cox, Paula Chakravartty, Jenn Fang, Brooklyne Gipson, VX, Sarah T. Hamid, Sarah J. Jackson, Akemi Kochiyama-Ladson, Audee Kochiyama-Holman, Priscillia Kounkou-Hoveyda, the organizers of *Aché* and *Phoenix Rising*, Joanie Leon Guerrero, Amita Manghnani, Mon M., Margo Okazawa-Rey aka DJ MOR Love and Joy and the feminist dance party crew, Yin Q, Zara Raven, Annie Tan, Vivian Truong, Diane Wong, Kate Zen, and many more brilliant. Rest in power, Cecilia Gentili.

NOTES

Preface: Toward Black and Asian Feminist Solidarities

1. bell hooks, *The Will to Change: Men, Masculinity, and Love* (New York: Atria Books, 2004), 17.

3. Understanding Disability, Ableism, and Incarceration More Expansively

1. Patty Berne, "Disability Justice—A Working Draft," *Sins Invalid* (blog), June 10, 2015, www.sinsinvalid.org/blog/disability-justice-a-working-draft-by-patty-berne.
2. See also Talila A. Lewis, "Working Definition of Ableism—January 2022 Update," *Talila A. Lewis* (blog), January 1, 2022, www.talilalewis.com/blog/working-definition-of-ableism-january-2022-update.
3. Berne, "Disability Justice."
4. See Talila A. Lewis, "Disability Justice in the Age of Mass Incarceration," in *Deaf People in the Criminal Justice System*, ed. Debra Guthmann et al. (Washington, DC: Gallaudet University Press, 2021), 220–303.
5. See Talila A. Lewis, "Disability Justice Is an Essential Part of Abolishing Police and Prisons," Abolition for the People, *Medium*, October 7, 2020; Liat Ben-Moshe, *Decarcerating Disability: Deinstitutionalization and Prison Abolition* (Minneapolis: University of Minnesota Press, 2020).
6. Kerima Cevik, "Catastrophic Encounters with Police: The Case of Tario Anderson and the Way Forward for Neli Latson," *Intersected* (blog), January 2, 2015, https://intersecteddisability.blogspot.com/2015/01/catastrophic-encounters-with-police.html; Victoria Law, "People with Mental Illness Face Acute Dangers During and After Police Encounters," *TruthOut*, July 11, 2021, https://truthout.org/articles/people-with-mental-illness-face-acute-dangers-during-and-after-police-encounters.
7. See also Bazelon Center for Mental Health Law, "Mayor Adams' Plan Will Not Help People with Mental Disabilities," December 12, 2022, www.bazelon.org.
8. See for example Helping Educate to Advance the Rights of Deaf people (HEARD), "HEARD Statement on Wrongful Conviction of Black/Disabled Deaf People," YouTube video, July 21, 2020; Talila A. Lewis, "MP Fireside Chat: Wrongful Conviction of Deaf and Disabled People," interview by Tricia Bushnell, Midwest Innocence Project, YouTube video, June 5, 2020; HEARD, "ASL Infographic: Wrongful Conviction of Deaf+Disabled People," YouTube video, December 12, 2019; Talila A. Lewis, "In Georgia, Imprisoned Deaf and Disabled People Don't Stand a Chance," ACLU, June 20, 2018, www.aclu.org/news/disability-rights/georgia-imprisoned-deaf-and-disabled.
9. Talila A. Lewis, "In the Fight to Close Rikers, Don't Forget Deaf and Disabled Peo-

ple," *TruthOut*, April 6, 2017, truthout.org/articles/in-the-fight-to-close-rikers-don-t-forget-deaf-and-disabled-people.

10. Ben-Moshe, *Decarcerating Disability.*
11. See James Kilgore, *Understanding E-Carceration: Electronic Monitoring, the Surveillance State, and the Future of Mass Incarceration* (New York: The New Press, 2022); Cobb v. Georgia Department of Community Supervision, ACLU of Georgia, Civil Action No. 1:19-cv-03285-WMR, www.acluga.org/en/cases/cobb-v-georgia-department-community-supervision.
12. Richard Dugdale, "The Jukes: A Study of Crime, Pauperism, Disease and Heredity," Buck v. Bell Documents, Paper 1, January 1, 1969, http://readingroom.law.gsu.edu/buckvbell/1.
13. "Decarcerating Care: The Evolution of Mental Health Surveillance," Institute for the Development of Human Arts, YouTube video, October 20, 2022.
14. For reference on manumission, see Benjamin Joseph Klebaner, "American Manumission Laws and the Responsibility for Supporting Slaves," *Virginia Magazine of History and Biography* 63, no. 4 (1955): 443–53; on public charge laws, see Talila A. Lewis, "Trump's Rule Attacking Disabled and Low-Income Migrants Has Violent History," *TruthOut*, August 27, 2019, truthout.org/articles/trumps-rule-attacking-disabled-and-low-income-migrants-has-violent-history; on vendue, see Benjamin Joseph Klebaner, "Pauper Auctions: The 'New England Method' of Public Poor Relief," *Historical Collections of the Essex Institute* 91, no. 3 (1859); on modern prison labor systems, see Leah Butz, "Prison Labor Is Remarkably Common Within the Food System," New York City Food Policy Center, Hunter College, September 15, 2021, www.nycfoodpolicy.org/prison-labor-is-remarkably-common-within-the-food-system.
15. See for example Dorothea Dix, *Memorial to the Legislature of Massachusetts* (Boston: Munroe and Francis, 1843), 7.
16. HEARD, "HEARD Victory: FCC Prison Phone Accessibility Vote—September 29, 2022," YouTube video, October 5, 2022.
17. See Lewis, "Disability Justice."

4. We Want Cop-Free Communities

1. See Moustafa Bayoumi, *This Muslim American Life* (New York: New York University Press, 2015); Deepa Kumar, *Islamophobia and the Politics of Empire: Twenty Years after 9/11* (New York: Verso Books, 2021).
2. See Chandan Reddy, *Freedom with Violence: Race, Sexuality, and the US State* (Durham, NC: Duke University Press, 2011).
3. See Kay Whitlock and Michael Bronski, *Considering Hate: Violence, Goodness, and Justice in American Culture and Politics* (Boston: Beacon, 2015).

5. Nail Salon Brawls and Boycotts

1. Long before COVID-19 and wide reports of anti-Asian violence, major news platforms have pushed narratives of Black-on-Asian crime, including coverage of the 1992 uprisings in Los Angeles and targeted assaults of Asian communities by Black criminals. This news coverage was often biased and lacked nuance. For examples of this news coverage, see "Korean Businesses Targeted During LA Riots," *NBC Nightly News*, YouTube video, April 28, 2017; "Black Admits to Targeting Asians but Says He's Not Racist," CBS 5 News, YouTube video, May 10, 2010.

2. See Chris Perez, "Botched Eyebrow Job Leads to Wild Nail Salon Brawl," *New York Post*, August 6, 2018, nypost.com.
3. New York Healthy Nail Salon Coalition, "New York Healthy Nail Salon Steering Committee Condemns Violence in Flatbush Nail Salon," Facebook, August 7, 2018.
4. Coalition for Asian American Children & Families, "Call for Unity and Justice for All Communities of Color," Facebook, August 10, 2018.
5. "These Boycotts Are Racist, and Wrong," *New York Times*, August 31, 1990, www.nytimes.com/1990/08/31/opinion/these-boycotts-are-racist-and-wrong.html.
6. Tracy Wilkinson and Frank Clifford, "Korean Grocer Who Killed Black Teen Gets Probation," *Los Angeles Times*, November 16, 1991.
7. Nigel Roberts, "Asian-Owned Beauty Supply Store Faces Boycott After Owner Attacks Black Customer," NewsOne, March 13, 2017, newsone.com.
8. Miliann Kang, *The Managed Hand: Race, Gender, and the Body in Beauty Service Work* (Berkeley: University of California Press, 2010), 199–200.
9. Joe Marino, "Protesters Target Second Nail Salon After Racially Charged Brawl," *New York Post*, August 6, 2018,nypost.com.
10. John Leland, Mariana Alfaro, and Aaron Robertson, "A Nail Salon Brawl Opened a Racial Rift Online. In Brooklyn, the Mood Is Calmer," *New York Times*, August 7, 2018, www.nytimes.com/2018/08/07/nyregion/brooklyn-nail-salon-brawl-protest.html.
11. Jonathan Rieder, "Trouble in Store," *New Republic*, July 2, 1990.
12. See Tamara K. Nopper, "On Anti-Black Terror, Captivity, and Black-Korean Conflict," this volume.
13. Diane Wong, interview by TD Tso, August 11, 2018.
14. Michelle Singletary, "Shopping While Black: African Americans Continue to Face Retail Racism," *Washington Post*, May 18, 2018, www.washingtonpost.com.
15. Miliann Kang, interview by TD Tso, August 12, 2018.
16. Diane Wong, interview by TD Tso, August 11, 2018.
17. In November 2014, New York City Police Department officer Peter Liang killed Akai Gurley in an unlit stairwell in an East New York public housing building. Liang's firearm went off as he pushed open a door, and the bullet ricocheted before it struck Gurley in the chest, killing him. The Chinese American officer was originally convicted of manslaughter, but his conviction was later downgraded to criminally negligent homicide. In the aftermath of the first manslaughter conviction, Asian Americans protested in droves, calling Liang a "scapegoat," as numerous white officers had their charges dropped in other cases involving police killings. This is one example of an incident in which Asian Americans activated toward a cause that blatantly disregards and disenfranchises Black Americans. To learn more, see Hansi Lo Wang, "'Awoken' by N.Y. Cop Shooting, Asian-American Activists Chart Way Forward," *Code Switch*, NPR, April 23, 2016, www.npr.org/sections/codeswitch.
18. Kat Chow, "'Model Minority' Myth Again Used as a Racial Wedge Between Asians and Blacks," *Code Switch*, NPR, April 19, 2017, www.npr.org/sections/codeswitch/2017/04/19/524571669/model-minority-myth-again-used-as-a-racial-wedge-between-asians-and-blacks; Shirley Leung, "Harvard Lawsuit Is About Affirmative Action, Not Asian Americans," *Boston Globe*, July 17, 2018, www.bostonglobe.com.

7. I Rememory You, Zheng Xianjuan

1. Alexis Pauline Gumbs, *Undrowned: Black Feminist Lessons from Marine Mammals* (Chico, CA: AK Press, 2021), 31.

2. Toni Morrison, *Beloved* (New York: Vintage, 1987); see also Jeong-eun Rhee, *Decolonial Feminist Research: Haunting, Rememory, and Mothers* (New York: Routledge, 2020), 2.
3. Centers for Disease Control and Prevention, "Leading Causes of Death – Females – Non-Hispanic Asian – United States," 2018, www.cdc.gov.
4. Dave Askins, "Rally in Support of Asian Community: 'Our Little Bubble at IU Bloomington Is Not and Never Has Been a Safe Place for Asian and Asian-American People,'" *B Square Bulletin*, February 4, 2023, bsquarebulletin.com.
5. Allison Klein and Lena H. Sun, "Teen Killed Outside Chillum Carryout," *Washington Post*, September 21, 2005.
6. Darcy Spencer and Gina Cook, "Mother Outraged Her Daughter's Killer Is Getting Out of Prison Years Early," NBC, November 26, 2019, www.nbcwashington.com.
7. Avis Thomas-Lester, "Asphyxiation Ruled in Trunk Death," *Washington Post*, January 31, 2007.
8. Jonathan Franklin, "Prince George's County Man Suspected of Killing Girlfriend Caught, Arrested in North Carolina," WUSA9, September 28, 2020, www.wusa9.com.
9. Drishti Pillai and Alyssa Lindsey, *The State of Safety for Asian American and Pacific Islander Women in the U.S.*, The Asian American Foundation, National Asian Pacific Women's Forum, and Korean American Community Foundation, https://search.issuelab.org/resource/the-state-of-safety-for-asian-american-and-pacific-islander-women-in-the-u-s.html; Drishti Pillai, Aggie J. Yellow Horse, and Russell Jeung, *The Rising Tide of Violence and Discrimination Against Asian American and Pacific Islander Women and Girls*, Stop AAPI Hate and National Asian Pacific Women's Forum, stopaapihate.org.

9. We Will Not Be Used

1. This piece is adapted from an essay originally published in Mari Matsuda, *Where Is Your Body? And Other Essays on Race, Gender, and the Law* (Boston: Beacon Press, 1997), 149–61.
2. Dr. Haunani Kay Trask alerted me to the new luna phenomena.
3. See, e.g., David Brand, "The New Whiz Kids: Why Asian-Americans Are Doing So Well, and What It Costs Them," *Time*, August 31, 1987; see, generally, Al Kamen, "Myth of 'Model Minority' Haunts Asian Americans; Stereotypes Eclipse Diverse Group's Problems," *Washington Post*, June 22 1992, A1.
4. Harry H. L. Kitano, *Asian Americans: Emerging Minorities* (Englewood Cliffs, NJ: Prentice Hall, 1995).
5. "Nihongo" is the Japanese word for the Japanese language.
6. For example, individuals such as columnist Arthur Hu have opposed affirmative action admissions programs at colleges, specifically criticizing race-based admission criteria at the University of California. See Arthur Hu, "Test Scores," Hu's on First, *Asian Week*, May 10, 1991, 26; Arthur Hu, Hu's on First, *Asian Week*, May 24, 1991, 12.
7. In 1985, only 35 (2.5 percent) of the 1,380 firefighters in the San Francisco Fire Department were Asian, while Asian men constituted 19.3 percent of the male civilian labor force. (Women were not hired by the SFFD until 1987.) U.S. v. City and County of San Francisco, 656 F. Supp. 276, 286 n. 10 (1987). A consent decree required hiring Asian Americans. As of August 5, 1990, Asian firefighters still constituted only about 4 percent of the SFFD. U.S. v. City and County of San Francisco, 748 F. Supp.1416,1428 n. 10 (1990).
8. According to a 1990 census data and a report by Leadership Education for Asian Pacifics, Asian Americans are widely dispersed along the economic spectrum and face

discrimination at all levels of employment. Further, Asian Americans earn less income, per capita, than white people, even though they are often better educated. See Elizabeth Llorente, "Asian Americans Finding Many Doors Closed to Them," *Record* (New Jersey), October 23, 1994, A1. The federal "glass ceiling report" (*Good for Business: Making Full Use of Human Capital* [Washington, DC: Federal Glass Ceiling Commission, 1995]) stated, "Despite higher levels of formal education than other groups, Asian and Pacific Islander Americans receive a lower yield in terms of income or promotions."

9. See, e.g., Brenna B. Mahoney, "Children at Risk: The Inequality of Urban Education," *New York Law School Journal of Human Rights*, no. 9 (1991): 161 (reporting the "declining numbers of urban minority high school graduates . . . pursuing postsecondary educational opportunities" and the increasing percentage of poor and minority students performing below grade level in mathematics and reading); Augustus F. Hawkins, "Becoming Preeminent in Education: America's Greatest Challenge," *Harvard Journal of Law and Public Policy*, no. 15 (1991): 367 (noting that the United States is falling behind other countries in virtually all educational areas, particularly mathematics and the sciences).
10. In the 1870s, white workers resentful of Chinese laborers (who worked for lower wages and in worse conditions), pressured politicians into enacting a series of anti-Chinese laws that culminated in the Chinese Exclusion Act of 1882. US Commission on Wartime Relocation and Internment of Civilians, *Personal Justice Denied: Report of the Commission on Wartime Relocation and Internment of Civilians: Report for the Committee on Interior and Insular Affairs* (Washington, DC: US Government Printing Office,1982), 42–44. See also Mari J. Matsuda, "Looking to the Bottom: Critical Legal Studies and Reparations," *Harvard Civil Rights–Civil Liberties Law Review*, no. 22 (1987): 363–68 (describing the internment of Japanese Americans during World War II and their subsequent claims for redress); Vincent Chin, a Chinese American, was murdered in Detroit in 1982 by assailants (unemployed autoworkers) who thought he was a Japanese person responsible for their loss of jobs. See US Commission on Civil Rights, *Recent Activities against Citizens and Residents of Asian Descent*, 1987, 43–44 (giving a brief history of this case).
11. This popular union song based on an old hymn, "I Shall Not Be Moved," was first sung in 1931 by miners; later versions added newer verses appropriate to the Civil Rights and antiwar movements. See Tom Glazer, *Songs of Peace, Freedom, and Protest* (New York: D. McKay, 1970), 332–33. For an example of antieviction struggle, see, e.g., Chester Hartman, "San Francisco International Hotel: Case Study of a Turf Struggle," *Radical America*, no. 12 (June 1978): 47–58 (describing activists struggling against the eviction of Chinese American tenants in San Francisco's Chinatown).
12. The International Longshore and Warehouse Union is a progressive, multiracial union active on the West Coast and in Hawaiʻi. See Edward Beechert, *Working in Hawaii: A Labor History* (Honolulu: University of Hawaii Press, 1985); Sanford Zalburg, *A Spark Is Struck: Jack Hall and the ILWU in Hawaii* (Honolulu: University of Hawaii Press, 1979); Thomas Almaguer, "Racial Domination and Class Conflict in Capitalist Agriculture: The Oxnard Sugar Beet Workers' Strike of 1903," *Labor History* 25 (1984): 325–50.
13. See Mari Jo Buhle, Paul Buhle, and Dan Georgakas, eds., *Encyclopedia of the American Left* (New York: Garland Publishing, 1990), 19–20 (chronicles the general history of the American Committee for Protection of the Foreign Born).
14. See, generally, Karen Umemoto, "'On Strike!' San Francisco State College Strike, 1968–69: The Role of Asian American Students," *Amerasia* 15 (1989): 3–41 (recounting the events at the San Francisco State College strike and Senator Hayakawa's attempt to end it).
15. Umemoto, "'On Strike!'" 19.

16. John Berry, "Survey Says Asians Are Dream Customers," *San Francisco Chronicle*, March 5, 1990, C1.

10. Recognition and Liberation for CHamoru People

1. In the United States, Pacific Islanders and Native Hawaiians are lumped into the "Asian American Pacific Islander" (AAPI) racial demographic, along with other variations of the term, resulting in the erasure and sidelining of these ethnic groups within a large, heterogeneous racial categorization. For more, see Lisa Kahaleole Hall, "Which of These Things Is Not Like the Other: Hawaiians and Other Pacific Islanders Are Not Asian Americans, and All Pacific Islanders Are Not Hawaiian," *American Quarterly* 63, no. 3 (2015): 727–47.

11. "Peace and Freedom—Inseparable"

1. See Carole Boyce Davies, *Left of Karl Marx: The Political Life of Black Communist Claudia Jones* (Durham, NC, and London: Duke University Press, 2007).
2. Editors' note: Notably amid anticommunist fervor, Jones's activism was seen as such a threat to US national security that she was deported and arrested, which also reflected a larger pattern of state containment of Black radicalism.
3. Steven Casey, *Selling the Korean War: Propaganda, Politics, and Public Opinion in the United States, 1950–1953* (New York: Oxford University Press, 2008), 132.
4. Claudia Jones, "International Women's Day and the Struggle for Peace (Women in the Struggle for Peace and Security)," in *Claudia Jones: Beyond Containment*, ed. Carole Boyce Davies (Banbury: Ayebia Clarke, 2011), 92–95.
5. Claudia Jones, "For the Unity of Women in the Cause of Peace," in *Claudia Jones: Beyond Containment*, 105–8.
6. Elisabeth B. Armstrong, *Bury the Corpse of Colonialism: The Revolutionary Feminist Conference of 1949* (Oakland: University of California Press, 2023), 19–20.
7. Claudia Jones, "'I Was Deported Because . . .' (Claudia Jones Interview by George Bowrin)," in *Claudia Jones: Beyond Containment*, 16–19; Charisse Burden-Stelly, "Constructing Deportable Subjectivity: Antiforeignness, Antiradicalism, and Antiblackness During the McCarthyist Structure of Feeling," *Souls: A Critical Journal of Black Politics, Culture, and Society* 19, no. 3 (2017): 346–49.
8. Denise Lynn, "Deporting Black Radicalism: Claudia Jones' Deportation and Policing Blackness in the Cold War," *Twentieth Century Communism*, no. 18 (2020): 56.
9. Davies, *Left of Karl Marx*, 141–47.
10. Claudia Jones, "Their Cry for Peace Is Heard," *West Indian Gazette and Afro-Asian Caribbean News*, August–September 1964.
11. Claudia Jones, "Anti-Bomb Meeting Blow to Imperialism," *West Indian Gazette and Afro-Asian Caribbean News*, August–September 1964.
12. "Armed Liberation and Peace," *West Indian Gazette and Afro-Asian Caribbean News*, August–September 1964.
13. Jones, "Anti-Bomb Meeting."
14. Nicola Hosburgh, *China and Global Nuclear Order: From Estrangement to Active Engagement* (Oxford: Oxford University Press, 2015), 51–53.
15. *Renmin Ribao* (People's Daily) is the official newspaper of the Central Committee of the Chinese Communist Party.
16. "WIG Editor Hails Chinese A. Bomb Test," *West Indian Gazette and Afro-Asian Caribbean News*, November 1964.

17. Jones, "Anti-Bomb Meeting."
18. Zifeng Liu, "Decolonization Is Not a Dinner Party: Claudia Jones, China's Nuclear Weapons, and Anti-Imperialist Solidarity," *Journal of Intersectionality* 3, no. 1 (2019): 32–34.
19. "W.I.G. Editor Visits Asia," *West Indian Gazette and Afro-Asian Caribbean News*, November 1964.
20. "WIG Editor Hails Chinese A. Bomb Test."
21. Claudia Jones, "First Lady of the World: I Talk with Mme Sun Yat-Sen," *West Indian Gazette and Afro-Asian Caribbean News*, November 1964.
22. Jones, "First Lady of the World."
23. A. Manchanda, "Dear Claudia, We Will Hold High Your Banner of Anti-Imperialism," *West Indian Gazette and Afro-Asian Caribbean News*, December 1965.

12. At the Intersections of Race, Gender, and Class

1. "About the Venceremos Brigade," Venceremos Brigade, https://vb4cuba.com/about-the-venceremos-brigade.
2. Ariane Vani Kannan, "The Third World Women's Alliance: History, Geopolitics, and Form" (PhD diss., Syracuse University, 2018), 49, https://surface.syr.edu/cgi/viewcontent.cgi?article=1907&context=etd.
3. Kannan, "Third World Women's Alliance," 3.
4. "Baker, Ella Josephine," Martin Luther King, Jr. Research and Education Institute, Stanford University, https://kinginstitute.stanford.edu/baker-ella-josephine.
5. Transcript of interview with Frances Beal, Voices of Feminism Oral History Project, Sophia Smith Collection of Women's History, SSC MS 00535, Smith College Special Collections, Northampton, Massachusetts.
6. Beal, interview, 24–26.
7. Kannan, "Third World Women's Alliance," 45.
8. *She's Beautiful When She's Angry*, directed by Mary Dore (Netflix, 2014), www.shesbeautifulwhenshesangry.com.
9. "Student Nonviolent Coordinating Committee," Martin Luther King Jr. Research and Education Institute, Stanford University, updated April 8, 2024, https://kinginstitute.stanford.edu/student-nonviolent-coordinating-committee-sncc.
10. Ashley Farmer, "The Third World Women's Alliance, Cuba, and the Exchange of Ideas," *Black Perspectives* (blog), April 7, 2017, www.aaihs.org/the-third-world-womens-alliance-cuba-and-the-exchange-of-ideas.
11. Kannan, "Third World Women's Alliance," 47.
12. "Nation: Women on the March," *Time*, September 7, 1970.
13. "Angela Davis," Biography.com, updated April 23, 2021, www.biography.com/activists/angela-davis.
14. Patricia Romney, "How NOW Attempted to Exclude the Third Women's Alliance from Feminist History," *Literary Hub*, October 13, 2021, https://lithub.com/how-now-attempted-to-exclude-the-third-womans-alliance-from-feminist-history.
15. "Frances M. Beal," Profile of Resistance, School of Education and Human Development, University of Virginia, January 2021, https://educatingfordemocracy.education.virginia.edu/sites/educatingfordemocracy/files/2021-01/Frances_Beal.pdf.
16. Linda Burnham and Erica Tatnall, *Paving the Way: A Teaching Guide to the Third World Women's Alliance*, CD-ROM, 2008, quoted in Kannan, "Third World Women's Alliance."
17. Barbara Crow, ed., *Radical Feminism: A Documentary Reader* (New York: New York University Press, 2000), 46.

18. Kimberlé Crenshaw, "Demarginalizing the Intersection of Race and Sex: A Black Feminist Critique of Antidiscimination Doctrine, Feminist Theory and Antiracist Politics," *University of Chicago Legal Forum*, no. 1 (1989): 139–67.
19. Beal, interview, 43–44.
20. Kannan, "Third World Women's Alliance," 50–51.
21. Grace Kyungwon Hong, "Research on Third World Women and Women of Color Activism at the Sophia Smith Collection at Smith College," UCLA Center for the Study of Women, June 22, 2016, https://csw.ucla.edu/2016/06/22/research-third-world-women-women-color-activism-sophia-smith-collection-smith-college.
22. "Sharing Sorrow," Women of Color Resource Center's Downfall Community Taskforce Findings, March 2011, http://jamalarogers.com/wp-content/uploads/2017/03/Women-Color-Resource-Demise.pdf.

13. "We're Here Because You Were There"

1. Excerpts from this introduction were originally published at *Black Women Radicals*, Jaimee Swift, "On the Power of Stella Dadzie: A Radical Pioneer of the Black Women's Movement in Britain," *Black Women Radicals*, May 24, 2020, www.blackwomenradicals.com/blog-feed/on-the-power-of-stella-dadzie-a-radical-pioneer-of-the-black-british-feminist-movement.
2. Stella Dadzie, interview by Samenua Sesher, *Respect Due*, Museum of Colour, https://museumofcolour.org.uk/stella-dadzie-transcript.pdf.
3. Organisation of Women of Asian and African Descent, "OWAAD Draft Constitution," 1978, https://artsandculture.google.com/asset/owaad-draft-constitution-the-organisation-of-women-of-asian-and-african-descent-owaad/xgHiqAbfrKfOTg?hl=en.
4. OWAAD, "OWAAD Draft Constitution."
5. The Windrush generation was a mass-migration movement of predominantly Black communities across the British Empire who arrived in the United Kingdom between 1948 and 1971. According to BBC.com, those of the Windrush generation "were encouraged to move to the UK to help with post-War labor shortages and rebuild its battered economy." See Adina Campbell, "Who Were the Windrush Generation and What Is Windrush Day?" BBC, updated June 20, 2025, www.bbc.com.
6. Olive Morris (June 26, 1952–July 12, 1979) was a Jamaican-born British political activist and feminist leader who was active in the British civil rights movement and the feminist and squatters' movements. A member of the British Black Panther Movement, she also was a founding member of the Brixton Black Women's Group (BBWG). Also a founding member of OWAAD, Morris traveled to China in 1977, and she documented her travels to the country in her report, "A Sister's Visit to China!" which was printed in the BBWG's newsletter *SpeakOut!* See Olive Morris, "A Sister's Visit to China!" *SpeakOut!* Brixton Black Women's Group, 1977, https://rememberolivemorris.files.wordpress.com/2021/04/dyrom_morris_china_trip.pdf.
7. Inspired by the Black Panther Party (BPP) and the Black Power movement in the United States, the Black Panther Movement (later the Black Workers Movement) was founded in Notting Hill, London, in 1968. Formed to address racial discrimination, prejudice, and police brutality enacted against Caribbean, African, and South Asian communities, the group, while influenced by the BPP, was not officially affiliated with the organization; however, the BBPM became the first Panther organization outside of the United States, "adopting the Panthers' symbols of military jackets, berets, and raised fists." See Diane Pien, "British Black Panther Party (1968–1973),"

BlackPast.org, July 2, 2018, https://www.blackpast.org/global-african-history/british-black-panther-party-1968-1973.

8. "The Brixton Black Women's Group (BBWG), which existed from 1973 until 1985, identified itself as a socialist feminist organization, and was one of the first Black women's groups to be established in the UK. The aim of the BBWG was to create a distinct space where women of African and Asian descent could meet to focus on political, social, and cultural issues as they affected Black women. BBWG published its own newsletter, *Speak Out!*, which kept alive the debate about the relevance of feminism to Black politics and provided a Black women's perspective on immigration, housing, health and culture." Milo Miller, *SpeakOut! The Brixton Black Women's Group* (New York: Verso, 2023).
9. For more information on the Brixton Black Women's Group, see "Black Women Organizing: Brixton Black Women's Group," *Feminist Review* 17, no. 1 (July 1984): 84–89, https://doi.org/10.1057/fr.1984.30.
10. For more information on virginity testing, see Madhulagna Halder, "A Historical Account of the 'Virginity Tests' in the UK on South Asian Women," *Feminism in India*, November 11, 2022, https://feminisminindia.com/2022/11/11/virginity-tests-uk-indian-pakistani-women.

14. Our Solidarity Is a Lifeline

1. The title of this interview is in reference to June Jordan's poem "Solidarity," which details how four women—two Black and two Asian—were discriminated against while in Paris, France. The four women were Jordan, Angela Davis, Pratibha Parmar, and her partner, Shaheen Haq. The poem can be found in Adrienne Rich, *What Is Found There: Notebooks on Poetry and Politics* (New York: W. W. Norton, 1993).
2. According to Leila Kassir, "Sheba Feminist Publishers (Sheba) was founded in 1980 by seven women and, over a fourteen-year period, published a range of feminist fiction, non-fiction, poetry, and children's books. Sheba consciously differed from many other women's publishers of the era (such as Virago and the Women's Press) as they were formed as a workers' collective, were independent, and focused on publishing new writers. Most importantly, Sheba was a political project, publishing works that originated within the struggles and activism of the women's movement, and with an emphasis on class and race." See Leila Kassir, "Sheba Feminist Publishers: A Conscience of the Feminist Publishing Industry," School of Advanced Study, University of London Student-Led Body, March 13, 2023, https://sasiety.co.uk/womens-history-month-sheba-feminist-publishers.
3. Inspired by the Black Power movement and the Black Panther Party, Dalit communities organized as Dalit Panthers to fight against caste injustices in India.
4. June Jordan, "Poem About Police Violence," in *Passion* (Boston: Beacon, 1980). Jordan wrote this poem in 1978 after the murder of Arthur Miller in Brooklyn, New York.
5. The Grunwick Strike of 1976 was a protest led by South Asian women against exploitative and poor working conditions in a British factory. See "The Grunwick Dispute," Striking Women, www.striking-women.org/module/striking-out/grunwick-dispute.

15. Revisiting a Press of Our Own

1. See Barbara Smith, "A Press of Our Own: Kitchen Table: Women of Color Press," *Frontiers: A Journal of Women Studies* 10, no. 3 (1989): 11–13.
2. Interview edited by Rachel Kuo.

3. Out of the fury and grief in this moment, Lorde wrote the poem "Need: A Chorale for Black Woman Voices" to open community dialogue on sexual and gender violence. "My lasting image of that spring, beyond the sick sadness and anger and worry, was of the women whom I knew, loved, and trembled for: Barbara Smith, Demita Frazier, Margo Okazawa-Rey, and women whose names were unknown to me," she writes in the preface to a new edition of "Need." See Rudolph Byrd, Johnnetta Cole, and Beverly Guy-Sheftall, eds., *I Am Your Sister: Collected and Unpublished Writings of Audre Lorde* (Oxford: Oxford University Press, 2011), 177.
4. As described by Barbara Smith during our interview on the significance of the Modern Language Association: "The MLA is probably [one of the] largest academic associations of any in the United States, because in most college curricula, students are required to take English, composition, literature, or something in that area and then, of course, different languages too. So unlike, say, political science, you don't have to take political science to get out of college and you don't have to take geography to get out of college. But in most cases, at least in the old days, and probably still in the current day, you have to take something that is writing, literature, or language."
5. See also Emily Bernard, "Audre Lorde Broke the Silence," *New Republic*, March 25, 2021, https://newrepublic.com/article/161595/audre-lorde-warrior-poet-cancer-journals.

16. Exploring Black and Asian American Lesbian Archives

1. Saidiya Hartman, "Venus in Two Acts," *Small Axe* 12, no. 2 (June 2008): 1–14, muse.jhu.edu/article/241115.
2. Tiffany Florvil, "Beyond Shorelines: Audre Lorde's Queer Belonging," *Black Perspectives* (blog), African American Intellectual History Society, February 15, 2021, www.aaihs.org/beyond-shorelines-audre-lordes-queered-belonging.
3. Newsletters are from author's personal archives.
4. This essay was originally published on March 25, 2021, as part of Black and Asian Feminist Solidarities, an Asian American Writers' Workshop project on *The Margins*.
5. Amy Sueyoshi, "Breathing Fire: Remembering Asian Pacific American Activism in Queer History" in *LGBTQ America: A Theme Study of Lesbian, Gay, Bisexual, Transgender, and Queer History*, ed. Megan E. Springate, (National Park Foundation and National Park Service, 2016), 20, www.nps.gov/subjects/lgbtqheritage/upload/lgbtqtheme-asianpacific.pdf; Sophia Yuet See, "Finding Community in the Past: Discovering a 1980s San Francisco Newsletter for and by Asian/Pacific Lesbians," *Futuress*, November 20, 2020, https://futuress.org/stories/phoenix-rising.
6. Sueyoshi, "Breathing Fire."
7. "2017 Honorees: The Founding Editors of Phoenix Rising," Asian Pacific Islander Queer Women and Transgender Community (APIQWTC), https://apiqwtc.org/phoenix-award-honoree/2016-the-founding-editors-of-phoenix-rising.
8. "2017 Honorees: The Founding Editors."
9. Jaimee Swift, "Exploring Black and Asian American Lesbian Archives: *Aché* and *Phoenix Rising*," *Margins, Asian American Writers' Workshop*, March 25, 2021, https://aaww.org/exploring-black-and-asian-american-lesbian-archives-ache-and-phoenix-rising.
10. Sueyoshi, "Breathing Fire."
11. Sueyoshi, "Breathing Fire," 15.
12. Kitty Tsui is the first out Chinese American lesbian to publish a book, *Words of a Woman Who Breathes Fire*, in 1983. Not only was Tsui a pioneer in the Asian American lesbian movement, but she was also a member of the Asian/Pacifica Sisters and an editor of

Phoenix Rising. See Sueyoshi, "Breathing Fire," 17; Nancy Hom, "Unbound Feet presents 'Yellow Daughters'" (screen print poster for a lecture at University of California Berkeley, Asian American Studies Department, 1981), www.abaa.org/book/855258322.

13. Kitty Tsui, "Breaking Silence, Making Waves and Loving Ourselves: The Politics of Coming Out and Coming Home," in *Lesbian Philosophies and Cultures*, ed. Jeffner Allen (Albany: SUNY Press, 1990), 55.
14. Jeffner Allen, ed. *Lesbian Philosophies and Cultures* (Albany, NY: SUNY Press, 1990), 55.
15. Patricia Romney, *We Were There: The Third World Women's Alliance and the Second Wave* (New York: Feminist Press at CUNY, 2021).
16. Kitty Tsui, "An Open Letter to All of the Retreat Participants," *Phoenix Rising: The Asian/Pacifica Sisters Newsletter* (June/July 1987) in the author's personal archives; Tsui, "Breaking Silence, Making Waves," 49–61, Tsui revealed that Oñang passed away from cancer in spring 1986.
17. Tsui, "Open Letter."
18. Wikipedia, s.v. "Shamakami," last edited June 23, 2024, 17:08, https://en.wikipedia.org/wiki/Shamakami. Prior to *Shamakami* was *Anamika*, considered to be the first South Asian American lesbian newsletter. Based in Brooklyn, New York, the creators of *Anamika*, Utsa and Kaya, spoke with journalist Susan Heske about the plight of South Asian lesbians in an interview titled "There Are, Always Have Been, and Always Will Be Lesbians in India." The transcription was published in *Conditions*, a lesbian feminist literary magazine in 1986 (pages 135–46). *Trikone* was another South Asian gay newsletter and organization founded in San Francisco in 1986 by activists Arvind Kumar and Suvir Das (V. K. Aruna, "South Asian Lesbians Stop APL Retreat," *Phoenix Rising: The Asian/Pacifica Sisters Newsletter* [August/September/October 1990]). The first issue of *Shamakami*, titled "Identifying Ourselves," was published in June 1990.
19. Jaimee A. Swift's personal archives of *Phoenix Rising.*
20. Chiou-ling Yeh, *Making an American Festival: Chinese New Year in San Francisco's Chinatown* (Oakland: University of California Press, 2008), 174.
21. *Aché: The Bay Area's Journal for Black Lesbians* 2, no. 1 (February 1990), www.lesbianpoetryarchive.org.
22. Rae Alexandra, "The Oakland Poet Who Brought Lesbian Feminism to the Fore," KQED, April 30, 2018, www.kqed.org/pop/102855/rebel-girls-from-bay-area-history-pat-parker-lesbian-feminist-poet-and-activist.
23. *Aché* 2, no. 1.
24. Heather Cassell, "Nia Collective Celebrates Its Silver Anniversary," *Bay Area Reporter*, November 14, 2012, www.ebar.com/story.php?ch=news&id=243075.
25. Online Archive of California, Black Lesbian Newsletter/Onyx Collection, 1979–1989 GLC 102, https://oac.cdlib.org/findaid/ark:/13030/c86w9ffz.
26. Heather Cassell, "Black Lesbians Display Their Sapphic History," *Bay Area Reporter*, December 16, 2009, www.ebar.com/story.php?ch=news&sc=&id=240374.
27. Krü Maekdo, "The *Aché* Project," Black Lesbian Archives, Prezi presentation, December 5, 2021, https://prezi.com/view/wx8Q7rJCOXY6pTh2rqIP.
28. *Aché: The Bay Area's Journal for Black Lesbians* 4, no. 1 (February/March 1992).
29. Gabrielle Hickmon, "What Audre Lorde Learned in Berlin About Afro-German Identity," *Literary Hub*, December 10, 2019, https://lithub.com/what-audre-lorde-learned-in-berlin-about-afro-german-identity.
30. Amal Ahmed, "How Audre Lorde Weathered the Storm," *JSTOR Daily*, March 13, 2019, https://daily.jstor.org/how-audre-lorde-weathered-the-storm.

31. Audre Lorde, "A Letter from St. Croix," *Aché* 2, no. 1: 27.
32. The majority of the footage in Jennifer Abod's documentary *The Edge of Each Other's Battles: The Vision of Audre Lorde* (2002) was from the I Am Your Sister: Forging Global Connections Across Differences conference.
33. *Aché: The Bay Area's Journal for Black Lesbians* 2, no. 6 (November/December 1990).

17. Reviving the History of Radical Black-Asian Internationalism

1. Sax Rohmer, *The Mystery of Dr. Fu-Manchu* (London: Methuen, 1913).
2. Despite subsequent inquiries by the World Health Organization and other authorities, the origins of COVID-19 remain unclear. For studies on its circulation prior to the first documented cases in December 2019, see "COVID-19 Origin: University of Calgary Research Shows SARS-CoV-2 May Have Been Evolving Slowly Since 2013," *Firstpost*, June 27, 2020, www.firstpost.com/health/covid-19-origin-university-of-calgary-research-shows-sars-cov-2-may-have-been-evolving-slowly-since-2013-8529141.html; "Novel Coronavirus Circulated Undetected Months Before First COVID-19 Cases in Wuhan, China," UC San Diego Health, news release, March 18, 2021, https://health.ucsd.edu/news/releases/Pages/2021-03-18-novel-coronavirus-circulated-undetected-months-before-first-covid-19-cases-in-wuhan-china.aspx.
3. Marc Ramirez, "FBI Says Texas Stabbing That Targeted Asian American Family a Hate Crime," *Dallas Morning News*, April 1, 2020; Alexandra E. Petri and Daniel E. Slotnik, "Attacks on Asian-Americans in New York Stoke Fear, Anxiety and Anger," *New York Times*, February 26, 2021, www.nytimes.com/2021/02/26/nyregion/asian-hate-crimes-attacks-ny.html.
4. For a more in-depth examination on how Orientalism has structured US discourses of national sovereignty and American freedom, see Ju-Hyun Park, "The Alien and the Sovereign: Yellow Peril in Pandemic Times," *Evergreen Review*, www.evergreenreview.com/read/the-alien-and-the-sovereign-yellow-peril-in-pandemic-times.
5. The 1895 lithograph was titled *Peoples of Europe, Guard Your Most Sacred Possessions*. For more on the long history of yellow peril discourse, see John Kuo Wei Tchen and Dylan Years, *Yellow Peril! An Archive of Anti-Asian Fear* (New York: Verso, 2014).
6. See Vince Schleitwiler, *Strange Fruit of the Black Pacific* (New York: New York University Press, 2017), 37–71.
7. Quoted in Julia H. Lee, *Interracial Encounters: Reciprocal Representations in African and Asian American Literatures, 1896–1937* (New York: New York University Press, 2011), 135.
8. See Soya Jung, "The Endurance of the Color Line," Othering and Belonging, www.otheringandbelonging.org/endurance-color-line.
9. For more on the Asian American Political Alliance and its relationship to Black revolutionaries, see Daryl Maeda, "Black Panthers, Red Guards, and Chinamen: Constructing Asian American Identity Through Performing Blackness, 1969–1972," *American Quarterly* 57, no. 4 (2005), 1079–1103.
10. Taylor Weik, "The History Behind 'Yellow Peril Supports Black Power' and Why Some Find It Problematic," NBC News, June 11, 2020.
11. See Maeda, ""Black Panthers, Red Guards, and Chinamen."
12. Langston Hughes, "Roar, China!," *New Masses*, February 22, 1938, 20.
13. Benjamin Young, "Juche in the United States: The Black Panther Party's Relations with North Korea, 1969–1971," *Asia-Pacific Journal* 13, no. 3 (March 30, 2015); "Statement from the US Peoples' Anti-Imperialist Delegation to Korea," 1970, History and

Public Policy Program Digital Archive, University of California, Berkeley, Bancroft Library, BANC MSS 91/213 c, The Eldridge Cleaver Papers, 1963–1988, Carton 5, Folder 4, obtained for NKIDP by Charles Kraus, https://digitalarchive.wilsoncenter.org/document/114495. For more, see Judy Tzu-Chun Wu, *Radicals on the Road: Internationalism, Orientalism, and Feminism During the Vietnam Era* (Ithaca, NY: Cornell University Press, 2013).

14. For more on this framing of Asian Americans, see Ellen D. Wu, *The Color of Success: Asian Americans and the Origins of the Model Minority* (Princeton, NJ: Princeton University Press, 2015); Cindy I-Fen Cheng, *Citizens of Asian America: Democracy and Race During the Cold War* (New York: New York University Press, 2013).
15. Dean Itsuji Saranillio, *Unsustainable Empire: Alternative Histories of Hawai'i Statehood* (Durham, NC: Duke University Press, 2018).
16. Naoko Shibusawa, *America's Geisha Ally: Reimagining the Japanese Enemy* (Cambridge, MA: Harvard University Press, 2010).
17. Andrew Yang, "We Asian Americans Are Not the Virus, but We Can Be Part of the Cure," *Washington Post*, April 1, 2020, www.washingtonpost.com/opinions/2020/04/01/andrew-yang-coronavirus-discrimination.
18. Assemblymember Grace Lee, "Bill to Integrate AANHPI History into New York's Public Schools," press release, May 23, 2023, accessed April 19, 2024, https://nyassembly.gov/mem/Grace-Lee/story/107275.
19. Catherine Thorbecke, "NYC Launches $100,000 Effort to Combat Anti-Asian Discrimination in COVID-19 Era," ABC News, May 26, 2020, https://abcnews.go.com.
20. Kimmy Yam, "Critics Fear NYPD Asian Hate Crime Task Force Could Have Unintended Consequences," NBC News, September 2, 2020. On abolitionist critiques of anti-Asian hate crimes, see Dylan Rodríguez, "The 'Asian Exception' and the Scramble for Legibility: Toward an Abolitionist Approach to Anti-Asian Violence," *Society + Space*, April 8, 2021, www.societyandspace.org/articles/the-asian-exception-and-the-scramble-for-legibility-toward-an-abolitionist-approach-to-anti-asian-violence.
21. This phrasing, of course, gestures to Martin Luther King Jr.'s language in his "Beyond Vietnam" speech at Riverside Church in New York on April 4, 1967. See Clayborne Carson et al., eds. *Eyes on the Prize: A Reader and Guide*, (New York: Penguin, 1987), 201–4.
22. Euny Hong, "Why I've Stopped Telling People I'm Not Chinese," *New York Times*, May 15, 2020.
23. For an extended engagement with the "allyship" frame of Asian American politics, see Hyejin Shim, "Questions on (the Limits and Effects of) (Asian American) Allyship," *Medium*, Aug 22, 2017, https://shimhyejin.medium.com/questions-on-the-limits-effects-of-asian-american-allyship-bb545f019117.
24. Andy Liu, "About Those 'Letters to My Asian Parents About Anti-Black Racism,'" *Time to Say Goodbye*, June 17, 2020, https://goodbye.substack.com/p/about-those-letters-to-my-asian-parents?s=r.
25. Vijay Prashad, "The Third World Idea," *Nation*, June 4, 2007, www.thenation.com/article/archive/third-world-idea.
26. Ben Norton, "BLM Platform Blasts 'U.S. Empire,' Militarization, War on Terror, AFRICOM," *Salon*, August 12, 2016, www.salon.com/2016/08/12/blm-platform-blasts-u-s-empire-militarization-war-on-terror-africom.
27. Stuart Schrader, "Yes, American Police Act Like Occupying Armies. They Literally Studied Their Tactics," *Guardian*, June 8, 2020, www.theguardian.com/commentis-

free/2020/jun/08/yes-american-police-act-like-occupying-armies-they-literally-studied-their-tactics; Austin C. McCoy, "The Struggle Against Police Is International. Our Solidarity Must Be Global," *TruthOut*, June 13, 2020, https://truthout.org/articles/the-struggle-against-police-is-international-our-solidarity-must-be-global.

28. Lara Jakes and Edward Wong, "U.S. Diplomats Struggle to Defend Democracy Abroad amid Crises at Home," *New York Times*, June 8, 2020, www.nytimes.com/2020/06/06/us/politics/protests-diplomats-coronavirus.html.
29. Nicole Gaouette and Jennifer Hansler, "US Embassy in Seoul Removes Black Lives Matter Banner and Pride Flag," CNN, June 15, 2020, www.cnn.com/2020/06/15/politics/us-embassy-seoul-blm-banner/index.html.
30. Penny M. Von Eschen, *Race Against Empire: Black Americans and Anticolonialism, 1937–1957* (Ithaca, NY: Cornell University Press, 1997).
31. Critical Resistance, "Abolitionist Platform in Response to COVID-19," accessed October 2, 2020, https://web.archive.org/web/20201002161358/http://criticalresistance.org/abolitionist-platform-in-response-to-covid-19-point-5.

20. "We Lead the World's Liberation"

1. See Matt Tracy, "Weekend Demos Focus on Black Sex Workers, Anti-Trans Violence," *Gay City News*, August 3, 2020, https://gaycitynews.com/weekend-demos-focus-on-black-sex-workers-anti-trans-violence.
2. Edited by TD Tso.
3. Red Canary Song (@redcanarysong), "Yesterday's Black Sex Workers Teach-In," Twitter, July 25, 2020, https://twitter.com/RedCanarySong/status/1287410873707962368.
4. SX Noir, "SX Noir: 'We Must Decriminalise Sex Work, and This Includes Digital Space,'" *i-D*, September 21, 2020, https://web.archive.org/web/20201202194624/https://i-d.vice.com/en_uk/article/v7ga78/sx-noir-we-must-decriminalise-sex-work-and-this-includes-digital-space.
5. "Digital Rally for International Whores' Day," Kink Out Events, June 2, 2020, www.kinkoutevents.com/events/international-whores-day-nyc-digital-rally.

21. "We Have More in Common Than Not"

1. Lindsay Whitehurst and Michelle Price, "Stigmas on Race, Gender and Sex Overlap in Atlanta Slayings," Associated Press, March 18, 2021, apnews.com.
2. This term is used to describe nonwhite people across the world, given that Black, Indigenous, and people of color account for over 80 percent of the global population. The decolonial phrase counters labels like "minority" or "people of color" that center whiteness as the default. See Cambridge Dictionary Online, s.v. "global majority," accessed August 6, 2024, https://dictionary.cambridge.org/us/dictionary/english/global-majority.
3. Martin Luther King Jr. famously said "It's all right to tell a man to lift himself by his own bootstraps, but it is cruel jest to say to a bootless man that he ought to lift himself by his own bootstraps." Martin Luther King Jr. "The Hammer of Justice," transcript of speech delivered at Ohio Northern University, January 11, 1968, www.onu.edu/mlk/mlk-speech-transcript.

23. Searching for Care and Justice

1. South Asian SOAR, *Together We Rise: Voices from the Frontlines of South Asian Gender-Based Violence Work*, October 2022, www.togetherwerise.report.

2. Sakhi for South Asian Survivors, "Mourning the Loss of Mandeep Kaur," August 9, 2022, https://sakhi.org/mourning-the-loss-of-mandeep-kaur.
3. Jennifer Rajkumar, "Assemblywoman Jenifer Rajkumar Gives Keynote Speech at Mayor's Office Roundtable on Domestic Violence in South Asian Diaspora," New York State Assembly, October 19, 2022, https://nyassembly.gov/mem/Jenifer-Rajkumar/story/104315.
4. Rajkumar, "Keynote Speech."
5. Margaret Abraham, *Speaking the Unspeakable: Marital Violence among South Asian Immigrants in the United States* (New Brunswick, NJ: Rutgers University Press, 2000).
6. Kristin Bumiller, *In an Abusive State: How Neoliberalism Appropriated the Feminist Movement Against Sexual Violence* (Durham, NC: Duke University Press, 2008); Beth E. Richie, *Arrested Justice: Black Women, Violence, and America's Prison Nation* (New York: New York University Press, 2012); INCITE! Women of Color Against Violence, *Color of Violence: The INCITE! Anthology* (Durham, NC: Duke University Press, 2016); Emily L. Thuma, *All Our Trials: Prisons, Policing, and the Feminist Fight to End Violence* (Champaign: University of Illinois Press, 2019).
7. Garrine P. Laney, "Violence Against Women Act: History and Federal Funding Note," Congressional Research Service, February 26, 2010, https://hdl.handle.net/1813/77645; Nancy Whittier, "Carceral and Intersectional Feminism in Congress: The Violence Against Women Act, Discourse, and Policy," *Gender and Society* 30, no. 5 (October 2016): 791–818.
8. South Asian SOAR, "Executive Summary," *Together We Rise.*
9. For just one example of this at work in New York City, see the New York Civil Liberty Union's 2023 report detailing systemic racial discrimination in the Administration for Children's Services, www.nyclu.org/en/campaigns/racism-every-stage-data-shows-how-nycs-administration-childrens-services-discriminates.
10. South Asian SOAR, *Together We Rise.*
11. South Asian SOAR, *Together We Rise.*
12. INCITE!, *Color of Violence.*

24. Beyond Gilded Cages

1. Mon Mohapatra, "Good Design . . . for Whom?" *New Inquiry*, March 27, 2019, https://thenewinquiry.com/good-design-for-whom.
2. See Talila A. Lewis, "Understanding Incarceration and Dis/Ableism"; Minju Bae and Mark Tseng-Putterman, "Reviving the History of Radical Black-Asian Internationalism"; Asian American Feminist Collective, "We Want Cop-Free Communities: A Letter," all in this volume.
3. Bae and Tseng-Putterman, "Reviving the History."
4. Lindsay Beyerstein, "Beyond the Hate Frame: An Interview with Kay Whitlock and Michael Bronski," Political Research Associates, July 27, 2015, https://politicalresearch.org/2015/07/27/beyond-the-hate-frame-an-interview-with-kay-whitlock-michael-bronski; Raja Krishnamoorthi, "Congressman Krishnamoorthi Denounces Hate Crime Against Women of South Asian Descent in Plano, Texas," August 27, 2022, https://krishnamoorthi.house.gov/media/press-releases/congressman-krishnamoorthi-denounces-hate-crime-against-women-south-asian.

25. Not Victims

1. The Page Act of 1875 was the first US law that restricted immigration; it prohibited the arrival of unfree laborers and women for "lewd and immoral purposes" and primarily

targeted Chinese women under the assumption that all of them were sex trafficked or engaging in sex work. The Page Act of 1875, Sect. 141, 18 Stat. 477 (March 3, 1875).

2. These are all harmful stereotypes and archetypes perpetuated about Asian femmes in media, legislation, and our daily lives. For more in-depth analysis on these stereotypes, see Celine Parreñas Shimizu, *The Hypersexuality of Race: Performing Asian/American Women on Screen and Scene* (Durham, NC: Duke University Press, 2007).
3. A common accusation made by SWERFS (sex worker exclusionary radical feminists) is that sex worker organizers want to expand the sex trade and sex trafficking. To learn more about the accusation, see Frankie Miren, "Sorry, UK Sex Work Protesters, There's No Such Thing as a 'Pimp Lobby,'" *Vice*, February 11, 2015, www.vice.com/en/article/nnqx48/the-pimp-lobby-292.
4. Butterfly 迁蝶 (@butterflycsw), "Quotes from Asian massage workers and Asian sex workers," Instagram, March 15, 2022, www.instagram.com/p/CbIr4QaNvlo.
5. Sex worker rights activists argue for decriminalization, or the removal of criminal penalties for the buying and selling of sex, as the means to reduce violence in the sex industry. To learn more about decriminalization and its arguments, see Chanelle Gallant and Elene Lam, *Not Your Rescue Project: Migrant Sex Workers Fighting for Justice* (Chicago, IL: Haymarket Books, 2024).
6. "International Sex Worker Rights Day," Events, Global Network of Sex Work Projects (NSWP), www.nswp.org/event/international-sex-worker-rights-day.
7. Bharati Dey et al., "Sex Work in a Transnational Context," *Hacking // Hustling*, livestreamed on April 12, 2021, https://hackinghustling.org/sex-work-in-a-transnational-context.
8. With thanks to Sanchari Sur for translation of audio from "Sex Work in a Transnational Context."
9. Durbar Mahila Samanwaya Committee (DMSC), "Short History of DMSC," 1998, submitted by NSWP on February 26, 2011, https://nswp.org/resource/member-publications/short-history-dmsc.
10. Dey et al., "Sex Work in a Transnational Context."
11. "Sex Workers Demand Respect for Their Fundamental Rights in a Parallel Summit to the AIDS 2012," UN AIDS, July 25, 2012, www.unaids.org/en/resources/presscentre/featurestories/2012/july/20120725asexworkers.
12. Global Network of Sex Work Projects (NSWP), "Introduction: the Sex Worker Freedom Festival," *Solidarity Is Not a Crime* (2012): 2, www.nswp.org.
13. Grace Kamau et al., "Sex Work in a Transnational Context," *hacking // hustling*, livestreamed on April 12, 2021, https://hackinghustling.org/sex-work-in-a-transnational-context.
14. Global Network of Sex Work Projects (NSWP), Sex Worker Academy Africa (SWAA) (2015), www.nswp.org.
15. Similar to Asian migrant workers in the United States, sex workers in Thailand are often presumed to be and treated like victims of human trafficking. To learn more, see Leo Bernardo Villar, "Unacceptable Forms of Work in the Thai Sex and Entertainment Industry," *Anti-Trafficking Review* 12 (2019): 108–26. Sex tourism in Thailand has been a massive market since the 1960s, when US Army members would travel from Vietnam for "rest and relaxation." To learn more about sex work in Thailand and EMPOWER's organizing, see Charlotte England, "The Thai Women Behind the First Bar Run Entirely by a Sex Workers' Collective," *Vice*, October 19, 2015, www.vice.com/en/article/ezjwd7/the-bar-owned-and-run-entirely-by-a-thai-sex-workers-collective.

16. Liz Cameron and Pompit Pakmai, *Bad Girls Dictionary* (Bangkok: Empower University Press, 2007), 25–26.
17. Asia Pacific Social Forum, "Sex Worker Criminalisation in Cambodia, India, Nepal, Sri Lanka and Thailand," Zoom, February 18, 2022.
18. Asia Pacific Social Forum, "Sex Worker Criminalisation."

26. Taking Up Each Other's Cause

1. Mistir Sew, "'The Sadism Is Very Disturbing': Two Months on the Run in Tigray," *Ethiopian Insight*, February 8, 2021, www.ethiopia-insight.com/2021/02/08/the-sadism-is-very-disturbing-two-months-on-the-run-in-tigray.
2. "One Year On, Peace Holds in Tigray, but Ethiopia Still Fractured," *Al Jazeera*, November 2, 2023, www.aljazeera.com/gallery/2023/11/2/photos-one-year-on-peace-holds-in-tigray-but-ethiopia-still-fractured.
3. ADF Staff, "Fano Attacks Threaten Return to War in Ethiopia," *ADF*, October 10, 2023, https://adf-magazine.com/2023/10/fano-attacks-threaten-return-to-war-in-ethiopia.
4. Lucy Kassa, "Ethiopian Troops Accused of Mass Killings of Civilians in Amhara Region," *The Guardian*, September 8, 2023, www.theguardian.com/global-development/2023/sep/08/ethiopian-troops-accused-mass-killings-amhara-civilians-region-fano-militia.
5. Srinagar Smart City, https://srinagarsmartcity.in; Hakeem Irfan Rashid, "Srinagar to Get Eight WiFi Zones," *Economic Times*, June 4, 2023, economictimes.indiatimes.com.
6. "Surveillance Concerns as India Issues New Digital IDs in Kashmir," *Al Jazeera*, January 26, 2023, www.aljazeera.com/news/2023/1/26/surveillance-concerns-as-india-issues-new-digital-ids-in-kashmir; "'Smart'" Settler Colonialism —The Srinagar Smart City Project," Stand with Kashmir, November 29, 2023, https://standwithkashmir.org/smart-settler-colonialism-the-srinagar-smart-city-project.

28. Celebrating a Hundred Years of Yuri Kochiyama

1. Yuri Kochiyama, *Passing It On: A Memoir* (Los Angeles, CA: UCLA Asian American Studies Center Press, 2004).
2. Connie Gentry, "Going for Broke: The 442nd Regimental Combat Team," National World War II Museum, September 24, 2020, www.nationalww2museum.org/war/articles/442nd-regimental-combat-team.
3. "May 19, 1921: Yuri Kochiyama Born," This Day in History, Zinn Education Project, www.zinnedproject.org/news/tdih/yuri-kochiyama-was-born.
4. "Asian American and Pacific Islander Heritage Month 2021," YWCA Utah (blog), May 13, 2021, www.ywcautah.org/ywca-utah/blog/2021/05/13/asian-american-pacific-islander-heritage-month-2021.
5. "The Passionate Harlem Activist Yuri Kochiyama, New York, 1921–2014 (Video)," *Harlem World Magazine*, July 7, 2020, www.harlemworldmagazine.com/harlem-activist-yuri-kochiyama-ny-1921-2014.
6. Diane C. Fujino, *Heartbeat of Struggle: The Revolutionary Life of Yuri Kochiyama* (Minneapolis, MN: University of Minnesota Press, 2005).
7. See Akemi Kochiyama, "Reflections on My Grandma Yuri, Malcolm X, and the Future of Black-Asian Solidarity," *TWR Journal*, www.twrjournal.com/nonfiction-akemi-kochiyama (Akemi speaks more about her upbringing, her grandmother, and Black and Asian solidarity).
8. Jennifer Lee and Tiffany Huang, "Why the Trope of Black-Asian Conflict in the Face

of Anti-Asian Violence Dismisses Solidarity," Brookings Institute, March 11, 2021, www.brookings.edu/articles/why-the-trope-of-black-asian-conflict-in-the-face-of-anti-asian-violence-dismisses-solidarity.

9. "Yuri Kochiyama."

29. Meditations on Black/Asian Locations

1. See TD Tso, "Nail Salon Brawls and Boycotts: Unpacking the Black-Asian Conflict in America," and Tamara K. Nopper, "On Anti-Black Terror, Captivity, and Black-Korean Conflict," in this volume for more detail on the Family Red Apple boycott and histories of Black-Korean conflict.
2. Lisa Lowe, *The Intimacies of Four Continents* (Durham, NC: Duke University Press, 2015).
3. Lowe, 31.
4. Lowe, 35.
5. Hanif Willis-Abdurraqib, "In Defense of 'Trap Queen' as Our Generation's Greatest Love Song," *Seven Scribes*, June 5, 2015, https://sevenscribes.com/in-defense-of-trap-queen-as-our-generations-greatest-love-song.

30. Academia and Activism

1. Claire Jean Kim states, "Being invisible is about as good as it can get because it's a sign that you're assimilated—it's a sign that you're integrated, at least to some degree." Weishun Lu, "Framing Asian Suffering in an Anti-Black World: A Conversation with Claire Jean Kim," *Edge Effects*, updated October 10, 2022, https://edgeeffects.net/claire-jean-kim.
2. Christina Sharpe, "Against Renewal," *Wading* 13 (September 2022): 12, Society for the Diffusion of Useful Knowledge, www.blackwoodgallery.ca/publications/sduk/wading/against-renewal.

32. From the Other Coast, with Love

1. Lucille Clifton, "won't you celebrate with me," in *Book of Light* (Port Townsend, WA: Copper Canyon Press, 1992), 25.
2. Zen Buddhist proverb.
3. Audre Lorde, "Coal," in *The Collected Poems of Audre Lorde* (New York: W. W. Norton, 2000), 6.
4. June Jordan, "A Powerful Hatred," in *Affirmative Acts: Political Essays* (New York: Anchor, 1998).

33. The Breadfruit Does Not Float Far from the Tree

1. "CHamoru" is the orthographically correct spelling, as opposed to the Spanish spelling "Chamorro."
2. See Karim Ganem Maloof, "The Breadfruit Tree," trans. Joel Streicker, *Stranger's Guide*, May 14, 2021, https://magazine.tablethotels.com/en/2021/05/the-breadfruit-tree.

34. Finding Solidarity and Survival Within a Transnational, Intergenerational Zoom Dance Party

1. This article was written in April 2021, following the targeted shootings of Asian spas in the Atlanta area on March 16 and the mass shooting that took place soon after at a FedEx facility in Indianapolis on April 15, all amid the ongoing COVID-19 pandemic. Both atrocities impacted Asian American and immigrant communities and were weighing heavy on me as I wrote this piece.

2. See anthology introduction, as well as our first interview conducted for the Black and Asian Feminist Solidarities column for *The Margins*. Jaimee Swift, "On The Radical Possibilities of Leading with Love: An Interview with Dr. Margo Okazawa-Rey," *The Margins*, August 27, 2020, https://aaww.org/on-the-radical-possibilities-of-leading-with-love-an-interview-with-dr-margo-okazawa-rey.
3. "Virtual Book Club with Dr. Margo Okazawa-Rey," Asia Society, Zoom event scheduled for August 6, 2020, https://asiasociety.org/triennial/events/members-only-event-virtual-book-club-dr-margo-okazawa-rey.
4. In February 2021, Myanmar's military staged a coup d'etat following the 2020 election of National League for Democracy leader Aung San Suu Kyi, imprisoning her and returning the Tatmadaw (Myanmar Armed Forces) to power. For more, see "Myanmar Military Seizes Power, Detains Elected Leader Aung San Suu Kyi," Reuters, February 1, 2021, www.reuters.com/article/world/myanmar-military-seizes-power-detains-elected-leader-aung-san-suu-kyi-idUSKBN2A00VB.
5. On April 20, 2021, former Minneapolis police officer Derek Chauvin was convicted on all charges for the 2020 murder of George Floyd, an unarmed 46-year-old Black man. Floyd's murder reignited the Black Lives Matter uprisings in the summer of 2020. For more, see Eric Levenson, "Derek Chauvin Found Guilty of All Three Charges for Killing George Floyd." CNN, April 21, 2021, www.cnn.com/2021/04/20/us/derek-chauvin-trial-george-floyd-deliberations/index.html.
6. Combahee River Collective, The Combahee River Collective Statement, April 1977, www.blackpast.org/african-american-history/combahee-river-collective-statement-1977.
7. See "Black & Asian Feminist Solidarity Playlist," Spotify, www.tinyurl.com/bafs-playlist.

35. A Black Feminist Perspective on the Politics of Care

1. Combahee River Collective, The Combahee River Collective Statement, April 1977, www.blackpast.org/african-american-history/combahee-river-collective-statement-1977.
2. Jennifer C. Nash, "Practicing Love: Black Feminism, Love-Politics, and Post-Intersectionality," *Meridians* 11, no. 2 (2011): 3, https://doi.org/10.2979/meridians.11.2.1.
3. Audre Lorde, *A Burst of Light and Other Essays* (Mineola, NY: Ixia, 2017), 130.
4. Joy James, "The Womb of Western Theory: Trauma, Time Theft and the Captive Maternal," *Carceral Notebooks*, no. 12 (2016): 26.
5. See Lorde, *A Burst of Light*.
6. Jennifer C. Nash, *Birthing Black Mothers* (Durham, NC: Duke University Press, 2021).
7. Nina Martin and Renee Montagne, "Black Mothers Keep Dying After Giving Birth. Shalon Irving's Story Explains Why," *All Things Considered*, NPR, December 7, 2017, www.npr.org/2017/12/07/568948782/black-mothers-keep-dying-after-giving-birth-shalon-irvings-story-explains-why.

36. On Healing Through Nature, Kink, and Communion

1. Edited by TD Tso.
2. See W. E. B. Du Bois, *The Souls of Black Folk; Essays and Sketches* (Chicago: A.G. McClurg, 1903).
3. Cathy J. Cohen, "Deviance as Resistance: A New Research Agenda for the Study of Black Politics," *Du Bois Review: Social Science Research on Race* 1, no. 1 (2004): 27–45.

37. On Dalit Dreaming and Rebellious Joy

1. Katherine McKittrick, *Dear Science and Other Stories* (Durham, NC: Duke University Press, 2021), 7.
2. Kumud Pawde, *Antasphot* (1981) (out of print).
3. Christina Sharpe, *In the Wake: On Blackness and Being* (Durham, NC: Duke University Press, 2016).
4. Billy-Ray Belcourt, *NDN Coping Mechanisms: Notes from the Field* (Ontario: House of Anansi Press, 2019).
5. Eve Tuck and C. Ree, "A Glossary of Haunting," in *Handbook of Autoethnography*, ed. Stacey Holman Jones, Tony E. Adams, and Carolyn Ellis (New York: Routledge, 2016), 639–58.
6. B. R. Ambedkar, *Castes in India: Their Mechanism, Genesis and Development* (Jullundur City: Bheem Patrika Publications, 1916).

38. Reimagining the Autistic Mother Tongue

1. Lydia X. Z. Brown, "Huxley's Adoption Story Is Part of a Much Larger Narrative About Race, Disability and Abuse," *gal–dem* (blog), May 29, 2020, https://gal-dem.com/huxley-adoption-story-youtube-stauffers-is-part-of-a-larger-narrative-race-disability-and-abuse.
2. See Sianne Ngai, *Our Aesthetic Categories: Zany, Cute, Interesting* (Cambridge, MA: Harvard University Press, 2012).

40. Unapologetic Agreements

1. Editors' note: We highly recommend and encourage reading Sonia Renee Taylor's *The Body Is Not an Apology* in its entirety to better understand radical self-love and embody its values—as ending body terrorism and body shame brings us all closer to solidarity as feminists of color.
2. Pillar 4, collective compassion is the "being" part of radical self-love. It is our internal compass, quickly alerting us when we are off course. Not only does collective compassion provide an internal structure of governance (i.e., the rules that guide our personal work), it is also the bridge to the *socially* transformative power of radical self-love. Collective compassion guides us toward how we ought to treat ourselves, but as importantly, it is our directive for "being" with others.
3. Matthew Inman, "You're Not Going to Believe What I Am About to Tell You," *The Oatmeal* (webcomic), July 23, 2017, http://theoatmeal.com/comics/believe.
4. Jon Lee Anderson, *Che Guevara: A Revolutionary Life* (New York: Grove, 2010), 178.
5. Alcoholics Anonymous, "Promises," in *Big Book* (1976), https://step12.com/promises.html.

41. Dreaming Is Our Radical Inheritance and "radical imagiNation"

1. "About Us." Abolition Is... https://abolition-is.com/about.
2. Alicia Garza, "Wrap It Up and Back It Up with Dr. Connie Wun," *Lady Don't Take No*, Spotify, April 2, 2021.
3. Ruth Wilson Gilmore, "Making Abolition Geography in California's Central Valley with Ruth Wilson Gilmore," interview by Léopold Lambert, *The Funambulist*, December 20, 2018, https://thefunambulist.net/making-abolition-geography-in-californias-central-valley-with-ruth-wilson-gilmore.
4. Diane Fujino, *Heartbeat of Struggle* (Minneapolis: University of Minnesota Press, 2005).
5. Fujino, *Heartbeat of Struggle*.

42. Nā Wāhine Noho Mauna

1. Because gender identity is influenced by personal, lived experiences, folks who are referenced in this article may identify as wāhine without using the word "womxn" as a translation. The word "māhū" in Hawaiian language and culture describes someone who embodies kane (male) and wahine (female) energies. Historically, Kanaka Maoli cared less about gender and sexual identities than about one's contribution to their community. In many contemporary Hawaiian language spaces, any Kanaka who is transgender, gender nonconforming, homosexual, or is part of a gender and/or sexual minority may identify as māhū. One of the most beautiful explanations of "māhū" has been offered by Kalani'ōpua Young, who shares a story that māhū are like sunsets, brilliant phenomena between day and night.
2. When kia'i mobilized in June 2015 to protect the mountain from the construction, thirty-one people were arrested. In 2019, thirty-eight elders were arrested.
3. Māhū scholars and community organizers are also expanding the language we use to talk about gender identities. For instance, the acronym MVPFAFF+ centers Pasifika languages and gender diversity, where "LGBTQIA+" does not. Coined by Niuean activist Phylesha Brown-Acton, MVPFAFF+ calls up Māhū (Tahiti and Hawai'i), Vaka sa lewa (Fiji), Palopa (Papua New Guinea), Fa'afafine (Samoa and Tokelau), Akava'ine (Cook Islands), Fakaleiti (Tonga), Fakafifine (Niue). These terms are more than gender categories. They refer to relational ways of being that are rooted in Pasifika communities, histories, and ancestral knowledges. New scholarship is also exploring the emergence of "Ka Māhūi" as a signifier for the collective mana of māhū in the Hawaiian movement. See Ka'imina'auao Kahikina, "No Ka Māhūi Aloha: Unsettling Homo/Hetero-Nationalist Logics of Belonging," *American Quarterly* 76, no. 3 (2024): 515–40.
4. Here I use *jurisdiction*, in the capacious sense that Shiri Pasternak writes about when she says, "Jurisdiction is the authority to have authority . . . the very substance of what authorizes law" (5). Jurisdiction is not just derived from or is an extension of state sovereignty. Jurisdiction comprises the practices that undergird and construct sovereign authority and political leadership in the first place. In *Grounded Authority*, Pasternak describes how "a dense patchwork" of settler state divisions crowd Algonquin ancestral territories and assert settler sovereignty through a kind of "jurisdictional commotion" that works to "undermine, erase, and choke out the exercise of Indigenous jurisdiction" (18–25). We witnessed this kind of settler state confusion among the occupying state's "microgoverning authorities" on Maunakea, who were often perplexed about which one of them controlled the road, could construct a gate, or make arrests.
5. Epeli Hau'ofa, "Our Sea of Islands," in *A New Oceania: Rediscovering Our Sea of Islands* (Suva: School of Social and Economic Development, University of the South Pacific, 1993), 16.

43. Toward Transnational Feminist Futures

1. Loretta J. Ross, Lynn Roberts, Erika Derkas, Whitney Peoples, and Pamela Bridgewater Toure, eds., *Radical Reproductive Justice: Foundations, Theory, Practice, Critique* (New York: Feminist Press, 2017).
2. Edited by TD Tso.
3. The Peace Corps is criticized for being another arm of American imperialism, white saviorism, and neocolonialism. To learn more about the critiques levied against the Peace Corps, see Lara Weber, "The Peace Corps Should Address Its 'White Savior' Problem, but It Shouldn't Be Abolished," *Miami Herald*, March 2, 2021, www.miamiherald.com.

4. The first known use of the phrase "women's rights are human rights" came from a Gabriela campaign against the dictatorship of Ferdinand E. Marcos in the Philippines. For more, see Lisa Levenstein, "The Forgotten Origins of 'Women's Rights Are Human Rights,'" Open Global Rights, September 29, 2020, www.openglobalrights.org/the-forgotten-origins-of-womens-rights-are-human-rights.
5. See Asian Communities for Reproductive Justice, "A New Vision for Advancing Our Movement for Reproductive Health, Reproductive Rights, and Reproductive Justice," 2005, https://forwardtogether.org.
6. NARAL was established in 1969 as the National Association for the Repeal of Abortion Laws.
7. Loretta J. Ross, "African-American Women and Abortion: A Neglected History," *Journal of Health Care for the Poor and Underserved* 3, no. 2 (1992): 274–84.
8. Recent statistics from 2016 show that 28 percent of US abortion patients were Black. To learn more, see "U.S. Abortion Patients Infographic," Guttmacher Institute, May 9, 2016, www.guttmacher.org/infographic/2016/us-abortion-patients.
9. This is in reference to Latasha Harlins, a 15-year-old Black girl who was murdered in 1991 in Los Angeles by Korean shop owner Soon Ja Du, who accused her of stealing a bottle of orange juice. To learn more, see Angel Jennings, "How the Killing of Latasha Harlins Changed South L.A., Long Before Black Lives Matter," *Los Angeles Times*, March 18, 2016, https://www.latimes.com/local/california/la-me-0318-latasha-harlins-20160318-story.html.
10. See Mari Matsuda, "We Will Not Be Used," this volume.
11. The Hyde Amendment, passed in 1976, blocks the use of federal Medicaid funding for abortion services.
12. The Jane Collective was an underground network in Chicago that helped women obtain abortions between 1969 and 1973 when *Roe v. Wade* made the procedure legal across the United States. For more, see Claire Lampen, "The Underground Network That Helped Women Get Abortions When No One Else Would," *Vice*, January 29, 2018, www.vice.com/en/article/43qjwj/abortion-jane-collective-heather-booth-underground-network.
13. See Resist, "Resist Newsletter, Dec. 1990" *Resist Newsletters* 229 (1990), Trinity College Digital Repository, https://digitalrepository.trincoll.edu/resistnewsletter/229.
14. The full quote by Toni Cade Bambara is "As a culture worker who belongs to an oppressed people my job is to make revolution irresistible." Thabiti Lewis, *Conversations with Toni Cade Bambara* (Jackson: University Press of Mississippi, 2012).

44. Collective Reproductive Freedom Is Racial Justice

1. N. T. Ellis and N. Chavez, "'We Are Not Surprised': Women of Color Say the Courts Have Never Served Their Communities," CNN, June 26, 2022, https://www.cnn.com/2022/06/26/us/women-of-color-roe-wade-decision/index.html.
2. Deirdre Cooper Owens, *Medical Bondage: Race, Gender, and the Origins of American Gynecology* (Athens: University of Georgia Press, 2018).
3. Laura Briggs, *Reproducing Empire: Race, Sex, Science, and U.S. Imperialism in Puerto Rico* (Berkeley: University of California Press, 2003).
4. Priya Kandaswamy, "Race, Reproductive Justice, and the Criminalization of Purvi Patel," in *Asian American Feminisms and Women of Color Politics*, ed. Lynn Fujiwara and Shireen Roshanravan (Seattle: University of Washington Press, 2018): 218–40.
5. Sital Kalantry, "Replacing Myths with Facts: Sex Selective Abortion Laws in the

United States," Cornell Legal Studies Research Paper No. 14–34, June 5, 2014, http://dx.doi.org/10.2139/ssrn.2476432.

6. See Talila A. Lewis, "Understanding Incarceration and Dis/Ableism," in this volume.
7. Eugene Declercq et al., "The U.S. Maternal Health Divide: The Limited Maternal Health Services and Worse Outcomes of States Proposing New Abortion Restrictions," Commonwealth Fund, December 14, 2022, www.commonwealthfund.org/publications/issue-briefs/2022/dec/us-maternal-health-divide-limited-services-worse-outcomes.
8. Priya Agrawal, "Maternal Mortality and Morbidity in the United States of America," *Bulletin of the World Health Organization* 93, no. 3 (March 2014): 135.
9. "Working Together to Reduce Black Maternal Mortality," US Centers for Disease Control and Prevention, updated April 8, 2024, www.cdc.gov/womens-health/features/maternal-mortality.html.
10. See Diana Greene Foster, *The Turnaway Study: The Cost of Denying Women Access to Abortion* (New York: Scribner, 2020).
11. Foster, *The Turnaway Study.*
12. Aubrey Hirsh, "The Economic Case for Abortion Rights." *Vox,* June 25, 2022, www.vox.com/the-highlight/23182150/abortion-rights-economic-justice.
13. Rafia Zakaria, *Against White Feminism: Notes on Disruption* (New York: W. W. Norton, 2021), ix.

45. *Siyah,* Hypervisible in Silence Is Violence

1. Social gatherings at friends' or relatives' homes.
2. *Manteau* for coat and *roussari* for veil, is the Islamic outfit required from girls and women in the Islamic Republic in Iran.
3. *Bamazeh* is funny.
4. *Hamman* is the baths, and *kisse* is a rugged washcloth.
5. Traditional Iranian checkers; wheat-leavened flatbread.
6. Nigger.
7. Iran-Iraq War, 1980–88.
8. Khoda is another name for God.
9. Audre Lorde, "Poetry Is Not a Luxury," in *Sister Outsider: Essays and Speeches* (New York: Ten Speed 1984), 36–39.
10. As a reference to Abadan, a town in the southern province of Khuzestan where many populations of African descent live.
11. Neighborhoods of Black people in towns like Bandar Bushehr, Bandar Abbas, Abadan, and across the southern Iranian coast.

47. "Commitment Is the Key"

1. Ideas from this essay about Boggs's understanding of revolution as protracted struggle are discussed in further detail in Rachel Kuo, *Movement Media: In Pursuit of Solidarity,* (New York, NY: Oxford University Press, 2025)
2. This version and date refers to a copy located in James and Grace Lee Boggs Papers (UP001342), Walter P. Reuther Library, Archives of Labor and Urban Affairs, Wayne State University, Detroit, MI (Box 4, Folder 17) alongside guidelines for a revolutionary study group. The essay was published anonymously in 1972 in the New Afrikan journal *Vita Wa Watu* until she wrote an updated introduction in 2011.

Afterword: Tough Love

1. I first heard the utterance of "tough love solidarity" in a recent conversation for transnational feminists from Dr. Vanessa Thompson, Black feminist scholar activist based in Europe and Canada.
2. Lorraine K. Bannai, "80 Years after Executive Order 9066, the Supreme Court Still Shuts Its Eyes to Reality," Just Security, February 18, 2022, www.justsecurity.org/80236/80-years-after-executive-order-9066-the-supreme-court-still-shuts-its-eyes-to-reality.
3. On South African apartheid, see "Honorary Whites," Generalist Academy, October 18, 2021, https://generalist.academy/2021/10/18/honorary-whites; on Five Civilized Tribes, "Five Civilized Tribes," Encyclopedia.com, updated on August 24, 2016.
4. Anika Raju, "Black and Asian Solidarity in American History: The Power of Unity Exemplified by 5 Major Events," Advancing Justice, *Medium*, February 25, 2021, https://medium.com/advancing-justice-aajc/black-and-asian-solidarity-in-american-history-the-power-of-unity-exemplified-by-5-major-events-391025bbf228.
5. Kim Tran, "The History of Solidarity Between Asian And Black Americans," interview by Alisa Chang, *All Things Considered*, NPR, April 2, 2021, www.npr.org/2021/04/02/983925014/the-history-of-solidarity-between-asian-and-black-americans.
6. Yuichi Oshiro, "The Presence of (Black) Liberation in Occupied Okinawa," in *Transpacific Antiracism: Afro-Asian Solidarity in 20th-Century Black America, Japan, and Okinawa* (New York: New York University Press, 2013), 138–82.
7. Kumiko Makino, "Afro-Asian Solidarity and the Anti-Apartheid Movement in Japan," in *Global History of Apartheid 'Forward to Freedom' in South Africa*, ed. Anna Konieczna and Rob Skinner (New York: Palgrave Macmillan, 2019), 265–80.
8. June Jordan, "Poem for South African Women," in *Passion* (Port Townsend, WA: Copper Canyon, 2021).

ABOUT THE EDITORS AND CONTRIBUTORS

Cecile A is a writer who is inspired by her chosen family, all survivors of colonization everywhere, and flowers that come back every spring. Her poetry appears in *Boston Accent Lit* and the *Manzano Mountain Review*.

Minju Bae is a historian of Asian America with a focus on community-engaged histories of capitalism, racialization, and US imperialism. Her work investigates the politics of labor, racial difference, and the urban-based global economy. She also writes about the Korean War and its impacts.

Moya Bailey is interested in how race, gender, and sexuality are represented in media and medicine. She is the digital alchemist for the Octavia E. Butler Legacy Network and the board president of Allied Media Projects, a Detroit-based movement media organization.

Salonee Bhaman is a scholar whose work delves into questions of gender, sexuality, race, social welfare, and law. She is a co-leader of the Asian American Feminist Collective and works as both an academic and public historian.

Rosa Bordallo is a native Chamorro/CHamoru from the island of Guam in the Mariåna Islands. She has written poetry zines and recorded music under the moniker Manett. Her solo albums *Reef Walker* and *Isidro* are available on major streaming platforms.

Nana Brantuo is an interdisciplinary researcher and education specialist with a PhD in education policy and leadership and an MEd in curriculum and instruction. She is the founder of Diaspora Praxis, LLC, and currently leads several research projects with the Ohio Immigrant Alliance and the African Women's Development Fund.

Sharon Bridgforth is a 2023 United States Artists Fellow, 2022 Winner of Yale's Windham Campbell Prize in Drama, a 2020–2023 Playwrights' Center Core Member, and a 2022–2023 McKnight National Fellow. She is a Doris Duke Artist and author of *bull-jean & dem/dey back* (53rd State Press).

Beverley Bryan is a British-Jamaican educator, writer, activist, and coauthor of *Heart of the Race: Black Women's Lives in Britain* with fellow activists Stella Dadzie and Suzanne Scafe. The book, first published in 1985, is considered a groundbreaking work that explores the experiences, struggles, and contributions of Black women in Britain.

Butterflymush is the artist moniker of Andrea Acevedo, a Colombian-born, American-raised multimedia artist.

Franny Choi is a poet and essayist. Their books include *The World Keeps Ending, and the World Goes On* (Ecco, 2022) and *Soft Science* (Alice James Books, 2019). Franny is also a coeditor of *We the Gathered Heat: Asian American and Pacific Islander Poetry, Performance, and Spoken Word*. They are the founder and codirector of Brew & Forge.

Stella Dadzie is coauthor of *The Heart of the Race: Black Women's Lives in Britain*, which won the 1985 Martin Luther King Award for Literature and was recently republished as a Verso Feminist Classic. She is a founding member of OWAAD (Organisation of Women of African and Asian Descent) and is described as one of the "grandmothers" of Black feminism in the UK.

Jamy Drapeza is a first generation FilAm and fourth-generation healer, descended from albularyos and caregivers to serve as a therapist and operations professional. Their areas of expertise include healing intergenerational trauma, transgender wellness, ethical non-monogamy, and navigating pathways to our next favorite self.

Samah Serour Fadil is an Afro-Palestinian writer, editor, and translator who resides in Tiohtià:ke/Montreal.

Demita Frazier, JD, is a cofounder of the Black radical feminist Combahee River Collective. She is a coauthor of the Combahee River Collective Statement, considered a groundbreaking Black feminist treatise that has, since its publication in 1977, laid the foundation for the emergence and development of global Black feminist movements.

Noelani Goodyear-Kaʻōpua is a Kanaka Maoli who works as a politics professor at the University of Hawaiʻi at Mānoa. Her books include *The Seeds We Planted: Portraits of a Native Hawaiian Charter School*, *A Nation Rising: Hawaiian Movements for Life, Land and Sovereignty*, and *Nā Wāhine Koa: Hawaiian Women for Sovereignty and Demilitarization*.

Zuri Gordon is a gay, Caribbean American, feminist poet from the Bronx. She has a bachelors degree in English/creative writing and women's, gender, and sexuality studies and a masters degree in higher education and student affairs. Zuri lives and works in New York City. "From the Other Coast, with Love" is her first published poem.

Beverly Guy-Sheftall is a Black feminist scholar, writer, editor, and founding director of the Women's Research and Resource Center and is the Anna Julia Cooper Professor of Women's Studies at Spelman College, a historically Black, women's liberal arts college in Atlanta, Georgia.

Simone Devi Jhingoor, cofounder and codirector of Jahajee: Indo-Caribbeans for Gender Justice, is a poet, activist, healer, and embodied leadership coach. She is committed to building the power of survivors of intimate partner and sexual violence to fight for gender justice, in her community and beyond.

Monaye Johnson is a Black feminist researcher looking at reproductive health and justice for Black women and girls. She received her master's in gender studies and public policy from George Washington University.

Simi Kadirgamar is a reporter and fact-checker. Her areas of interest include the impacts of war, militarization, and ethnonationalism. Her writing on South Asia includes stories about the occupation of Kashmir and the transnational networking of Hindu supremacist organizations.

Eunsong Kim is a poet, writer, and scholar whose practice spans literary studies, critical digital studies, poetics, translation, visual culture, and critical race and ethnic studies. She is the author of *The Politics of Collecting: Race and the Aestheticization of Property* (Duke University Press 2024).

Julie Ae Kim (she/her) is a writer and organizer from Queens, New York. Her work has been published in *Witness*, *Joyland*, *Harper's Bazaar*, and elsewhere. She has received support from the Greater Columbus Arts Council, Kundiman, and the Mendocino Coast Writer's Conference. She is also a cofounder of the Asian American Feminist Collective.

Akemi Kochiyama-Ladson is a scholar-activist and community builder who currently serves as the director of Advancement at Manhattan Country School. She is also codirector of the Yuri Kochiyama Archives Project and coeditor of *Passing It On: A Memoir by Yuri Kochiyama*.

Priscillia Kounkou-Hoveyda is a Black Iranian Cape Town-based filmmaker and creative director and founder at the Collective for Black Iranians and House of Salone, a production and creative agency for critically conscious storytelling. She is a PhD candidate at the University of Cape Town and its departments of African feminist studies and fine arts. Her area of research is the Black Iranian gaze: constructions of racial Blackness in Iran.

Vijeta Kumar teaches English at St. Joseph's College (Autonomous), Bangalore. She writes at rumlolarum.com.

Rachel Kuo writes and teaches about race, feminism, media, social movements, and digital technology. She is author of *Movement Media: In Pursuit of Solidarity* (Oxford University Press, 2025) and a cofounder of the Asian American Feminist Collective.

Talila A. Lewis is a Black, queer, multilingual abolitionist, artist, organizer, educator, writer, griot, and community lawyer from the Deep South who was raised and lives all over the world. Lewis founded the cross-disability abolitionist organization HEARD; cofounded the Harriet Tubman Collective (& drafted its charter document); and is a *very proud* legacy of the Black southern recitation, oration, and griot traditions. Join Lewis here: www.talilalewis.com

Sinnamon Love is a visual storyteller, community organizer, Black Feminist pornographer, and executive director of BIPOC Collective, an organization providing financial assistance and increased access to mental health and wellness resources for Black and Brown sex workers.

Zifeng Liu is an intellectual historian of the twentieth-century Africana world, with specializations in Black internationalism, anticolonial thought, and Afro-Asian solidarity. His work explores Black leftist women's understandings of race, class, gender, sexuality, and empire in Cold War geopolitical contexts. He is an assistant professor of history at Hong Kong Baptist University.

Mari Matsuda is a critical race theorist and intersectional feminist. She is a writer and an artist. Art is at marimatsudapeaceorchestra.com.

Karla Méndez is an arts and culture writer. She writes about the histories of Black and Latin American women and their representation in art, performance, and poetry. She holds an MA in American studies from Brown University and a BA with honors in interdisciplinary studies from the University of Central Florida.

Mon M. is an abolitionist researcher, poet, and spadeworker. Her work focuses on national and local jail moratoriums, supporting an end to caste apartheid, antisurveillance obfuscation practices, and building intergenerational, interclass organizing capacity for abolitionist work in the so-called United States and beyond.

SX Noir is a self-proclaimed "thot leader" leading the conversation on the intersection of sex work and sex tech. SX hosts the podcast *Thot Leader Pod* in an attempt to hack the conversation on sex, love, dating, and tech.

Tamara K. Nopper is a sociologist, educator, writer, and editor. Her research focuses on Black-Korean conflict, the racial and gender wealth gap, financialization, criminalization, and technology. She is the editor of *We Do This 'Til We Free Us: Abolitionist Organizing and Transforming Justice*, a book of Mariame Kaba's writings and interviews.

Margo Okazawa-Rey, professor emerita San Francisco State University, is a transnational feminist activist and educator working on issues of militarism, armed conflict, and violence against women examined intersectionally. She is a founding member of International Women's Network Against Militarism, Women for Genuine Security, and the Combahee River Collective.

Pratibha Parmar is a writer, director, and producer and has directed award-winning films for BBC, Channel 4, ITVS, PBS, and European broadcasters. Her work has also had theatrical distribution.

Shaista Aziz Patel is a Pakistani Shi'i Muslim feminist scholar. Her scholarly and all other political investments are in several questions that draw upon theories in Indigenous (to North America and South Asia), Black, Dalit, anticaste, Muslim, and transnational feminist studies.

Shreerekha Pillai is a professor of humanities. She is author of *Women Writing Violence: The Novel and Radical Feminist Imaginaries* (SAGE, 2013) and editor of *Carceral Liberalism: Feminist Voices Against State Violence* (University of Illinois Press, 2023).

Yin Q is a parent, writer, media producer, and core organizer with Red Canary Song and founding member of Kink Out. Yin's writing has been published in *BUST, Apogee Journal, We Too: Essays on Sex Work and Survival* (Feminist Press at CUNY, 2021), and *Afro Asia* (Duke University Press, 2008). Their media work includes "Mercy, Mistress" and *Fly in Power.*

Loretta J. Ross is a professor at Smith College, feminist, and activist for reproductive justice. Ross was the national coordinator of the SisterSong Women of Color Reproductive Justice Collective from 2005 to 2012 and a 2022 MacArthur Fellow.

Jane Shi is a poet, writer, and organizer living on the occupied and stolen unceded territories of the Musqueam, Squamish, and Tsleil-Waututh peoples. She organizes Crips for eSims for Gaza and founded Masks4EastVan. Her debut poetry collection is *echolalia echolalia* (Brick Books, 2024).

Barbara Smith is an independent scholar and was cofounder of Kitchen Table: Women of Color Press. She has been writer in residence and taught at numerous colleges and universities for over twenty-five years. She is also a cofounder of the Combahee River Collective and coauthor of the Combahee River Collective Statement.

Shaé Smith is a decolonial therapist, visual artist, and writer who currently lends their passion work to a community-based collective serving queer and trans West Indian, Afro-Latinx, and Afro-Indigenous communities; one that honors Black, queer, and trans parenthood; and a Black-owned therapeutic private practice.

Senti Sojwal is a writer, digital strategist, and reproductive justice advocate based in Brooklyn. She is communications director at Planned Parenthood of Greater New York and is a cofounder of the Asian American Feminist Collective.

Chandanie Somwaru is an Indo-Caribbean poet from Queens, New York. She is author of the chapbook *Urgent \\ Where the Mind Goes \\ Scattered* (Ghostbird Press, 2021) and was the 2024 recipient of the Ruth Lilly and Dorothy Sargent Rosenberg Poetry Fellowship. Her writing has been published in *Poem-A-Day, Honey Literary, Solstice, SWWIM, The Margins* and other outlets.

Jaimee A. Swift is the founder and executive director of Black Women Radicals and the School for Black Feminist Politics. She is the coauthor of the forthcoming biography of Black feminist icon Barbara Smith.

Nate Tan is a codirector at Asian Prisoner Support Committee. He has led and supported antideportation campaigns for dozens of Asian Americans facing deportation and has seen the release of more than one hundred people out of prison and ICE.

Courtney Faye Taylor is the author of *Concentrate* (Graywolf Press, 2022), which won the Cave Canem Poetry Prize, the T.S. Eliot Four Quartets Prize, and the Hurston/Wright Legacy Award and was a finalist for the NAACP Image Awards and Lambda Literary Awards.

Sonya Renee Taylor is a *New York Times* bestselling author of seven books, transformational thought leader, world-renowned activist, award-winning artist, and founder of the international movement The Body Is Not an Apology.

Angel Trazo is a Bay Area author, illustrator, and interdisciplinary researcher with an avid interest in combining Asian American studies and visual storytelling.

Mark Tseng-Putterman is a historian of Asian American community politics, Cold War imperialism, and social movements. His essays on Asian America, racial politics, and US empire have appeared in *The Atlantic*, *Boston Review*, and *ROAR Magazine*, among others.

TD Tso is a writer and editor, cultural organizer, and community gardener. She is a cofounder of the Asian American Feminist Collective.

Kai Naima Williams is a multidisciplinary writer and performing artist based in Harlem, New York. She is the author of *The Bridges Yuri Built: How Yuri Kochiyama Marched Across Movements* (Kaepernick Publishing, 2024) and poetry chapbooks *He Tried to Drown the Ocean, I Waved* (Hyacinth Girl Press, 2018) and *Tomorrow Maps* (Hunger Press, 2023).

J Wortham is a sound healer, reiki practitioner, herbalist, and community care worker oriented toward healing justice and liberation. J is also a staff writer for the *New York Times Magazine*, cohost of the podcast *Still Processing*, and editor of the visual anthology *Black Futures* (One World, 2020), along with Kimberly Drew.

VX is a black feminist sound theorist and abolitionist educator.

Kate Zen is a community organizer, artist, and software developer. Born in Shanghai and raised in Spanish Harlem, Kate cofounded the Chinatown Literacy Project at age fifteen. She was also executive director of Chinatown Youth Initiatives and a cofounder of Red Canary Song.

CREDITS AND PERMISSIONS

In order of appearance:

"Five Memorials for Latasha" is excerpted from *Concentrate*. Copyright ©2022 by Courtney Faye Taylor. Reprinted with the permission of Graywolf Press, Minneapolis, Minnesota, www.graywolfpress.com.

The poems "Field Trip to the Museum of History" and "On How" are from *The World Keeps Ending and the World Goes On* by Franny Choi. Copyright 2022 by Franny Choi. Used by permission of HarperCollins Publishers.

"Understanding Disability, Ableism, and Incarceration More Expansively" is adapted from a two-part interview series with George Yancy and Talila A. Lewis originally published at *TruthOut* under "Ableism Enables All Forms of Inequity and Hampers All Liberation Efforts" (January 3, 2023) and "Incarceration and Ableism Go Hand in Hand, Says Abolitionist Talila Lewis" (January 8, 2023).

"We Want Cop-Free Communities: A Letter" was originally self-published by the Asian American Feminist Collective on *Medium* in August 2020 with updated signatories as of September 3, 2020. It has also been republished in *Frontiers: A Women's Studies Journal* 45, no. 1 (2024): 114–18.

TD Tso's "Nail Salon Brawls and Boycotts: Unpacking the Black-Asian Conflict in America" is adapted from original publication on Refinery29 on August 21, 2018.

Tamara K. Nopper's "On Anti-Black Terror, Captivity, and Black-Korean Conflict" is an edited reprint from *Decolonization: Indigeneity, Education & Society* (blog), September 24, 2015.

"Dear Indo-Caribbean People" by Chandanie Somwaru is adapted from original publication in *Mochi Magazine* on September 4, 2020, for the Black Allyship @ Mochi column.

"We Will Not Be Used" is adapted from original publication as "We Will Not Be Used: Are Asian Americans the Racial Bourgeoisie" in Mari Matsuda, *Where Is Your Body? and Other Essays on Race, Gender, and the Law* (Boston: Beacon, 1997), 149–61.

Excerpts from Karla Méndez's essay on the Third World Women's Alliance were originally published for *Black Women Radicals* blog on July 22, 2021.

Several essays are adapted and updated from original publication for the Asian American Writers' Workshop's magazine *The Margins*, under the Black and Asian Feminist Solidarities project and A World Without Cages project (in order of appearance in the anthology):

Jaimee A. Swift, "Exploring Black and Asian American Lesbian Archives: *Aché* and *Phoenix Rising*," March 25, 2021; VX, "Lessons Learned: Building a Police-Free Future with Abolition Park," December 11, 2020; Kate Zen and SX Noir, "'We Lead the World's Liberation': A Conversation with Sex Work Activists," October 29, 2020; Mon M., "Beyond Gilded Cages: South Asians for Abolition," December 16, 2020; TD Tso, "Not Victims: On Global Sex Worker Organizing," April 6, 2022; Simi Kadirgamar, "Taking Up Each Other's Cause: A Conversation on Tigray and Kashmir," November 8, 2021; Akemi Kochiyama-Ladson and Jaimee A. Swift, "Celebrating a Hundred Years of Yuri Kochiyama," May 19, 2021; Zuri Gordon and Cecile A, "From the Other Coast, with Love," January 28, 2021; and TD Tso, "Finding Solidarity and Survival Within a Transnational, Intergenerational Zoom Dance Party," April 29, 2021.

Minju Bae and Mark Tseng-Putterman's essay "Reviving the History of Radical Black-Asian Internationalism" was first published July 21, 2020, in *ROAR Magazine*.

Nate Tan's letter to Ny Nourn is adapted from original publication in 18MillionRising's Love Letters to Movement Leaders. It has also been republished in *Frontiers: A Women's Studies Journal* 45, no. 1 (2024): 124–25.

"Then, a Palestinian was born" by Samah Serour Fadil was first published in *Mizna* magazine 23, no. 2.

Butterflymush's illustration was originally published as the cover image for the anthology *But I Am Here: Writing and Art from the Sex Worker Movement in NYC*.

Rosa Bordallo's "The Breadfruit Does Not Float Far from the Tree" was first published in 2023 in *Recipes for Radical Hospitality*, a digital zine for Allied Media Projects.

Shaista Aziz Patel and Vijeta Kumar's "On Dalit Dreaming and Rebellious Joy" is adapted from the original publication on April 13, 2022, in *The Funambulist* 41 (May–June 2022) for a special issue on "Decentering the US," commissioned and edited by Léopold Lambert and Shivangi Mariam.

Jane Shi's "Reimagining the Autistic Mother Tongue" was originally published by Disability Visibility LLC on June 13, 2021, edited by Alice Wong.

"Unapologetic Agreements" is excerpted with permission from Sonya Renee Taylor, *The Body Is Not an Apology: The Power of Radical Self-Love* (Oakland: Berrett-Koehler, 2021).

Kai Naima Williams, "radical imagiNation" was originally published at *Abolition Is* in January, 2021, https://abolition-is.com/kai-naima-williams-feature-page-2021.

Sections of Noelani Goodyear-Ka'ōpua's piece "Nā Wāhine Noho Mauna: Leadership, Solidarity, and Gender on Maunakea" are adapted from the article "Protecting Maunakea Is a Mission Grounded in Tradition," coauthored with Yvonne Mahelona, originally published on September 5, 2019, for Zora at *Medium*.

Senti Sojwal's "Collective Reproductive Freedom Is Racial Justice" is adapted from original publication on December 12, 2022, for PBS Thirteen under "Abortion Rights Are Racial Justice."

INDEX

Page numbers in *italics* refer to images.

ABOUT HAYMARKET BOOKS

Haymarket Books is a radical, independent, nonprofit book publisher based in Chicago. Our mission is to publish books that contribute to struggles for social and economic justice. We strive to make our books a vibrant and organic part of social movements and the education and development of a critical, engaged, and internationalist left.

We take inspiration and courage from our namesakes, the Haymarket Martyrs, who gave their lives fighting for a better world. Their 1886 struggle for the eight-hour day—which gave us May Day, the international workers' holiday—reminds workers around the world that ordinary people can organize and struggle for their own liberation. These struggles—against oppression, exploitation, environmental devastation, and war—continue today across the globe.

Since our founding in 2001, Haymarket has published more than nine hundred titles. Radically independent, we seek to drive a wedge into the risk-averse world of corporate book publishing. Our authors include Angela Y. Davis, Arundhati Roy, Keeanga-Yamahtta Taylor, Eve Ewing, Aja Monet, Mariame Kaba, Naomi Klein, Rebecca Solnit, Mohammed El-Kurd, José Olivarez, Noam Chomsky, Winona LaDuke, Robyn Maynard, Leanne Betasamosake Simpson, Howard Zinn, Mike Davis, Marc Lamont Hill, Dave Zirin, Astra Taylor, and Amy Goodman, among many other leading writers of our time. We are also the trade publishers of the acclaimed Historical Materialism Book Series.

Haymarket also manages a vibrant community organizing and event space in Chicago, Haymarket House, the popular Haymarket Books Live event series and podcast, and the annual Socialism Conference.

ALSO AVAILABLE FROM HAYMARKET BOOKS

All Our Trials
Prisons, Policing, and the Feminist Fight to End Violence (Revised Edition)
Emily L. Thuma, foreword by Sarah Haley

Care: The Highest Stage of Capitalism
Premilla Nadasen

Corridors of Contagion
How the Pandemic Exposed the Cruelties of Incarceration
Victoria Law

Enemy Feminisms: TERFs, Policewomen, and Girlbosses Against Liberation
Sophie Lewis

The Gate of Memory
Poems by Descendants of Nikkei Wartime Incarceration
Edited by Brynn Saito and Brandon Shimoda, foreword by Mitsuye Yamada

How to End Family Policing: From Outrage to Action
Edited by Erin Miles Cloud, Erica R. Meiners, Shannon Perez-Darby, and C. Hope Tolliver

Iran in Revolt: Revolutionary Aspirations in a Post-Democratic World
Hamid Dabashi

Not Your Rescue Project: Migrant Sex Workers Fighting for Justice
Chanelle Gallant and Elene Lam
Foreword by Harsha Walia, afterword by Robyn Maynard

#SayHerName: Black Women's Stories of Police Violence and Public Silence
Kimberlé Crenshaw and African American Policy Forum
Foreword by Janelle Monáe

We the Gathered Heat
Asian American and Pacific Islander Poetry, Performance, and Spoken Word
Edited by Franny Choi, Bao Phi, No'u Revilla, and Terisa Siagatonu

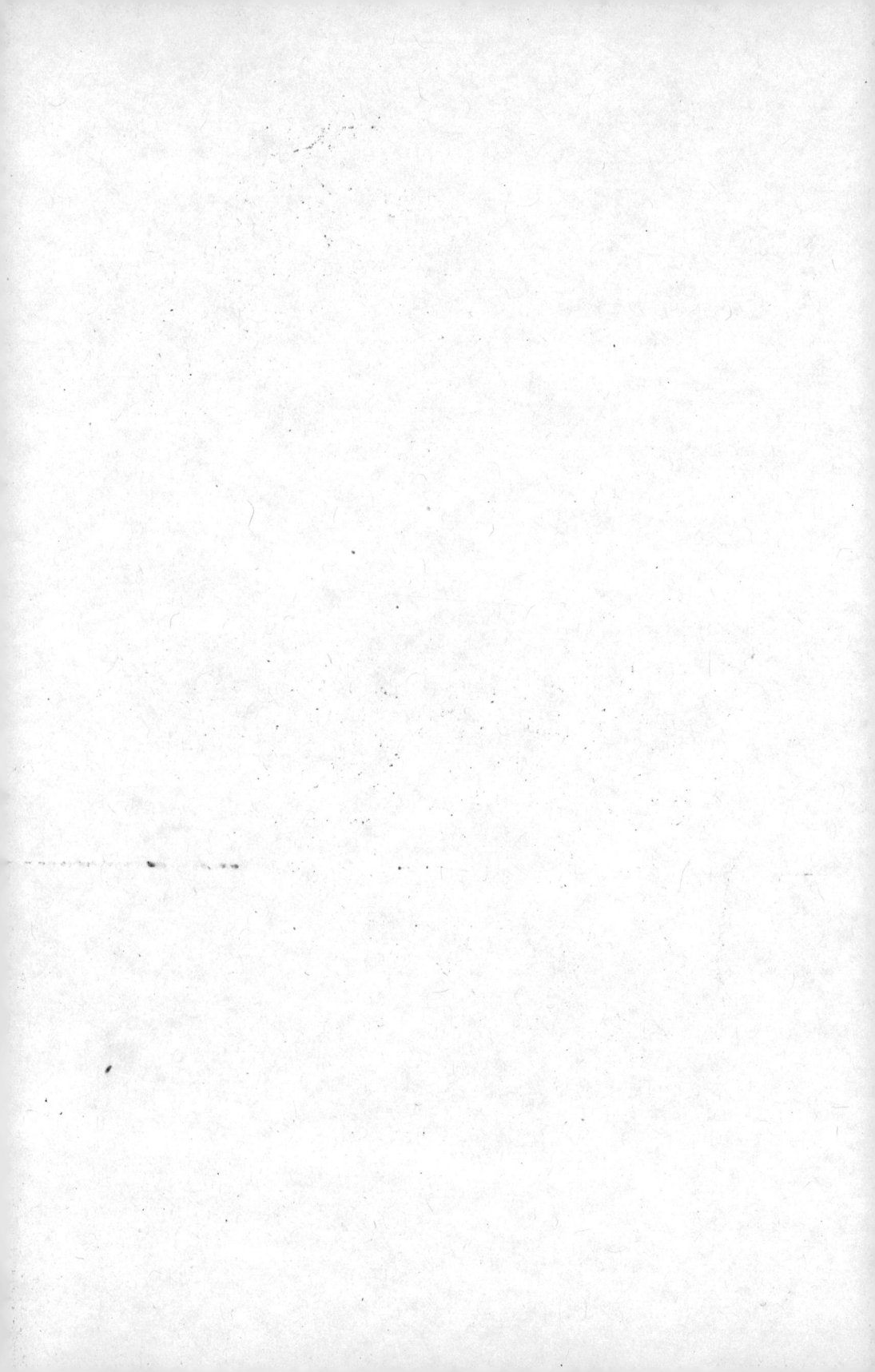